Savage Frontier

Volume II

1838–1839

Other Books by Stephen L. Moore

Battle Surface! Lawson P. "Red" Ramage and the War Patrols of the USS Parche. Annapolis, MD: Naval Institute Press, 2011.

Savage Frontier: Rangers, Riflemen, and Indian Wars in Texas. Volume IV: 1842–1845. Denton, TX: University of North Texas Press, 2010.

European Metal Detecting Guide: Techniques, Tips and Treasures. Garland, TX: RAM Books, 2009.

Presumed Lost. The Incredible Ordeal of America's Submarine Veteran POWs of World War II. Annapolis, MD: Naval Institute Press, 2009.

Last Stand of the Texas Cherokees: Chief Bowles and the 1839 Cherokee War in Texas. Garland, TX: RAM Books, 2009.

War of the Wolf: Texas' Memorial Submarine, World War II's Famous USS Seawolf. Dallas, TX: Atriad Press, 2008.

Savage Frontier: Rangers, Riflemen, and Indian Wars in Texas. Volume III: 1840–1841. Denton, TX: University of North Texas Press, 2007.

Spadefish: On Patrol With a Top-Scoring World War II Submarine. Dallas, TX: Atriad Press, 2006.

Eighteen Minutes: The Battle of San Jacinto and the Texas Independence Campaign. Plano, TX: Republic of Texas Press, 2004.

Savage Frontier: Rangers, Riflemen, and Indian Wars in Texas. Volume 1: 1835–1837. Plano, TX: Republic of Texas Press, 2002.

Taming Texas. Captain William T. Sadler's Lone Star Service. Austin, TX: State House Press, 2000.

With William J. Shinneman and Robert W. Gruebel. *The Buzzard Brigade: Torpedo Squadron Ten at War*. Missoula, MT: Pictorial Histories Publishing, 1996.

For more information,visit www.stephenlmoore.com

Savage Frontier

Volume II
1838–1839

Rangers, Riflemen, and Indian Wars in Texas

Stephen L. Moore

University of North Texas Press
Denton, Texas

Manufactured in the United States of America

10 9 8 7 6 5 4 3 2

The paper used in this book meets the minimum requirements of the American National Standard for Permanence of Paper for Printed Library Materials, Z39.48.1984.

Library of Congress Cataloging-in-Publication Data

Moore, Stephen L.
Savage frontier II: rangers, riflemen, and Indian wars in Texas/ Stephen L. Moore.
p. cm.
Includes bibliographical references and index.
ISBN-13: 978-1-57441-205-5 (cloth:alk. paper)
ISBN-10: 1-57441-205-1 (cloth: alk. paper)
ISBN-13: 978-1-57441-206-2 (pbk: alk. paper)
ISBN-10: 1-57441-206-X (pbk. alk. paper)
1. Indians of North America—Wars—Texas. 2. Indians of North America—Texas—Government relations. 3. Texas Rangers—History. 4. Frontier and pioneer life—Texas—History. 5. Texas—Politics and government—1836-1846. I. Title
E78.T4 M675 2006
976.4—dc21
Volume I: 2002000480

Cover design based on Vol. I creation by Alan McCuller
Layout and typesetting by Stephen L. Moore

About the Author

Stephen L. Moore, a sixth generation Texan, is the author of a dozen other books on Texas, military history and relic hunting. He has been featured at the Texas Book Festival and has been a contributing writer for the Texas Ranger Hall of Fame and Museum's online *Dispatch* magazine and The Texas State Historical Association's *Southwestern Historical Quarterly*. He currently serves as the marketing and advertising director for an electronics manufacturing company. Steve, his wife Cindy, and their children Kristen, Emily and Jacob live near Dallas in Lantana, Texas.

Contents

Volume 2

Prologue

If I fight, the whites will kill me. If I refuse to fight, my own people will kill me.

Chief Bowles, leader of the Texas Cherokees, to peace commissioners in June 1839.

If you are friendly with the wild Indians and Mexicans, we will be forced to kill your people in defense of our frontier. You are between two fires. If you remain, you will be destroyed.

Major General Thomas Jefferson Rusk on July 11, 1839, during peace negotiations with twenty-one Indian leaders on Council Creek.

★ ★ ★ ★ ★

Volume I of *Savage Frontier* traced the early days of the Texas frontier defense system. Ranger battalions were organized in 1835 by acts of the provisional government of the Republic of Texas. Ranger companies were in the field continuously from October 1835 through 1837. At its peak in mid-September 1836, the service had boasted some thirteen ranger companies, comprising approximately 450 men in four battalions.

By early 1838, however, the Texas Rangers were in danger of disappearing altogether. They had suffered losses at the Post Oak Springs Massacre and at Stone Houses. As enlistments expired, the frontier forces had dwindled to one battalion under Major William H. Smith, which was based on the Colorado River. President Sam Houston, a proponent of a conciliatory policy towards the Indians, had no interest in maintaining such frontier units.

Major Smith retired from the ranging service, as did his top company commanders, and the senior lieutenant left in service discharged the balance of his rangers in April 1838.

Within months of the disbanding of the Texas Rangers, Major General Thomas Rusk began authorizing the use of his revamped Texas Militia. During 1838, the Texas Militia was out in force on a number of expeditions. In between periods of alert, Rusk allowed his militia brigades to maintain small battalions of mounted rangers.

A few units consisted primarily of Tejanos, or Texas citizens of Mexican and Spanish descent. There were even Indian units which served as scouts and rangers, including Indians from Cherokee, Shawnee, Choctaw, Lipan Apache, and Delaware tribes.

These ranger battalions and the militia conducted offensive expeditions to the Kickapoo village in East Texas, up the Trinity River to the Cross Timbers area of present Dallas and Fort Worth, and even chased Caddo Indians across the United States border into Louisiana.

The militia and the ranging companies which operated during 1838 consisted of citizen soldiers. The men mobilized for temporary duty in fighting whatever crisis existed at the time. In most cases, the lack of funding, the lack of subsistence, or lack of interest compelled the men to return to their homes as promptly as possible.

Continued depredations throughout Texas motivated new President Mirabeau Lamar to adopt an extermination policy toward hostile Indians upon his taking office in December 1838. He immediately appropriated funds to build up a new Frontier Regiment of the Texas Army, comprising both infantry and cavalry. During early 1839, Lamar's Congress also authorized numerous companies of Texas Rangers to serve the more troubled counties. One such unit in Houston County was that of Captain John Wortham. According to the legislation which established it, Wortham's ranger company was "organized to protect and defend lives and property and whose duty was to die in such defense thereof."

The year 1839 was very active in the Indian wars of Texas. Depredations were particularly deadly for settlers, but they aggressively retaliated. Campaigns and offensive strikes were carried out by the army, cavalry, rangers, militia, and even hastily assembled civilian volunteer groups.

The new Frontier Regiment made two major offensive thrusts during the year: the Cherokee War during the summer and another campaign in December. Ranger companies also had a number of encounters during the year. Lamar authorized several other expeditions against Comanches and other hostile tribes. By year's end, the Cherokees had been largely driven from Texas and the Shawnees had been removed. The Comanches, however, would remain a formidable presence for some time.

Volume II continues the in-depth study of the expeditions, battles, and leaders of the Texas frontier defense system. As often as possible, the events are allowed to be told first-hand through the participants, whose stories were captured in newspaper articles, diaries, letters or by early historians. Such recollections are even more powerful when accurate dates are added via the use of available republic-era documents. Unfortunately, few accounts exist to paint a picture from the point of view of the Native Americans involved in these 1830s battles.

Original letters and documents are quoted in the language of the original authors. However, I have chosen to correct spelling and add punctuation in many cases for readership. No words are added to such quotes, with any exceptions denoted by [ ] brackets. These quotes are more significant when the reader can clearly understand what was being expressed in the writer's limited grammar and spelling abilities.

Many of the muster rolls presented here are courtesy of the Texas State Archives. Countless other key ranger records, army papers, muster rolls, and military documents were lost when the Adjutant General's office was burned in 1855 and during a fire in the Texas Capitol in 1881. Other records have disappeared from the Texas Archives over time. Reconstructing some of the missing muster rolls was accomplished via careful study of the Republic of Texas Audited Claims, Public Debt Claims, Pension Papers, and Unpaid Debt microfilm series. These files contain the original service papers filled out by the men and their companies during their service period. These documents give insight into the locations of companies, their tenure of service, payroll information, personnel losses, recruitment efforts, and eyewitness accounts of various battles or skirmishes.

I began studying the early Texas Indian wars to learn more about my ancestors. Great-great-great grandfather Thomas Alonzo Menefee and his father Laban Menefee both served as Texas Rangers during the Indian campaigns of 1839. Great-great-great-great-great grandfather John Morton served in an 1839 Houston County ranger battalion and fought in the Cherokee War that summer. Great-great-great grandfather William Turner Sadler was active in the 1830s Indian wars in two ways: as a ranger and as a captain of both militia and army. Great-great-great-great grandfather Armstead Bennett, a veteran rifleman of the 1811 battle of Tippecanoe in Indiana, supplied early ranger and militia companies with goods from his fortified home, known as Bennett's Fort, in present Houston County.

This modern perspective on the Texas Indian wars should aid genealogists tracing their own ancestors' adventures on the early frontier. It does not seek to justify the persecution or prejudices that prevailed in the 1830s. My own ancestry, in fact, includes both a Cherokee great-great-great grandmother and a number of ancestors who served in the Texas Rangers and Texas Militia.

The early Texas frontier freedom fighters of the late 1830s still did not have the superior repeating weapons that would reach them during the 1840s. Among the tactics they most frequently depended on were: strength in numbers, organized firing of their rifles, good defensive positioning, or sometimes just sheer courage to charge against a superior foe during some of their more deadly battles.

The 1830s frontier fighters deserve the in-depth focus of the first two volumes of *Savage Frontier* for one to fully appreciate how the Texas Rangers developed into such a respectable service during the 1840s. The Texas Indian wars did not end with 1839. Depredations would continue for years all across the Republic of Texas, but the areas of conflict began to move more south and westerly after the Cherokee War in East Texas. Perhaps a third volume will be needed to explore the increasing conflict with the Comanches during the early 1840s and the rise of Jack Hays as the ideal ranger leader.

Acknowledgments

This volume is dedicated to my father Marshall Lee Moore Jr. (1940–2004), who was never too busy to make a road trip to take photos or to help with research.

As with Volume I, Donaly Brice of the Texas State Library and Archives Commission in Austin was a key source during the writing of Volume II. He continually fulfilled search requests for muster rolls and various archival documents which helped fill in the blanks in this manuscript.

For the illustrations, I appreciate John Anderson of the Texas Archives for his assistance and advice. Thanks also to Tom Shelton, Photo Archivist at the University of Texas Institute of Texan Cultures in San Antonio, and Linda Peterson, Photographs Archivist for The Center for American History, The University of Texas at Austin.

Eliza Bishop of the Houston County Historical Commission provided a biography and photo of her great-grandfather, Major John Wortham. Edwin G. Pierson Jr. provided numerous muster rolls and other information concerning the service of his great-great grandfather, Captain John G. W. Pierson. Thanks also to Eagle Douglas of the American Indian Heritage Center for his continued support.

For offering advice and for reviewing the first volume of *Savage Frontier* prior to its publication, special thanks are due to historians Chuck Parsons, Bill O'Neal, Donaly Brice, and Allen Hatley. For their early reviews and critical comments which improved this second volume, I thank Professor James E. Crisp of North Carolina State University, Paul N. Spellman of Wharton Junior College, and Texas historian Jack Jackson.

Aside from primary archival data, research for this book was greatly aided by published works of the leading authorities of Texas

Indian Wars history. These authors had the foresight to record much of the eyewitness accounts, folklore, and memoirs of the early frontiersmen. Such crucial guides included John Henry Brown's *Indian Wars and Pioneers of Texas* (1880); J. W. Wilbarger's *Indian Depredations in Texas* (1889); James T. DeShields' *Border Wars of Texas* (1912); and A. J. Sowell's *Texas Indian Fighters* (1900) and *Rangers and Pioneers of Texas* (1884). More recently, Dr. Walter Prescott Webb's *The Texas Rangers* (1965) was the forerunner of the modern histories of this state's fabled lawmen.

CHAPTER 1
The Texas Militia Takes the Field

December 1837–August 19, 1838

Colonel Henry Karnes, the cavalry commander stationed in San Antonio, hoped to negotiate peace with the hostile Indian tribes of Texas. He had most recently concluded a peace treaty with three Tonkawa Indian chiefs in San Antonio on November 22, 1837. Just days after this accord, Colonel Karnes was notified that more of the aggressive local Indians were proposing to come in to work out a treaty similar to that agreed upon by the Tonkawas.

Karnes' command was in a sad state by this time, however. The Texas Cavalry had dwindled to forty-seven enlisted men by the end of 1837. When Karnes was promoted to command of the cavalry, some in San Antonio resented his taking the local control from his new subordinate, Lieutenant Colonel Juan Seguín, a hero of the Texas Revolution. Such dissatisfaction even forced Karnes to dishonorably discharge two dozen men. Almost all of his remaining cavalrymen were without horses and ill-prepared to fight in case of a crisis.[1]

Karnes therefore notified the senior Texas Ranger commander, Captain William Eastland, to bring his men into San Antonio to help deal with the Indians. Suspicious of a ruse, Colonel Karnes wanted to be prepared. Eastland, who had been an officer on Colonel John Henry Moore's 1835 ranger campaign, had recently led his own expedition into Indian territory.

Captain Eastland, knowing of former ranger Noah Smithwick's friendship with the Comanches from the previous summer, invited him to come along as a spokesman. "Owing to the scarcity of money, the blacksmith business was not very remunerative," recalled Smithwick.[2]

He substituted into Eastland's company for ranger Isham M. Booth, who had enlisted on April 27, 1837, for twelve months.

Smithwick took over Booth's remaining four months on December 1, 1837, and "once again cast my lot with the Texas rangers."[3]

Eastland led his men to San Antonio in early December, where they remained in camp for several days waiting for the Indians to come in to treat. When they failed to appear, Eastland broke up camp and led his men back toward Fort Houston on the Colorado River. During their return, his men encountered a band of Comanches who had recently killed a Mexican vaquero and had driven off a herd of horses. While a portion of the Comanches kept the rangers engaged, the rest got away with the stolen horses. There were no known losses on either side and Eastland apparently felt his numbers inferior to try pursuing the Indians.[4]

Such aggressive Indians were an issue with the Texas Congress during December 1837. The Senate's Indian Committee, which had been appointed in May 1837, was headed by former ranger leader Isaac Burton. In October, Chairman Burton's committee had found President Sam Houston and John Forbes' February 23, 1836, treaty with the Cherokees to be null and void. Burton wrote that operation of this treaty would not only be "detrimental to the interests of the Republic, but would also be a violation of the vested rights of many citizens." The Senate then officially nullified the Houston/Forbes treaty in December.

An unrelated item of interest passed by the Texas Congress on December 8, 1837, was an act changing the name "Mina" to "Bastrop" for both the town and the county of that name. Many early Republic documents refer to Mina but as of late 1837 this area became legally known as Bastrop.[5]

★ ★ ★ ★ ★

Frontier Forces Dwindle

During the month of December, the enlistments of many of the men attached to the frontier ranging service expired. The mounted gunman battalion of Colonel Joseph Bennett, approved in June for a six-month period, never reached desired strength. The men whom Bennett did raise were discharged during December. Captain John Bowyer's mounted gunman company was disbanded on December 18, 1837. The discharge papers of Private P. B. Norton were signed in Houston by First Lieutenant A. B. Vanbenthuysen, who had only recently returned from his ill-fated Indian encounter at Stone Houses.[6]

The Colorado River area ranger battalion remained in service, but the number of men enlisted began dwindling significantly by year's end. Payment records for Major William Smith show that he completed a full year's service as major of this battalion and was paid $484 for service between December 14, 1836, and December 14, 1837. Another record, filed by Major Smith on December 2, 1837, with the War Department in Houston by Barnard Bee, shows that he was allowed total payments of $1,435.90, after deducting $48.90 for clothing and rations.[7]

Also departing the ranger service during December 1837 were many of the officers instated by Congress the previous year. Among them were captains Tommy Barron, Micah Andrews, and Daniel Monroe. Andrews was paid as a ranger captain through January 5, 1838, although he did not serve at Fort Houston after August 1837.[8]

Eastland's former first lieutenant, John L. Lynch, had been promoted to captain of rangers on November 28, 1837, to help fill the void in senior officers. Lynch had continued recruiting for his company into the new year. In an affidavit from February 20, 1838, in Bastrop County, it is seen that "John B. Berry enlisted under my command in the ranging service of Texas for the term of three months, commencing January 6, 1838, and ending this day."[9]

Captain Lynch's company was disbanded on February 20 "by order of the Secretary of War."[10] A search of Republic of Texas audited military papers reveals the names of some of the other rangers serving under Captain Lynch to be Allen J. Adkisson, Marquis Ambrose, Wilson H. Biggs, Miles J. Cook, Daniel O. Etheridge, Joseph Hornsby, Malcolm M. Hornsby, Reuben Hornsby, Galand Jones, Johnson Jones, Samuel Luther, Dennis Mahoney, Fielding McKay, George Neill, William Robertson, and Patrick Sullivan.

★ ★ ★ ★ ★

The Revamped Texas Militia

Under Sam Houston's leadership, Congress had first passed legislation on December 6, 1836, which established the essential militia structure for frontier defense, but thereafter refused to appropriate any money to support this effort.

President Houston had furloughed most of the Texas Army during 1837, and the decline of the ranger service during the latter part of the year further exposed the outlying settlements to Indian depredations. By December, the republic's military forces had been stretched so thin that the Second Congress of Texas had to address the issue.

Despite the veto of Sam Houston, Congress passed a supplemental militia act on December 18, 1837. This act reduced the militia to only one division, which would be headed by a major general. The militia would then be divided into four brigades with a brigadier general for each who reported directly to the major general. Congress then proceeded to hold elections for these five positions on the same day.[11]

Thomas Rusk, who had commanded the Texas Army in 1836 following San Jacinto, was elected major general of the militia. Direct authority of the actions of the militia, much to the displeasure of President Houston, passed from the Republic's chief executive to General Rusk. The actions of the Texas Militia were presided over by Colonel Hugh McLeod, a friend of Rusk's who was named the adjutant general or chief militia officer.

For the four brigadier generals, Congress elected Edward Burleson, Moseley Baker, Kelsey H. Douglass and John H. Dyer, commanding the first to fourth brigades, respectively. The original brigade districts for 1837 were as follows: the First Brigade under Burleson included all areas west of the Brazos; the Second Brigade under Baker included the territory between the Brazos and Trinity; the Third under Douglass included the country between the Trinity and the Sabine; and the Fourth under Dyer the area north of the Sabine and up to the Red River.

By its new standards, the militia would accept able-bodied male citizens of the Republic who were over seventeen and under fifty years of age. Young men coming of age or men newly moving into a district were required to enroll in a militia company in their county. Within ten days of enrolling in a company, men were required to provide themselves with their own equipment, which was to include: a good musket, a suitable bayonet, belt, six flints, knapsack, and cartridge box with twenty-four suitable ball cartridges. If the militiaman chose to arm himself with a rifle, yager, or shotgun, he must then provide his own knapsack with a shot pouch, powder horn, fifty balls suitable to the caliber of his gun, and half a pound of powder.[12]

The supplemental militia law of December 18, 1837, specified that companies would include one captain, two lieutenants, four sergeants, four corporals, one drummer, and one fifer or bugler. The captain and lieutenants were elected by members of the company. The captain thereafter was responsible for appointing the noncommissioned officers and musicians. The company should at no time consist of fewer than thirty-two privates. If it ever did, then the company should merge with other companies while such deficiencies existed.

In order to maintain the militia, each Texas county was to be divided into militia precincts. The number of precincts varied by county, depending on the number of men who were subject to militia duty. One company of at least fifty-six men was to be raised in each precinct. Companies of the militia were subject to duty at the discretion of the president and they could be called to perform a tour of duty when deemed expedient. The normal limit for such a tour was three months and no militia company was to serve more than two tours without discharge. While in service, the militia was to be governed by the articles of war and the rules and regulations adopted by the army. The militiamen would also receive the same pay and rations as soldiers in the army.[13]

Rusk's militia did not immediately organize following this new legislation. Unlike the ranger service, his troops would not even perform duty until being called up in times of crisis. The early Texas Militia companies used their hometown as an organizational hub and elected a captain to lead the unit. If the population was great enough to form three full companies, a major was elected to command all three companies.

The establishment of a proper militia was an important move by Congress. It would be used extensively during 1838 and 1839 to combat the rising Indian hostilities, particularly in East Texas.

★ ★ ★ ★ ★

The General Land Office of the Republic of Texas opened on January 4, 1838. A new land law of December 14, 1837, had established the land office and other county land offices. The opening of the land office created a flood of land claimants and surveying parties who invaded what was previously Indian-held territory. The resulting flood of surveying parties into the fields would lead to renewed Indian encounters during 1838.

The Lipan Indian tribe signed a peace treaty with Texas on January 18, 1838, at Live Oak Point. Chief Cuelgas de Castro represented the Lipans and James Power acted in behalf of the Texas government. The treaty provided the Indians with $250 in gifts and for trading houses to be established among them. In return, neither the Lipans nor the whites would attack one another.[14] The Lipans, in fact, would become respected scouts who fought on the side of the Texas frontier forces against Comanches in 1839.

President Sam Houston desired further treaties to be made with other warlike Indian tribes. He visited Nacogdoches in February for peace talks, hoping to soothe tensions with the Cherokees and their associate tribes, who were becoming restless with the Congress of the Republic of Texas for refusing to recognize their 1836 treaty.

From Houston on February 4, Barnard Bee appointed Albert Sidney Johnston and Lysander Wells as "commissioners to meet and hold conference with the Comanche Indians." They were to assure the Comanches of friendly feelings with them felt by the whites, a desire to open trading houses with them and to end violence. Johnston and Wells were to invite "seven or eight of their chiefs to visit the Executive and both houses of Congress at the next session" on April 21.

Bee added that President Houston himself had just left for Nacogdoches "to enter into an arrangement with the Cherokees." Colonel Henry Karnes was added as a colleague of Wells and Johnston on April 12 but it was almost two months after the initial appointments that the Comanche talks were actually held.

★ ★ ★ ★ ★

Ranger Battalion Expires: April 1838

During early spring 1838, the remaining rangers who had enlisted under Colonel Coleman and Major Smith during 1836 and 1837 saw their service periods ending. Captain Eastland remained the most senior officer of this battalion in service during early 1838. Payment vouchers and war department memos of Eastland show that he remained in constant service with the ranger service from December 14, 1836, through March 2, 1838. Another memo from Secretary of War Bernard Bee shows that Eastland was "entitled to four dollars each" for enrolling twenty-nine men into the ranging service as of January 21, 1838.[15]

After Captain Eastland's departure, First Lieutenant William Moore became acting commander of his Company D. Within a few months, Moore would be the most senior officer left in the service of the Texas Rangers. Some of the rangers completed their service requirements during March, such as Private Henry Wilson, who drew his last payment from Company D on March 29, 1838. One of the last men in service with Eastland's former company was Private Richard J. Lloyd, who was honorably discharged when his enlistment expired on April 25, 1838.[16]

Lieutenant Moore and the remnants of the ranger battalion created nearly two years prior closed out service operating from Fort Houston on the Colorado River. Private Noah Smithwick, who had re-enlisted in the service on December 1, 1837, was honorably discharged by Moore on April 26, 1838. Smithwick had "honestly and faithfully discharged his duty in the said corps" and was thereby "entitled to the whole year's pay." Moore signed this voucher as "1st Lt. Commanding Rangers" and noted "there being no field officer at this time," he discharged Smithwick. Secretary of War Bee sanctioned this discharge.[17]

For each twelve-month service enlistment, a ranger was given 1,280 acres of land. Smithwick was actually awarded three separate grants of this land, one for his original service and one more for each of the two enlistments he finished by substituting in for other rangers who had departed. "No one cared anything for land those days. I gave one of my certificates for 1,280 acres for a horse which the Indians relieved me of in less than a week."[18]

As the government rangers declined, the settlers in Bastrop and along the Colorado River soon were left to fall back to their own defenses. Spurned by Mexican rebels, the Indians would soon step up their attacks on the white settlers in central Texas in 1838. The lack of a regularly maintained ranging service would soon show its effect.

The mere presence of the 1837 ranging companies in this area had had a great effect on checking Indian depredations.

★ ★ ★ ★ ★

Indian Actions: April–May 1838

Secretary of War Bee and Colonel George Washington Hockley managed to sign a treaty of peace with the Tonkawa Indians at Houston on April 11. Chiefs Placido, Benavido, Campos, and Oquin represented the Tonkawas. They agreed that the Tonkawas would not permit one of their own to commit depredations against white Texas settlers yet could still enjoy their hunting grounds and homes in peace. In return, the Republic of Texas would appoint an agent to superintend their business, protect their rights, and see that the treaty was complied with. A further stipulation was that five Tonkawa chiefs should visit the seat of Texas government twice a year to talk with the President and "amicably adjust all differences."[19]

Four days after this treaty of peace was signed, Indians began committing violence against men working land claims in the northeastern territories. From Nacogdoches, Richard Sparks had departed in early April 1838 to locate land on the Trinity River. He moved to Parker's Fort and from there out into the fields near the Three Forks of the Trinity in the area of present Dallas. Sparks and a small group of men were attempting to catch up with a surveyor who had preceded them by a few days.

A party of about seventy Kickapoos attacked Sparks' camp. Three men were killed in camp and a fourth was killed while fleeing from the Indians. Several others managed to escape. A letter dated April 16, 1838, from Robertson Colony citizen Thomas Dillard to Sterling C. Robertson described some of this attack.

> Barry was in the middle of a prairie surveying and discovered persons on horses and some on foot but could not distinguish whether they were Americans or Indians for some time, but at length made the discovery and endeavoured to make the timber.[20]

The other white surveyors fled for the timber when the Indians charged them. A man named Chairs had the fastest horse, and he escaped in company with a Mr. Kay. In camp, a man named Hunter was the first to be killed. According to Dillard's account, Mr. Barry was killed next, and "Sparks [was] the third person killed at camp," the latter suffering a shot through the head.

The surviving surveyors returned to Fort Parker and en route found the body of Francis Holland, who had been employed as a hunter for the party and had disappeared a few days prior to the attack at their campsite.[21]

Dillard noted that two other surveying parties under captains Joseph B. Chance and Sam Davis were still out in the field as of April 16. In a postscript to his letter, Dillard added that Robertson's colonist Henry Moss had his horse shot out from under him about 1:00 p.m. on April 15. The Indians then killed and scalped Moss within a half mile of his own father.[22]

The Robertson County citizens residing high on the Brazos and Navasota rivers immediately signed a petition asking their government for help for their "exposed frontier." They were

> daily and hourly exposed to the mercy of the merciless savages. Our surveyors have been murdered together with their hands and within the last two days one of our neighbors was inhumanly butchered and his scalp borne off in triumph by the Indians.

The citizens felt that the lack of regular resistance had made the Indians become even bolder. They asked for some means of protection and suggested that artillery pieces be sent to the larger frontier settlements.

The *Telegraph and Texas Register* reported on April 25 that the inhabitants of the frontier about sixty miles above Washington-on-the-Brazos were "forsaking their farms and collecting at the forts in that quarter." The murders of the surveyors and Henry Moss had left many young men who "would rejoice to be permitted to punish these marauders."

Just days after the Robertson County petition, residents of Milam County sent their own petition to Congress. They stated that they were "almost daily visited and harassed by a savage foe, who seeks and avails himself of every opportunity to embrue his hands in the blood of the white man." They described how their citizens had "fallen victims to the tomahawk and scalping knife," and how others had been taken into captivity. The citizens asked their government "for the immediate passage of a law" to call out the militia to "repel the enemy—or for the authorizing of a corps of mounted volunteers to be raised for their immediate protection."

This petition was read before the Texas Congress on April 28. As the people of Robertson and Milam counties were asking for help, the militia was trying to organize itself. Brigadier General Edward Burleson, elected into his position on December 18, 1837, was trying to organize his First Brigade at this time. He enthusiastically planned to establish eight battalions within his area, which covered all areas west of the Brazos River. Citizens of Brazoria, Fort Bend, Austin, Washington, Milam, Bastrop, Matagorda, Colorado, Fayette, Jackson, Victoria, Goliad, Gonzales, and Béxar counties would form the eight battalions. Adjutant General Hugh McLeod reported in April that Burleson planned to have the elections of field officers for these militia battalions held on June 15 at the seat of justice for each county within his First Brigade boundaries.

One of the two surveying parties still in the field during April, that of Captain Joseph Chance, had its own Indian encounter shortly after the murders of the Sparks party surveyors. Chance, who had commanded rangers during the Texas Revolution, had organized his party of fifteen men and set out from Washington-on-the-Brazos to explore the upper Brazos. His party included James Cook, James Shepherd, James Evitts, Sam Evitts, Henry Eustace McCulloch, and Samuel McFall.[23]

McCulloch had come to Texas from Tennessee with his brother Benjamin McCulloch in the fall of 1835. Both would make names for themselves in Texas, Henry as an Indian fighter and ranger captain for years on the southwest frontiers.

Captain Chance's party reached the Little River and then moved upstream, scouring the country along the waters of the Leon, San Gabriel, Lampasas, and other Little River tributaries. While out hunting by themselves one day on this expedition, McCulloch and Samuel McFall encountered a party of five Indians and attacked. They killed two and chased the other three into the bottom lands of the San Gabriel. This was the first Texas Indian engagement for young Henry McCulloch, but would be far from his last.

★ ★ ★ ★ ★

"Nothing Will be Gained by War": May 1838

Indian commissioners Sidney Johnston, Lysander Wells, and Henry Karnes did manage to meet with the Comanches near San Antonio in May. A band of about 150 Comanches led by chiefs Essowakkenny and Essomanny came in to hold talks with them. The basics of peace and frontier trading posts were discussed and the chiefs were invited to appear before Congress. Chief Essowakkenny, a man of about twenty-eight years, replied that he would not go, but that his brave brother Essomanny would go. Gifts of friendship were exchanged and the meeting was broken up. Following these talks, Colonel Karnes went with the Comanches with a supply of goods which he sold among them.[24]

Another citizen petition was read before Congress on May 1, this one from the Robertson County citizens of Parkers' Fort. They informed the government that the Indians had recently committed depredations in the area and continued to steal horses and cattle from the settlers. The petitioners had information from Indian traders that the Indians intended to "attack the fort and various other parts of the frontier with strong forces." The people asked for an artillery piece to be sent to Parker's Fort and that the militia be called out to campaign against the Indians.[25]

The next Indian incident mentioned in Robertson County occurred a few days prior to May 14, 1838, when a young man named Taylor was shot just at the edge of the town of Nashville in Mr. Bell's field. According to resident A. S. McCoy, Taylor was pursued two or three miles by three Indians, but was not dangerously wounded.

Congress approved on May 15, 1838, an act to authorize President Houston to raise a "Corps of Cavalry." This was in response to Indian depredations and the increased lawlessness on the southwestern frontier, where unofficial trading had sprung up with northern Mexico.

Other factors for this decision included an outbreak of Federalist revolutionary activities in northern Mexico and the establishment of a French blockade of Mexican ports.[26]

This cavalry corps was to consist of not more than 280 men, or five companies, whose recruits would enlist for no less than one or no more than three years service. The tenure of service was left to the discretion of the president. This cavalry corps would be "for the purpose of protecting the Southwestern Frontier" and "shall, at no time, be quartered within fifteen miles of any town." In order to carry this into effect, Congress appropriated fifty thousand dollars in promissory notes.[27]

Cavalry recruiting stations were established and manned in Houston, Galveston, and Matagorda during the second half of 1838. Recruiting was a slow process, although several companies recruited in Brazoria and Galveston were mustered in Houston during mid-October 1838. These companies were thereafter stationed near Béxar and Gonzales for protecting the western counties. News from the western frontier brought intelligence of new depredations being committed by lawless Texans or raiding Mexican forces.[28]

Congress tried to provide again for the Texas Rangers by passing an act to provide companies of mounted gunmen to be maintained within each militia brigade. They would "commence active operations against the hostile Indians on the frontier." President Houston reviewed this act of the House on May 25, however, and found it "in every feature objectionable."[29]

Houston felt that it was legally *his* duty to decide *when* to call out the militia. He felt that the scarcity of food supplies on the frontiers at the present time would limit their effectiveness and he seriously questioned the ability of mounted militiamen to decide which Indians were truly hostile and worthy of attack.

Houston cited expeditions made against the Indians during the previous winter and spring in which "the blood of some of our best citizens has paid" for the aggressiveness of ranger officers who went against the Indians. The president therefore refused to sign this act for raising 280 mounted gunmen, promising to call up the militia when the "safety of the country may require it." He firmly believed in working out treaties with the Indians versus a show of force.

"Everything will be gained by peace," Houston wrote, "but nothing will be gained by war."

Another Indian treaty was signed in Houston just days after the president rejected the act for more frontiersmen. Soon after Henry Karnes' visit among the Indians, a large party of more than one hun-

President Sam Houston (1793–1863) wearing a cowboy duster in this early daguerreotype. Houston preferred a policy of treating with the hostile Indians and opposed the ability of Major General Thomas Rusk to call up the Texas Militia without presidential consent.
Texas State Library and Archive Commission.

dred Comanches came into Bastrop during late May to trade with the citizens. They moved on through San Felipe de Austin on their way to Houston, where they planned to make a peace treaty with the Texas government.

The Indians spent several days in San Felipe while their guide recovered from illness. The Indian women were all dressed in doeskin trousers and jackets. Many of the women wore crude gold rings on their fingers and spun-glass bead necklaces. The men wore buffalo skins or wrapped themselves in large dye-colored blankets. Some wore a large bracelet of copper or gold below their elbow, from which hung their collections of human scalps.

Convinced by Colonel Karnes to join the congress while in session, the Comanches arrived in Houston on May 26. The citizens of Texas' capital city gathered in numbers to stare at these frontier warriors. Such opportunities to view the Comanches in town were very rare. The Indian women and children busied themselves with collecting the trash of the white people while their men conducted peace talks. The leading Comanche chief wore a Mexican hat which he greatly treasured, a hat that he had reportedly taken from a Mexican officer he had previously killed.[30]

Talks before congress went well, for a treaty was signed at the capital in Houston on May 29, 1838. Secretary of State Robert Anderson Irion, and Dr. Ashbel Smith represented Texas, while chiefs

Muguara, Muestyah, and Muhy represented the Comanches. The Comanches agreed to "stand by the white man and be his friend against all of his enemies." They also promised not to steal from or kill white settlers and to visit the seat of government on the second Monday of October of every year to discuss matters of mutual interest and to settle grievances.[31]

The Comanches departed Houston and made their way back toward the west Texas frontiers. When the Comanche party passed back through San Felipe, a Frenchman named Frédéric Leclerc noted that their chief was "in an unbelievable state of exaltation" over the gifts bestowed on him and his men by President Houston. Most of the gifts were glass beads, blankets, red cloth, and gunpowder. Leclerc wrote that their joy would not, however, compel the Comanches to honor the treaty they had just signed.

> The flag which the old chief bore was evidence enough of the success of the peace-treaty mission, but the Comanches were not to keep it long. This same band which was welcomed in San Felipe was, a few days after, to steal every horse it could find in the vicinity of San Antonio. Three Texians lured by the spirit of adventure, the desire to make money, and to open up new lanes of commerce, had accompanied the Indians to their savage strongholds. These unlucky souls were never to return; it was learned that one of them had been murdered long before the Comanches reached their wigwams, and nothing more was heard of the other two.[32]

★ ★ ★ ★ ★

Frontier Indian Skirmishes: May–July 1838

During the last days of May 1838, a skirmish took place between a party of settlers from the vicinity of Fort Oldham and a number of Indians concealed in a thicket near Tenoxtitlán. Fort Oldham, the fortified home of William Oldham, was located in present Burleson County on the the road joining Independence, Tenoxtitlán, and Franklin.[33]

A charge was made by the Indians and they killed two men, Joseph Reed and Dr. Bigham. They also wounded a man named Lawson. This fight was recorded in the May 30 issue of the *Telegraph and Texas Register*. The Indians were reportedly armed with short barrel yagers and rifles.

> A company of six or seven men went the next day to reconnoiter the ground, and found the bodies of the two individuals who had been killed, lying where they had fallen; they had not been scalped, but a part of their clothing had been taken away, and the gun of one had been broken to pieces. The barrel and lock had been taken but the breech was left! These Indians were well armed with rifles and yagers.

Indian encounters were experienced by other Texas settlers living in the northern settlements during the spring of 1838. One of these early fights was recorded by pioneer Samuel Dalton, who had come to Texas on May 24, 1837, and settled in present Lamar County near Paris. Following the murder of the Crookers family near Fort Inglish, a small volunteer party went out against the Indians who had committed the killings, as Dalton relates.

> It was in the winter of 1837 or 1838. Family by the name of Crookers were murdered at or near Fort Inglish, about daylight in the morning, when they were attacked. The father was shot at his horse lot, his little son in the yard and little daughter at or near the door. The mother, confined to her bed, was there murdered. She was found that morning, dead in a gore of her own blood and her infant child, the only one left of the family, covered with blood, crying and trying to get its mother's breast.
>
> Some eight or ten of us started in pursuit of them, as it was the custom in those days for every man to be in readiness to start at a minute's warning. We followed on their trail two days and nights. We came upon and surprised them the third morning about daylight, killed four and wounded a squaw accidentally. Three or four made their escape. They proved to be Caddo Indians.
>
> We recaptured the stolen horses and captured all their ponies and equipage. No one of us got hurt. David Rice, brother of Wm. M. Rice of Houston, Thomas C[o]usins, W[ash] Doss, and myself besides three others constituted our company.
>
> In 1838, the greater portion of this year, I was in a ranging company under Capt. Wm. M. Williams better known then as Buck Skin Williams. We had several little skirmishes with the different tribes of but little importance.[34]

During July 1838, settlers in Red River County were involved in yet another skirmish with hostile Indians. Thomas Ragsdale, an early citizen of this area, wrote that the Indians in the upper Red River areas often stole horses from the white settlers and even killed on occasion. When a white settler was killed, the locals formed a pursuit posse. Several pursuits had been made prior to 1838, but none had resulted in a fight with the Indians. "The Indians as much as twice offered to fight," Ragsdale wrote, "but owing to the Indians being too strong for our men, they declined fighting them until July 1838."[35]

When Indians were reported in July to be camping on Cypress Creek with stolen American horses, a Red River County volunteer force was put together to go after them. Upon reaching the creek, the men did not find any horses that they could recognize as being stolen. The Texans were "unorganized" and "rather in confusion" over whether to fight these Indians or not, according to Ragsdale.

Some of the Texans were intent upon fighting, while others were for moving out and leaving well enough alone. The men appointed their own committee to decide which way to act. Ragsdale, William Becknell, Claiborne Chisum, M. D. Wright, James Bourland, and Mathis Click were appointed to make this decision. Three of the committee "was for fighting" with Bourland declaring that "they had stolen all of his horses and that he would have some horses before he left."

Those who were opposed to fighting, amounting to about seventeen men, departed for home. Bourland then went to the Indian chief and told him that his braves had stolen one of his horses and that he must pay Bourland with some of these horses. "The chief agreed for Bourland to take twenty horses and keep them until the 15th of September," recalled Ragsdale. If the chief's men did not bring in his horses by that date, Bourland would keep the Indian horses.

Bourland and his small company of men proceeded to drive off the twenty Indian horses. As they did so, the Indian warriors immediately commenced an attack on them. Eight men engaged in the fight, including Bourland, Abner Netherey, M. D. Wright, Thomas Ragsdale, James Adkinson, and Mathias Click. In the fight which ensued, the Bourland party managed to kill three Indians with "no hurt done on our side," stated Ragsdale.

The Red River men drove off the Indian horses after the fight. Sam Houston was reportedly displeased with this company for their actions. As expected, the September 15 deadline passed without a further word on the return of Bourland's horses.

★ ★ ★ ★ ★

Buildup of Córdova's Rebellion: July–August 1838

The first true test of the Texas Militia's effectiveness was put in motion during the summer of 1838 by an uprising later dubbed the "Córdova Rebellion." At the beginning of 1838, northern Mexico was under the military command of General Vicente Filisola, who made his headquarters near the Rio Grande in Matamoros. In order to continue the war against Texas settlers, Filisola was determined to win the friendship of the various Indian tribes of Texas and unite them in an effort to drive the white men from their territory.

A Mexican agent named Julian Pedro Miracle was sent from Matamoros to work through the various Indian groups and Mexican Texans to unite them against the white Texas settlers. Miracle's force included Vicente Córdova, a former Mexican judge and *alcalde* (mayor) of Nacogdoches who had been forced out of office when the Republic of Texas was established. Córdova, born in 1798, had been captain of a citizens' militia company in the August 2, 1832, battle of Nacogdoches. Córdova and other Nacogdoches Tejanos had since become frustrated by the new Anglo majority which failed to protect their property and acknowledge their political voice. Córdova had left Nacogdoches due to his differences with the Anglo authorities and had since been commissioned by General Filisola to help raise Indians as "auxiliaries" to the Mexican army. Accompanying Miracle and Córdova was a force of seventy-two men, which included thirty-four Mexican soldiers, twenty Cherokee and Caddo Indians, two other Indians, and sixteen citizens from Matamoros.[36]

Moving into Texas, Miracle's party was joined on June 3 by Juan de la Garza, who brought food and ammunition for the group. During their travels, these rebels managed to capture fifteen horses and a valuable stash of tobacco from a party of smugglers. Miracle's party camped on June 17 at the Pastel, where they killed two Irishmen, a woman, and her children. On June 19, they encamped on the Arroyo Blanco and spent the next few days scouting out American forces near La Bahía. Miracle continued on past the Guadalupe and Colorado rivers, finally meeting with the Kickapoo Indians in the woods between the Brazos and Navasota rivers on June 27.

By July 9, they had reached Chief Bowles' Cherokee village and soon thereafter a conference was held among several Indian chiefs. Among the other tribes Miracle was known to have met with were representatives of the Choctaws, Cherokees, Kickapoos, Kichai, Chickasaws, Caddos, Wacos, and Tawakonis. In these councils, Miracle would smoke the peace pipe with Indian leaders and then distribute gifts of tobacco, powder, and lead to them. Miracle's direct orders from General Filisola instructed him to "propose to them that they and their friends should take up arms in defense of the integrity of the Mexican territory in Texas." The Indians would be "rewarded according to their merits" in arming themselves for a war against the Texas settlers. The ultimate scheme would then involve Filisola leading his army into Texas to join the Indians in overthrowing the young republic. Upon the completion of this campaign, Mexico would reward the Indians with "possession of the land they are entitled to."

Visiting the Mexicans and Cherokees in the vicinity of Nacogdoches in early August, Miracle was joined by a number of revolutionary Tejanos who resided about Nacogdoches, including Juan Flores, Juan Cruz, Juan Jose Rodriguez, Carlos Morales, Juan Santos Coy, Jose Ariola, Jose Vicenti Micheli, and Antonio Corda. He was also instrumental in enlisting former slave Joshua N. Robertson and a few Tejano-loyal whites such as Nathaniel Norris and John Norris. These were added to his entourage of Tejanos and Indians which now numbered more than two hundred rebels. Miracle's force by late July had made their campground on the Angelina River about twenty miles southwest of Nacogdoches.

The *Nacogdoches Chronicle* reported of Córdova's force that "a dozen leaders of the Mexican population in Nacogdoches have renounced the Constitution and expressed their desire to have revenge. Other reports state 200 men are now in arms."[37]

The citizens of Nacogdoches County had grown accustomed to watching out for Indians, who became increasingly bold during the Córdova Rebellion. San Jacinto veteran Stephen Franklin Sparks later wrote his impressions of living on Indian frontiers outside of Nacogdoches during 1838.

> The Indians became very troublesome. During the moonlit nights they would make raids, and in one night they would steal all the horses in a whole settlement . . . The Cherokees and Shawnee Indians lived about thirty miles north of the settlement. They pretended to be at peace with the whites, but they were probably interested in the stealing . . .
>
> I bought a piece of land on the outside of the settlement, and my wife, mother-in-law, and I moved out there. We had three or four negroes with us. We never knew at what moment we would be attacked, and I slept with my gun at the head of my bed, where I could lay my hands on it. I hired a young man by the name of B. F. Sills to live with me, as much to help protect my family as to work for me. We would take our guns

> with us to the field to plough, and we would leave one gun at one end of the rows and one at the other; then we ploughed so that he would be at one end and I at the other, so they could not cut us off from both our guns at the same time.[38]

The first outbreak of violence from Córdova's rebellion happened on August 4, 1838, following a raid in which a number of horses were stolen from the white settlers. A small group of settlers rode down to Córdova's settlement in Nacogdoches County, where they found a Tejano man herding some of their horses.

The Texan party arrested this Tejano and started home with their horses. They had not made it two miles down the road toward home when a party of rebels fired about thirty shots at them. Nacogdoches citizen Frank Hamilton was killed and the others fled rapidly for a small pioneer fort only a few miles away. Another party was sent out to recover Hamilton's body and word of this attack was passed along to Tom Rusk and Kelsey Douglass, commanders of the militia in this area.

On August 7, Captain John Durst informed Major General Rusk that at least one hundred armed Tejanos, headed by Córdova and Nat Norris, were encamped on the Angelina River. Córdova's force is known to have also included his brother Telesforo Córdova, Juan Galán, and Guillermo Cruz, the latter reporting later that the Nacogdoches Tejanos had been treated as "dogs long enough." Another report from Captain Antonio Menchaca, who had actually been in the Córdova camp, gave their number as 120 Mexicans and twenty-five Biloxi and Ioni Indians.[39]

★ ★ ★ ★ ★

Karnes' Arroyo Seco Fight: August 10, 1838

On the southwestern frontier during 1837 and 1838, Colonel Henry Karnes was in command of the Texas Cavalry. In the summer of 1838, he led a volunteer company of twenty-one men, including San Jacinto veteran Benjamin F. Cage, out from the San Antonio area. West of the Medina River, they halted on the Arroyo Seco. While resting their horses here on August 10 they were suddenly approached by two hundred mounted Comanche Indians charging toward them.

Karnes quickly ordered the men to secure their horses and take station for the fight. They were slightly protected by a ravine and chaparral brush, from which they fired in alternate platoons, by which method one-third of their guns were constantly loaded to meet attackers at close quarters.[40]

Volunteer Jack Hays helped to divide the assailants by dropping their chief from his horse. Hays, who had served in 1837 with Captain Deaf Smith, had since been involved as a surveyor and scout in southwestern Texas. The Indians dropped out of rifle range to regroup, then signaled their next advance with a flurry of arrows. The Texans were good shots and managed to drop a number of their assailants on their second pass. Heavily favored in number, the Comanches would not give up the fight easily. Launching another barrage of arrows, they charged in for a third pass on Karnes' men. During this pass, they picked up their dead and wounded before galloping away. Losing at least twenty killed and an equal number wounded, the Indians had apparently had enough. One of the Comanche Indians reportedly killed was Chief Essowakkenny, a leader who had met with Karnes and Johnston in May in San Antonio for a peace treaty.[41]

While fearlessly leading his men, Colonel Karnes exposed himself to Indian fire on a number of occasions and was himself wounded. He was struck by an arrow while standing atop the bank for a better view of the battle. No other men from his party were wounded, although most of their horses were wounded or killed by the numerous arrows launched at them. In so standing their ground, Karnes and his men won the continued respect of the citizens of San Antonio and the Texas Southwest.[42]

★ ★ ★ ★ ★

Rusk's Militia Mobilizes

Nacogdoches was a bustling town in the days following Captain Durst's August 7 report of Córdova's forces building up on the Angelina River. President Sam Houston, while in Nacogdoches at this time, issued an order on August 8 for the Mexicans and Indians to disperse or to be considered enemies of the Republic.

These rebels replied to Houston on August 10 that they were not familiar with "the existing laws" of the Republic, that they were well armed, and were "ready to shed the last drop of the blood" in defense of their principles. These men claimed that they were not in favor of violence but only wanted their property rights respected by the government. The signers of this bold letter to Houston were Córdova, Nat Norris, Juan Arista, José Vicente Micheli, Juan Santos Coy, Antonio Corda, Carlos Morales, Joshua Robertson, Juan José Rodriquez, José de Labome, Antonio Caderon, Julio Lasarin, James Quinelty, Antonio Flores, Guadalupe Cárdenas, Napoleon de Valtz, William Donavan, and Juan José Acosta.[43]

Another attack was made during August by Córdova's forces. Two brothers, Matthew and Charles Roberts, were shot down in the road. A third man, believed to be William Finley, escaped with a bullet having torn his clothing. The attackers were said by Finley to be Indians, although the *Nacogdoches Chronicle* that month stated "we think he was mistaken" about this identity.[44]

While Rusk's companies served as field reinforcements, President Houston worked in Nacogdoches to keep the Cherokees from the rebels. He wrote letters to the Indians with whom Texas had standing treaties. Chief Bowles and Sam Houston considered themselves brothers and Houston sent his nephew John Bowles back to the Cherokees to warn them. He also sent a letter on August 10 to Chief Big Mush's village stating that "There is now some trouble between the Mexicans and the Americans. I wish you to stand by the treaty which I made with you."[45]

Houston wrote a letter to Chief Bowles on August 11, cautioning him to "not be disturbed by the troubles which are around you, but be at peace." Houston also advised Bowles that surveyor Elias S.

Thomas Jefferson Rusk (1803–1857) served as major general of the Texas Militia during 1838 and 1839. He had previously served as secretary of war, had been brigadier general commanding the Texas Army in 1836 and was among the signers of the Texas Declaration of Independence.
Texas State Library and Archives Commission.

Vansickle, despite the current heated situation, was running the promised survey line near the Cherokee territory. Vansickle, who had served as a ranger in 1836 under Captain Costley, was later captured by Córdova's rebels, however, and held as their prisoner.

General Rusk was impatient to go after the rebels while Houston negotiated. The company stationed at the Angelina stayed on the east side while Córdova's forces occupied the west side. On August 10, a report was received that about three hundred Indians had joined Córdova. Having sent their decree to Sam Houston, Córdova's rebels then began to move up river toward the Cherokee Nation.

Rusk had not been sitting idle while Sam Houston negotiated. He had started organizing companies and putting out the word for volunteers to form an expected expedition against these rebel forces. The earliest company formed for this expedition was that of Captain Hiram B. Stephens, who organized a force of mounted rangers on August 4. This was on the day that Nacogdoches citizen Francis Hamilton had been killed by Córdova's men.

The following day, August 5, two companies of mounted volunteers under captains James D. Long and Lewis Sanchez had been mustered into service. These companies served on Rusk's campaign under Colonel William Sparks and were under the direct supervision of Major Baley C. Walters.

On August 6, Captain Wesley W. Hanks' Mounted Riflemen and Captain David Laird's Mounted Gunmen were organized for service, followed by a Nacogdoches area volunteer company under Captain Samuel C. Box which mustered in on August 7.

The bulk of the companies under Rusk were organized in and near Nacogdoches on August 8 and August 9. Captains Robert W. Smith, David Rusk, Alexander Horton, David Muckleroy, and George W. Hooper organized parties of mounted volunteers. In addition, Captain James Reily took charge of the "Nacogdoches Guards" and Captain William M. Keeling was elected leader of a dismounted infantry unit.

In San Augustine, other militia companies were formed as news of Córdova's rebellion reached that area. The volunteers from San Augustine were organized under Major Alexander G. Hale. The first mounted volunteer company under Captain Henry W. Augustine, destined to join Major Rusk's campaign, had mustered into the service by August 8. One of the volunteers of Augustine's company was John Salmon Ford, a doctor who had been born in South Carolina in 1815 and arrived in San Augustine in June 1836. In his memoirs, Ford gives an interesting look at how the early Texas Militia companies were organized.

In his memoirs, Dr. John Salmon "Rip" Ford (1815–1897) offers some interesting anecdotes of this 1838 Texas Militia campaign. Ford was later a respected leader of the Texas Rangers and a Texas statesman.
Texas State Archives and Library Commission. Original photo from 1875 Constitutional Convention.

It was the custom in those days for men able to do military duty to outfit themselves with arms, ammunition, and provisions. It was usual to meet at the county seat and organize. Elections were primitive affairs. For instance, when two candidates were in the field for captain, they were placed some distance apart. At the word "march" the friends of the respective candidates fell into line by the side of their favorites. A count was made and the result declared. The captain of the San Augustine company, to which the writer belonged, was H. W. Augustine.[46]

As the number of militia companies increased, General Rusk split his forces for this expedition. Colonel Samuel S. Davis was put in charge of the First Regiment and Colonel William Sparks and Lieutenant Colonel James Carter were given command of the companies of the Second Regiment, both regiments falling under Brigadier General Kelsey Douglass' Third Militia Brigade. Rusk's command staff, elected on August 9, included Brigadier Inspector Archibald Hotchkiss, Adjutant Peter Tipps, and aides de camp Isaac Campbell, David Spangler Kaufman, and Charles S. Taylor.

General Rusk, in company with Adjutant General Hugh McLeod, had thus organized fourteen companies by August 9, all in direct defiance of the orders of Sam Houston in Nacogdoches. Colonel McLeod, a New York-born Georgian who had graduated last from the 1835 class at West Point, had previously served in the U.S. Army. Named the adjutant general of Texas in May 1838, he was responsible for keeping army records and handling administrative matters.

Many of Rusk's men grew restless as they awaited the word to march out against the Mexican and Indian rebels. In camp, the citizen soldiers humored each other by poking fun at the younger recruits who were not used to being out in the wilderness. John Ford of Captain Augustine's company later wrote of these lighter moments.

> The "greenies" suffered as usual. A sentinel named [Private Selden G. Purce] Purce one night mistook the noise made by a rat while packing sticks to complete a nest for the furtive tramp of a savage, and fired. The line of battle was speedily formed, an investigation set on foot, and the truth was ascertained. Every once in a while someone would bawl out: "Who shot the rat?" A multitude of voices would respond: "Purse!" He grew tired of the fun and swore a goodly lot of extra oaths, but the cry ceased not.[47]

When Córdova's bold letter was received on August 10, the militiamen were eager to move out. The notice that Córdova's forces were moving from their Angelina River camp compelled General Rusk to order Captain Henry Augustine's mounted unit to follow the rebels' movements. Córdova was reported to be moving up towards Chief Bowles' Cherokee country. Augustine's company performed its reconnaissance without incident, maintaining a vigilant night guard to avoid being surprised.

The Texas spies followed the Mexican and Indian party upriver while Rusk's main body of troops marched out from Nacogdoches along the Old San Antonio Road. Rusk's men camped out on the Angelina River, where Rusk wrote a letter to Chief Bowles on August 13. He explained how the Mexican rebels who had stolen horses, killed a Nacogdoches settler, and then threatened war were now hiding in the Cherokee Nation. Rusk sent this message via courier Joseph Durst and encouraged Bowles to send word back with Durst. Rusk assured Bowles that he did not intend to harm the Cherokees, but they were wrong to harbor enemies of Texas.[48]

Captain Augustine's men camped out nearly two days at Lacy's Fort, a fortified farmhouse located near present Alto along the road which led to Washington-on-the-Brazos. The main house sat on an elevation overlooking a vast extent of territory.

On the second day, Captain Augustine's company learned that Córdova's forces were close by and numbered approximately four hundred. He moved his company from Lacy's Fort and encamped that night in a patch of timber which was surrounded by prairie on all sides. The following morning, he started his company marching along in twos in pursuit of Córdova.

General Rusk's main body of troops caught up to Augustine's advance scouts that morning beyond Lacy's Fort. The men of Augustine's company were at first alarmed when they spotted Rusk's main body marching across the prairie in their direction, as Private Ford later wrote.

> The order was given: "Front into Line!" We moved at a gallop. An elderly gentleman, Mr. [William] Shofner, seemed to feel the necessity of going into battle with a full stomach. He detached a piece of dried beef from the cantle of his saddle, made a vigorous effort to fill his mouth. The ground was "sidling," his horse began stumbling, was unable to recover, and fell a long distance, leaving the rider on the ground behind him. The prostrate man made a desperate effort to finish his meal. It did not take long to learn the force in sight was General Rusk's main command.[49]

Rusk's militia force had grown during the second week of August. Another mounted volunteer company under Captain Charles Mote Walters had joined Colonel Sparks' Second Regiment by August 10. Several more companies were created over the next few days. From the eastern extremes of the Third Militia Brigade, Colonel Willis H. Landrum soon arrived with three more companies under his charge. Captain Robert Kemp Goodloe's San Augustine Mounted Gunmen and Captain David Renfro's Sabine County Mounted Volunteers were mustered into service on August 12, while Captain James F. Timmins' Mounted Volunteers were organized on August 14. Colonel Landrum was placed in command of the Third Regiment of Mounted Volunteers of the Third Militia Brigade forces.

The final company to join General Rusk's expedition on August 16 was the mounted volunteer unit of Captain Andrew Caddell, who became part of Colonel Sparks' Second Regiment. Payroll records of these companies show that captains were paid at the rate of seventy-five dollars per month, first lieutenants at sixty dollars per month, second lieutenants at fifty dollars per month, orderly sergeants at forty dollars per month, and privates at twenty-five dollars per month.

Captain Augustine's Texas scouts soon located Córdova's rebels some two miles from Chief Bowles' Cherokee village. Rusk and Douglass moved from Lacy's Fort on to Fort Houston on August 14. Several Fort Houston area residents joined Rusk's expedition. Among those present at Fort Houston was the family of former ranger superintendent Garrison Greenwood, who had felt safe in venturing out to visit old friends in the area due to Rusk's strong show of forces. His fourteen-year-old son John Harvey Greenwood enlisted as a volunteer in the company of Captain Samuel Box on August 14.[50]

Captain Box's company was one of two volunteer cavalry companies raised under the direction of Major Leonard H. Mabbitt of the San Augustine Municipality. Mabbitt had served during the Texas Revolution in the volunteer company of Captain Thomas Lewellan and had been active in the Texas Army during 1836.[51]

Messenger Joseph Durst returned from Bowles' village on August 14 and informed Rusk that he had met with Bowles, Chief Big Mush, and the Mexicans. He had found the Mexicans and some of the Indians armed and seemingly ready for battle.[52]

From Fort Houston, Rusk's militiamen then pushed ahead up to the village of Chief Bowles. Sam Houston wrote to Bowles on August 14, urging him to give up the idea to fight. The Texas Militia marched through the Cherokee village before setting up its own temporary camp nearby while Rusk talked with Bowles.

Ten Indian chiefs were present for the peace talks on August 15. As a result of the talks, the Córdova's Mexicans postponed their operation for a short time. John Ford of Captain Augustine's company was impressed with Chief Bowles during these negotiations.

> He was standing at a short distance from his house, a comfortable appearing log cabin, conversing with some of our officers, perhaps General Rusk. An interpreter was present. Bowles' face had somewhat the contour of a Caucasian. The nose was rather on the aquiline order. He impressed one with the idea that he possessed force of character and great firmness. He denied all connection with the movement set on foot by Córdova and his Indian allies. As far as his people were concerned, we were induced to form a different opinion very soon thereafter.[53]

Rusk wrote to Sam Houston on August 16 from his camp. He stated that he wished to avoid "raising an Indian war," but did not like "remaining idle until our enemy has had time to make all his arrangements and concentrate his forces." That night, William Goyens, a free mulatto loyal to Rusk, and Leonard H. Williams disguised themselves as Indians and slipped into Bowles' village. They successfully met with the old chief, who assured them that his men would take no part in the uprising.[54]

Rusk soon received word that Córdova's rebels had broken camp and were fleeing westward toward the headwaters of the Trinity River, while the rest were planning to filter back into their settlements. Texas scouts pursued the fleeing rebels, while most of the militiamen remained camped at the Neches Saline. Private Ford noted the enemy's trails "grew smaller as we advanced."

William Young Lacy of Captain Bob Smith's company felt that Chief Bowles had sent Córdova's men away, wanting nothing to do with his mischief. This was due to the fact that

> there were 500 to 600 white men within three miles and the sooner they got away the better. [Córdova's] camp broke up and they left in double quick order. We pursued them about 40 miles, found his men had scattered, and supposing that they had left the country and gone to Mexico, we returned home, disbanded our forces with the exception of two companies of cavalry, commanded by L. H. Mabbitt, and sent [them] to Fort Houston for the protection of that frontier.[55]

Sam Houston sent a letter to Rusk on August 18 ordering him to disband his militia. Houston hoped that the "brave men who will have so promptly rallied to their country's defense" would soon be discharged to return to their homes.[56] He admitted that Córdova's forces, although dispersed, "may again unite at some point, so as to annoy a portion of our population."

The majority of Rusk's militia companies began disbanding on August 21 and continued to do so over the next week per Houston's orders. The Third Regiment companies under Colonel Landrum were several days longer in reaching their extreme eastern Texas homes before they were discharged.

Colonel Hugh McLeod, the adjutant general of Texas and strongly loyal to Tom Rusk, endorsed the Texas Militia leader's action and criticized President Houston for hindering Rusk's work "in every way with his orders." Rusk wrote Vice President Lamar that this "timely demonstration of force" through Indian country stirred up fear in the Indians.

Houston's diplomacy had prevented a major war for the moment but Rusk and Lamar's efforts to exterminate Indians of questionable loyalty would not be long subdued.

Major General Rusk's Indian Expedition into Cherokee Nation

Field and Staff, Third Militia Brigade: August 9–27, 1838

Thomas J. Rusk	Major Gen.	Archibald Hotchkiss	Brig. Inspector
Hugh McLeod	Adj. General	James M. Smith	Sgt. Major
Kelsey H. Douglass	Brig. Gen.	Kindred H. Muse	Quartermaster
Samuel S. Davis	Colonel	Isaac Campbell	Aide de Camp
William C. Sparks	Colonel	David S. Kaufman	Aide de Camp
James Carter	Lt. Colonel	Charles S. Taylor	Aide de Camp
Baley C. Walters	Major	George S. Hyde	Surgeon
Peter E. Tipps	Adjutant		

Capt. Hooper's Mounted Volunteers: August 9–27, 1838

Captain:
George W. Hooper
First Lieutenant:
Henry Clay
Second Lieutenant:
Charles Haley
Orderly Sergeant:
James N. Candler
Privates:
Samuel G. Atkinson
David Blankenship
John M. Bradley
William G. Branson
John M. Britton
James F. Brown
Tyme Buckley
David R. Cannon
Mason G. Cole
Harrison Davis
Nathan Davis
Eli Dumer
William H. Dunn
William T. English
Allen Haley
John R. Haley
John R. Haley Jr.
Mark Haley
Raburn Haley
Richard Haley
Thomas Haley
James Hall
Samuel N. Hall
Andrew Harvey
Redmond Hughes
Brian Humphries
Lewis Latham
Berry Lindsay
Samuel Lindsay
Thomas Lindsay
John Little
Baley Lout
Robert O. Lusk
Andrew Martin
Jefferson McCluskey
William Morton
Thomas Pondrill
Peter Whitstone
Howard L. Wiggins
Rodrick Wiggins

Capt. Timmins' Mounted Volunteers: August 14–25, 1838

Captain:
James F. Timmins
First Lieutenant:
Hampton Anderson
First Sergeant:
John Ray
Privates:
Bailey W. Anderson Jr.
Heusam Anderson
James Asher
Howard Dillard
James Dillard
E. W. Gibbs
J. L. Gibbs
David Gilleland
Kelly Hamilton
Jacob Harmark
Daniel Little
Shad Owen
John Rivo
Edward Smith
Hancock Smith
Isaac Stout
James S. Stout
Stephen B. Trader

Capt. Sanchez's Mounted Volunteers: August 5–27, 1838

Captain:
Lewis Sanchez
First Lieutenant:
William W. Umsted
Orderly Sergeant:
Santiago Rabia
Privates:
Howard W. Bailey [1]
Jose Maria Chavana [2]
Santiago Chavana [1]
Rafael de la Cruz [1]
Jose Falcon [1]
Jacinto Magano [1]
Delores Martinez [1]
John Randolph [1]
David Sanchez [1]
Simon Sanchez [1]
Ygancio Sanchez [1]
Benigo de los Santos [3]
Desiderio Saucedo [1]
Henry Webb [1]
Peter Welden [1]

[1] Joined August 12.
[2] Joined August 20.
[3] Joined August 23.

Capt. Goodloe's San Augustine Mounted Gunmen: Aug. 12–Sept. 1, 1838

Captain:
Robert Kemp Goodloe[1]
First Lieutenant:
John McAda
Second Lieutenant:
William Fisher
Orderly Sergeant:
Frederick W. Ogden
First Sergeant:
H. Campbell
Second Sergeant:
T. McLamore
Third Sergeant:
P. Hinds
Fourth Sergeant:
A. M. Langham
First Corporal:
Anthony Blythe
Second Corporal:
David Reynolds
Third Corporal:
James B. Woodsworth
Privates:
Lorenzo Dow Baker
George Barber
Robert G. Cartwright
William P. Conner
A. M. Davis
G. Fisoph
William Hobby
John Hunt
Nathaniel Hyden
H. C. Irvine
H. Johnson
A. T. Jones
Hugh B. Kelly
Isaac H. Kendrick
William Lakey
S. D. Lansome
George W. Lewis
William Munford
George N. Palmer
P. Pantallion
G. Payne [2]
James Ship
Thomas Shoemate
Francis M. Stovall
William H. Taylor
H. Thompson [2]
S. Tinsley
David F. Webb

1 Promoted from First Lieutenant when Captain J. Sims resigned.
2 Went to the army.

Capt. Hanks' Mounted Riflemen: August 6–October 20, 1838 *

Captain:
Wesley W. Hanks
First Lieutenant:
J. M. Justice
Second Lieutenant:
Wilson W. Baker
First Sergeant:
Frederick W. Ogden[1]
Second Sergeant:
Robert A. Barkley
Third Sergeant:
H. Cantfield
Fourth Sergeant:
C. H. Langhorn
First Corporal:
T. J. Quesenberry
Second Corporal:
Anthony Blythe [1]
Third Corporal:
David Reynolds
Fourth Corporal:
James B. Woodward
Privates:
William Army
D. N. Barkley
Thomas D. Brooks
Newton H. Brownfield
Archer Browning
George M. Casey
H. D. Conn
James Dillard
Henderson Duncan
William French
Augustus B. Hardin
Benjamin Herrige
T. J. Holland
Levi Hopkins
B. F. Howard
James Biddle Langham
John H. Lewis
Lewis Mason
William McKnight
R. W. Moore
C. J. Neely
William Norris
Isaac Parker
A. Phelps
Thomas Platt
William R. Powell
Wiley Rogers
John Sanders
James Simmons
Daniel Smiley
Thomas Smiley
Eli B. Stephens
S. Talada
William Thompson
Frederick A. Tibbles
Thomas Tobin
Joseph Walker
William G. Walker
John Warden
Russell Warner
C. C. White
Hansel Wright

* Hanks' company was reorganized on August 22 and continued to serve through October 20, 1838.
1 Transferred from Capt. Goodloe's company.

Captain Laird's San Augustine Gunmen: Aug. 6–22, 1838

Captain:
David Laird
First Lieutenant:
Charles Epps
Second Lieutenant:
T. Southern
First Sergeant:
Corley T. Crawford
Second Sergeant:
J. C. Moses
Third Sergeant:
J. Scarborough
Fourth Sergeant:
William Moon
First Corporal:
William Phillips
Second Corporal:
M. M. Stewart
Third Corporal:
Andrew J. Berry
Fourth Corporal:
Oran Ham
Privates:
James Alexander
William Anderson
T. D. Barber
H. A. P. Berry
Jacob D. Black
D. A. Boon
B. M. D. Borough
T. Burk
Allen Dilliard
George W. Forbes
Bartlett Fry
M. Gentry
J. Gentry
William Johnson
C. Martin Loggins
William G. Long
James Martin
J. Matthews
Mereda McCabe
M. Mebane
David Meradith
John D. Miller
M. Miller
W. Montgomery
John Moore
W. Perry
J. C. Ray
E. P. Richards
N. D. Ridgway
A. W. Rowe
J. D. Russell
J. N. Shofner
Henry C. Sossaman
T. J. Stockdon
W. Switchall
J. Wallace
J. Wallen
John White
W. A. Willis

Capt. Keeling's Nacogdoches Infantry Company: August 9–23, 1838

Captain:
William M. Keeling
First Lieutenant:
Isham Sims
First Corporal:
H. Craber
Second Corporal:
David F. O'Kelly
Privates:
Hayden S. Arnold
J. C. Bradford
C. Campbell
Philip Carroll
N. Carson
J. L. Clark
J. D. Coffee
John M. Dorr
Lewis Duvall
James Eakin
C. Emerick
Oscar Engledow
John Gann
George Hamilton
Vincent Hamilton
James Hart
Calvin Henderson
Charles Hotchkiss
William Jones
Robin Kasey
John Lambert
Thomas Lampkin
William Manwarren
Artimon L. Martin
John W. McCobb
G. F. A. Meide
Benjamin Miller
Sylvester Moreland
Alexander Parks
R. H. Pinney
George Pollett
James Pollock
James Condy Raguet
Henry Raguet
James Reid
Simon Schloss
James Sims
Augustus W. Slawson
Michael Snyder
Thomas Stanford
John Stewart
I. Sturock
James C. Thompson
John S. Thorn
George W. Welch
J. Wilbourn
Samuel W. Wilds
Moses Williamson
L. W. Wilson
George Von Wrede
Charles Yordt

Capt. Muckleroy's Mounted Volunteers: August 9–22, 1838

Captain:
David Muckleroy
First Lieutenant:
Bartlett M. Hall
Second Lieutenant:
Alfred Walling
First Sergeant:
James M. Draper
Second Sergeant:
Henderson Draper
Third Sergeant:
Abram Odell
Fourth Sergeant:
Elijah Chism
Privates:
S. D. Baker
David Barron
William A. Beard
Bluford Bell
Charles N. Bell
James Bell
William Bell
William W. Bell
Alfred Berry
George Brandon
John N. Brimberry
Willis H. Bruce
Samuel Caldwell
Wiley Caldwell
Claiborn Chism
John R. Chism
Wililam P. Chism
Jesse Cole
Sidney Cummings
David Curry
Thomas Curry
Pleasant Davis
James Goodin
James Gilliland
Samuel Gilliland
James Goodin
Green Hall
Isaac Hamby
George Humphreys
John Hunter
Henry Jacobs
James Jacobs
James Jones
Michael P. Kelley
Isaac Lee
William McClure
J. W. McFarland
Joseph Nations
Bernard Pantalion
John S. Perttilier
James Pharis
Solomon Royle
Reuben Russell
John Sample
William Sasser
William F. Shannon
Bartlett H. Simpson
James Simpson
Isaac C. Skilling
Benjamin Strickner
Lewis Walker
James Walling
Jesse Walling
John Walling
John C. Walling
Thomas J. Walling
Thurston M. Walling
Elijah Wiatt

Capt. Reily's Nacogdoches Guards: August 9–24, 1838

Captain:
James Reily
First Lieutenant:
James S. Mayfield
First Sergeant:
Warren Angus Ferris
Second Sergeant:
Daniel Lacy
Third Sergeant:
Benjamin F. Moore
Sergeant:
Thomas T. McIver
Sergeant:
William Hart
Privates:
___ Abraham
Thomas Adams
William Adams
Nathaniel Amory
Robert Bean
Thomas Young Beauford
A. Bierman
Leo Bondies
Christopher Y. Buford
Lewis Buford
John S. Caruthers
Albert G. Corbin
H. Crutchir
William Dankworth
Lewis Dufore
Gibson J. Dyer
Albert Emanuel
Charles M. Gould
W. Hanson
William Harrison
Rinaldo Hotchkiss
John Hansford Hyde
Hugh Kenner
John H. Kerchoffer
Joel Langham
Alexander McIver
Stewart Meradith
____ Moore
Richard Parmalee
Moses L. Patton
Edgar Pollitt
Henry M. Rogers
Antonio Sanchez
Henry Sibley
Edwin P. Sims
Matthew F. Sims
James Harper Starr
William Sturock
James Triplett
Frances Voderhoys
Fred Weider

Capt. Walters' Mounted Volunteers: August 10–30, 1838

Captain:
Charles Mote Walters
Privates:
Andrew Ables
Harrison Ables
Joseph S. Ables
T. T. Ables
T. B. Atwood
Thomas Goss
Alexander Z. Walters
Andrew C. Walters
Anthony W. Walters
Tillman Walters
Wade Hampton Walters
William Warnell

Capt. Renfro's Sabine Co. Mounted Volunteers: August 12–26, 1838

Captain:
David Renfro
First Lieutenant:
Alston H. Payne
Second Lieutenant:
James H. Thompson
First Sergeant:
J. T. O. Levine
Second Sergeant:
William Renfro
Third Sergeant:
Dennis Dykes
Fourth Sergeant:
Enoch P. Chisholm
First Corporal:
J. W. Cobble
Second Corporal:
B. H. Zachary
Third Corporal:
Daniel Estep
Fourth Corporal:
E. Devinney
Privates:
William B. Birks
Owen H. Bishop
R. H. Bloomfield
John Boyd
William C. Bullock
Joseph Chrisman
Wiliam Clark
John C. Cole
Jacob Crawford
W. H. Davis
R. H. Dement
John T. Dennis
Richard Devinney
William Donaho
William Earle
Charles Eaton
E. H. Evans
William O. Flowers
Alex L. Frazer
W. B. Frazer
E. P. Gaines
John B. Gaines
Malcolm Givin
Larkin Groce
W. V. Haney
T. J. Hatton
John Higgins
E. W. Hocket
Josephus Irvine
William D. Irvine
George Lane
Lott Lee
R. L. Love
Roland McKenny
J. C. McLean
James B. McMahan
John B. McMahan
John M. Mitchell
T. W. Mitchell
Lipscomb Norvell
William Oneal
Benjamin Payne
William J. Ragsdale
J. H. Ridgway
Martin Rumph
T. W. Slaughter
Jackson Smith
Robert Stephens
Andrew Tippett
Robert Tippett
Francis M. Weatherred
William C. Weatherred
B. White
James T. White
M. D. White
Ed Wilder
J. W. Williams
John Yoce

Capt. Box's Volunteers: August 7–September 24, 1838

Captain:
Samuel Charles Box
First Lieutenant:
Alford G. Sims
Second Lieutenant:
W. L. Selman
First Sergeant:
W. B. Blackburn
Privates:
George A. Bass
Isaac T. Bean
Jeremiah Blackwell
Zachariah W. Bottoms
John Andrew Box
George W. Click
William Davis
Zaccheus Gibbs
Beverly Greenwood
John Harvey Greenwood
Thomas M. Hughes
Adam Johnson
John Johnson
Jesse C. Kincannon
Joseph Luce
Amos Quinn
John Ridens
John Roark
Russell Roark
Tenese Sanchez
William W. Sims
Eli M. Thomason
Samuel W. Wyles

Capt. Rusk's Nacogdoches Mounted Volunteers: August 8–22, 1838

Captain:
David Rusk
First Lieutenant:
Jacob Snively
Second Lieutenant:
Abner Alvis
First Sergeant:
James W. Cleveland
Second Sergeant:
Jacob Matchesen
First Corporal:
John Noblett
Second Corporal:
Charles Worthington
Privates:
John Aldrich
Bennett Blake
Joseph Buffington
James C. Carr
Asa Dorsett
Abram E. Dowdle
John Forbes
Henry Gough
William Gowen
Allen Greer
Elias Edley Hamilton
Samuel M. Hyde
William Johnson
Zachariah C. Johnson
Dyer Little
J. Little
James McCormick
Aquilla M. Mead
George Miliken
John Miliken
John C. Morrison
Henry Myers
Benjamin Nance
Isaac G. Parker
William R. Powell
James Power
Dimer W. Reeves
John Rivers
____ Ryan
L. Sample
James Shea
Levi B. Shrader
Thomas Sims Sr.
Thomas Sims Jr.
Berry Smith
Stephen Stanley
Willeford Stanley
Wiley Stone
Samuel Taylor
Leonard M. Thorn
Jackson Todd
Nathan Wade
J. VanCalvert
John M. White
William Williams
George H. Wright
Solomon Wright Sr.

Capt. Smith's Nacogdoches Mounted Volunteers: August 8–21, 1838

Captain:
Robert W. Smith
First Lieutenant:
John Bingham
Second Lieutenant:
Stephen F. Sparks
Orderly Sergeant:
Leander E. Tipps
Privates:
Elijah Anderson
John Bailey
E. K. Black
James Brewer
William Brewer
Williamson Bromley
Thomas D. Brooks
Henry C. Cook
Ambrose Hulen Crain
Robert Cummings
Edward Davis
William C. Davis
James Dickerson
Theodore Dorsett
William Duford
James Edwards
Ambrose B. Eubank
Elias Newman Eubank
Edward V. Eubank
Hartwell Frazier
Archibald C. Graham
William Graham
Sylvester Gray
Samuel Haynes
William F. Henderson
Lewis Knight
David Knowles
William Young Lacy
J. T. Langham
Madison H. Langham
Monroe P. Langham
Pascal C. Langham
John Lively
James McAnulty
Mack McRoy
James McWilliams
James B. Murray
Robert Patterson
Charles L. Price
George W. Ritter
James W. Robertson
Samuel Rogers
W. B. Shaw
Henry Madison Smith
Eli G. Sparks
James Hawkins Sparks
William W. Taylor
Thomas G. Timmons
J. H. Urby
Meriweather L. Ware
Robert W. Watkins
Madison G. Whitaker

Capt. Stephens' Nacogdoches Mounted Rangers: August 4–21, 1838

Captain:
Hiram B. Stephens
First Lieutenant:
Daniel Weeks
Second Lieutenant:
James Fisher
First Sergeant:
Edwin Corbitt
Second Sergeant:
Benjamin Moore
Third Sergeant:
John W. Fowler
Fourth Sergeant:
John C. Moss
Privates:
Levin Cadenhead
David Cook
Thomas Cook
Samuel Craft
William Curl
B. P. Despallier
James G. Dixon
Levi Ford
Asberry Griggs
Isaac Hicks
Thomas M. Hughes
Jesse T. Jones
J. N. Lewis
Francis C. McKnight
John A. Medford
Ishum Medford
Isaac Medkeff
Daniel Meradith
Joseph Meradith
James Moore
Pleasant Palmer
Adolphus Riemann
Eli Russell
A. M. Walters
George T. Walters
Robert Walters
Charles Weaver
Joseph Williams
James Windsor
William W. Wornell

Capt. Horton's Mounted Volunteers: August 8–September 22, 1838

Captain:
Alexander Horton
First Lieutenant:
Lewis M. Crow
First Sergeant:
Reuben D. Woods
Privates:
Charles Anderson
Bushwood W. Bell
David Brown
B. M. D. Burrows
James Daniel
William Daniel
Charles Epps
Redding Gaines
F. S. Green
Oran Ham
Nathaniel Hamilton
Cyrus Hard
Thomas Hendrick
William W. Holman
William M. Hurt
James Lansing
Edwin O. LeGrand
Felix G. Lemmon
W. Linville
Elijah A. Loyd
William Loyd
Thomas Martin
William D. Ratcliff
H. G. Richardson
Joseph Shanks
J. N. Shannon
M. H. Shryock
L. D. Simmons
Jordan Smith
Harrison E. Watson
William Weeks

Capt. Caddell's Mounted Volunteers: August 16–September 29, 1838

Captain:
Andrew Caddell
First Lieutenant:
Abraham Lewis
Second Lieutenant:
John T. Rawls
First Sergeant:
Ransom Sowell
Second Sergeant:
Freman Prather
Third Sergeant:
Daniel M. Evans
Fourth Sergeant:
Daniel C. Payne
Privates:
John C. Caddell
Andrew J. Caldwell
William Caldwell
Armsted Chumley
John Clark
Daniel Ferris
John C. Gallion
Thomas J. Griffin
Nathaniel Hunt
William Isaacs
Silas Keithley
John Maginnes
John Martin
George Massingill
John Massingill
John C. McFarlan
John M. Neely
Thomas Payne
Thomas Smith
Zachariah L. Stringer
James Walker
Robert C. Wilson

Capt. Augustine's Mounted Volunteers: August 8–22, 1838

Captain:
Henry W. Augustine
First Lieutenant:
John D. Nash
Second Lieutenant:
N. K. Kellum
First Sergeant:
John G. Berry
Second Sergeant:
John Neely
Third Sergeant:
L. W. Wright
First Corporal:
Zeb Payne
Second Corporal:
George F. Martin
Third Corporal:
C. Rodo
Privates:
H. B. Achols
James Alexander
John Allison
John W. Anderson
William G. Anderson
Peter Anthony
Nelson Ashmore
William Bates
G. W. Berry
Oliver P. Bodine
John Borders
F. N. Brooks
Samuel Brooks
Joseph Broyles
John Bryant
J. Burdett
Jesse Burdett
Newel Burdett
Newton W. Burdett
William B. Burdett
L. T. Burnes
F. P. Cabler
J. Camell
J. S. Cartwright
Thomas Chumley
Gerrett G. Cole
Levi Cole
H. Corzine
Rodden Taylor Crain
Ezekiel W. Cullen
S. L. Davidson
A. P. Davis
George W. Davis
Jesse Davis
R. Davis
L. T. Delle
L. T. Dew
M. Dial
Alford Douthard
William M. Ewing
Williston E. Ewing
John Salmon Ford
T. F. French
Benjamin Fuller
Ponton Fuller
Thomas H. Garner
Milton Garrett
William Garrett Jr.
D. W. Gilbert
John B. Gray
H. H. Green
Joseph T. Green
Horatio Griffith
Daniel Griggs
Jefferson Hagerty
H. Hall
Calvin Hamilton
Jacob E. Hamilton
Blackstone Hardeman Jr.
William N. Hardeman
Anthony Harris
Charles Haywood
R. H. Hibbitt
James Higgins
Don Holloway
Simpson Holloway
J. W. Hooker
H. H. Horn
James Gray Hyde
Joseph Irwin
W. G. Irwin
W. N. Jackson
R. J. Johnson
Nealy Kimbro
William Kimbro
Walter Paye Lane
W. W. Lanier
A. A. Lewis
W. Lockhart
G. H. Love
G. C. Lucas
E. W. Martin
George W. Martin
J. Martin
J. F. Martin
Morris May
Daniel C. McFarland
W. T. McGrew
John Mitchell
William Nash
Wiley W. Parker
J. F. Parmer
Anthony B. Patton
George W. Payne
Gilford Payne
W. W. Payne
Thomas J. Pittie
Alfred Polk
John Polk
Benajmin B. Pulliam
Selden G. Purce
Charles Richards
John Richards
William Richards
B. Riley
Joseph Rowe
Levi Sanders
Thomas M. Scott
G. W. Sharp
Joseph D. Sharp
H. R. Shearer
W. D. Shelton
William Shofner
Henry Shores
L. D. Simmons
David Skelton
John C. Smith
Samuel Smith
W. S. Smith
C. R. Sosman
Francis M. Stovall
Henry W. Sublett
H. R. Temple
Benjamin Thomas
Jackson Thomas
H. L. Thompson
Thomas Thompson
C. Trobridge
Sidney Vandiver
B. L. Vivian
Barkley M. Walker
D. O. Warren
L. Wells
J. T. Whiteman
O. H. Willis
Archibald Yancy

Capt. English's Mounted Volunteers: August 10–26, 1838

Captain:
George English
First Lieutenant:
Jesse Amason
Second Lieutenant:
R. B. English
First Sergeant:
Joseph Hall
Second Sergeant:
C. L. Mann
Privates:
James Alford
Jefferson Anderson
Jonathan Anderson
Jefferson Ashabram
J. R. Beauchamp
R. L. Biggar
Ahira Butler
A. L. Castleberry
Stephen Castleberry
John Choate
James Davenport
James T. Denton
Joseph Dial
L. W. Edwards
William A. Eliot
A. H. English
James English Jr.
John English Jr.
Stephen English
William T. English
Samuel Farrow
John H. Forsythe
Alfred Gates
William Gates
George L. Graham
John J. Hammond
John M. Hansford
William B. Hicks
James Hinton
Jeremiah Holman
Albert C. Horton
Thomas Hough
John Houston
Hartwell Howard
Hiram Inman
John Inman
Thomas Jester
Alvey R. Johnson
E. D. Johnson
R. A. Jordan
C. B. Lindsey
Varner Lout
Aaron Lowry
John Lowry
John May
Berry Merchant
Edward A. Merchant
John D. Merchant
Frederic H. Miller
John E. Myrick
Robert Parmer
William Porter
Isaac Raines
John D. Raines
William Riddle
Augustus Ryans
John A. Smith
James M. Sperry
James J. Standefer
Martin Taylor
Samuel Todd
William Van
William Walker
Zachariah C. Walker
Anderson Whetstone
Hedley White
Henry White
Reuben White
J. C. Williams
William Williams
Arthur Willis
Joseph C. Yates

Capt. Long's Mounted Volunteers: August 5–23, 1838

Captain:
James D. Long
First Lieutenant:
Levi B. Dikes
Second Lieutenant:
James M. Sanford[1]
First Sergeant:
John Walker
Second Sergeant:
Thomas H. Stovall
Third Sergeant:
Isaac Durst
Privates:
Zachariah W. Bottoms
James Brown
George W. Click[2]
John Dean
Elbridge G. Sevier
Lawrence W. Simpson
M. R. Springfield
Theodore B. Starkes

1 Joined August 10.
2 Joined August 11.

Sources: Each muster roll from Major General Rusk's campaign was compiled from available pay roll and muster roll records, furnished courtesy of the Archives and Information Services Division of the Texas State Library.

Author has attempted to record names as accurately as possible, but these documents were often handwritten with poor penmanship and frequently misspelled names. Where possible, cross-reference audited military claims and county census information were used to fill in names and correct spellings. The service dates for each company indicate the particular muster and pay rolls referenced.

CHAPTER 2

"Shoulder Your Arms and Chastize the Enemy"

August 20–October 9, 1838

Two days after Rusk was ordered to disband his militiamen documentary evidence was obtained that proved the Mexican agents had been making proposals to Indian leaders in Texas. On August 20, the chief Mexican agent, Captain Julian Pedro Miracle, was killed on the Red River by a Spanish man named Alexander Peñeda who had recently been held by Miracle as a prisoner. The journal and papers of Miracle were translated by Dr. A. G. Wright. These papers made their way into the hands of Daniel Montague, a Texas Militia leader of the Fourth Brigade, Fannin County Deputy Surveyor Seth Parker, and Asa Hartfield.[1]

Word was quickly spread of what was found on Miracle. In addition to his detailed journal, instructions from General Vicente Filisola were found which instructed him to visit with the leaders of the Indians of Texas. Miracle's correspondence showed that he had recently visited both the Kickapoo and Cherokee villages in east Texas and that he had held a meeting between Chief Bowles, Córdova, and rebels from Nacogdoches. Miracle had similarly visited with the Chickasaws, Caddos, Kichais, and Shawnees, while attempting to arrange meetings with the Wacos and Tonkawas.[2]

The Miracle papers caused enough outrage that even President Houston could not ignore them. For militia leader Tom Rusk, the papers provided ample support for him to maintain a strong force in the field to deal with the Córdova Rebellion.

Two new militia companies were created in Nacogdoches on August 22. One was a twenty-two-man company under Captain Isham Sims which was employed to guard about twenty Mexican prisoners being held in town for their involvement with Córdova's rebellion. The group of Mexicans had come back to Nacogdoches

County and surrendered themselves as prisoners of war to Rusk.[3] Captain Daniel Weeks also formed a twenty-five-man mounted company of August 22, many of his enlistees taken from the newly returned and disbanding companies, such as from Captain Stephens' company.

During August 1838, President Houston also received word in Nacogdoches of a different threat to his young nation. News of a planned Mexican incursion into Texas via the port at Corpus Christi provided a new challenge for him. Houston authorized Colonel George Hockley, the secretary of war, to take necessary steps to force these troops from Texas. Houston suggested Colonel Henry Karnes, stationed in San Antonio, or Lieutenant Colonel Lysander Wells as the best choices to lead this movement. A regimental force of up to 280 men was to be dispatched to the lower Nueces.

Colonel Pinckney Caldwell and a company of his mounted men had been followed to near the Nueces River by a division of approximately 150 Mexican cavalrymen from Matamoros. Although Caldwell put together a force of volunteers for possible action, the whole issue was resolved peacefully when it turned out to be merely a landing of Mexican supplies.[4]

★ ★ ★ ★ ★

Development of Douglass' Third Militia Brigade

The twenty companies which participated in Rusk's August Indian campaign had been disbanded by September 1, 1838, with only a few exceptions. Captain Andrew Caddell's mounted volunteers served through September 29. Captain Alexander Horton's mounted volunteers served through September 22. Captain Samuel Box's men served through September 24 and operated for some of this time out of Fort Houston. Lieutenant H. R. Shearer, formerly of Captain Augustine's company, organized an infantry company on August 30 that would serve for three months. The bulk of Captain Robert Goodloe's San Augustine company was disbanded on September 1, but his junior officers transferred into a new company under Captain Wesley Hanks on August 22. Hanks' revamped mounted gunman unit served in East Texas through October 20, 1838.

During early September, Rusk approved General Kelsey Douglass to organize new mounted volunteer companies in the Third Militia Brigade. The muster roll of his staff shows that they were paid for service from September 5, 1838, through February 28, 1839. Douglass' leading officers included Brigadier Inspector Archibald

Hotchkiss, Aide de Camp James S. Mayfield, volunteer aides de camp Alfred P. Walden (a former ranger captain of Colonel Coleman's battalion), William C. Duffield and W. A. Sims. Leander E. Tipps served as assistant quartermaster.

Captain Eli Russell commanded a small mounted spy company under Major Baley Walters from September 2–November 15, 1838. In its prime during October this unit consisted only of seven members. Captain Lewis Sanchez, who had recently commanded volunteers on the August campaign, raised another ranger-type mounted company on September 7 which served through January 27, 1839. Captain Charles Walters, who had commanded a company during the August campaign, commanded another company of the Second Regiment of the Third Brigade from September 4–October 12, 1838.

The need for rangers at Fort Houston was strongly requested by the local citizens. The Indians in their area had been incited by the Mexican rebels and were drawing blood. Shortly after General Rusk's militiamen returned to Nacogdoches, a letter was drafted by the leading men of the fort on August 25, 1838, and sent to President Houston.

> We the undersigned citizens of the town of Houston (Houston County) & its vicinity, beg leave respectfully to represent to your excellency that our property has been stolen, our houses & farms infested and surrounded, our families alarmed & ourselves compelled to desert our homes on account of depredations committed by our Indian neighbors.

The settlers claimed that the Kickapoo Indians were rumored to be the most aggressive of those in their neighborhood. To Houston they stated that frontier protection was "earnestly but strongly solicited in our truly unpleasant and distressing situation."[5]

The appeal from Fort Houston was taken to heart, for Major Leonard Mabbitt was dispatched in September by Sam Houston to operate from this settlement with two mounted ranging companies. It is unknown exactly when they first arrived but available company records show that Mabbitt's troops were definitely operating from Fort Houston by late September.

The ranging system had been allowed to lapse in April 1838. Efforts of Congress to revive the Texas Rangers within militia brigades had been rejected by Sam Houston in late May. Córdova's Rebellion, however, gave Major General Rusk the justification he needed to keep small units of mounted gunmen or rangers within the Third and Fourth Militia Brigades.

Major Mabbitt's command was referred to on muster roll and payroll receipts as the "First Regiment of Mounted Gunmen" of the Third Militia Brigade or "Mabbitt's Battalion of Volunteer Rangers." At the close of Rusk's August Cherokee Nation campaign, Captain Champion Blythe had managed to raise a small force of men on August 30. Under Mabbitt's leadership, Blythe turned command of his company over to Captain Squire Brown, formerly the second lieutenant, on September 22. Privates Corley T. Crawford and George F. Martin were also promoted on September 22 to first lieutenant and second lieutenant, respectively.

This restructuring likely took place at Fort Houston upon the arrival of the other two companies of Mabbitt's new regiment. Captain Blythe transferred into the mounted ranger company of Captain Jacob Snively, taking the rank of private. Snively, a surveyor who had settled in Nacogdoches in 1835, served in the Texas Army during the revolution and had risen to the rank of acting secretary of war the following year. His nearly fifty-man company had been organized the previous week on September 14.

Captain Brown's muster roll shows that new volunteers from Fort Houston began joining his company on September 27, making it the largest unit of Major Mabbitt's gunman regiment. Eight of the twenty-five men who had sent the August 25 appeal to President Houston joined Brown's company during late September and early October: James Edward Box, Daniel LaMora Crist, William Frost, Alexander McKenzie, Lacy McKenzie, Jacob Morrow, John Wilson, and John W. Carpenter.

Mabbitt's first two companies comprised just over one hundred men upon arrival at Fort Houston in late September. Within two weeks, he would add the volunteer ranging companies of captains James Bradshaw and William T. Sadler–who had commanded rangers at Fort Houston during the Texas Revolution–to his regiment and increase his strength to roughly 175 men.

Mabbitt's First Battalion companies were technically attached to the Texas Militia but truly functioned as rangers, just as the Second Congress had hoped to authorize in May. They ranged the frontiers of Houston County from the Trinity eastward toward the Neches. These men soon found evidence that the effects of Córdova's Rebellion were still present. These rebels had successfully enlisted the Kickapoos, whose village was located north of Fort Houston in the northeastern corner of present Anderson County, to their cause. The Kickapoos and other Indians were still aroused shortly after Rusk had been ordered to disband his companies in Nacogdoches.

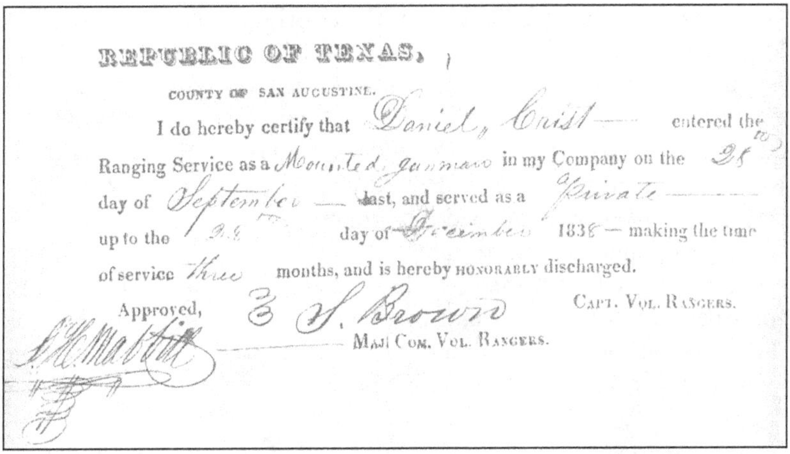

REPUBLIC OF TEXAS,

COUNTY OF SAN AUGUSTINE.

I do hereby certify that Daniel, Crist entered the Ranging Service as a Mounted gunman in my Company on the 25th day of September last, and served as a Private up to the 25 day of December 1838 — making the time of service three months, and is hereby HONORABLY discharged.

Approved, E S. Brown CAPT. VOL. RANGERS.

L. H. Mabbitt MAJ COM. VOL. RANGERS.

This service voucher attests to Major Leonard Mabbitt's Third Militia Brigade mounted gunmen battalion, which included companies under captains Brown, Bradshaw, Sadler and Snively. Mabbitt's rangers fought two battles with Mexican and Indian rebels during October 1838.
Daniel L. Crist PP, R12, F 211. Texas State Library and Archives Commission.

General Rusk felt that the Indians were stockpiling whiskey, lead, and powder during this lull, and Texas scouts soon discovered that Indian camps were on the move. Mabbitt's reports to General Rusk helped encourage the general to recall his forces in early October.

★ ★ ★ ★ ★

General Dyer Mobilizes Fourth Militia Brigade

On September 2, 1838, an Indian peace treaty was signed between Texas and the Wacos, Tawakonis, Kichais, and Towash (Pawnee) Indians. Holland Coffee negotiated this deal at the Shawnee village located near the mouth of the Washita River in Fannin County.[6]

Coffee was a commissioner on the part of the Republic of Texas and they both promised to maintain peace, for which the Indians received gifts for signing the treaty. Coffee, Silas C. Colville, Daniel R. Jackson, and A. O. Houston signed for Texas. The Indian signers were Chief Oso of the Kichais, Chief Tocarawate of the Tawakonis, Towash captains Carawatta and Orahsta, and Waco captains Ichata and Wakka.[7]

Within days of this treaty, General John Dyer had organized a full battalion of companies of his Fourth Militia Brigade, just as General

Douglass had organized his own Third Brigade. Dyer's new First Regiment of Mounted Riflemen was formally mustered into service on September 6, 1838. Direct command of the battalion was given to Colonel Samuel W. Sims and his staff. Company commanders were captains John Robert Craddock, William Edmondson, James Gillian, Robert S. Hamilton, James E. Hopkins, and Joseph R. Mix. Including field and staff, the first expedition organized by Dyer on September 6 comprised just over three hundred men.

When the new rifleman battalion was organized it replaced a tiny four-man mounted ranger unit that had been on duty in the area for the previous months. Claiborne Chisum had received orders from General Dyer on May 28, 1838. Chisum was

> appointed Capt. of a squad of spies and as such will act to the best of your skill and abilities. You will choose you four men to act with you that you can place the utmost confidence in and as soon as practicable proceed to range on the frontier of this county and make all the discovery that you can and report every trip to Major Peters as he is convenient. You can make a trip every two weeks if you can conveniently do so.[8]

Captain Chisum enrolled privates James S. Johnson, George Hall, and John C. Harris on June 9. These four rangers served through September 9 under orders of the First Regiment of the Fourth Brigade. They were formally discharged from service by Colonel Sims on September 9.

A second small ranger unit was also replaced at this time by Sims' new companies. Captain James R. O'Neal had commanded Empson Hamilton, Peter Laflore, John Seymore, Richard Sowell, and Jesse Stiff for five months. According to his muster roll, Captain O'Neal's Company of Fannin County Spies "was mustered into service by order of Brig. Gen. John H. Dyer and placed on the frontier of Fannin County the 8th day of April 1838." His men "furnished their own rations, horses, guns, [and] ammunition" until discharged on September 8.

Colonel Sims' new battalion was necessitated by a recent rise in violence. For William B. Stout, the Red River County frontier had changed before his eyes in the past two years. Born in Virginia, he emigrated to Texas from Illinois in February 1836 during the Texas Revolution. Following the battle of San Jacinto, Stout felt this northern Texas area had been basically peaceful. It was not until "the fall of 1837 [that] the Indians commenced stealing on the Red River."[9]

When General Dyer and Colonel Sims organized the new battalion of mounted riflemen on September 6, William and his brother Henry Stout both joined Captain James Hopkins' company as privates. The First Regiment marched out to challenge hostile Indians along the upper Trinity River. Upon reaching the Sabine River, Dyer halted his forces to gather intelligence.

William and Henry Stout were sent out ahead on horseback to reconnoiter the area for Indian villages and hiding places in the area. The brothers ran across eight "enemy on the Elm Fork of the Trinity; one of which was killed." The other Indians fled. At this point, the brothers parted company, with William Stout moving towards the Cross Timbers.

En route, he met a party of Kickapoos, who informed him "that the country was full of Caddos." They advised him "to go back and in haste, too." Based on the plentiful signs of hostile foes in the area, Stout took this advice. Returning back to the main encampment of Dyer's forces, he met his brother Henry, who had also returned without discovering much.

While these men were out scouting, other riflemen from Colonel Sims' forces had captured an Indian and brought him into camp. William Stout relates:

> This Indian informed the Texans of a village on the waters of the Sabine, and piloted Captain William Scurlock with twelve men to it. He found only eight Indians in the village; naked and singing, four of whom were killed. The Indian pilot, on their way back, rushed upon a Shawnee Indian (who was friendly to the whites and had gone with Scurlock as a pilot also) and, snatching a knife from the Shawnee's belt, attempted to stab him.
>
> The Shawnee parried the blow and the assailant immediately fled. He was fired upon by several and killed.

Scurlock was actually serving as first lieutenant of Captain Joseph Mix's Company C of Mounted Riflemen. The reference to him by Stout as captain is accurate, as Scurlock did assume command of the company from Mix in November 1838.

After the Indian encounter, Lieutenant Scurlock's party returned to General Dyer's main camp. The general was content to wrap up the field expedition for the time being and move his battalion back to the settlements. Twenty of Captain Mix's men were discharged from service on September 23 after the troops had returned to the settlements.

After sending the First Regiment back to protect the settlements, Dyer moved to join up with the Second Regiment. Lieutenant Colonel Daniel Montague of Fannin County had been given command of the Second Regiment of the Fourth Militia Brigade on September 14, just a week after the Fourth Brigade's First Regiment had been organized. His adjutant was James O'Neal, who had just completed commanding a ranger company the previous week.

Born in Massachusetts, Montague had settled during 1837 on Choctaw Bayou near a deserted stockade on the Red River built by Abel Warren the previous year as an Indian trading post. Montague and William Henderson opened a general merchandise store and this rapidly settled area became known as Warren. The settlement was also designated the county seat when Fannin County was organized in the spring of 1838.[10]

General Dyer moved with a small group of about eight men to join Montague. Dyer was accompanied by Major Clement Johns, aide Lemuel Peters and surgeon John F. Smith of his staff. The general's staff was accompanied by several members of the First Regiment, including Private William Stout of Captain Hopkins' company.

These eight men soon joined the two ranging companies of the Second Regiment on Pilot Grove Creek. General Dyer found that Lieutenant Colonel Montague's men had already had their share of excitement with Indians.

★ ★ ★ ★ ★

Montague's Rangers Take Scalps

Lieutenant Colonel Montague had recruited approximately eighty men and placed Fannin County's first two volunteer companies into service on September 14, 1838. They were commanded by captains Nathaniel T. Journey and Robert Sloan.

Captain Journey's company was organized on September 13 at the home of Jonathan Anthony. This home was located eight miles south of Fort Inglish, a two-story blockhouse surrounded by a stockade that had been built in the summer of 1837 by Bailey Inglish on the western edge of the Red River frontier where Bonham now stands.[11]

According to one militiaman, most of Captain Journey's men that night were in "high glee under the influence of strong drink." During the night, Journey's charger and two other horses were stolen by Caddo Indians. The men spent the next day securing horses for the three that had been lost during their stupor.[12]

Journey's company rendezvoused with Captain Sloan's new Fourth Brigade company on the night of September 14 at Linsey's Springs on Bois d'Arc Creek. Cattle were slaughtered for rations and preparations were made for Montague's two companies to depart in the morning for the Indian village located on the west forks of the Trinity River.

The companies made camp for the night with sentries posted about the perimeters. Many of the rangers broke into groups to swap stories and pass the time. One of the guards fired his gun during the evening, sending everyone scrambling for their guns, shot pouches, and ammunition. The guard reported to Captain Journey that he had fired at an Indian trying to steal horses. No sign of a wounded Indian was found, but the camp was much more alert during the remainder of the night.

Companies of Lieutenant Colonel Montague's 2nd Regiment, 4th Militia Brigade September–December 1838

Field and Staff: September 14, 1838–January 1, 1839

Lieutenant Colonel:
Daniel Montague
Major:
James B. Shannon
Adjutant:
James R. O'Neal
Quartermaster:
Joseph Sowell
Surgeon:
E. C. Rogers

Captain Sloan's Fannin Co. Rangers: Sept. 14, 1838–January 14, 1839

Captain:
Robert Sloan
First Lieutenant:
Mark R. Roberts
Orderly Sergeant:
Arch H. Fitzgerald
Second Sergeant:
L. W. Fitzgerald
Privates:
H. S. Allen [1]
Wilson B. Allen [2]
William Anderson [7]
Jonathan Anthony
Timothy E. Carpenter
William Cose
Thomas Cousins [6]
James Crowder [7]
John Dameron [3]
J. M. Davis
John Davis
William Davis [4]
Charles Doherty
Benjamin J. Fuller
Asa Hartfield
James Martin
William M. McCarty
Allen McKinney [5]
David Mouser
Henry Mouser
Jason H. Petigrew
William R. Rice
Abram Shelly [1]
William R. Slack
Joseph P. Spencer
David Strickland
Henry Viser [6]
James Washburn

[1] Enrolled 10/17/38.
[2] Enrolled 10/4/38.
[3] Enrolled 10/8/38. Served through 1/1/39.
[4] Enrolled 10/3/38.
[5] Enrolled 10/16/38.
[6] Enrolled 10/17/38. Served through 1/1/39.
[7] Served through 1/1/39.

Captain Journey's Rangers: Sept. 13, 1838–March 13, 1839

Captain:
Nathaniel T. Journey
First Lieutenant:
Richard H. Sowell
Second Lieutenant:
Bushnel Garner
Orderly Sergeant:
Solomon Chambless
Second Sergeant:
Joshua Sharpless
Corporals:
M. Gibson
Jefferson Ivy
Gibson May
Privates:
Santa Argo
Spencer Asburry [1]
William W. Boon
Isaac Camp
Nicholas Canto [2]
William Cosley
Franklin Davis
John Ferguson
William Foster [3]
James M. Garner [4]
George Ivy [2]
Daniel Jackson [2]
James Jeffries
Hardin Jones
W. M. Kenneda
P. L. Lankford
John Leyman
William Martin
John McClanahan
Jose S. Morea [5]
Garret Pangburn
Taylor Patterson
James Pearson [6]
Andrew Penara
James Roland
John Russell [7]
William Scott [1]
John M. Thurston
Lorenzo Tula
William Tyler
James Ward
William Winlock
John Yates

Note: Journey, Isaac Camp and John Ferguson were present on 9/13. All others were mustered in on 9/14 unless otherwise noted.

[1] Enrolled 10/20/38.
[2] Enrolled 1/1/39.
[3] Enrolled 2/12/39.
[4] Enrolled 2/25/39.
[5] Enrolled 1/15/39.
[6] Enrolled 10/1/38.
[7] Enrolled 11/10/38.

Capt. Hart's Mounted Gunmen: November 19, 1838–January 1, 1839
Second Regiment, Fourth Brigade under Lt. Colonel Montague

Captain:
John Hart
First Lieutenant:
Richard H. Lock
Second Lieutenant:
W. D. Pace
First Sergeant:
L. M. Blodgett
Second Sergeant:
Free L. Hart
First Corporal:
Berry H. Reed
Second Corporal:
Martin D. Hart
Third Corporal:
Hiram B. Bush
Privates:
William Allen
J. Slater Baker
Jacob D. Black
Green Clift
Daniel Dugan
George Dugan
George W. Duncan
John Duncan
John R. Garnett [2]
Hardin Hart
F. S. Holcomb
Thomas Jouett [2]
Thomas G. Kennedy
Yelverton "Yell" Kerr
M. H. Langford
Thomas Mahurin
A. J. McGowen
Curtis Moore [2]
Jose Morea
Sestin Pace [2]
Alexander Russell
Felix G. Sadler
Daniel Slack
Thomas S. Smith
John Stephens Jr.
John Stephens Sr. [1]
Joseph Swaggerty
William Washburn

[1] Horse lost; valued $100.
[2] Absent without leave as of November 20.

Captain Stiff's Fannin Co. Mounted Gunmen: Dec. 1–29, 1838
Second Regiment, Fourth Brigade under Lt. Colonel Montague

Captain:	William R. Caruthers	Thomas R. Shannon
Jesse Stiff*	John Cornelison	W. E. Sprague*
Second Lieutenant:	William Davis	James Thompson [2]
William C. Caruthers*	Neely Dobson	Samuel Wachard
Sergeant:	William Foster	
Joseph Murphy*	Joseph Jeffries*	
Privates:	Robert McIntyre	
Renny Allred	Bastin Oliver*	
William Bailey	Seth Parker	
James Blagg[1]	James Seymore	

* Served through Dec. 29. All others discharged between December 11 - 27, 1838.
[1] Joined December 9.
[2] Joined December 21

Lt. Simpson's Fannin Co. Mounted Gunmen: Dec. 1, 1838–Jan. 14, 1839
Second Regiment, Fourth Brigade under Lt. Colonel Montague

First Lieutenant:	George Dawson [1]	Joseph Rogers [2]
John P. Simpson	Joel C. Fuller	Joseph D. Rogers [3]
Privates:	Mabel Gilbert	Andrew Thomas
Carter Bolin	Bailey Inglish	Samuel Young
Wesley Chisum	Jacob Keechum	
Mitten Darnell	Thomas Lindsey [1]	
William Darnell	Samuel McFarland [1]	

[1] Discharged Dec. 20
[2] Discharged Dec. 11
[3] Discharged Dec. 15

Journey and Sloan's companies mounted their horses and rode for the Trinity River on the morning of September 15, led by an experienced pilot. Lieutenant Colonel Montague's little expedition proceeded up the Trinity for three days without finding sign of hostile Indians. General Dyer's staff and several other volunteers joined Montague on Pilot Grove Creek on the headwaters of the Trinity during this time.[13]

The rangers made camp on the night of September 17 on the upper Trinity. Volunteer John P. Simpson recalled another "alarm by the pickets during the night," but no one was injured in the resultant shooting. Having encountered no Indians thus far, Montague and Dyer's men thus decided to raid the Caddo village known to be located on the west forks of the Trinity. Simpson recalled that the men fully expected a major conflict.

> Next morning a council of war was held, scouts were sent ahead to spy out the village. The scouts returned and reported

> the village near at hand. Now we must try our bravery or run —three hundred Indian warriors fortified in their huts, to defend themselves, squaws and children, and only ninety whites to attack and enter into deadly conflict with them. Columns of attack were formed and the charge ordered. Many a pale face was to be seen in the ranks.[14]

The Caddo village attacked on September 18 did not turn out to be as heavily populated as expected, however. William Stout, one of the men with General Dyer who had just joined Montague's expedition, found it to be only "a small encampment of the Caddos on the Clear Fork of the Trinity." This village was located in present Arlington in Tarrant County. Major Jonathan Bird would build Bird's Fort on this location in 1841.

In the resulting Caddo village attack, Stout reported that the Texans killed three of them. Simpson recorded that Montague's rangers suffered one man wounded and one of their horses killed. One of the volunteers, John Hart, took the opportunity to remove scalps from the slain Caddos. Among the camp goods seized by the Texans were the stolen horses of Captain Journey and the two others.

After the battle, one wounded Indian still lay in the tall grass, concealed with a tomahawk in his hand. One of Captain Journey's men, Garrett Pangburn, was surprised by the Indian, as J. P. Simpson later recalled.

Lieutenant Colonel Daniel Montague (1798-1876) commanded the Second Regiment of the Fourth Militia Brigade. His Fannin County rangers attacked a Caddo village near present Fort Worth on September 18, 1838.
Originally published in History of Montague County.

> A man by the name of Pangburn (usually called "Brandy," from the quantity of that article he drank) was on the lookout for the wounded Indian and came up on him so close he couldn't shoot. The Indian rose with tomahawk in hand, striking at Pangburn's head. The latter wheeled and ran, shouting for help at every jump. One gun was fired from our ranks, the Indian fell, and Captain Hart was on him in an instant and took his scalp.

Hart was elected captain of another ranger company under Lieutenant Colonel Montague several weeks after the Sloan-Journey Expedition returned to Fannin County. Following this Tarrant County Indian village raid, General Dyer concluded it was time to turn his men back toward home. According to volunteer William Stout, the men were out of provisions and half starved by the time they reached home.

On the third night after the battle, the men under captains Sloan and Journey camped on Bois d'Arc Creek near where Orangeville now stands. They found that Indians had been into this settlement in recent days and killed one of the area's more prominent citizens, William Washburn.

Following Montague's brief campaign, his original Fannin County ranger companies remained on duty throughout the year and into 1839. General Dyer returned to the Clarksville area to begin making plans for another extended Indian campaign.

★ ★ ★ ★ ★

Rusk Strengthens Third Brigade: October 1, 1838

President Houston worked during the fall of 1838 to pacify the Cherokee Indians of East Texas. He sent instructions to Indian agent Charles H. Sims to proceed with the surveying and marking off of the boundary lines that had been agreed upon with the Cherokees in their February 23, 1836, treaty with Houston, despite the fact that Congress had negated this treaty.

Sims was informed that he would help surveyor Zach F. Worley complete the task. Sims was to also notify Chief Bowles of the work in progress. Houston notified Thomas Rusk on October 10 that this line "should be done immediately" to prevent any future problems with the Indians. Houston warned that failure to mark off the Cherokee Nation and abide by its boundaries would cause "another runaway scrape and Eastern Texas will be desolated."[15]

The Indians and Mexicans of Córdova's forces on about October 1 captured Elias Vansickle, who was working on surveying the Cherokee boundaries. In a deposition before the county court of Nacogdoches on January 25, 1839, Vansickle's testimony was read by Chief Justice Charles S. Taylor.[16]

> He was taken prisoner at the Saline, Nacogdoches County, by a party of Mexican[s], Biloxi, and Shawnee Indians, and kept by them until the 21st of December following, when he made his escape.

While a prisoner of Córdova's rebels, Vansickle would witness the comings and goings of Indians from various East Texas tribes. Likely in response to this abduction, President Houston appointed Colonel Alexander Horton, who had recently participated in Rusk's August campaign, to supervise the Indians in this area. A company of mounted gunmen under Captain David Renfro was enrolled on October 7 for frontier service under Horton. Renfro's company was assigned to patrol along the Cherokees' boundaries and served in this role through November 9, 1838.

The information of Vansickle's capture was passed on to Thomas Rusk via courier from the Fort Houston rangers under Major Mabbitt. He was informed that Córdova's Mexican and Indian forces were camped near the Kickapoo village north of Fort Houston. Major General Rusk decided to mount another campaign against these rebels. He responded to the latest appeal for help from Mabbitt's Fort Houston rangers from his "Headquarters Nacogdoches" on October 1. "In consequence of the information received" from Fort Houston, Rusk called on "the Citizens of the County of Houston" to prepare for a new campaign.

> I have authorized raising of from two to three hundred volunteers to defend the country and chastize the Indians. The repeated depredations, the thefts and sundries which have been committed in your county by a faithless and insignificant foe has called loudly for exemplary punishment upon the Indians and you are loudly called upon by every consideration of regard to your country and your frontier of helpless women and children to shoulder your arms and chastize the enemy.[17]

Rusk sent similar orders to General Douglass and to Major Elisha Clapp in San Augustine on October 1. Clapp, a ranger captain in 1836 and the third senior officer on Rusk's August expedition, was asked to raise 150 volunteers for protection of the frontier and to go against the Indians. After rounding up volunteers, Clapp was instructed to join General Kelsey Douglass and his volunteers at Fort Houston on Monday, October 15.

Major Clapp was very successful in his efforts to organize new militia companies. He held a meeting in San Augustine on October 5 and had thirty-six of forty men present volunteer for duty. Clapp sent a message to Rusk on the evening of October 5.

> I have not heard from Fort Houston since you received express from Maj. Mabbitt. I have no doubt but that the Indians and Mexicans are embodied near Kickapoo village and in all probability we can get a fight near home. We are in the need of ammunition & cannot effect a campaign without it. I would like to hear of Maj. Douglass' success in raising volunteers. It may be that we need all that we can get. I would go against them myself but I do not think it would be a prudent measure unless I have a larger force. Your order to raise men for our protection I must inform you met with universal hallelujahs & hurrahs, it being the first legal order of the kind ever sent forth officially to our country.[18]

★ ★ ★ ★ ★

The Killough Massacre: October 5, 1838

Recent tragedy generally worked in favor of those raising militia forces during the early days of the Republic of Texas. Major General Rusk would be given no better motivator to raise men during early October than the horrible "Killough Massacre" carried out in present Cherokee County on October 5, 1838.

The Killough family had moved from Talladega County, Alabama, and settled in Texas on Christmas Eve 1837 on a creek just inside the Cherokee claim south of the Neches Saline. Aware of the presence of Córdova's forces in the area, Isaac Killough Sr., his four sons, and their families went to their fields to harvest their crops before winter. An unarmed group of the family was ambushed and killed en route to the fields. The rest of the Killoughs and their neighboring families fled for their lives as the Indians descended and began slaughtering the families.[19]

Isaac Killough Sr. was killed in his yard by eighteen bullet wounds, and the entire George Wood family was gone when the massacre ended. Urcery Killough, wife of Isaac Sr., asked the Indians to kill her after they had slain her husband. The Indians refused, cursing the woman and ordering her into her house.

Between the Wood, Barakias Williams, and Killough families, at least sixteen family members were murdered or captured on October 5. More than half the family members managed to escape and find horses for the long ride to safety with their wives and children.

The Indians claimed that they had no interest in killing the women, and they allowed three widows and one of their children to escape the scene. Barakias Williams initially joined the women but he was chased through the woods and killed. The surviving quartet made its way through the wilderness to Fort Lacy, some forty miles away. They were Urcery Killough, Jane Killough, and Narcissa Killough, widows of Isaac Sr., Isaac Jr., and Samuel Killough, respectively. Narcissa Killough carried her one-year-old son William B. Killough with them during their harrowing travel through Indian country. William "Billy" Killough later wrote of the ordeal of his mother and other relatives.

> When night came they started for Ft. Lacy, travelling as best they could, as they had to leave the path often as Indians were coming up all through the night. There was one serious drawback to them—one that might have proven fatal to them at any time. They had an infant one year and eight days old, and a small fist dog along. The cry of one or the bark of the other would have been fatal, but it seems that both knew that there was something wrong, for when they would stop the dog would hover under their skirts like he was trying to keep out of danger. In starting, they did not know what to do with the dog. They could not leave it, and didn't have the heart to kill it, nor anything to kill it with.[20]

After several days in the wilderness, these Killough women made their way to Fort Lacy and safety. Fort Lacy was located along the Old San Antonio Road on the southern boundary of Cherokee land on the outskirts of present Alto on Highway 21. Martin Lacy, who as a private in Captain Costley's company had helped to build Fort Houston during late 1836, had fortified his farmhouse-turned-trading house during 1838 after the local Kickapoo and Biloxi Indians had become increasingly hostile.

Those killed in the massacre had been Isaac Killough Sr.; son Allen Killough, his wife and five children; son Isaac Killough Jr.; son

At least sixteen settlers were killed in the Killough Massacre of October 5, 1838. This vandalized marker and a native stone monument stand near the community of Mount Selman in northern Cherokee County. *Author's photo.*

Samuel Killough; son-in-law George W. Wood, his wife and two children; Barakias Williams; son-in-law Owen C. Williams' daughter; and Elizabeth Killough.

The Indians also stole all firearms belonging to these families, a horse carriage, two horses, a wagon, and a number of cattle. All of the food, furniture, farming utensils, and other property of these families was either carried off or destroyed.

The massacre, the largest and bloodiest in East Texas history, took place about one and a half miles west of the old town of Larissa in Cherokee County. The site was located about six miles east of the Kickapoo Village, which was located in the extreme north of present Anderson County. Several historical accounts state that this depredation was carried out by Shawnees and Biloxis, but evidence more strongly points to supposedly friendly Cherokees who lived in this vicinity. Among those Indians reported by survivor Billy Killough to have participated in the massacre were an Indian named Dog Shoot and Chief Sam Benge, the latter among those who had participated in the Sam Houston peace treaty of 1836.

Further evidence that the Killough massacre was carried out by Cherokees can be found in the testimony of Elias Vansickle, who had been taken prisoner by Córdova's rebels on about October 1 in Nacogdoches County. While hostage in this camp, Vansickle also heard the plans of a major Indian attack against the East Texas settlements in the works.

> Dogshoot, a Cherokee, came to the enemy some time before [the Kickapoo battle of October 16] and brought a scalp which he said belonged to one of the Killough family, who had been murdered about the same time in the Cherokee Nation. The Cherokees, Dogshoot and others, said that in three days from that time, thirty besides those then in camp would join them, and unite with them in a war upon the white settlements.[21]

The resulting excitement caused General Rusk to make a strong call for volunteers to gather at Fort Lacy. Surviving brother Nathaniel Killough would quickly become involved in the East Texas Indian campaign.

Indian attacks were not limited to East Texas during October. The *Telegraph and Texas Register*'s Saturday, October 6, issue warned of hostilities closer to present Houston.

> The country between the Colorado and Gonzales is very much infested with Indians. It is not safe to go from Columbus to Gonzales in companies smaller than five or ten persons. A citizen of the neighborhood by the name of Davis, who had been on the Colorado on business, was killed on the 11th inst. by Comanches while on his way home.[22]

Major Elisha Clapp, busy recruiting volunteers for General Rusk's next militia offensive, received notice of the bloody Killough attack. He quickly ordered Captain William Sadler's volunteer ranger company of Houston County to move to Fort Houston to join Major Mabbitt's mounted battalion. Before departing the area near Brown's Fort, Sadler and the other men old enough to have families left their loved ones in the care of older men and women. Several of the families of his men were gathered in the home of Tennessee native John Edens near the present community of Augusta on San Pedro Creek.

Mabbitt's men would not be long in finding a fight with the hostile Indians and Córdova's rebels.

★ ★ ★ ★ ★

Surveyors' Fight: October 8, 1838

Three days after the Killough Massacre, Indians in Navarro County perpetrated an attack against a surveying party which resulted in an equally costly massacre of Texans.

During the fall of 1838, the northernmost town between the Brazos and Trinity rivers was a settlement known as Old Franklin, located between the present towns of Calvert and Bryan. Old Franklin, which included a blockhouse to protect the settlers, had become the rendezvous site of choice for surveying parties of this area of Texas.[23]

Surveying the lands near present Dallas was extremely dangerous in 1838. Several surveyors working the areas north of Fort Parker had been killed in April. The next major surveying expedition organized into this area was one led by William Fenner Henderson. Twenty-one years of age, he had arrived in Texas in 1835 and served in the Texas Army in Lieutenant James T. Sprowl's infantry company.[24] Originally settling in the Nacogdoches area, Henderson had also participated in Major General Rusk's August 1838 Indian campaign.

In late September, Henderson organized his surveying party of twenty-five men at Old Franklin (also called Fort Franklin). At least two of the men, Samuel Allen and Joseph Jones, had served as rangers in 1836. They departed for what is now the southeastern part of Navarro County. After camping at the site of old Fort Parker, the surveyors passed Tehuacana Springs and proceeded up to the Richland Creek area. En route, the men passed a number of Indians in small groups and others in larger groups. In their immediate area, there were about three hundred Kickapoo Indians engaged in supplementing their buffalo meat supply. After arriving at the desired location, Henderson's men began running survey lines without incident on the first day.[25]

When a compass was found to be defective on the second day, Henderson sent William Jackson and William M. Love back to Parker's Fort to secure a magnet to correct the needle. While the surveyors continued their work during the morning hours, they carelessly noted Indians moving to and fro in their vicinity, some apparently in consultation. The men stopped to take a breakfast break around 11:00 a.m. While they were eating, a group of about fifty Kickapoo Indians warned them that a party of about seventeen Ioni Indians was planning on attacking the whites this day, October 8, 1838. Knowing that Ionis only armed themselves with bows and arrows, Henderson's men remarked that they were not afraid of such a threat.

After the breakfast break, the men returned to running their survey lines across a stretch of prairie that paralleled a ravine. During this time some more Indians moved close enough to them to mutter comments at them and one even begged a piece of tobacco from San Jacinto veteran Walter P. Lane. After this Indian crossed back over the ravine, the surveyor party was immediately fired upon by forty or more Indians who had been lying concealed in the bushes growing on the banks of the ravine. Thus began the fight that became known as the Surveyors' Fight or the Battle Creek Fight.

According to the *History of Navarro County,* command of the surveying party was given to Captain James Neil Sr., a surveyor who had settled in the present Grimes County area. He led the twenty-three-man group which came under Indian fire this day. As events shaped up, he would not survive to live on the land he claimed, but his son, James Neil Jr., later came to claim land that his father had surveyed in Grimes County and would be involved in organizing the county seat of Corsicana.

Of the accounts that were left of this fight, Lane claims that Neil was in command of the men from the start of the expedition; Henderson later stated that the men elected Neil as commander when the Indians made their attack. According to Lane, the Texans made an initial charge against their attackers until another one hundred Indians "showed themselves in the timber behind them."[26]

The surveyors collected their instruments and fell back in formation to the nearest timber, about a mile distant. The Indians immediately surrounded them and fired bullets and arrows from all sides.

Upon reaching the woods, Captain Neil's men found Indians already occupying the timber. The surveyors then retreated to a ravine in the prairie and took up a defensive position. A lone cottonwood tree stood at the juncture of two ravines. With four- and five-foot banks dotted with small bushes along the top, the gully offered the men a chance of holding their ground. The heavy firing by this point had already wounded or killed most of the Texan horses.[27]

According to Henderson, Captain Neil was wounded soon after reaching the ravine and he appointed Euclid M. Cox as captain of the men. Of the twenty-three Texans, many were wounded at this point. Entrenched in the small ravine on the open prairie, the surveyors were heavily surrounded by upwards of three hundred Kickapoos, Tawakonis, Ionis, Wacos, and Caddos. The Indians obviously viewed these surveyors as breaking up territory that had traditionally been theirs; their intent, therefore, was to kill all of their enemy.

Captain Cox's men had little chance in their predicament. The resourceful Indians climbed trees and fired down over the lip of the ravine. Little by little, more of the Texans fell wounded or dead. Seeing the necessity to remove the Indian snipers from the trees, new captain Cox took up a position behind the lone cottonwood tree. In

William Fenner Henderson (left), one of only seven survivors of the Surveyors' Fight on Battle Creek on October 8, 1838. Walter Paye Lane (right), who escaped with a shattered leg bone, later served as a brigadier general for the Confederacy.
Both images originally published in James DeShields' Border Wars of Texas.

the course of the next hour, he reportedly killed about ten Indians on his own. While exposing himself for another shot, however, he was finally shot through the spine and fell back from the tree.

"I ran up the bank, took him by the shoulder, and, under heavy fire dragged him to the ravine," wrote Walter Lane. Cox died within two hours from his wound, but begged Mr. Button to give his wife one of his pistols. Button later honored this request and as of 1885 it was in the possession of Hill County Sheriff John P. Cox, son of Captain Cox, of Hillsboro, Texas.[28]

Without a leader once again, the surviving Texans decided to remain together and use their discretion in their defense. Upon seeing Cox fall, the Indians sent up shouts of joy and proceeded to charge the ravine. Only a deadly fire from the surveyors' pistols and rifles kept the survivors from being totally overrun.

At this same time, about fifty mounted Indians appeared on a ridge about 250 yards away. They called to the surveyors, "Kickapoos good Indians, come to Kickapoos." Mr. Spikes, an old man of eighty-two years, decided to test the Kickapoos' loyalty. He mounted one of the remaining horses and rode out toward them, only to be killed by the Indians.

Surveyors' Fight on Battle Creek: October 8, 1838

James Neil, Capt. [1]	Alexander Houston [1]	William Tremier [1]
Euclid M. Cox, Capt. [1]	Elijah Ingram [1]	John T. Violet [2]
Samuel Tabor Allen [1]	William Jackson [3]	J. W. Williams [1]
Nathan W. Baker [2]	Joseph P. Jones [1]	
Thomas Barton [1]	P. M. Jones [1]	
J. Bulloch [1]	Walter Paye Lane [2]	
____ Button	William M. Love [3]	
David Clark [1]	____ McLaughlin	
Richard Davis [1]	Asa T. Mitchell [1]	
J. Hard [1]	William Smith [2]	
William F. Henderson	_____ Spikes [1]	

[1] Killed in battle.
[2] Wounded.
[3] Sent to Parker's Fort; not present for battle.

Note: some sources list a Rodney Wheeler among those killed.

Another wounded Texan, Richard Davis of San Augustine, mounted his horse and attempted to run the gauntlet of fire. He, too, was shot dead within sight of the other surveyors.

The Indians kept the survivors surrounded and pinned down even after dark. Finally, between 11:00 p.m. and midnight, after more than twelve hours of fighting, those left decided to use the cover of darkness to make a break for the timber bordering Richland Creek. Unfortunately, there was a full moon up this night, which made the prairie very bright. According to the reports of Lane and Henderson, there were only two or three horses left alive at this point. Some time about midnight, those still alive made ready to go.

The four most seriously wounded were loaded on the horses. The ten survivors at this point were Henderson, Neil, McLaughlin, Button, Lane, Elijah Ingram, Joseph Jones, John Violet, William Smith, and Tom Barton, the latter five all being wounded. As the surveyors rose from the ravine to leave, the Indians let out a yell and charged in a half circle toward them. The Texans fired back during their slow retreat toward the timber. The Indians proceeded to shoot man after man from the horses.

Joseph Jones and Elijah Ingram were both shot from a horse during the early moments of the escape. Lane and a companion helped Captain Neil onto a horse. He made less than ten steps before the Kickapoo shot down Neil and his horse. William Smith, favoring a wounded arm, raised Thomas Barton up behind him on one of the other horses. They raced only fifty yards before this final horse was shot out from under them. Smith survived, but Barton jumped up just before dying and cried out, "Lord, have Mercy on me!"[29]

Baker and Smith managed to escape through the timber together, eluding the Indians and ultimately reaching the Falls of the Brazos on their own. Another surveyor, a young man named McLaughlin, did not leave the ravine when the other nine made their break. He instead took up hiding in the bushes growing on the bank until the Indians had departed. When the Indians pursued the main party of Texans, McLaughlin fled down the ravine and ultimately reached the settlements on the Trinity River.

In addition to Baker, Smith, and McLaughlin, four others from the main party of Texans survived after fleeing from the ravine: Henderson, Lane, Violet, and Button. Of these seven, Button, Smith, Violet, and Lane were injured, with John Violet's injury being the most severe.

Walter Lane was shot through the leg during this escape, with the bullet shattering his leg bone. He managed to hobble on his heel and keep going. He reached the thicket with Henderson and Button, who had both escaped being wounded.

> We got into a deep ravine that led to the creek. I called to Henderson to stop and tie up my leg as I was bleeding to death. He did so promptly. We went down some distance and heard the Indians following us. We climbed on the bank and lay down with our guns cocked. Twelve of them passed so close I could have touched them. We got on the creek an hour before day, and followed down till we found some muddy water. We left the creek and went on the bank till we found a log reaching to a brushy island. We crossed over it and lay hidden all day. We could hear the Indians on the bank looking for us.[30]

According to Henderson's account, he and his party included the badly injured John Violet. Violet suffered from a broken thigh, which prevented him from crawling any further. He was left near Richland Creek with the promise that the other three would send him help. After hiding out from passing Indians searching for survivors, the trio started for Tehuacana Hill, which was twenty-five miles distant. Three days after the fight, on October 11, Henderson, Lane, and Button ran across six Kickapoo Indians, whom they told they had been fighting Ionis. Henderson offered one of them his Bowie knife if they would take them to water, which they did.[31]

After drinking water, the trio was taken to the Indian camp, where they were fed. After spending a night, the Texans were anxious to leave the next morning, fearing that one of the Kickapoos from the

The victims of the Surveyors' Fight are buried near Battle Creek in this little cemetery in Navarro County beneath this giant old cottonwood. Captain Euclid Cox's sons later erected this marble shaft in honor of the Surveyors' Fight victims. *Photo by Marshall L. Moore Jr.*

battle would alert these Indians that these were their enemy. Henderson then offered one of the Indians his rifle to lead them to Parker's Fort and allow the wounded Walter Lane to ride a pony. Lane was forced to walk, but the Kickapoos did lead them to Parker's Fort by the next day, October 12.

The surveyors then followed the Navasota River for a mile and proceeded on foot on toward Old Franklin. On October 14, they were discovered by Love and Jackson, who had been sent to repair the com-

The names of five of those who escaped (left) are chiseled on the south face of the marker.
Photo by Marshall L. Moore Jr.

pass days before. These men took the wounded on their horses on to Old Franklin, about fifteen miles away. Thereafter, a company of about fifty men was organized at Old Franklin by William Love. They went back to the scene of the battle to bury the dead. En route, they stopped at Tehuacana Springs, where they found poor John Violet with his broken thigh. He had gone six days with little food or water and had crawled more than twenty-five miles from where he had originally been left on Richland Creek.

Love's party found and buried the bodies of the surveyors, which had been badly savaged by wolves in the past week. They also found considerable blood from the firing points of the Indians, evidence that the Texans had taken their share of lives.

The slain Texans were buried beneath the spreading branches of the lone tree on the embankment under which they had so desperately fought. A memorial to the Battle Creek Fight victims was erected in 1881 by Captain Euclid Cox's sons, John P. Cox and Reverend J. Fred Cox, at the site of the battle in which their father was killed. Inscribed on it are the names of seventeen killed and five who escaped, a list now considered incomplete.

The exact number of surveyors involved in the fight varies by whose account one relies on. The number of those killed also varies between fourteen and twenty. By best count from all sources, sixteen men were killed, with a seventeenth man (Rodney Wheeler) likely.

Standing one mile west of Dawson on State Highway 31 in Navarro County is a Texas historical marker which identifies the Battle Creek Burial Ground.[32] Also standing as of this writing is the massive tree which provided cover for the besieged surveyors in 1838.

CHAPTER 3

The Kickapoo War

October 9–18, 1838

As the Surveyors' Fight survivors were struggling back to civilization, Major General Rusk was preparing his Texas Militia for another foray against the hostile Indians in East Texas. Almost all of the men who had followed him on the previous August 1838 expedition had been discharged back into civilian life. Word of the Killough Massacre would help him secure new volunteers to assist Major Mabbitt's Fort Houston forces.

At 2:00 a.m. on October 11, Rusk was awakened from his bed in Nacogdoches by a courier of Indian agent Charles H. Sims. The letter from Sims was sent from Fort Lacy. It informed Rusk that Sims had visited the village of Chief Bowles, the war chief of the Cherokees, the previous day. He had found that the Indians had packed up and were in the process of departing.[1]

"I wrote a communication to Bowles," Rusk wrote, "in very positive terms, demanding to know the cause of the movement." He sent this letter back to the Cherokees via messenger William Goyens, a son of a free mulatto from North Carolina. Goyens had first come to Texas in 1820 and had became a trusted Indian agent for the Mexican government. He had also come to be trusted with Indian dealings by the Anglo-American settlers of East Texas.

Around daybreak on October 11, Rusk received a second messenger, this from Captain Alexander Jordan in the field. Jordan reported that all the houses of Chief Big Mush, the Cherokee's political chief in East Texas, had been found deserted the day before. The Indians had carried off all of their belongings. Rusk's immediate reaction was, "If the Cherokees intend war, not a moment was to be lost."

Rusk sent word to Captain Jacob Snively's ranger company, which had been in service since September 14, to be in readiness to march by 10:00 a.m. He then requested veteran militia officer Robert W. Smith "to collect as many men as he could, and march at the same time." Captain Smith quickly rounded up twenty-three men and he was joined by another twenty men under Major Baley Walters. Another eight or ten volunteers fell in with Rusk, who departed before lunch on October 11 with just over fifty men.

Rusk's messengers were very active, for as his men marched out, Goyens brought back word from Chief Bowles, who wrote to Rusk that "the reason of his removal was threats made by the Mexicans and Indians against him." At about the same time, Rusk received a letter from Chief Big Mush, who stated to him that the Indians and Mexicans were "encamped in force near the Kickapoo town."

Rusk immediately took up the line of march toward the Kickapoo town, intending to reach that point by way of the Angelina River and Fort Houston. His meager forces had organized into companies under the command of captains Bob Smith, Jacob Snively, William Charles Brookfield, and Joseph Williams. They planned to join with Major Mabbitt, who was operating from Fort Houston with his First Regiment of Mounted Gunmen.

En route, Rusk's volunteers were joined by more men. Another company under Captain John Durst joined at the lower crossing of the Old San Antonio Road over the Angelina River. These men had gathered at Durst's Fort, his fortified homestead at this river crossing. The settlement about his home was known as Mount Sterling and was located about sixteen miles west of the town of Nacogdoches. Durst's home was a large house "protected by blockhouses, which were refuges for the entire neighborhood" during Indian troubles.[2]

Major Mabbitt would supply welcome reinforcements in the form of four volunteer ranging companies stationed at Fort Houston totalling more than 175 men. Rusk sent orders for Mabbitt to meet him at Fort Duty, located four miles west of the Neches River and about ten miles from Fort Houston. Early settlers used the fortified home of Richard Duty for shelter during Indian disturbances. Duty had built his twenty-four-foot square two-story cabin in 1837 near Snake and Stills creeks. United with Mabbitt, Rusk planned to march to the Kickapoo village to meet Córdova's rebels.

★ ★ ★ ★ ★

Mabbitt's Rangers Ambushed: October 12, 1838

Leonard Mabbitt moved his volunteer rangers out from Fort Houston on October 12 for Fort Duty. Leading the procession were the companies of captains James Bradshaw and Jacob Snively, followed by the Houston County volunteer rangers under Captain William Sadler. Bringing up the rear of the formation was the largest company, that of Captain Squire Brown. Due to a narrow trail that led from Fort Houston toward the Neches River and Fort Duty, the companies filed along one behind the other.

The trailing forces of Mabbitt's command were attacked about six miles east of Fort Houston. The ambushing party was a group of Indian and Mexican rebels of Córdova's forces led by Juan Flores and Juan Cruz.[3] They had apparently spied on the Texan forces on the move and then staked out an advantageous spot in the forest to attack.

The rearmost company of Captain Brown, marching about a mile behind Mabbitt's forward guard, was caught completely off guard by a sudden hail of gunfire. His men fought back valiantly, but suffered half a dozen casualties.

Private John W. Carpenter, a San Jacinto veteran who had joined Brown's company at Fort Houston only a week previous, pursued a Caddo chief into the woods during the furious fight. He followed the Indian almost a half mile from the scene of the main battle before the two exchanged a final, fatal round of fire with each other. The bodies of Carpenter and the chief were found about thirty yards apart, where each opponent apparently delivered a deadly shot simultaneously.

Other Texans moved into the woods to join the fight after the initial shock of the ambush passed. The companies under Bradshaw, Snively, and Sadler rushed back to assist, but their opponents quickly fled through the forest. It was impossible for Mabbitt to accurately gauge the number of the rebel forces which had attacked his men. Flores and Cruz's men were apparently more intent on making a hit and run statement that would throw fear into some of the volunteers.

The Texans managed to kill at least five Indians in the short battle, including the Caddo chief. Some Indian bodies were dragged away from the battlefield, leaving blood trails. Captain Brown's company suffered four men killed: Carpenter, Julius Bullock, Thomas M. Scott, and John Wilson. Two other rangers, First Corporal David F. Webb and Private Lacy McKenzie, were wounded.

Major Mabbitt certified that Webb had "entered the ranging service of the Republic of Texas in the fall of 1838 in my command." In the fight with Córdova's rebels, he had lost his horse pistols, saddle, and a blanket, collectively valued at $130. His "property was lost in a battle which I had with the Mexicans and Indians combined near Fort Houston, where the said Webb received wounds which will make him a cripple for life."[4]

The mounted gunman regiment regrouped and Mabbitt resumed the march toward Fort Lacy to meet General Rusk's Nacogdoches militia forces. Rusk had made camp at the Jack Still place, east of present Palestine, where Mabbitt's men caught up with them after dark on October 12. William Lacy, son of Indian agent Martin Lacy and a member of one of Rusk's companies, recalled the rangers' arrival. "That night we were reinforced by Col. Mabbitt's command from Fort Houston," wrote Lacy. "On his march to join us, his rear guard was attacked by (Córdova's) forces and a sharp little fight ensued in which Mabbitt lost three men."[5]

Rusk and Mabbitt's forces broke camp on the morning of October 13 and marched westward back toward Fort Houston. En route, they passed back over the battlefield of the previous day. The volunteers found the bodies of John Carpenter and the Indian chief he had killed. The bodies of the four Texans killed in the Córdova skirmish were collected and transported back to Fort Houston. These casualties were buried in unmarked graves in the little Fort Houston cemetery.[6]

Rusk's companies camped in and around Fort Houston that night. Major General Rusk's report of the Kickapoo War, published in the *Telegraph and Texas Register*, states: "On the 14th, I arrived at Fort Houston, having been joined by Major Mabbitt and several men having fallen in on the way and at Fort Houston, my force amounted to about two hundred men."

The following day, October 14, was spent organizing and preparing the troops for battle with Córdova's main rebel force, still reported to be inhabiting the Kickapoo village north of Fort Houston. A new mounted spy company was created under the command of twenty-four-year-old Captain James Edward Box, a San Jacinto veteran. Box had fought valiantly two days prior as a member of Captain Brown's company. First Sergeant William Lacy, second senior officer of Box's "mounted riflemen," joined from Rusk's forces. Most of the other members of this new company were pulled from the ranks of the large volunteer ranger company of Captain Sadler.

Thomas Rusk wrote a last-minute letter postmarked "Head Quarters Fort Houston" to his brother David in Nacogdoches late on October 14. He wrote that his companies were "taking up the line of march from this place to the place where the Indians are said to be encamped about twenty-five miles from here."[7]

The Texans were unaware of exactly what odds they would face. Rusk noted that Córdova's forces had been estimated to be anywhere from one-hundred-and-fifty warriors to six hundred while "my effective forces will be under two-hundred men." He confided in his brother his resentment toward President Houston for hindering his efforts with the Texas Militia.

> If General Houston and some others had been guided by feelings of patriotism and not by low & selfish purposes, I should have had in the field at least five-hundred men; but let success or misfortune attend my efforts. I have the consolation of knowing that all my efforts have been directed to my country's good.
>
> If the Indians are not routed, the frontier will be laid in ruins and if that is done the people of Texas will have to fight two-thirds of the Indians on the U.S. frontier. Towards the people of Texas I have no unkind feelings. They have more than remunerated me by their good feelings for all the sacrifices I have made and the services I have rendered them. To a few demagogues and speculators, who while I was doing all I could for the country were slandering me and speculating on the resources of the country, I wish no greater harm than they may be changed into honest men.

Major General Rusk promised to send his brother news of the expected battle in four days. Should he be killed in action, he would leave his wife and children "much less than many men have sold lots for in the city of Houston, who never paid anything for them except a sacrifice of Principle."

★ ★ ★ ★ ★

Battle at Kickapoo Village: October 16, 1838

Major General Rusk's volunteer forces moved northeasterly from Fort Houston during the morning hours of October 15. The Texan forces moved across present Anderson County for the Neches River and the old Kickapoo village where Córdova's rebels were rumored to be camping out.

Against an unknown number of enemy, Rusk had at his disposal about 260 men by best count. Some accounts claim that Rusk had up to seven hundred men with him on this campaign, which was later referred to as the Kickapoo War. In reality, his entire command amounted to only nine self-armed and provisioned companies under majors Leonard Mabbitt and Baley Walters of Nacogdoches. General Rusk's small command staff included Major Isaac Burton, the ranger captain who had captured the Mexican schooners in Copano Bay in 1836.

Also accompanying Rusk's offensive expedition was Texas' adjutant general, Colonel Hugh McLeod, who was eager to punish Córdova's followers. McLeod would write a detailed campaign report to President-Elect Mirabeau Lamar on October 22.

THE "KICKAPOO WAR" CAMPAIGN
SUMMARY OF FORCES: THIRD MILITIA BRIGADE

Sources: Each of the following company rosters, unless otherwise noted, was compiled from available pay roll and muster roll records, furnished courtesy of the Archives and Information Services Division of the Texas State Library.

Major General Rusk's Command Staff
October 11–21, 1838

Major General:
Thomas Jefferson Rusk
Adjutant General:
Hugh McLeod, Colonel
Volunteer Aides-de-Camp:
Isaac Watts Burton, Major
David Spangler Kaufman, Major
James Reily, Major
Charles Stanfield Taylor, Major

Surgeon:
Calvin Sanderson
Commissary:
Hiram B. Stephens
Quartermaster:
John S. Roberts
Assistant Quartermaster:
Leander Erwin Tipps

SECOND REGIMENT, THIRD MILITIA BRIGADE

Major Baley C. Walters

Captain Box's Mounted Riflemen: Oct. 14, 1838–Jan. 14, 1839

Captain:
James Edward Box
First Sergeant:
William Young Lacy [1]
Privates:
John Bascus
Samuel Charles Box
Thomas Griffin Box
George W. Browning
Daniel Murry Crist
Balis Edens
Darius H. Edens
William M. Frost [1]
John C. Gallion
Amos H. Gates [1]
Alfred M. Hallmark
Mathew D. T. Hallmark
William C. Hallmark
Green Benjamin Hardwick
John A. Harris
James Head
Spencer Hobbs
Pleiades O. Lumpkin
Alexander McKenzie[1]
Thomas Mitchell
Jacob S. Morrow [1]
Elijah B. Reneau
Hiram C. Vansickle
William W. Wilkinson [2]

[1] Joined from Captain Brown's company.
[2] Joined from Captain Brookfield's company. All others joined from Captain Sadler's company.

Captain Brookfield's Mounted Rangers: October 12–24, 1838

Captain:
William C. Brookfield
First Sergeant:
Presley Gossett
Second Sergeant:
William Gossett
Orderly Sergeant:
John Allbright

Privates:
Refugio Ballensweller
John P. Barnett
John E. Clapp
Mills I. Eason
Ira P. Ellis
Richard B. Finch
James L. Gossett
George W. Hanchett
Joseph Lopez
Alfred M. Liles
Zachariah Maddan
John A. Muncriff
Ira C. Shute

Captain Durst's Mounted Volunteers: October 10–20, 1838

Captain:
John Durst
First Sergeant:
James D. Long
Orderly Sergeant:
Theodore B. Starkes
First Corporal:
Solomon Harkil
Second Corporal:
Russell Roark

Privates:
Isaac T. Bean
Robert Bean
Wily Burrow
Levi B. Dikes
Asa Dorsett
Peter Harper
Julian Harby
Adam Johnson
Jackson Little
Hugh Rennerd
John Roark
Antonio Sanchez
Elbridge G. Sevier

Capt. Smith's Nacogdoches Mounted Volunteers: October 10–21, 1838

Captain:
Robert W. Smith
First Lieutenant:
Stephen F. Sparks
Second Lieutenant:
William W. Taylor
First Sergeant:
Eli G. Sparks

Privates:
Elijah Anderson
Howard W. Bailey
Jeremiah Bailey
Williamson Bromley
Ambrose Hulon Crain
Theodore Dorsett
Delores Martinez
James McAnulty
Edward Price
Henry M. Rogers
Samuel Rogers
Lewis Sanchez
Hiram B. Stephens
Heartwell Twaisime
Robert H. Watkins
Daniel Weeks

Captain Williams' Mounted Volunteers: October 9–19, 1838

Captain:
Joseph Williams
First Lieutenant:
James Fisher
Second Lieutenant:
John Deen
Orderly Sergeant:
William Laucer

Privates:
John Able
Durham Avant
R. P. Banks
Zachariah W. Bottoms
Henry Mitchell Brewer
James Brewer
John Brewer
William Brewer Jr.
James Brown
Levi P. Cadenhead
Davis Cook
Thomas Cook
Thomas Cox
William Curl
Levi Ford
James Foster
Asbury Griggs
Thomas Grison
Isaac Hicks
Jesse C. Kincannon
George W. Knox
John Lively
Joseph Looce
Lyman H. Matthews
John A. Medford
Daniel Meredith
Isaac Stokely
George T. Walters
Robert Walters
Tillman Walters
Wayne Walters
William Wasnell
Joseph E. White
James Windsor
Martin Windsor

FIRST REGIMENT OF MOUNTED GUNMEN

Major Leonard H. Mabbitt

Capt. Bradshaw's Mounted Riflemen: October 10–December 1, 1838

Captain:
James Bradshaw
First Sergeant:
James Allison
Privates:
William Allison Jr.
Andrew Jackson Click
Dr. Elisha J. DeBard [1]
Beverly Greenwood
James Hall [1]
George Isaacs [1]
Nathaniel Killough [1]
B. Lacey
John Marshall
Jacob Pruett
Len Pruett
Martin J. Pruett
William Robinson
Benjamin A. Vansickle [2]
Dr. James J. Ware [1]
Elijah Wheeler
Alexander White
John "Young" Williams
Leonard Williams
Thomas Williams [1]

[1] Wounded October 16.
[2] Joined October 18.

Capt. Brown's Mounted Gunmen: August 30–December 28, 1838

Captain:
Champion Blythe [1]
Squire Brown [2]
First Lieutenant:
A. J. Blythe [1]
Corley T. Crawford [3]
Second Lieutenant:
George F. Martin [3]
First Sergeant:
Samuel Brooks
Second Sergeant:
H. Gilliland
Third Sergeant:
Eler D. Hanks
Fourth Sergeant:
Charles Shanks
First Corporal:
David F. Webb [4]
Second Corporal:
C. C. White
Third Corporal:
Thomas Hanks
Fourth Corporal:
William Thompson
Privates:
L. L. Artage
William Bates
Thomas Berry [6]
A. W. Blythe [1]
James Edward Box [7]
Newton Brownfield
Daniel Buez
Julius Bullock [5]
John W. Carpenter [5]
James Cartwright
Daniel LaMora Crist[6]
Calvin J. Fuller
Ponton Fuller
Amos H. Gates [8]
James Gilliland
William P. Gilliland
Charles Gilmore
Isiah Hamilton
Thomas J. Hanks
Augustin B. Hardin
E. R. Harris
Charles Johnson
A. T. Jones
Harland Jones [9]
Jesse H. Looney
Mathew Mabin
Daniel Marteth
Lacy McKenzie [4]
John D. Miller
John Mitchell
John P. Moseley
James O'Neal
M. L. Phillips
T. J. Quesenberry
Isaac Raines
Joel D. Raines
John D. Raines
Wiley Rogers
Thomas M. Scott [5]
William Scott
Joseph Shanks
Daniel Smiley
J. Smith
J. H. Smith
Robert Waggoner
Joseph Walker
William G. Walker
B. W. Watson
James Weeks
John White
John Wilson [5]

[1] Transferred to Capt. Snively's Sept. 21.
[2] Promoted from 1st. Lt. on Sept. 22.
[3] Promoted on Sept. 22.
[4] Wounded Oct. 12.
[5] Killed Oct. 12.
[6] Wounded Oct. 16.
[7] Promoted from the company Oct. 14.
[8] Transfer to Lieutenant Shearer's Oct. 4.
[9] Deserted.

Captain Sadler's Mounted Rangers: September–November 7, 1838

Captain:
William T. Sadler
First Lieutenant:
John Wortham
Second Lieutenant:
John Edward Nite
Orderly Sergeant:
Thomas Hays
Privates:
Britton H. Adams
Cephus Adams
Solomon Adams
William H. Adams
Stephen Bennett
Reuben Brown
Jacob Crist
John Crist
Stephen Crist
John Silas Edens
John Crawford Grigsby
William G. W. Jowers
Joseph Kennedy
James Madden
Robert Madden
John Murchison *
Benjamin Parker
Daniel Parker Jr.
Dickerson Parker
William H. Pate
Dr. William Perry
P. T. Robinson
William T. Smith
John Walker
Martin A. Walker
Phillip Walker
Samuel G. Wells
George W. Wilson

* Wounded October 16.

No muster roll available. This muster roll based on author's research of Audited Claims of the Republic of Texas and known participants of the Kickapoo War.

Capt. Snively's Mounted Rangers: September 14–December 13, 1838

Captain:
Jacob Snively
First Lieutenant:
John H. Davis [1]
James W. Cleveland
Second Lieutenant:
William W. Umsted
First Sergeant:
Marquis D. Boyd [2]
Second Sergeant:
Jackson Ward
Third Sergeant:
John Jacobs
Fourth Sergeant:
J. D. O'Kelly
First Corporal:
John W. Fowler
Second Corporal:
B. Steward
Bugler:
William W. Wade
Privates:
James Alexander
A. J. Blythe
A. W. Blythe
Champion Blythe
George A. Box
Sebastian Box
Joseph Buffington
Charles Chevallier
Josiah Taylor Childers
William Cobb
H. D. Conn [3]
Delores Cortinez
James Dickerson
James G. Dixon
Joseph Durst
Henry Gough
Oscar L. Holmes [4]
John Hunter
James G. Hyde
Michael P. Kelley [2]
Joel Langham
William McKaughn
Mack McRoy [2]
Joseph Meradith
Stewart Meradith
Benjamin Moore
John C. Morrison
O. R. Powell [5]
Dimer W. Reeves [3]
Asa Rolling
Louis Rose
John Rovan
John Rowan
Justus Shearwood
Augustus W. Slawson
James Triplett [2]
Samuel Turner
Wm. Henry Vardeman
Juan Jose Via [6]
Moses Wells
George Washington Welsh
Samuel W. Wilds
John Wright

[1] Resigned commission. Served balance of his service as private.
[2] Wounded October 16.
[3] Joined October 28.
[4] Joined October 20.
[5] Joined November 1.
[6] Joined November 9.

> The General resolved to move on at once after the enemy, seeing that a victory was necessary to give the people breathing time and confidence. He did not march direct to the Saline, as he feared they would perceive his approach and retire before him. He marched first to Fort Houston, laid in what supplies he could procure, and marched then across towards the Saline.[8]

The Kickapoo village was located roughly thirty miles to the north-east of Fort Houston, 2.5 miles south-southeast of present Frankston. The ride was largely uneventful, although Major Mabbitt's men did spot a few Indian braves in the afternoon while moving toward the Kickapoo village. The Indians were believed to be carrying meat to Córdova's forces.[9]

The Texans did not encounter the main body of enemy forces. Major General Rusk decided to make camp at the abandoned Kickapoo Village shortly before sundown. It was obvious to him that hostile forces were in the area, who were no doubt very aware of the presence of the rangers and militiamen.

The fading hours of October 15 were spent setting up camp. The old Indian village was located perhaps a half mile northwest of the Neches River on a horseshoe bend of Kickapoo Creek in the extreme northern corner of present Anderson County. The bending creekbed was selected as a defensive area that was hoped to prevent surprise attacks.

Colonel Hugh McLeod (1814–1862), the adjutant general of Texas, joined Major General Rusk's forces for the October 1838 Kickapoo campaign. *Texas State Library and Archives Commission.*

Sleep would be a precious commodity during this night, as spies of Córdova were watching Rusk's camp. At 10:00 p.m., they attempted to torch the woods surrounding the Texan camp. This technique had been devastating for Lieutenant Vanbenthuysen's rangers in 1837. Fortunately this time the forest was not dry enough and the fires died out before posing a serious threat to the men or their horses.

The Texans arranged their camp in a defensive setup along Kickapoo Creek to prepare for the conflict which now appeared imminent. The men tied off their horses in the center of camp with one armed guard positioned to prevent a stampede and other sentinels posted at each corner of the camp. The setup resembled a rectangle. Córdova's spies kept tensions at a premium through the night. Two men moved in close enough at one point during the night that Texan guards fired upon them and managed to seize one of their horses.[10]

The spies had seen enough to size up the Texan camp. During the final hours prior to dawn, hundreds of Indian and Mexican rebels slipped silently through the forest around Major General Rusk's camp and took up position. Just after daybreak on October 16, the forest around the militia camp suddenly exploded with the sounds of gunfire and war whoops.

For the second time in four days, Major Mabbitt's rangers found themselves under a surprise attack in the woods. Conditions favored the attackers, who had given their eyes plenty of time to adjust to the conditions. A light, misty rain was falling as the first light of dawn tried to peek through the tall pines and leaf-barren hardwoods of the East Texas forest near Kickapoo Creek. Colonel McLeod noted that the "woods were very open and the trees large, affording an admirable opportunity for their favorite tactics of fighting behind a cover."[11]

The shape of the attack caused those companies which had slept in the extreme northern end of the camp to bear the brunt of the initial attack. These were the companies of captains Box, Bradshaw, Sadler, and Snively.[12] Most of these men had been involved in the previous surprise attack on Mabbitt's gunmen on October 12. Fortunately for the Texans this morning, Hugh McLeod felt that it was the "closest shooting I ever saw to do so little execution." Nearly every man caught under fire at the head of the camp had his clothes ripped in at least one place by rifle balls.

In his report after the conflict, McLeod drew a sketch to help illustrate the three-pronged attack the Texans endured.

> On the morning of 16th just after day break at the Kickapoo Town, we were attacked. Our camp was an oblong

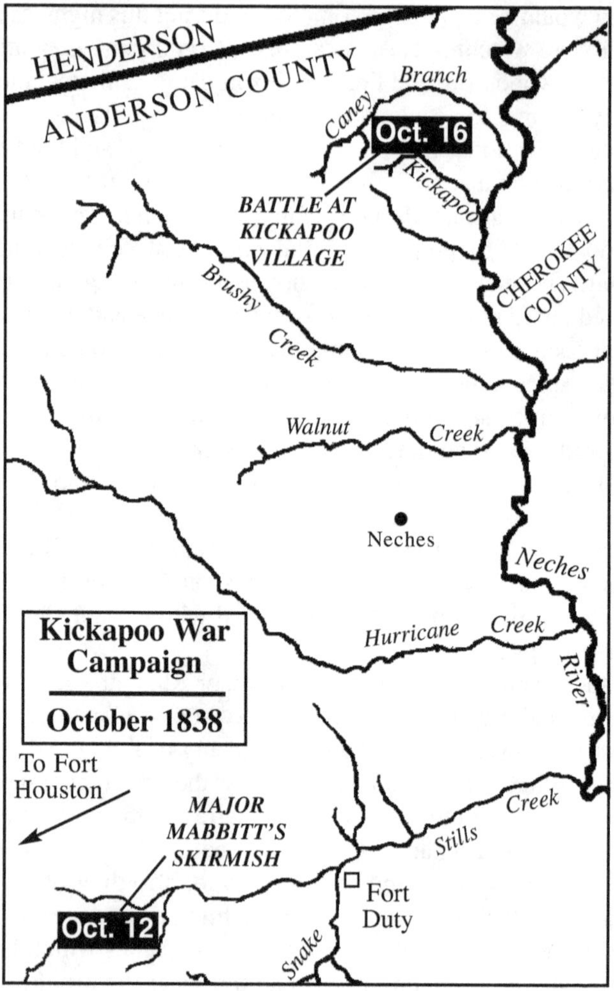

square, with the horses at the center. The attack was made principally on the head of the square within forty yards of the guard, but they displayed around three sides as marked and compelled us to maintain the square. For this reason the troops at the head had to bear the brunt of the action.[13]

No Texan was killed outright, but thirteen men were wounded in varying degrees. More than a quarter of Captain Bradshaw's men were wounded. The tightly packed horses in the camp no doubt saved many a man's life during the early shooting, where dozens of the animals were wounded.

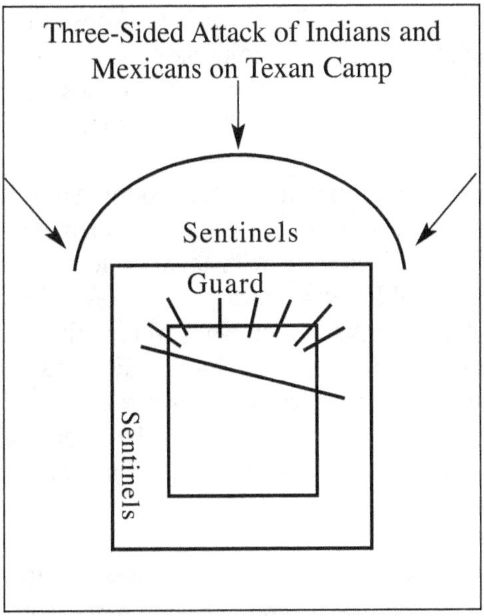

This illustration is based on the original sketch by Colonel Hugh McLeod in his Kickapoo campaign report.
See Gulick, *Lamar Papers,* II: 266.

Captain Sadler's Houston County company suffered only one casualty in the firefight. Private John Murchison, Sadler's brother-in-law, was literally shot between the eyes. Anderson County historian Andrew J. Fowler later wrote an historical sketch which included the involvement of San Pedro Creek settlement residents in quelling Córdova's Rebellion.

> Near[ly] all the available force of that settlement volunteered their services and elected W. T. Sadler, a San Jacinto veteran, as their captain. Among this number were the Madden brothers, Robert and James, two or three young Edenses and young John Murchison, who, it will be recollected, was wounded at the Battle of Kickapoo.
>
> He there received a ball in the forehead between the eyes, which knocked him down, but did not penetrate the skull. The thick, bony structure in the region of the eye arrested the force of the ball, which was partially spent. The ball lodged in the socket of the left eye against the eyebrow. Whence it was extracted, the wound resulted in no permanent injury to health or vision. Those who know the determined will of the man, jocularly remarked that his head was too hard to be penetrated by a bullet.[14]

The attacking force was later estimated to number several hundred warriors. In addition to Córdova and his rebel Mexicans, his party was believed to include Kickapoo, Delaware, Caddo,

Coushatta, Kichai, and Cherokee Indians. Surveyor Elias Vansickle, being held prisoner by Córdova's rebels, was soon able to shed some light on the composition of the enemy forces. Vansickle's deposition was read on January 25, 1839, by Chief Justice Charles Taylor.

> He states that he was in their camp at the Kickapoo town at the time of the battle between General Rusk's forces and them, and that there was then fifteen Cherokees with them, who all joined in the attack upon General Rusk's camp . . .
>
> Several Shawnees—five, he thinks, in number—were at the hostile camp some days previous to the battle. Fifteen Coushattas were in the battle against us, led by Benash, a chief. Another chief was killed a few days before in an action between Major Mabbitt's command and the Indians, in which it is well known the latter made the attack.[15]

Córdova's forces were well positioned to inflict losses on the Texans. In addition to stationing shooters behind the large trees, Tom Rusk noticed that the Indians had mounted warriors waiting on a hill just out of gun range. He felt that these cavalrymen were waiting to ride down upon any Texans who tried to flee the camp ambush. Angered by the enemy he could scarcely see, Rusk attempted to draw some of his attackers into the open. He boldly moved twenty paces out from camp and shouted, "You damned cowardly bastards! Come out and show yourselves like men!"[16]

The Indians whooped and fired their rifles, but did not rush into the open as Rusk had hoped. The firing began to die down around the camp after about fifteen minutes. Seizing the chance, Rusk rallied his troops and ordered a large portion of his men to charge the enemy. Another portion of the men were left behind to guard the camp and the remaining horses. The rangers and militiamen charged ahead into the thicket and sent the rebels fleeing on foot and on horseback ahead of them. Several enemy were shot down in their flight.

Major General Rusk allowed pursuit to continue about three-quarters of a mile through the forest before he called a halt. His enemy was on the run and protecting camp from another counterattack was more sensible at this point. "The force of the enemy I had no means of ascertaining," Rusk wrote, "but it must have been very considerable, as the ground occupied by them was near half a mile in length."[17]

The Texans returned to camp to tend to their wounded. Nearly a dozen Indian and Mexican bodies were left lying about the battlefield,

A Texas Centennial Marker stands at the site of the October 16, 1838, Battle of Kickapoo along Highway 19 near Frankston in northeastern Anderson County. *Author's collection.*

most killed within fifty feet of the Texan camp. Blood trails were found in the grass where other dead or wounded warriors had been dragged away. Rusk felt that his men had wounded at least seventy Indians who were helped from the area. The survivors quickly scattered into the forest and evaded further contact with Rusk's forces. Colonel McLeod noted the losses in his battle report.

> Among the dead and the nearest to our camp was a Cherokee named Tail. Bowl[es] says he was a bad Indian, that he never could manage him, and that he was well killed. They left on the ground 11 killed, and the grass full of trails of blood; we have since heard they lost about 30.[18]

Private Isaac T. Bean, who had come to Texas in 1823 and had served in Rusk's August expedition, was among Captain John Durst's company in the fight. He saw the bodies of at least two of his opponents.

> We had as well as I can remember some ten or twelve men [were] wounded; none killed dead on the battlefield and but one that died of wound[s]. Jefferson Ware was one of the wounded. We killed one Mexican and one Indian that we got. There was a great deal of blood on the trails.[19]

Texan Casualties of October 16, 1838
Battle of Kickapoo

Name / Rank:	*Company:*	*Remarks:*
Thomas Berry, Pvt.	Capt. Brown	Wounded.
Marquis D. Boyd, 1st Sergeant	Capt. Snively	Wounded.
Daniel LaMora Crist, Pvt.	Capt. Brown	Shot in hip and hand.
Dr. Elisha J. DeBard, Pvt.	Capt. Bradshaw	Wounded.
James Hall, Pvt.	Capt. Bradshaw	Mortally wounded.
George Isaacs, Pvt.	Capt. Bradshaw	Wounded.
Michael P. Kelly, Pvt.	Capt. Snively	Wounded.
Nathaniel Killough, Pvt.	Capt. Bradshaw	Shot in shoulder.
John Murchison, Pvt.	Capt. Sadler	Shot in the face.
Mack McRoy, Pvt.	Capt. Snively	Wounded.
James Triplett, Pvt.	Capt. Snively	Wounded.
Dr. James Jefferson Ware, Pvt.	Capt. Bradshaw	Wounded.
Thomas Williams, Pvt.	Capt. Bradshaw	Wounded.

The two surgeons, Dr. William Perry of Major Mabbitt's ranger battalion and Dr. Sanderson of Rusk's staff, were kept busy treating the wounded men in the wake of the battle. Perry operated on Daniel Crist of Captain Brown's company to remove rifle balls that had lodged in his hip and hand.[20]

Private James Hall from Captain Bradshaw's company was badly wounded, but Dr. Sanderson felt that he would pull through. Billy Killough, a survivor of the Killough Massacre, later wrote that his uncle Nathaniel was "wounded in the Kickapoo fight, being shot through the shoulder."[21]

Major General Rusk, short of horses and confident that his men had inflicted serious losses on their enemy, decided that his forces should withdraw. The wounded Texans were transported on litters from Kickapoo Creek back to Fort Houston. On the day of the battle, the men were furnished corn and fodder by local resident George W. Wilson, who lived near Fort Houston. His receipt of October 16 for forty-two dollars was signed by Quartermaster John Roberts and his assistant, Leander Tipps.[22]

After returning to Fort Houston, Dr. Elisha DeBard of Captain Bradshaw's company was nursed back to health with assistance from his wife. Learning of her husband's wounds, she packed provisions and traveled on horseback with a faithful servant from Nacogdoches to Fort Houston.[23] Private James Hall, critically wounded in the Kickapoo fight, later died of his wounds on December 17 and was buried in the Fort Houston cemetery.

George H. Duncan of Fort Houston was later paid by the Republic of Texas for boarding Hall and another severely wounded man. Another seriously wounded Texan, Sergeant Marquis Boyd, returned to Nacogdoches, where he was boarded and fed by Dr. James Cook for seventeen days while he recovered.[24]

Major General Rusk wrote an account of the Kickapoo battle to the *Telegraph and Texas Register* in Houston, which was published in the newspaper on November 3, 1838.

> We had eleven men severely wounded—none killed, and about twenty-five or thirty horses so badly shot as to be unfit for use. Among the enemy's dead were found Caddos, Coushattas, Biloxies, one Cherokee and two Mexicans. They dropped on their flight a number of guns, blankets . . . It would be difficult to find language to do justice to the officers and men: all fought with a spirit and determination seldom equalled. The officers in the action were Adj. Gen. McLeod, Maj. Kaufman, Maj. Reily, and Maj. Burton, Volunteer Aides-de-Camp, Majors Walters and Mabbitt, Captains Box, Bradshaw, Snively, Smith, Williams, Durst, Sadler, Brookfield, and Brown.

Counting both the October 12 and October 16 fights with Córdova's rebels, the Texans had suffered five killed and fourteen wounded. In exchange, they felt sure that they had killed at least three dozen and wounded dozens more of their opponents.

At Fort Houston, claims were issued for those who had lost their horses in combat. From Captain Sadler's company, audited claims show that privates Robert Madden, John Murchison, and John Walker each lost a horse in the October 16 fight. Their papers were signed by Sadler and Rusk on October 19 at "Headquarters, Fort Houston." From other companies, men known to have lost a horse or a mule at the Kickapoo fight include George Hanchett, Joseph Walker, Theodore Dorsett, and Darius Edens.[25]

General Rusk marched back to Nacogdoches with his Third Militia Brigade volunteers. Captain Williams' company was discharged on October 19 and Captain Durst's men had reached Mount Sterling by October 20. Captain Smith's Nacogdoches company was discharged upon arrival in town on October 21. The mounted gunman battalion under Major Mabbitt, however, remained on duty in the Fort Houston area.

Shortly after returning to Nacogdoches, Rusk wrote to Chief

Bowles of the Cherokees, telling him that he had "punished" the Mexicans and Indians and that his men had killed one Cherokee. He warned Bowles to keep his tribe from the Mexicans and advised the Cherokee chief to come to Nacogdoches soon with Chief Big Mush to hold a talk on the matters.[26] The Cherokees would later explain that they had been absent from their village during the Kickapoo battle because they had heard of the first fight on October 12. Chief Bowles feared that the whites would blame his people and come to destroy them and their villages.

Rusk's October campaign was later commonly referred to among Texans as the "Kickapoo War." Today, only a centennial marker stands along Highway 19 south of the town of Frankston in northeastern Anderson County in testament of the 1838 battle. The battlefield along Kickapoo Creek is believed to be located on the farm behind this sign. Once the Texans had Córdova's rebels on the move, the battle actually carried on over some distance in the vicinity of the old Indian village, Kickapoo Creek and the Neches River. Residents along a rural farm-road that follows the creek for some distance claim to still occasionally find arrowheads and other evidence of the early battle.

The Texans had held their own against the Mexican and Indian forces. It was a telling defeat for Vicente Córdova, and his rebellion had been effectively quelled for the time being by the strong showing of Texas forces. Córdova himself returned to Mexico, where he would remain until he and Flores could organize a new rebel force the following year.

CHAPTER 4

To the Border and Beyond

October 18–December 1838

News of Tom Rusk's big battle at the Kickapoo village spread quickly. In Nacogdoches, Colonel William Sparks' Second Regiment of the Third Militia Brigade of Texas was called back into service on October 17, 1838. Sparks had commanded the Second Regiment during Rusk's August campaign to Chief Bowles' Cherokee village, but his staff had been discharged on August 22.

Determined to aid Rusk's efforts, Colonel Sparks and Lieutenant Colonel James Carter organized their staff. The other members were Major Baley Walters, Adjutant Peter Tipps, Sergeant Major Joel Burditt Crain, Quartermaster Thomas B. Garrett, First Surgeon James Harper Starr, and Assistant Surgeon Henry M. Rogers.

Before the Second Regiment could join Rusk, another band of Indians struck a deadly blow in Houston County only miles from where Rusk's troops were at Fort Houston. On the night of Thursday, October 18, 1838, a group of eleven Indians attacked the frontier home of John Edens. He and three other older men were protecting fifteen women and children, many of whose husbands and fathers were presently serving with Captain William Sadler's volunteer rangers.[1]

The Indians who carried out this raid appear to have been the Kickapoos. Elias Vansickle, a captive of Córdova's rebels, had been held hostage near Kickapoo Town during the battle of Kickapoo. A short time after the battle, he noted that, "Some Kickapoos, a large number, came in and stated that they had killed the families of Eden[s] and others, near Mustang Prairie, Houston County."[2]

The Indians waited to commence their attack until the men had retired to one room of the dogtrot cabin for the night. Several Indians guarded the door to the room occupied by the men while others burst into the cabin occupied by the women and children. Using guns, tomahawks, and scalping knives, the Kickapoos began slaughtering their helpless victims.

Mrs. John Edens, Sarah Murchison, and Mary Murchison Sadler were quickly murdered. Lucinda Edens Madden and Nancy Halhouser Madden were both severely wounded and left for dead. The men in the adjacent room fought their way free but apparently felt too outnumbered to fight the well-armed Indians without their weapons. John Edens, James S. Madden, Elisha Moore, and Martin Murchison were pursued for some distance but escaped with their lives.

The men were later criticized for not fighting to their own deaths. Such sharp words likely paled in comparison to the losses each felt upon returning to the scene of the depredation. After slaughtering most of the women and children, the Indians set fire to the dogtrot cabin and burned it down.

Two daughters of John Edens were killed. Two sons of James and Lucinda Madden were killed, as were a daughter of Robert and Nancy Madden and a daughter of William and Mary Sadler. A seventh child, that of Martin Murchison, may also have been killed. The fire burned so fiercely that only charred remains were to be found. For some of the children, it would remain unknown if they were murdered, burned to death, or carried away by the Indians.

An Edens family servant named Patsy helped the two severely wounded Madden women to escape from the blazing home. She also rescued a young daughter of John Edens. The only other child to survive was nine-year-old Balis Erls Edens, who crawled from the house during the slaughter and hid all night in a hog bed behind the slaves' quarters.

Other families in the area heard the horrible screams and shooting from the Edens home. They fled into the forest and hid in the creekbeds. Others fled toward Fort Houston, where word reached General Rusk's militia by the following morning, October 19.

Captain Sadler's men and many men of Captain Box's ranger company rode to the Edens home to behold the smoldering ruins where some of the men had left their families for safety. Both Sadler and one of his privates, Robert Madden, had lost their wives and young daughters. Several of the Edens sons returned to find that they had lost their stepmother and two sisters.

The men held a small ceremony for the ten victims of what became known as the Edens-Madden Massacre. What remained of the victims' bodies, mostly ashes, was buried 150 yards south of the burned home. The State of Texas erected two markers to honor these victims. The first was a centennial marker at the massacre site, located in the woods a few miles off FM 2022 near Augusta on the south side of San Pedro Creek, about thirteen miles northeast of Crockett, Texas. A more accessible and more accurate marker was erected in 1972 in the Houston County community of Augusta.

★ ★ ★ ★ ★

Captain Cage's Fight on the Leon: October 20, 1838

October 1838 was equally violent in other areas of Texas. A party of Mexican and white surveyors camped at Leon Creek, about four miles from San Antonio, were attacked by Comanches on October 18. At least five of these men were killed, including Cornelius Skinner, a Mr. Jones of Bastrop, and San Jacinto veteran Moses Lapham. Mr. Earnest and others escaped on foot to town. Their scalped and mutilated bodies, some with arrows protruding, were found the next day. Two Mexicans, Francisco Antonio Ruiz and Nicolas Flores Ruiz, were taken prisoner this day. One was never heard from again, but the other man succeeded in escaping and making his way back to San Antonio.[3]

When word reached San Antonio, Hendrick Arnold, a former scout under Deaf Smith, took command of a few men and they quickly rode out to reconnoiter. These men managed only a slight skirmish with the Comanches.

In the meantime, another volunteer group was fitted out in town to pursue these Indians. Major Valentine Bennett, quartermaster for the cavalry, helped supply horses for the men. A party of nine men under Captain Benjamin Franklin Cage, a San Jacinto veteran, was put together. The *Telegraph and Texas Register* on Wednesday, November 14, 1838, stated that, "He was also second in command under Col. Karnes in the recent engagement with the Comanches on the Arroyo Seco."[4]

As Captain Cage's party headed out toward the Leon Creek massacre sight, other men followed along until the party numbered thirteen men. This pursuit party included General Richard G. Dunlap from Tennessee, Judge Joseph L. Hood of San Antonio, Dr. Henry G. McClung, San Jacinto veteran John Pickering, former Deaf Smith cavalryman Peter Conrad, an Irishman named James Campbell, Robert Montgomery Lee, Daniel O'Boyle, Alexander Bailey, Robert Patton, and two men whose names have been recorded only as King and Green.

En route to the Leon, the small party was approached by a party of Comanches several miles out of town. Dunlap quickly proposed that the group move from the open prairie into some nearby timber to fight under cover of tree protection. Captain Cage, however, would have nothing of this and proposed fighting the Comanches on the spot.

Cage's small party was quickly surrounded by more than one hundred Indians. Cage and O'Boyle dismounted at a tree to fight, while the others chose to fight from horseback. Hood and Bailey made a charge through the Indians and then back to their own comrades. In the process, Judge Hood was wounded by an arrow. The first judge of Viesca, thirty-five-year-old Hood had also served on the General Council in 1835 and had been involved with recruiting ranger companies during the Texas Revolution. Hood's wounds were not life threatening. He was later elected Sheriff of Béxar County in 1839 but died during the famous Council House Fight in 1840.[5]

Less fortunate than Judge Hood were Captain Cage and Daniel O'Boyle, both of whom were killed on the ground. Robert Lee, a twenty-four-year old Connecticut native who was a merchant from Houston, was killed on horseback. Robert Patton was sliced through the arm and had his horse wounded. Bailey's gun took this ill opportune time to fail to fire.

At this point, a number of the Texans had fallen dead and the situation was hopeless. The Indians opened the way toward town and the survivors seized the moment to flee on horseback as their only chance to escape. It was a race for life toward town with the Indians closing in on their flanks all the way. Some of the Texan volunteers were killed as the mad retreat commenced. General Dunlap was lanced during the chase and his bay steed was severely wounded. The chase only ended as the Indians literally chased the surviving whites right into town before turning away. One badly wounded, naked Tejano man later managed to crawl back into town from the fight.[6]

Eight of the thirteen men were killed outright, and four of the others were wounded. The survivors made their way back to Béxar with great difficulty. Those killed were Captain Cage, Lee, Dr. McClung, Conrad, O'Boyle, Pickering, King, and Green. General Dunlap survived his spear wound and was recovering rapidly a week later. Colonel Lysander Wells of the Texas Cavalry carried the news to Houston, whereupon it was reported in the November 3 issue of the *Telegraph*.

On October 20, a mounted party of Tejanos and Texas settlers under Captain Mauricio Carrasco went out to the battle scene. They found the bodies of Cage's slain men and those of the surveyors and brought them back into town.

Major Bennett helped improvise coffins for them, as lumber was very scarce at the time. Judge James W. Robinson delivered the funeral oration on October 21 and the men were buried in a single grave in the town's American cemetery (just outside the Catholic cemetery near present Milam Square in San Antonio).[7]

"On the 21st, we buried them outside the walled cemetery," wrote Miles Squire Bennett, son of Major Bennett, in his diary. "All in the cold, drizzling rain."

★ ★ ★ ★ ★

Development of Third Militia Brigade Regiments

In East Texas, Tom Rusk was as eager to take the fight to the Indians as Captain Cage had been. He found greater challenges to overcome in properly equipping his men for the campaign he desired to carry out.

He planned to use three of four militia brigades in a combined sweeping effort to drive the hostile Indian forces from the northern and eastern regions of Texas. He would move General John Dyer's Fourth Brigade down from the Red River, Kelsey Douglass' Third Brigade up from Nacogdoches, and Moseley Baker's Second Brigade from the Trinity. Rusk's planned October campaign fizzled when President Houston refused to release money from the treasury to organize and equip the troops.[8]

In the wake of the Kickapoo battle, James Reily informed Rusk that the Kickapoo Indians appeared to have remained on friendly terms, refusing to join with the hostile Indians. Those in Houston County felt relief after the Kickapoo War, but Major General Rusk moved on to San Augustine to raise more troops.

After doing so, he proceeded back to Fort Houston to join the troops he hoped to take on a campaign after the hostile Indians, who were believed to be retiring northward. Some companies which fought at Kickapoo were broken up shortly after the fight. Captain John Durst's Mount Sterling company was disbanded at Durst's Fort shortly after the fight. General Rusk was encouraged to pursue his campaign against the Indians without the president's funding or approval. He promised his men only that they could expect to be paid for their service sometime in the future.

Additional militia forces assembled in Houston County during late October while Rusk set up his temporary headquarters in the Fort

Houston area. Captain William C. Duffield of Nacogdoches arrived at Murchison's place on October 23 with nineteen men. There, he found General Douglass with eighty men. Duffield wrote on October 24 of Douglass:

> He is desirous of fighting the Indians who are assembled in force at the Saline, of from one to two thousand. Serious reports, no doubt all magnified. We will leave here tomorrow for Anglin's place and from there we will go to the Saline and give them a fight anyhow.[9]

Duffield, Douglass, and their men planned to wait at Anglin's until more reinforcements under Colonel Horton, expected at around one hundred more men, could arrive. According to Duffield, the Indians were "sorry that they retreated so soon" during the Kickapoo village battle, and they felt that Rusk's troops would have withdrawn had the Indians made a more sustained charge.

Major Mabbitt and his forces remained at Fort Houston from October 19 through October 28, as evidenced by provisioning receipts signed by Mabbitt and his commissary, Amos H. Gates. Among the locals supplying corn, beef, pork, and other goods to the Fort Houston rangers during this time period were William Smith, Stephen Crist, Roland Box, Joseph Jordan, and Reason Crist. Captain Snively's company made at least one scout out to Fort Parker, where his company took on provisions on October 24, 1838.[10]

The lack of action following the Kickapoo village fight was enough to sway some volunteers to return to their homes. Captain James Box's ranging company saw many of its enlistees return to their farms, with fifteen men being discharged on October 28 alone. The balance of Box's men remained on duty at Fort Houston and would continue ranging Houston County for another year. A provisions document of November 27 at Fort Houston shows that Box signed for his troops as "Capt. of Spies."[11]

The Third Regiment of the Third Brigade was commanded by Colonel Willis Landrum. He first organized a mounted company under Captain George English on October 10 and next Captain Richard Haley's Shelby County company on October 14 in response to Rusk's call for troops. English and Haley's men missed the Kickapoo fight, but would remain on constant service on the eastern Texas frontiers under Landrum's direction for three months.

As of October 30, Rusk's Third Brigade troops were still camped at a spot in northern Houston County called Murchison's Camp on

Murchison's Prairie. Volunteer ranger Captain William Sadler, whose farm lay close to the camp, was among those who offered supplies to the troops stationed there. Assistant quartermaster Leander Tipps recorded that Sadler supplied 142 bushels of corn from his farm at the rate of $3.50 per bushel "for the use of the troops now in the field." Another receipt shows that Sadler supplied fourteen "beeves" and three hogs worth $242 to the troops under Colonel Willis Landrum, commanding the Third Brigade.[12]

Others supplying militia forces with food during October and December at Murchison's Camp in Houston County were Armstead Bennett, Martin Murchison, Daniel Parker, and Joel Daniel Leathers. John Edens, who had lost his wife and other family members in the Edens-Madden Massacre, supplied the militia with $200 worth of corn fodder and beef in late 1838. He had previously supplied beef to Captain Sadler's rangers on October 1 prior to the Kickapoo battle.[13]

During the early days of November, General Rusk led his militiamen from the Fort Houston area to the Sabine River. There the troops camped for three days while scouts were sent out in all directions to seek information on Indian activities. The scouts reported back that they had seen no Indian signs, which made Rusk all the more nervous. He next marched his Third Brigade troops back down to Chief Bowles' village in Cherokee Nation, but also found it deserted.

Colonel Landrum, with the companies of captains English and Haley at his discretion, continued to recruit men. The forty-three-man Sabine County mounted militia company of Captain William P. Wyche was mustered into service on November 4, 1838, for three months' service. Captain Joseph Ferguson's thirty-two-man mounted volunteer unit was also added to Landrum's Third Regiment of the Third Militia Brigade on December 8 for three months. Each of Landrum's companies was formally part of General Douglass' Texas Militia brigade, but they more properly operated in the fashion of rangers. They equipped themselves with arms and provisions, ranged over unprotected territory, and remained in service even after the close of formal expeditions.

After marching back through the Cherokee village of Chief Bowles, many of the Third Brigade companies were disbanded. Colonel Sparks and his Second Regiment staff had returned to Nacogdoches by November 13 and ended their service. General Douglass remained on duty, as did Colonel Landrum. A number of new three-month companies were formed during early November in the Third Brigade.

Among them was that of Captain John Wortham, which was mustered into service on November 9, 1838, in Houston County from the remnants of Captain Sadler's company. Several other Kickapoo battle veterans from Captain Brookfield's former company joined Wortham's unit.

Third Brigade, Texas Militia
Companies in Service November–December 1838

Senior Officers:

Kelsey Harris Douglass	Brigadier General
William Crain Sparks	Colonel, Second Regiment
Willis C. Landrum	Colonel, Third Regiment
James Chessher	Colonel, Fourth Regiment

Companies in Service:

Commander:	*Service Tenure:*
Capt. Hayden S. Arnold	Oct. 3–Nov. 16, 1838
Capt. James Edward Box	Oct. 14, 1838–Oct. 18, 1839
Capt. James Bradshaw	Oct. 10–Dec. 1, 1838
Capt. Thomas D. Brooks	Oct. 29–Nov. 29, 1838
Capt. Squire Brown	Aug. 30–Dec. 28, 1838
Capt. Andrew Caddell	Nov. 1–15, 1838
Capt. Stephen Collins	Oct. 12–Nov. 26, 1838
Capt. James H. Durst	Dec. 1, 1838–Jan. 25, 1839
Capt. John Durst	Nov. 17–Dec. 16, 1838
Capt. George English	Oct. 10, 1838–Jan. 13, 1839
Capt. Joseph Ferguson	Dec. 8, 1838–Mar. 8, 1839
Capt. John B. Gaines	Nov. 1, 1838–Feb. 1, 1839
Capt. Richard Haley	Oct. 14, 1838–Jan. 10, 1839
Capt. James Hoggart	Nov. 1–18, 1838
James Gray Hyde, First Lieut.	Nov. 1–30, 1838
Capt. William Kimbro	Oct. 24–Nov. 25, 1838
Capt. Panther (Shawnees)	Nov. 25, 1838–Jan. 25, 1839
Capt. George Pollitt	Oct. 12, 1838–Jan. 2, 1839
Capt. David Renfro	Oct. 17–Nov. 9, 1838
Capt. Eli Russell	Sept. 2–Nov. 15, 1838
Capt. William Turner Sadler	Sept.–Nov. 8, 1838
Capt. Lewis Sanchez	Sept. 7, 1838–Jan. 27, 1839
H. R. Shearer, Lieut.	Aug. 30–Nov. 30, 1838
Capt. James Smith	Oct. 7–Dec. 1, 1838
Capt. Robert W. Smith	Nov. 8–20, 1838
Capt. Jacob Snively	Sept. 14–Dec. 13, 1838
Capt. James F. Timmons	Oct. 12, 1838–Feb. 6, 1839
Capt. Jackson Todd	Nov. 19–Dec. 1, 1838
Capt. Madison Guess Whitaker	Oct. 30–Nov. 11, 1838
Capt. John Wortham	Nov. 9 , 1838–Feb. 8, 1839
Capt. William P. Wyche	Nov. 4, 1838–Feb. 4, 1839

Back in Nacogdoches, Major General Rusk called on his senior officers to raise 300 militiamen who would be willing to join him in a march to the Three Forks of the Trinity River. He was armed with fresh intelligence from an Indian trader that in one village alone at the Three Forks of the Trinity, some 700 Indians had congregated. This included Wacos, Tawakonis, Hainais, Kichais, Caddos, Cherokees, and a few Seminoles. West of this village was another village containing some 300 Indians. Rusk hoped to take an expedition out to destroy these villages in the area of present Dallas.

To his great disappointment, Rusk found that only forty-five men were willing to join him on yet another march into Indian territory, this one all the way to the Three Forks. The approaching winter, the lack of provisions and lack of pay certainly contributed to the morale problems he faced in motivating these men. In addition, some of the men following Rusk had now made three marches against the Indians in just three months. An equally discouraged Adjutant General Hugh McLeod felt that President Houston was hindering the militia's effectiveness with its men. He explained to President-Elect Mirabeau Lamar on November 16, "We are all without commission, and had no means of forcing them."[14]

While McLeod and Rusk struggled to motivate weary men to go on expedition again, the Third Congress of the Republic of Texas had convened on November 6. Fortunately for the relentless general, Congress passed supportive resolutions to provide for the militia. One act appropriated $20,000 for Rusk to purchase arms, ammunition, clothing, and provisions for his troops. Another $20,000 was appropriated to fit out 250 men from General Moseley Baker's Second Militia Brigade.[15]

The Third Congress passed another resolution requesting President Houston to issue commissions to all duly elected and appointed militia officers. Further legislation promised to legalize the position of militia officers who had been elected by their men in the absence of regularly commissioned officers. Congress also promised to pay all citizens who volunteered for frontier service.[16]

These new laws would soon allow General Rusk to motivate another regiment of militiamen to follow him on expedition. More importantly, they helped to prevent Sam Houston from deterring Rusk's efforts to combat the hostile Indians of eastern and northern Texas. In order to avoid delaying efforts further, Congress authorized the militia leader to immediately use $10,000 from the customs collector at San Augustine.

Most of the companies operating in General Douglass' Third Militia Brigade were properly paid for their services thanks to this new legislation. Many of the companies which served in ranger fashion in between expeditions or without serving on a proper militia expedition were not completely paid at this time. A report of Paymaster General Jacob Snively to the Fourth Congress in 1839 lists the names of those Third Brigade companies and staff units which were not completely paid.[17]

Snively submitted an estimate of the funds needed to repay the militia companies which had served under "command of General T. J. Rusk, in the fall of 1838, and beginning of 1839." A summary of his estimate shows:

Capt. Jackson Todd	$190
Capt. William C. Brookfield	290
Capt. James F. Timmons	2,055
Capt. James F. Timmons (August 1838 campaign)	212
Capt. Alexander Horton	825
Capt. William P. Wyche	3,229
Capt. Joseph Ferguson	2,700
Capt. David Laird	514
Capt. John P. Applegate	300
Capt. John B. Gaines	1,100
Capt. William T. Sadler	200
Capt. Wesley W. Hanks	900
Major Leonard Mabbitt's rangers	5,050
Capt. George W. Hooper	953
Capt. Alexander Jordan	600
Capt. Richard Haley	400
Amount due on last payment	6,830
Colonels Willis Landrum and Samuel Davis' staff rolls	8,540
	$33,049.00

General Douglass was highly active in developing his Third Militia Brigade. With his own regiment in place and those of colonels Sparks and Landrum, he even added a fourth regiment in November 1838. This he placed under command of Colonel James Chessher, an early settler of the town of Jasper who had commanded a volunteer company during the 1835 Béxar siege and another Jasper-area volunteer company following the Alamo's fall.[18]

Colonel Chessher's Fourth Regiment of the Third Militia Brigade was based out of Bevil's Fort on the Sabine River. This early fortified home was likely that of John Bevil, the first settler of present Jasper County and *alcalde* of the 1834 Bevil Municipality. Bevil's Fort likely

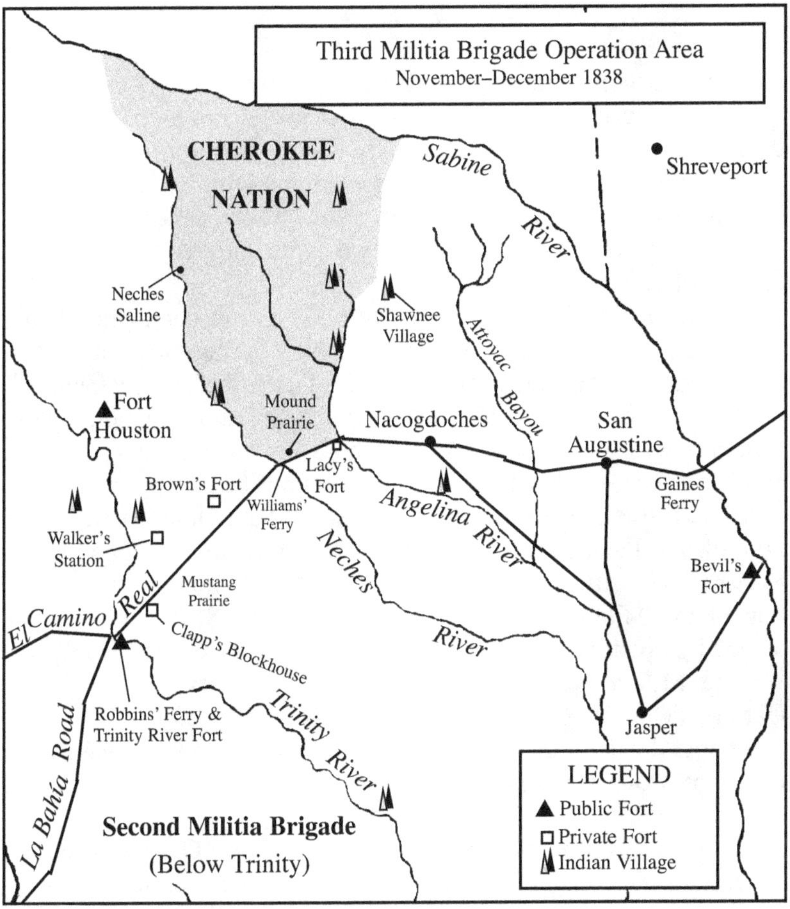

lay along the Jasper–Natchitoches, Louisiana Road in Newton County, west of the Sabine River.

Chessher himself was pleasantly surprised at General Douglass' new Fourth Regiment, as he wrote from "Bevil Fort, 30th Nov. 1838".

> Sir, I have unexpectedly received my commission from the Government, and have in compliance with your orders, divided the Regiment into 1st and 2nd Battalions and issued orders to the Lieut. Col. and Major to take charge of their respective command, and organized the Militia, without delay. Reports shall be forwarded to the Brigade Inspector and Secretary of War so soon as possible.

★ ★ ★ ★ ★

Bonnell Sends Rangers to Houston County

The renewed support from Congress would not help Tom Rusk through his immediate effort to mount an expedition to the Three Forks. While he struggled to organize men to conduct another November campaign, General Moseley Baker's Second Militia Brigade had successfully organized two companies for his use during the fall of 1838.

Major George Washington Bonnell was put in command of this 150-volunteer battalion as it was organized during November. The first company organized in Houston called itself the "Milam Guards."

This unit of well-armed men was commanded by Captain Joseph Daniels, twenty-nine, who had been born in Boston, Massachusetts, and had later served as first lieutenant of a military company in New Orleans. Daniels met the wounded General Sam Houston while the hero of San Jacinto was recovering in New Orleans. He then moved to Texas and settled in Houston in 1837. Daniels was appointed captain of the Milam Guards on November 9, 1838, his commission signed by President Houston and Secretary of War George Hockley.[19]

The Milam Guards had already been in service during late October. The *Telegraph and Texas Register* on October 27, 1838, noted that President Houston had arrived in the town of his namesake on the previous Monday.

> He was escorted into the city by the Milam Guards. Their commander, Capt. Daniels, has gained much credit for his untiring exertions in behalf of the company, and is reputed one of the best drill officers in the country.

In Houston, Daniels' company received orders on November 14 to "take possession of any public arms" available from the citizens to arm itself. Daniels' company fell under the supervising command of Major Bonnell, whose headquarters was located near the settlement of Samuel McCarley in what is now Harris County (along present FM 2920). Bonnell sent orders to Captain Daniels on November 29 via an express messenger.

> By order of Gen. Baker I am directed to rendezvous on the Little Brazos at the house of Jesse Webb, 20 miles above Nashville. You will repair to that post with all possible diligence. It is unnecessary to urge dispatch to a soldier.

> You will pass through a country infested with small bands of Indians, and it will be necessary to use every precaution to prevent them from stealing horses.

Daniels and his company reported to the Falls of the Brazos, where he found Major Bonnell, who was already supervising Captain George Briscoe's fifty-man Fannin Rangers. Briscoe's company was mustered into service on November 16, 1838, and served until it was discharged January 9, 1839, in Houston by orders of the secretary of war.[20]

After meeting up with Bonnell, the Milam Guards were ordered by Brigadier General Kelsey Douglass of the Third Militia Brigade to march to Fort Houston and take command of that post. Daniels' company stopped at Fort Lacy on December 4, where William F. Allison provided "one beef for use of the Milam Guards." This note was signed by company commissary Magnus T. Rodgers.[21]

At Fort Houston, Daniels' company joined the Houston County ranger company of Captain James Box. Immediately upon arriving, Captain Daniels was to "send out spies and ascertain where the enemy is, and if not found in numbers over one hundred you will give them battle." In the event that enemy forces were found, Daniels had orders to call in the ranger company of Captain John Wortham to assist in battle.[22]

Since assuming command of his ranger company on November 9, Captain Wortham had been busy. After organizing his company, he sent word to Major General Rusk via his orderly sergeant, Martin A. Walker. Rusk sent Walker back to Wortham on November 11 with orders to range the Houston County area for hostile Indians.[23]

As of December 4, John Wortham's rangers were based at Walker's Station (west of present Crockett) in Houston County. According to his first report to generals Rusk and Douglass, his men had already made several scouts for Indians in their first month.

> I have had portions of my company out in the wilds as many as three different times, but have not been able to discover any hostile Indians or sign thereof.
>
> Information reached me, however, on the 29th [November] of two Indians, having been seen on the Trinity near the mouth of Elkhart Creek. I immediately dispatched my first lieutenant [John Edward Nite] with a portion of the men to see and examine the place where they should have been seen. The person who should have seen the Indians being a new emigrant into

Captain Daniels' Milam Guards: Nov. 15, 1838–Feb. 14, 1839

Captain:
Joseph Daniels
First Lieutenant:
John W. White
Second Lieutenant:
William G. Kerley
First Sergeant:
Joseph C. Eldridge
Second Sergeant:
H. H. Brower
Third Sergeant:
Joseph F. Waples
Fourth Sergeant:
Timothy O'Neill
Fifth Sergeant:
James B. Shaw
First Corporal:
Lewis Way
Second Corporal:
Thruston M. Taylor
Third Corporal:
Elam Stockbridge
Fourth Corporal:
Lyman Tarbox
Commissary:
Magnus T. Rodgers
Musician:
Francis Bettinger
Privates:
Thomas Bryson
Bernard Carruther
William T. Carter
Thomas D. Cooke [1]
William M. Cooke
John Coughlin
W. Cruger
Patrick D. Cunningham
James Duncan
William G. Evans
Zachariah Forest
H. N. Gaston
Lewis B. Harris
Thurman Hart
Thomas Jeffries
William Jones
Alfred A. Lee
_____ Miller
John W. Moore
Rufus Muncus
Willard Post
John Smith
Thomas H. Spooner
Thomas Waring
Thomas Waters
William H. Weaver [2]
Joseph Wells
Tobias Wheeler

Notes:
Sergeant Robert Hamet Breedin accidentally killed on duty 1/14/39.
[1] Transferred in December to Major Bonnell's staff.
[2] Transferred from Capt. Briscoe's company when it disbanded in Houston.

Captain Briscoe's Rangers: Nov. 16, 1838–January 10, 1839

Captain:
George C. Briscoe
Second Lieutenant:
Duncan C. Ogden
Third Sergeant:
James L. Rudolph
Fourth Sergeant:
James G. Claud
Third Corporal:
Armaugh Frederick
Fourth Corporal:
Charles V. Taplin
Musician:
Henry Smith
Privates:
Henry Blut
William Brockner
John Brown
John Cahill
Charles Caliott
Ewen Cameron
John Campbell
John Carlton
John Day
Hubart Defau
Charles Gallaher
S. A. Gordon
Jackson H. Griffin
James Hawthorn
Lucas D. Isham
Lewis J. Jones
John Kellogg
George W. Lang
George M. Lee
Samuel W. Lincoln
William M. Logan
Alexander MacDonald
Thomas Martin
Moses Martindale
Joseph Mayor
Neill Robinson
Washington Simpson
John Snider
James Thomas
William H. Weaver
Robert Whitlock
William Williamson
B. G. Winn

Source: Partial roster based on author's research of audited military claims, Republic of Texas.

NOTE: Major George Bonnell's staff also included quartermaster James D. Cocke, assistant quartermaster James Wright Simmons, and surgeon Samuel Pilkington.

> the county could not find the place, and the corps have returned without making any discoveries.
>
> I intend starting out again in a day or two with all my disposable force, and shall make a general tour in the rear of the settlements. Should anything important be discovered or happen at any time, you shall have the earliest possible information given you of the facts.

Captain Wortham sent this letter with his Quartermaster Sergeant Stephen Horton on to General Rusk in Nacogdoches. In Rusk's absence, Horton was to visit the headquarters of General Douglass and await further orders for his company.

The heavy volume of militia troops camping out in Houston County during October and November of 1838 had virtually depleted the area of its crops and extra foodstocks. Wortham's rangers, therefore, found it very difficult to secure provisions.

> There has been such a devastation committed in this county by the troops under the command of Maj. Mabbitt and others that there has been produced thereby a great scarcity of the articles of subsistence and those who have them are unwilling to part with them upon any terms. There are some crops of corn and stocks of cattle here yet, belonging to persons who have fled the country in its time of need which I think ought to be appropriated to the public use but do not feel myself entirely at liberty to take such articles.

Captain Wortham had taken the liberty of commissioning David Campbell as his special "contractor" to secure items for his rangers. Campbell was sent

John Wortham (1804–1867) was captain of the Houston County Rangers from late 1838 into 1839. He was promoted to major of the Houston County battalion and served on Brigadier General Kelsey Douglass' staff during the Cherokee War. *Photo courtesy of Eliza Bishop.*

to Houston for such necessities as coffee, salt, sugar, and iron for shoeing horses. Orderly Sergeant Walker had already procured a keg of powder for the company. Wortham had additionally secured from Quartermaster Martin Lacy "seventeen pounds of powder and fifty bars of lead." Contractor Campbell was to secure "six dozen gunflints and one box of percussion caps," as the company used both types of firearms.

"This supply of ammunition will do for the present," Wortham wrote, "but would fall very far short of a sufficiency to comply with the law of June 1837." This 1837 law had required ranging companies to be armed with two hundred rounds of ammunition per man. Despite such difficulties in supplying his men, Captain Wortham expressed "great hopes of being able to give entire security in future to our own frontiers."

Neither Wortham's rangers nor Captain Daniels' Milam Guards managed to find a fight with the Indians during the early weeks of December. Major Bonnell thus ordered Daniels to give up scouting the countryside and return to Houston by the end of the year to serve in his own militia district.[24]

★ ★ ★ ★ ★

Central Texas Depredations

While the Indians were battled and pursued in eastern and northern Texas, the number of depredations in the fall and early winter of 1838 was low for the central Texas areas. One notable exception was the capture of five children on December 9, 1838, by Comanche Indians.

It happened near the Guadalupe River in present DeWitt County. A group of five individuals—Matilda Lockhart, thirteen, Rhoda Putman, seventeen, Elizabeth Putman, six, Juda Putman, two, and James Putman, ten—ventured out into the woods to gather pecans near the homes of their parents. The five children were captured and taken into captivity by the Indians.[25]

These Indians were encountered during their retreat by Captain John Tumlinson and his six-man surveying party then in the field. Tumlinson's party was pursued by the large body of Indians, but managed to return safely to Guadalupe River settlements. Upon crossing the river and reaching the home of William Taylor, they heard of the capture of the Lockhart and Putman children.

A volunteer company was immediately raised and it went in pursuit of these Comanches, but could not catch up with them. Matilda

Lockhart's father, Andrew Lockhart (brother of former ranger Captain Byrd Lockhart), had emigrated from Illinois in 1828. He would dedicate much time to searching for his lost child and would be involved in an early 1839 campaign against a Comanche village to attempt her rescue.

These young prisoners were treated terribly. Matilda Lockhart was later delivered to Texas commissioners in San Antonio in 1840. Elizabeth and James Putman were eventually reclaimed from the Indians, but their sister Juda remained a captive for some fourteen years before being ransomed to traders. By that time, she had all but forgotten the English language and even who she was. The final child, Rhoda Putman, became the wife of a chief and refused to leave the Indians.

Indian attacks had also occurred in the Bastrop area during late November 1838. On the night of Saturday, November 17, a party of Indians attacked two Bastrop citizens who were returning from the house of Pinkney Hill at about 8:00 p.m. Mr. Weaver was shot near the heart with a heavy rifle ball that killed him instantly. His companion, Mr. Hart, was hit by an arrow in the abdomen and managed to run into Bastrop and sound the alarm. Hart died about thirty-six hours later.[26]

Bastrop citizen Van R. Palmer, who had served as a ranger under Colonel Coleman and Major Smith during 1836–37, reported that before any pursuit could be made, the Indians fled into the darkness of the night. "The following morning a small party of our citizens took the trail," he wrote, "but not being able to overtake them, returned the next day."

The following week, on November 24, Indians struck the remote settlements again. A party of about a dozen Indians at the hour of midnight attacked the home of Mr. Chandler, who lived about eighteen miles above Bastrop. Chandler could not go for help, but bravely defended his family by exchanging shots with the Indians. None of his family were killed, although the Indians did kill several of his cattle.

This second attack was enough to make the Bastrop townspeople band together. Former ranger Van Palmer wrote of the situation on November 25.

> Tomorrow morning a company from Bastrop will start with me, to join a company raised above town and we intend to follow them as long as prudence and a determination to chastise them will allow us to do.

> I intend forthwith to remove back to their old range, the Tonkawas and Lipans—who have been for some weeks encamped on the Colorado above and below Bastrop—as the people generally are not satisfied to have them in too close proximity.

Captain Palmer's volunteer party did not leave Bastrop until November 27. He wrote to Mirabeau Lamar before departing that he intended to plot this frontier section of Texas and mark out locations most suitable for establishing military posts. Palmer deemed his party's prospects as "gloomy," as most men of Bastrop were guarding their own homes and families. Leaving everything to range against the Indians was considered by most to "be exposing his family to almost certain destruction."[27]

The Bastrop volunteers did not consider the latest attacks in their area to have been committed by the Comanches. The blame was instead focused on the "Northern Indians," the Wacos, Tawakonis, and Caddos. The neighboring Tonkawas and Lipans still appeared to remain friendly to the white settlers.

Captain Palmer and the other Bastrop area volunteers spent several days ranging the frontier during the late days of November and early days of December. There is no evidence to indicate that they found any conflict while in the field.

★ ★ ★ ★ ★

Rusk's Caddo Campaign: November–December 1838

General Rusk was disappointed by his failure to raise enough troops to conduct a campaign against the northern Indians during early November. Undaunted, he departed from his home in Nacogdoches on November 17, 1838, for the Red River. His plans were to gather Fourth Militia Brigade troops under General John Dyer there and conduct another campaign against the Indians that would "cripple them sufficiently to give breathing time for the adoption of a permanent means of defense."[28]

Before departing, Rusk wrote a letter to Mirabeau Lamar, urging him to take up the issue of frontier military defense as soon as he entered office. He enclosed copies of letters he had already sent out on his desire for a permanent infantry force of at least 500 men to be raised to operate against the Indians.[29]

Rusk departed Nacogdoches with Colonel McLeod and moved first to the Shawnee village, located just east of Cherokee Nation near present Henderson in what is now Rusk County. They arrived on November 20 and found that Chief Linney's Shawnees professed friendship, but were "alarmed at the threats made by the whites against the Indians." Linney claimed all existing difficulties should be blamed on Mexican agents. Hugh McLeod noted that the weather was cold. "The thermometer is at zero and fingers frozen." Rusk sent another letter to Lamar from the Shawnee village on November 20, in which he further advocated creating a new frontier regiment.

> If measures could be adopted this session of Congress to raise a force of about 300 Infantry and one hundred cavalry, I am clearly of the opinion that they could—by cutting a road across from Red River to the Brazos and establishing a chain of block houses or forts—put a termination to our present Indian difficulties in less than six months.

Rusk and McLeod held two talks with Chief Linney, who informed them that his Shawnees and the Choctaws, Kickapoos, Delawares, and Cherokees were friendly to the white men. "He does not, however, say much of the Cherokees," wrote Rusk the next day, "other than simply that they are friendly." The Shawnee chief related that the Kickapoos had moved their camp close to the Trinity.[30]

From "Shawnee Town" on November 21, Rusk wrote to Brigadier General Douglass of the intelligence he obtained. The Shawnee's chief further substantiated that Julian Pedro Miracle's Mexican rebels had recently been among the Indians.

> He also stated to me that while out some time ago, he saw twelve Mexicans who had just come from Matamoros to see the wild Indians.
>
> I have no doubt that correspondence has been held by the Mexicans with the various tribes here and in the United States and the only thing which has delayed a prompt action has been awaiting the arrival in the country of a Mexican Army.

The Shawnees claimed no connection with any enemy forces and even offered a guide for Rusk and McLeod as they moved on to Port Caddo. They were en route to meet up with Brigadier General Dyer, who had assembled some four hundred men from Clarksville for a campaign against the Indians on the Trinity and Cross Timbers. McLeod estimated on November 22 that they should rendezvous "in a few days."

McLeod and Rusk arrived at Port Caddo camp on the night of November 21 and set up their temporary headquarters. They found that a forty-man Fourth Brigade company recruited from present Bowie County under Captain Edward H. Tarrant had left at noon that day. Tarrant, forty-two, had served under General Andrew Jackson in several Indian campaigns and at the Battle of New Orleans before coming to Texas in 1835. He had also represented Red River County in the Second Congress during early 1838. According to McLeod, Tarrant's men had orders "to destroy a band of Caddos (60 men) camped near here—and if necessary, if they could not be found on our unquestionable territory to follow them across the line and exterminate them."

Rusk approved of General Dyers' orders to Captain Tarrant and he eagerly awaited the outcome of their expected battle. Word came to Rusk's temporary headquarters on November 23 that Tarrant's men had found the Caddos. The Indians had reportedly armed themselves in the United States and were planning to enter into Texas. The Caddos had been tipped off by "some white man" and had "retreated to a cane brake, and are awaiting an attack, fully prepared for it."[31]

General Rusk decided that they must be attacked, even though they had crossed into United States territory, as had Captain Tarrant's men. In an effort to justify such a foray beyond the Texas border, Colonel McLeod wrote President-Elect Lamar: "If the Captain retreats after this demonstration, this Country will be desolated by the Indians. Something therefore *must* be done at once." Rusk resolved to take the lead of the fight, and McLeod decided to join him for what he expected to be "a bloody affair, as the numbers are about equal."

Rusk and McLeod joined Captain Tarrant's company across the border of the Red River in Louisiana. They marched to the Caddo Indian town at Caddo Lake along the Louisiana border and found them in battle array in front of their camp. The advance force of Texans received several warning shots which were fired over their heads. The Caddos later explained that they fired on the Texans because they had been informed by an Indian agent that these were the men who had recently stolen some of their horses.

Rusk, McLeod, and an interpreter bravely advanced halfway to the Indian camp and met with their Chief Cissany and his principal man. Rusk informed the Caddo chief that he had only crossed the Louisiana line because the Indians had been committing depredations on his people. Rusk gave the Caddos the option of fighting to their deaths or going into Shreveport to deposit all their firearms with U.S. Indian agent Charles A. Sewell until the current Indian war was deemed over. Sewell agreed to keep the Caddos from coming over the line again into Texas.

The Caddos gave in and McLeod accompanied Chief Cissany to Shreveport, where his men turned in their firearms. He informed McLeod that the larger portion of the Caddo tribe which was actually committing some of the East Texas depredations was under a chief called Tarshar, or "the wolf." Satisfied that these Indians would be of no threat to the Texas frontier, Rusk, McLeod, and Captain Tarrant's company crossed back into Texas on December 1, 1838. They headed directly for the Three Forks of the Trinity, where they planned to meet General Dyer's Fourth Militia Brigade volunteers from Clarksville.

While riding through the night to join Dyer's men, Hugh McLeod was thrown from his horse and injured seriously. He remained at a spot about twenty-five miles west of Clarksville with some of Captain Tarrant's men for almost three weeks recovering. Rusk and some of Captain Tarrant's men moved on, intent upon joining General Dyer at the Three Forks of the Trinity in early December.

Tom Rusk's pursuit of the Indians into Louisiana stirred up controversy. The *Natchitoches Herald* published an article on December 16 with the headline "INVASION OF THE UNITED STATES BY TEXAS." The article reported of Rusk's disarming of the Caddos and stated that U.S. military forces had marched from Fort Jesup to insure that order was maintained.[32]

By the time the Jesup troops arrived, the tireless General Rusk had already returned to Texas and had rendezvoused with other troops to conduct yet another Indian expedition.

Capt. Tarrant's Mounted Riflemen: Sept. 6, 1838–Jan. 7, 1839

Captain:
Edward H. Tarrant
First Lieutenant:
Hiram Brinta [1]
Second Lieutenant:
Collin McAkin
Orderly Sergeant:
James Brown [2]
Second Sergeant:
William Burnside
Third Sergeant:
Fountain R. Floyd [3]
Fourth Sergeant:
Henry Bevins
Privates:
Henry L. Beasley
J. A. Beasley
Jonas Berry
Joseph Boman [4]
George Bunder
John C. Byers [3]
Lakin Calvin [5]
John Crow
William Crutchir
Thomas Davis
Ambrose Douthit [6]
John Downey
J. W. F. Elliott
John L. Henry
William Holland
H. L. Holm
E. J. Jackson [7]
David Jones [3]
H. L. Jones
J. E. Jones [3]
William C. Jones
Jacob R. Lacey
Peter Lamb
David Lane
John W. Lane
B. Loyd
Hiram Loyd
James McWharton [8]
Daniel Morris [3]
George Morris
Lee Morris
Robert B. Morris
Seth Morris
William A. Portman
Howard Raines
John Robbins
Thomas R. Scott
Absolom Sherwood
John W. Sherwood
William Tapp
Colman Watson [3]
Solomon Watson [9]
Thomas Wilson
John Wright

[1] Taken sick November 12.
[2] Removed November 12.
[3] Enrolled December 8.
[4] Left without leave Dec. 21.
[5] Died December 4.
[6] Elected 1st Lt. Nov. 12.
[7] Enrolled December 7.
[8] Refused to serve.
[9] Left without leave Dec. 7.

Source: Texas State Archives.

CHAPTER 5

Campaigns of the Red River Riflemen

December 1838–January 7, 1839

Scheme to Raid Nacogdoches Uncovered

Major Baley Walters had a certain ability to glean information from his Indian sources. Through careful scouting and persistent interrogation of friendly Indians in December, he was able to uncover a planned night raid on Nacogdoches.

Walters had served with Colonel Sparks' Second Regiment of the Third Militia Brigade until its staff had returned to Nacogdoches on November 13. He was then detailed by Brigadier General Kelsey Douglass to take some men and monitor Indian activities around the Cherokee Nation in East Texas.

During mid-December, he scouted in and near Chief Bowles' Cherokee Nation, including the Neches Saline. Walters worked much of the time from the big Shawnee village just east of the Cherokee land in present Rusk County. Douglass had successfully enlisted a thirty-man mounted Shawnee spy company under his command. Although Indian companies had not been employed by the Texas Militia thus far in 1838, Douglass certainly saw the value in having Native American rangers in his brigade. The Second Congress on June 12, 1837, had previously approved the use of a spy company composed of Shawnees, Delawares, Cherokees, or other "friendly" Indians to serve as scouts and spies. One of the leading Shawnees, Panther served as captain while Spy Buck served as interpreter for the whites. Captain Panther's Indian company would be instrumental as guides and in scouting out intelligence from the other northern Texas tribes. Chief Linney, Panther, and Spy Buck of the Shawnees had, of course, previously cooperated with General Rusk in late November.

From "Camp Shawnee Town," Walters wrote to General Douglass on December 14, 1838.

> Agreeably to instructions, I came on to this place last evening. I found the Shawnees prepared to fulfill their stipulation, but learn[ed] that a portion of the tribe had just returned from a predatory excursion, bringing with them about 30 horses which they say they captured from the wild Indians, six days' march west of Saline.
>
> It has been suggested that the Indians from whom these horses were taken will pursue them, and probably follow them into the settlements.[1]

Major Walters scouted up to the Neches Saline during the next week before returning to his camp at Chief Linney's Shawnee Town. "I got information that the Caddo Indians was yet at Shreveport," he wrote, "and would be held on at that place."[2] Walters also found from interpreter Spy Buck and a Shawnee brave named Washita that several tribes were in talks with Chief Bowles to join the Cherokees in a hostile raid into East Texas.

> When I arrived back to this place, the Shawnee chief had been absent for several days and has not returned yet. I learned from Spy Buck that two Shawnee Indians got in yesterday from Arkansas. [He] states that the Cherokee Indians has reinforced at [Chief] Harris' so as to make the number of Cherokees embodied at that place two hundred and fifty.
>
> The Delawares has reinforced from Washataw. The number he is not able to say. The Kickapoos has reinforced so as to make the whole number five hundred strong. Since your talk with the Shawnee chief, Bowles has sent three of his men to see the Shawnee chief and made application to said Shawnee chief to meet him, the said Bowles, at his house with all his men in order to make an attack on Nacogdoches—which was to be done about cock-crow, or between that and daylight.
>
> The Shawnee chief denied him and said he would not send any of his men, which made the Cherokees mad and went off. This information from Spy Buck and other Shawnee Indians that I can confide in.

Major Walters added a postscript to his letter, urging Douglass to lend him some more men. The previous volunteers had only signed on for one month, so he asked that new men come on "for a term not less than three months."

The Cherokees' hopes to raid Nacogdoches was alarming news to General Douglass. Just days after Walters' intelligence, Captain James Box sent even more disturbing news of Indian buildup. In command of the mounted rangers at Fort Houston, Box was surprised on Christmas Eve when four weary men made their way to his outpost.

One of the them was Elias Vansickle, who had been captured about October 1 while working on survey lines near the Neches Saline. He and three other prisoners managed to escape from their Indian captors on December 21 and flee toward Fort Houston. Vansickle arrived there with "two negroes belonging to Mr. [Elisha] DeBard and a Mexican by the name of Jose, all of whom for some time past have been prisoners with the Spaniards and Indians."[3]

The statements of Vansickle and his fellow escapees were taken down by the rangers at Fort Houston. Signing a note to General Douglass as captain of a "spy company," James Box passed along their intelligence.

> The Spaniards and Indians are embodied about one hundred miles from this place, West of the Trinity below the Three Forks some distance, and about forty miles from the river upon a large creek running into Trinity (I presume it to be in reality the West Fork of that River).
>
> According to their statement, there is 40 Mexicans, 150 Caddos, 300 Kickapoos, 100 Ionis, and Anadarkos—supposed to be 100 Biloxis, Coushattas, and Uwanies, and they are expecting 400 Choctaws from Red River. Their spies give an account of a considerable army in two days' march of the position they now occupy—which I supposed to be Genl. Rusk.
>
> From the account of the prisoners, the Indians and Mexicans design coming to the Neches Saline in twelve days from this date. They keep runners constantly passing between them and Bowles and a white man living on the Red River Road eight miles from Nacogdoches by the name of Henry Bailey. From these two, they receive most of their information in regard to what is passing among the whites and Cherokees.

Vansickle and his fellow prisoners felt that Chief Bowles and his Cherokees would continue to curry "favour and pretend friendship to the whites" until an alliance of Indians and Mexicans was ready to fight. Captain Box added, "They also think the object of the enemy will be Nacogdoches and the frontier nearest to the same."

General Douglass was obviously alarmed by the reports coming in from around Cherokee Nation. He had been busy during December rallying more troops in his Third Militia Brigade to join Major General Rusk for an Indian expedition. He reported to Secretary of War Albert Johnston on December 30, 1838, that he had readied some eight-hundred volunteers to join Rusk. Douglass felt that "the affairs of the Texas frontier were never in so critical a condition."[4]

To assess the immediate threat from the Indians, Douglass organized a ranger battalion on January 6, 1839, that would hold the peace in this area. Jacob Snively, who had commanded a three-month ranger company through mid-December, was made lieutenant colonel directly commanding the battalion. Snively's former first lieutenant, James W. Cleveland, mustered their former ranger company back into service on January 6.

In addition to Captain Cleveland, Snively could rely upon Captain Box's Fort Houston company and several Third Brigade companies still in service at his discretion. Near Crockett was the ranging company of Captain Wortham. When Lieutenant Colonel Snively marched toward the Neches Saline, he was accompanied by two other mounted gunman companies which had been in service for some time. One was that of Captain James F. Timmons, whose three-month company was due to disband on January 12. Captain Lewis Sánchez, who had been in service with the Third Brigade since September, had organized a small ranging company on November 18 which consisted largely of Tejanos from the Nacogdoches area. Sánchez, of Mexican and Indian ancestry, was living in Nacogdoches by 1831 and often served as an interpreter for Indian negotiations.

Lieutenant Colonel Snively would also have at his disposal a large number of allied Indians. Captain Panther's Shawnee company was largely disbanded after a month's service on December 20, although interpreter Spy Buck would continue to serve with fellow Shawnees Possum and Young Spy Buck through January 25, 1839. The Shawnees were paid the same as rangers, at the rate of twenty-five dollars per month. Panther was appropriately paid the sixty dollar per month rate of captains for his twenty-six total days of service.

Another company largely composed of Indians was organized on December 24, just after the former captives made their way to Fort Houston. Captain James H. Durst, who had been in service with Major Walters since December 1, mustered in a fifty-eight man ranger unit officered both by whites and friendly Indians. His company was largely Cherokee (with such names as Stanley Bowles), with perhaps a few Caddo or Shawnee volunteers. The company's muster roll shows many interesting Indian names, including Big Bone, Cat Floating, Coushatta Killer, Alloverbigness, Night Killer, and Shitass. These Indian rangers, who served a month's duty under Captain Durst, were paid at the same rate as the few white men in their company.

General Douglass' Texas Ranger Staff: January 6–February 2, 1839

Brigadier General:
Kelsey Harris Douglass
Lieutenant Colonel:
Jacob Snively
Adjutant:
Peter Tipps
Commissary:
George Pollitt
Assistant Commissary:
George Washington Jewell
Sergeant Major:
J. G. Grayham
Sergeant:
John Lee Witter
Bugler:
Albert A. Nelson

Captain Box's Mounted Rangers: January 15–March 25, 1839

Captain:
James Edward Box
Contractor/1st Lieutenant:
John Holmes
First Sergeant:
James Head
Privates:
Thomas Berry
Jeremiah Blackwell
Richard Dixon
Richard Duty
Harrison Farmer
Gibson Gaston
Alfred M. Hallmark
Spencer Hobbs
Daniel M. McKenzie
Dr. William B. Perry
Elijah B. Reneau
Luke Roberts
Mark Roberts

Source: Captain Box's muster roll of February 4–March 25, 1839. His previous muster roll ended on January 14, but his company is known to have served a full year in the field.

Captain Cleveland's Mounted Rangers: January 6–February 5, 1839

Captain:
James W. Cleveland
First Lieutenant:
Marquis D. Boyd
Second Lieutenant:
James Triplett
First Sergeant:
Josiah Taylor Childers
Second Sergeant:
John Roark
Third Sergeant:
George Bass
Privates:
Durham Avant [1]
R. P. Banks
William Brown
Delores Cortinez [2]
William Cobb
James G. Dixon
Balis Edens
Sylvanus Everett
Harrison Farmer
Archibald C. Graham
Benjamin P. C. Harrill
George W. Jewell [3]
Hugh Kenner [2]
Jesse C. Kincannon [4]
Artimon L. Martin
William Maxfield
A. W. McAlpin [2]
William. D. McKnight
Mack McRoy
Joseph Meradith
Moses L. Patton [2]
William Sasser
B. Steward
Elisha Tubbs
William W. Wade
Hammond Warfield
George Washington Welsh
Joel D. Wilburn

[1] Served 1/6–1/27/39.
[2] Served 1/6–1/9/39.
[3] Also served as assistant commissary.
[4] Hospital steward.

Captain Durst's Mounted Rangers: Dec. 24, 1838–Jan. 25, 1839

Captain:
James H. Durst *
First Lieutenant:
Justus
Second Lieutenant:
Cut Worm
Orderly Sergeant:
Hugh Kenner
Second Sergeant:
George A. Ross
Third Sergeant:
John Bags
Fourth Sergeant:
Moses L. Patton
Privates:
Alloverbigness
Back Bone
Big Bone
Big Rump
Stanley Bowles
Calawntalite
Cat Floating
Coffee
Early Cordery
Dolores Cortinez
Coushatta Killer
Dry
Ellis
Gizzard
Ground Hog
He Stops Them
He Throws Them Down
Hog Stones
Hot House
Jackson
James
Jesse
John
Krak Killer
Lightning Bug
Looking at Us
Louis
Wash Loura
Alexander McKelpin
Moses
Night Killer
Otastuke
Otterlifter
Over the Branches
Parrikeet
Pleasant
John Rogers
Sequeah
Shitass
Tekiansta
They have Shot the Dog
Turnover
Twister
Utalah
Uxtalle
Watch
White Man
William
Young Bird
Zekiel

* In active service from December 1, 1838.

Captain Panther's Mounted Shawnees: Nov. 25, 1838–Jan. 25, 1839

Captain:
Panther [1]
Interpreter:
Spy Buck [2]
Privates:
Big Field [1]
Buzzard [3]
Catawah [3]
Chewwackatah [1]
Chewwah [3]
Fox [1]
George [3]
Hood [1]
Howtiskey [3]
Jack [3]
Killawsha [3]
Kishescaw [3]
Lewis [1]
Little Jack [3]
Little Jim [1]
Little John [3]
Pachewe [3]
Pachilla [3]
Petitah [3]
Pocawah [3]
Possatatah [1]
Possum [2]
Robinson [3]
Solgis [1]
Thompson [3]
Whet Stone [3]
Yellow Jacket [3]
Young Spy Buck [2]

[1] Served from November 25–December 20, 1838.

[2] Served from Nov. 25, 1838–January 25, 1839.

[3] Served from November 25–December 9, 1838.

Sources: Each company roster was organized from available pay roll and muster roll records, furnished courtesy of the Archives and Information Services Division of the Texas State Library. The service dates for each company indicate the particular muster and pay rolls referenced.

Captain Sánchez's Mounted Rangers: Sept. 7, 1838–Jan. 27, 1839

Captain:
Lewis Sánchez
Second Lieutenant:
Jacinto Magano [1]
First Sergeant:
Santiago Rabia [1]
Second Sergeant:
Howard W. Bailey [2]
First Corporal:
Simon Sanchez [1]
Privates:
Francisco Acosta [3]
Jackson Anderson [1]
Nelson Chandler [4]
Santiago Chavana [1]
Francisco Cuellar [1]
Hartwell Frazier [1]
Antonio Garing [2]
Santiago Goscano [3]
Samuel Hawkins [4]
Thomas Hawkins [5]
Susano Hernandez [2]
Incarnacion Juarrez [2]
Cornelias Lopez [3]
Samuel Luper [2]
Juan Mata [3]
Thomas Maxwell [4]
James McKim [2]
Antonio Mendez [3]
Lorenzo Perez [2]
John Randolph [7]
Maximo Salazar [6]
David Sánchez [1]
Peter Welden [7]
Antonio Y'Barbo [1]
Jose Maria Y'Barbo [1]
Juan Y'Barbo [3]

[1] Enlisted Nov. 18, 1838.
[2] Enlisted Jan. 1, 1839.
[3] Enlisted Dec. 10, 1838.
[4] Enlisted Jan. 13, 1839.
[5] Enlisted Dec. 14, 1838.
[6] Enlisted Dec. 26, 1838.
[7] Served Sept. 13–16, 1838.

Captain Timmons' Mounted Gunmen: Oct. 12, 1838–Feb. 6, 1839

Captain:
James F. Timmins
First Lieutenant:
Hampton Anderson
Second Lieutenant:
Joseph Humphries
First Sergeant:
John Ray
Privates:
Bailey Anderson
Holland Anderson
James Asher
John T. Coplir
Eliazer Divinny
Benjamin Gage
Sam P. Hall *
Henry Harrold
Daniel Martin *
Daniel McCall
Henry J. McDonnell *
Robert Parmer
Alfred Reel *
James Reel *
Isaac Stout
James Stout
Josiah Thomas
Elijah Williams
John N. Williams

* Joined January 1, 1839.

Capt. Wortham's Houston County Rangers: Nov. 9, 1838–Feb. 8, 1839

Captain:
John Wortham
First Lieutenant:
John Edward Nite
Second Lieutenant:
Thomas Hays
First Sergeant:
Martin A. Walker
Second Sergeant:
Stephen Horton
Privates:
Britton H. Adams
Cephus Adams
Solomon Adams
William D. F. Adams
William H. Adams
John P. Barnett
J. L. N. Brown
David H. Campbell
Joel Clapp
John E. Clapp
George Crosby
Ira P. Ellis
J. L. B. Horton
John Irwin
John B. McIlyes
John McLaughlin
William H. Pate
Charles D. Taylor
Jesse G. Thompson
J. C. Vaughn
Philip Walker
R. A. Walker
Russell Warner

Lieutenant Colonel Snively's ranger battalion was encamped on the outer perimeters of Cherokee Nation as of January 13 at "Camp Williams." This site was likely at the trading post of Leonard Williams, who operated a ferry in Houston County at the Neches River crossing of the Old San Antonio Road. Snively issued a report this day to General Douglass.

> I am yet awaiting on the arrival of forces. Captain Wortham's company will arrive I hope in a few days.
>
> The Cherokees are in good spirits and anxious for the contest. I have all confidence in them. Captain Timmins' company, I am fearful, will leave the place for their homes. Their time has expired. I still hope to prevail on them to accompany me to the prairies. Dr. [John Lee] Witter has sent a requisition which I wish furnished.[5]

The next day, Snively's companies moved north and camped within a few miles of the Neches Saline at the old Killough settlement. From there, he sent his next report to Douglass that his "small command" was "tolerably well organized" with sufficient provisions to subsist for thirty days. Colonel Peter Tipps, the battalion's adjutant, sent a request that his brother Leander Tipps send "one fifty pounds of tobacco."[6]

Lewis Sanchez's mounted gunmen had lost one man to desertion by this date. "Captain Sanchez wishes you to take up Lorenzo Perez as a deserter and lodge him in jail," Snively wrote. As for the duty-weary company of Captain Timmins, Snively had "at length prevailed" on him to remain until "I receive a small reinforcement." To Douglass, he firmly requested, "Send volunteers. I must have them. These men will not move until they arrive."

Lieutenant Colonel Snively was fully prepared to take his rangers "to the prairies" in search of battle. There existed among his men, however, some distrust. Some of Captain Sanchez's men were distrustful of the loyalty of the Cherokees of Captain Durst's company. "The Mexicans are much more suspicious than the whites in regard to the intentions of the Cherokees," he wrote. Snively felt that his Indian rangers would ultimately carry out their promises.

> I am sorry to say that a great distrust exists among the whites. They are suspicious of the Cherokees. For my part, I have no such suspicions. I am positive they will do their duty nobly. Send me thirty more volunteers, and then I shall be able

to prevail on them to take up the line of march . . .

I am convinced that no hostile Indians are in this vicinity. My scouts have examined the country west of the Neches from the battleground, as far as they thought the enemy would be likely to make trails on this part of the frontier. I shall never turn my back on the enemy until I ascertain their position and give them battle.

★ ★ ★ ★ ★

Captain Stout's Work in the Settlements

At the time that Snively's Third Brigade rangers were just organizing to move to the Neches Saline, Brigadier General John Dyer's Fourth Militia Brigade was closing out a winter campaign through northern Texas.

After a brief expedition with Lieutenant Colonel Montague's Fannin County Rangers in September, General John Dyer had returned to the Red River settlements to prepare for another major Indian campaign. By November 24, he had raised more than four hundred men of the First Regiment, Fourth Militia Brigade and assembled them in Clarksville.

In addition to the general's staff and that of Colonel Sam Sims, General Dyer had the six companies that had participated in his first September 1838 expedition: those of captains Joseph R. Mix, John Craddock, William Edmondson, Robert Hamilton, James Gillian, and James Hopkins.

A seventh company of Colonel Mix's First Regiment of Mounted Gunmen had been already formed on November 17 under Captain George Birdwell, a forty-four-year-old Tennessee native. In addition to these companies, Dyer had assembled Captain William B. Stout's twenty-one-man Red River County Rangers. Stout's company had been organized on November 20 under orders of Dyer to serve for six months on the Red River frontiers. Red River County was vast in 1838, including all the territory from Arkansas and Louisiana to the east to Bois d'Arc Creek in the west, and south to Cypress Creek.

Captain Stout wrote that Dyer's campaign set out "with 500 men."[7] This number seems fairly accurate, as a best count of all men known to have departed with Dyer at this time is about 426.

The Fourth Brigade marched out on November 24, moving in the direction of the Indian villages at the Three Forks of the Trinity, the area of present Dallas. General Dyer's companies camped in present Lamar County on November 27 at Camp Chisum, located upon the farm of Claiborne Chisum, who was a member of Captain Edmondson's Company A.[8]

By December 5, 1838, Major General Tom Rusk had united with General John Dyer's Fourth Brigade at the Clear Fork of the Trinity River. Rusk had left Captain Edward Tarrant and most of his men to procure cattle to feed the troops, while proceeding ahead to the rendezvous with only a few men.

One of Dyer's 400-plus volunteers was fifteen-year-old Samuel M. Dalton, who had settled in present Lamar County in March 1837. Dalton was one of eight new recruits joining Captain Craddock's Company B on November 13 when the company was reorganized for the new campaign.

> In November of this year, our company was attached to a regiment, raised in Fannin, Lamar, Red River, and Bowie counties, under the command of Genl. Dyer and Col. Sam Sims. After we had gone as far as the Cross Timbers, Genl. Thomas J. Rusk came up with us and took command. [He] made a war speech to the boys, who would have followed him against an enemy, fifty to one. We following him during the month of December and January, saw no Indians, except a few friendly Kickapoos.[9]

Rusk, of course, was an old hand at motivational speeches. He and Sam Houston had given talks prior to San Jacinto that served to inspire their troops.

At Clear Springs, Rusk took command of Dyer and Sims' entire party. He then detached a group of men under Captain George Pollitt to stay with the camp baggage and await the "beeves" that were to be driven to the army by Captain Tarrant's company.[10]

Following its departure from Clarksville, the Fourth Brigade had undergone some personnel changes. On November 28, First Regiment Colonel Sam Sims and Sergeant Major James W. Sims resigned from Dyer's expedition. Joseph Mix, captain of one of the mounted rifleman companies, was promoted to colonel in command of the Fourth Brigade's First Regiment. Another of Captain Mix's company, George Clark, was promoted to sergeant major. First Lieutenant William Scurlock was promoted into command of Mix's company.

After rendezvousing with Major General Rusk, Captain James Gillian resigned command of his rifleman company on December 5. First Lieutenant Dickerson Dyer was elected captain in his place and several junior officers were promoted.

In order not to leave the frontier settlements exposed while this large force was in the field, General Dyer had stationed companies of Daniel Montague's Second Regiment at key posts in the Red River area. He also dispatched Captain William Stout's rangers on December 5 from the Fourth Brigade camp "to go to the cypress lying between the Sulphur and the Sabine."

Stout's company, numbering thirty men by this date, was apparently dispatched in response to word that Indians had killed a citizen named Joseph Harris earlier that morning. Harris had stopped at the Blundell residence before departing for Clarksville. From Blundell's he had only ridden about two miles on his way to an old farm where he planned to inspect the corn there which he wished to purchase. Just half a mile short of reaching this place, he was attacked and killed by Indians.

Captain Stout and his men arrived at the site of the killing on the evening of December 5 and they provided a proper burial for the body. "The Indians were pursued," wrote Stout, "but in consequence of the heavy rain which fell all night and day, they could not be trailed."

This killing alarmed the local settlement. Mr. Blundell, the family of Joseph Harris, and the whole settlement convened on Cypress Creek near the Cherokee Crossing. Under the protection of Stout's rangers, a new fortification was constructed and it was named Fort Sherman. Some eight or nine families took up shelter there. Leaving fifteen of his rangers behind, Captain Stout then proceeded to the Sabine River, and from there to Lyday's settlement on the Sulphur River.

Stout's rangers had spent more than a week at Fort Sherman. They arrived at Fort Lyday on or before December 19, on which date twenty-one new men from that settlement were enlisted into his ranger company.

At Lyday's, Stout found the settlement "in a state of alarm and on the eve of breaking up—in consequence of three men being killed in the neighborhood." Two of the men were brothers by the name of Washburn. In this settlement, there was an older dilapidated fort, which Stout and his rangers repaired. The fourteen or so families residing here now took this fort as their shelter from the Indians.

Isaac Lyday had been in charge of armed settlers at his namesake settlement as early as September 1, 1838. General Dyer had mobilized several ranging companies in this area of the country during September. Stout's account is flawed in stating that his was the only ranger company in service in this area.

Capt. Stout's Red River Co. Rangers: Nov. 20, 1838–May 26, 1839

Captain:
William B. Stout [1]
First Lieutenant:
John M. Watson [1]
Second Lieutenant:
H. G. McDonald [1]
First Sergeant:
A. S. Young
Second Sergeant:
Green H. Crowder [1]
Third Sergeant:
A. Jackson Click [4]
Fourth Sergeant:
Lewis Roark [1]
Privates:
Hugh Allen [2]
Joseph Allen [2]
John Avery [1]
John Brown [3]
Eli Burnett [4]
William M. Burns [1]
Andrew Coots [2]
David Coots [2]
George Coots [2]
John Crisp [4]
A. G. Crowder [5]
Benjamin Crownover [1]
Howard Ethridge [1]
Ambrose D. Foster [4]
Isaac Foster [4]
James Foster [4]
John Foster [4]
William G. Gavin [1]
Robert Haley [5]
Benjamin Hall [1]
John Harris [1]
Henry B. Hutchins [6]
A. McGee Jeffries [1]
James A. Jeffries [1]
Samuel Jeffries [1]
Hiram Jones [7]
Robert Jones [5]
Thomas Jones [8]
John Mathews [9]
W. O. Mathews [9]
Wilson McCrury [1]
Albert McFarland [5]
Jackson McFarland [5]
James McFarland [5]
Joseph Mickhel [4]
Harvey Milligan [10]
Henry Noble [4]
Thomas Noble [4]
William Noble [4]
Quintus C. Nugent [9]
Green Orr [4]
John Oustall [4]
John Patterson [1]
James M. Patton [5]
Ancel C. Peck [5]
Isaac Pennington [4]
Carey Regan [5]
Ambrose Ripley [8]
Lewis Roark [1]
James A. Sharp [1]
Eli J. Shelton [4]
Harvey Shelton [4]
John Simmons [4]
John Snyder [4]
Elisha W. Turner [3]
Madison Wade [5]
Isaac Ward [11]
Samuel B. Ware [12]
Joel D. Webb [4]
Warren Wilkerson [11]
Isaac Wilson [11]
Jason Wilson [4]
William Yates [4]

1 11/20/38–5/26/39
2 12/5/38–3/6/39
3 1/26–5/26/39
4 12/19/38–5/26/39
5 2/26–5/26/39
6 11/24/38–5/26/39
7 12/5/38–5/26/39
8 12/5/38–3/5/39
9 11/20/38–2/26/39
10 3/10–5/26/39
11 11/26/38–5/26/39
12 2/21–5/26/39

Source: Texas State Archives.

Lyday's military papers show that he was "duly elected Capt. of 3rd Comp. of Rangers of Red River County, stationed at Fort DeKalb." Captain Lyday's small ranger company served during the six month period of September 1, 1838, to February 28, 1839. General Dyer visited "Fort DeKalb" on November 29, signing Lyday's military papers authorizing the service of his company.[11]

This fort in Lyday's settlement was popularly known as Fort Lyday. It was renamed Fort DeKalb by November, likely in honor of Baron Johann DeKalb, a German general in the American

Revolution. It has been speculated that General Dyer may have been an admirer of DeKalb and thus selected this name. Once Lyday's ranger company was discharged in 1839, the frontier fortification became again known as Fort Lyday.

There is no extant muster roll of Lyday's rangers, but he continued to provide food for his men and add new recruits to his company during the half year period he commanded this post. The papers of Private Cornelius B. Tollett show that he enlisted for a term of three months with Lyday's company on October 16 at "Fort Lyday." He was paid at the rate of twenty-five dollars per month and was discharged at the fort on January 16, 1839, by Captain Lyday and Major Stephen Peters of the First Regiment, Fourth Militia Brigade. Another ranger, Curtis Jernigan, joined the company on November 29 and served until the unit was disbanded on February 28, 1839.[12]

Fort Lyday/DeKalb was smaller in size than other such pioneer fortifications, taking up only about a quarter acre. It was surrounded by the usual stockade fence. Inside along the north side were storerooms measuring ten by twelve feet. Running along the other walls were living quarters of about the same size. In the center of the fort was an open space with a large well. A corral for livestock was outside the stockade perimeter. The fort was located three-quarters of a mile east and one-half mile north of the old Lyday's crossing of the North Sulphur River in present southwestern Lamar County near the community of Dial.[13]

After assisting with Fort DeKalb, Captain Stout left ten of his rangers behind to supplement those of Captain Lyday. Stout then proceeded with his remaining men to Shelton's settlement, located about fifteen miles below Lyday's. He had received word that the pioneers of Shelton's settlement were packing up and preparing to flee from their homes due to the recent Indian hostilities. Stout later wrote that his company arrived on December 26, but his own muster roll would indicate that his men were at Shelton's by December 19. He found "the principle part of the settlement assembled at Shelton's, and debating what was best to be done."[14]

Fort Shelton, as this settlement was known, had been built by Jesse Shelton in 1837 near the banks of the North Sulphur River in southwestern Lamar County near the present community of Roxton. Soon after the Red River rangers arrived, Shelton's fortification was renamed Fort Rusk in honor of the Texas Militia's senior officer.[15]

The rangers decided that the Shelton settlers should help build Fort Rusk and learn to protect themselves.

> Captain Stout proposed that they should build a fort and that he would have the families protected, provided they would remain and the men would make a crop. To this they agreed. The fort was built. The arrangement for making a crop was this. They were to work for each other; five or six working today and five or six more working the next—thus taking it in rotation until all had done an equal portion of labor. As soon as one man's field was dispatched, they commenced on another's. Whilst the men were at work, a party of soldiers were station[ed] in the field as a guard against the Indians.[16]

Captain Stout, having been authorized by General Dyer to augment his force as necessary, obtained an additional nineteen ranger recruits from the settlement on December 19. This allowed him to garrison the fort and still have enough soldiers to protect the field laborers. In this manner, the settlers of Shelton's continued their practice from December 1838 until the fall of 1839—"when the families returned to their respective homes in security, with the fruits of a good crop, as good as had ever been raised in the settlement."

★ ★ ★ ★ ★

Montague's Second Regiment of Riflemen

In Fannin County, Lieutenant Colonel Daniel Montague still operated several companies of the Second Regiment, Fourth Brigade of the Texas Militia. These men served as ranger companies to protect the settlements while General Dyer's men were out on expedition.

Captain Jesse Stiff organized the Fannin County Mounted Gunmen on December 1. A sixteen-member detachment of the Fannin County Mounted Gunmen under First Lieutenant John P. Simpson was stationed at Fort Saline on this date. Also on duty as of December 1 under Montague's direction was Captain John Hart's thirty-two-man company of mounted gunmen. Hart had lost four men who had absented themselves without leave on November 20, following the first Dyer expedition.

Lieutenant Simpson later wrote that the further organization of Montague's battalion of Dyer's Fourth Brigade was in response to Indian depredations against the white settlers of the area.

> The citizens were up in arms and on the lookout for the foe; companies were organized, and every man was on the alert. A battalion was formed of the citizens of Lamar and

Fort Inglish was the rendezvous site for ranger companies of Brigadier General John Dyer's Fourth Militia Brigade during 1838. Built by Bailey Inglish in 1837, the early fort protected the settlers of Bois d'Arc, a Fannin County community that later became known as Bonham. The reconstructed Fort Inglish is now part of a museum in Bonham.
Photo by Marshall L. Moore Jr.

> Fannin counties, armed and equipped for service under the command of Gen. John H. Dyer of Red River County. The rendezvous was at Fort Inglish, near where Bonham now stands. This settlement, then consisting of eight or ten families, was forted up for mutual protection. When the army left in search of the Indians, the writer was left at the fort as Lieutenant in command of a squad of twenty men for the protection of the women and children.[17]

One of Simpson's rangers was Andrew Thomas, who narrowly escaped death during the early days of December 1838 after Dyer's battalion had taken to the field. Thomas and another man, William Dority, took Dority's son Andrew and the son of William McCarty with them to search for their hogs near present Kentuckytown, where they had lived previously.

The men found their hogs and soon started back with their pork in a wagon. En route, they stopped at a deserted house near Bois d' Arc

Creek near the present site of Orangeville in southwestern Fannin County. Andrew Thomas was cooking dinner when he heard the war whoops of Indians near the creek. The Indians surprised young McCarty at the creek and shot him full of arrows. The attackers proceeded to chop off the boy's head with their tomahawks.

The Indians, yelling and screaming loudly, then moved to surround the abandoned house where the other three men had camped. William Dority was shot through the left side and killed before he could reach the house. His young son Andrew Dority was shot through the elbow, a wound which would cripple his arm for life. Thomas was stopped short of reaching the house by several Indians bearing both rifles and tomahawks. One of them fired a volley which narrowly missed him. Being in such close proximity to the Indians, Thomas' only defense was to aggressively charge his attackers with a rifle in one hand and his fire poker in the other. He was too close to shoot his rifle, but used the fire poker as a weapon to bash several of his opponents to the ground.

This bold show of force was enough to intimidate the other Indians to retreat to the brush for safety. Thomas and the wounded Andrew Dority then raced for Fort Inglish, where Lieutenant Simpson and the other rangers were stationed. Some of the Indians trailed them, but Thomas was able to fend them off by presenting his loaded gun.

Dority and Thomas did reach the fort safely before dark. The company there mounted up and rode to the scene of the attack early the next morning. Lieutenant Simpson was moved by the carnage he saw.

> Arrived at the battle ground, there lay old man Dority in a pool of blood, three scalps having been taken from his head and the tomahawk having been sunk twice in the naked skull–a sight so horrible and appalling that you can have no conception of it without you had been an eyewitness. McCarty's son was not scalped, but his head was cut entirely off except a small ligament on one side. The bodies were brought to the fort next day and deposited in the graveyard at Fort Inglish, being the second burial at that place.

Another of Lieutenant Colonel Montague's Second Regiment companies, that of Captain Nathaniel Journey, remained in active service through March 13, 1839. On January 13, his men were operating from Camp Journey, which is believed to have been located on Journey's own farm in the Mulberry Bend of Red River, north of the mouth of Caney Creek in Fannin County. Caney Creek flows into Red River about twelve miles northwest of Bonham.[18]

Montague's Second Regiment of the Fourth Militia Brigade continued to operate into 1839 with ranger companies organized under captains John Emberson, Mark R. Roberts, and Joseph Sowell. Paymaster General Jacob Snively, in a Pay Department statement dated October 21, 1839, allowed $15,643 in payment for the Second Regiment frontiersmen. This included pay for Montague's field and staff and the companies of captains Journey, Roberts, Hart, Sloan, and Stiff and Lieutenant Simpson.[19]

Snively identified these companies under Montague as "rangers" who were paid "for services rendered on the Red River frontier, in 1838 and 1839."

★ ★ ★ ★ ★

President Lamar Creates Frontier Regiment

Even as the Fourth Militia Brigade was fortifying frontier settlements and conducting a major campaign during December, the new government of Texas was taking steps that would soon drastically change the republic's approach to Indian warfare.

The catalyst of the major change in Indian policy was Mirabeau Buonaparte Lamar, who was inaugurated as the new President of Texas on December 10, 1838. A hero of the battle of San Jacinto, Lamar had spent the past two years serving as vice president under Sam Houston. When he and new Vice President David Gouverneur Burnet took office, Lamar made it clear that he would not follow President Houston's policy of pacifying the hostile Indians of Texas.

In his first speech before the Third Congress in Houston on December 21, President Lamar set the tone for his administration's new stance on Indian policy. "As long as we continue to exhibit our mercy without showing our strength," he said, "so long will the Indians continue to bloody the tomahawk and move onward in the work of rapacity and slaughter."[20] He also pledged to remove from Texas the Western Cherokees, the tribe under Chief Bowles with whom Sam Houston had granted a land treaty in 1836 in eastern Texas. Lamar claimed that Indians had no legal claim to Texas lands and therefore had no reason to complain. The new Texas president saw the Native Americans as "wild cannibals" who committed killings with the "ferocity of tigers and hyenas."

Clearly, Lamar planned to be far more aggressive in his Indian policy, advocating an ethnic cleansing. He planned for his young republic to retaliate against the Indians by taking an "exterminating war" to bring about "their total extinction."

Soon after the new president had taken office, the Third Congress of Texas began work on acts that would properly protect the frontiers. The solutions ranged from a revamped army to new county-level ranging companies.

Some counties were eager to appoint new mounted ranger companies to patrol their territory. James Shaw and George Washington Hill, representing Milam and Robertson counties, gave written notice to Lamar on December 20, 1838, of the peoples' choices in officers for new companies. They proposed a company on the east side of the Brazos River in Robertson County to be under Captain William Love, First Lieutenant Albert Gholson, and Second Lieutenant William Sherrod. For a company west of the Brazos in Milam County, they preferred the officers to be Captain Lee Davis, First Lieutenant Charles Curtis, and Second Lieutenant W. L. Murray.[21]

The most significant legislation of the new administration was an act creating a new regular army, which was passed on December 21, 1838. This "Frontier Regiment" was charged with the duty of protecting "the northern and western frontier" of Texas. It was to consist of fifteen companies, a total of 840 men, which would be stationed along a military road that would be laid out from the Red River on the United States border to the Nueces River near the Mexico border. Along this route would be a string of forts for the protection of nearby settlements. Congress appropriated $300,000 in Republic promissory notes to help Lamar organize the army.[22]

The largest portion of this army would become infantrymen, but it was also to include cavalry. It was left to President Lamar's discretion "to make cavalry of as many" of the 840 men raised as "the public exigencies may demand, and to distribute them among the different stations." Each man providing his own horse would be paid a fair amount as judged by two sworn appraisers, but this amount was not to exceed $150.

Each of the fifteen infantry companies would have a captain, a first lieutenant, and a second lieutenant. The infantry would consist of one regiment, divided into two battalions. The First Battalion would include all detachments west of the Brazos River and the Second Battalion would consist of all detachments east of the Brazos. The army's regiments would be headed by a colonel, one lieutenant colonel, and a major, followed by company captains.

The Frontier Regiment was to be stationed in detachments throughout Texas, including one company at or near the Red River;

three companies near the Three Forks of the Trinity; two companies at or near the Brazos River; two at or near the Colorado River; one company at the San Marcos River; one at or near the headwaters of the Cibolo; one company at or near the Frio River; and the balance of the men at or near the Nueces River.

Detachments from these various stations were to traverse the country between stations daily. Those troops who had previously been enrolled in cavalry units under the law of May 15, 1838, "shall be deemed part of the regiment created by this act" and were to report to the post on the Nueces.

The earliest enlistees into this new Frontier Regiment were placed under command of captains George Thomas Howard and Samuel W. Jordan. Howard, Jordan, and Captain Louis C. D'Antignac had each commanded companies of Major James W. Tinsley's First Regiment of Cavalry during early 1838. Captain Martin K. Snell, a mustering officer for the Texas Army, continued to recruit new men from Matagorda into the cavalry during September and October.

A War Department note of December 23, 1838, shows that Secretary of War Johnston deployed these companies to help offset recent Comanche depredations. Captain Howard's company was ordered to occupy a position near Gonzales and Captain Jordan's company was posted near San Antonio "for the protection of the inhabitants of those districts."[23]

Captain Howard's Troop B, First Cavalry Regiment company proceeded to San Antonio to secure horses before returning to Gonzales to take up station. By January 10, 1839, Gonzales Station, later known as Post Gonzales, was established with the two cavalry companies of Howard and Jordan. As the Frontier Regiment developed, these companies were included as infantry companies during 1839 but remained on duty in Gonzales through the early months of the year.[24]

The senior officers for the Frontier Regiment were soon appointed, with noted Indian fighter Edward Burleson named as the colonel commanding. The majority of the leaders of this new Texas Army would be instated during January 1839. Realizing that the plan to establish military roads and proper military posts throughout the frontier would take some time for the new First Regiment to complete, the Third Congress moved to provide local protection from Comanche and other hostile Indians for the short term with another act. On December 29, 1838, Congress authorized President Lamar to use $75,000 to press eight "Companies of Mounted Volunteers" into service for six months' ranging duty.

Each company would consist of a captain, a first and a second lieutenant, three sergeants, and fifty privates, each for six-month terms. Each would be paid monthly in the same fashion "as Mounted Riflemen in the Ranging Service," which had been established by the act passed on December 10, 1836.[25]

This act also declared that the eight-company mounted volunteer battalion would constitute "one Regiment, to be commanded by one Colonel, one Lieutenant Colonel, and one Major, to be appointed by the President." Lamar was further authorized to use these troops "offensively or defensively, as in his opinion the interest of the country may require."

The commanding officers of this regiment were instated by Congress on January 9, 1839, as Colonel Henry Wax Karnes, Lieutenant Colonel Jerome Devereaux Woodlief, and Major William Jefferson Jones. Troops that were already enlisted, under the cavalry frontier protection act of May 15, 1838, were to proceed forthwith to the Nueces.[26]

Major Jones was ordered on January 21 to proceed with recruiting men through Columbia and Matagorda en route to Washington on the Brazos. A total of 450 men were needed "for the Corps of Rangers in which you have the honor of holding a command." Jones was to meet with Karnes and Woodlief to adopt "prompt and energetic measures" to raise the necessary rangers, who were designated to operate "against the Comanches and other hostile Indians." [27]

This set of orders best clarifies that the mounted battalion to be raised by Colonel Karnes, Woodlief, and Jones operated as true Texas Rangers. This battalion would eventually include mounted volunteer companies commanded by Mark Lewis, James Ownby, Greenberry Harrison, John Garrett, and John C. Neill.

Lamar and the Third Congress did not halt their military buildup with the army's new Frontier Regiment and Karnes' mounted battalion. Many three and six-month ranger companies were soon approved to assist the volunteer militiamen on the frontiers. Under Mirabeau Lamar, the frontier system would achieve record attention and the fabled Texas Rangers would write many new pages in their early history during 1839.

★ ★ ★ ★ ★

Rusk/Dyer Winter Expedition to the Three Forks

The recent military allocations by Lamar's new congress would be a welcome relief to aggressive Major General Tom Rusk. He had rendezvoused with General John Dyer's First Regiment of the Fourth Militia Brigade by December 5 in their quest to attack the Caddo and Wichita Indians living along the Trinity River.

Shortly after organizing the troops, Rusk, Dyer, and Colonel Joseph Mix moved their forces on toward the Cross Timbers. This well-known pioneer landmark consisted of two long, narrow strips of timber which extended parallel to each other from present Oklahoma down through central Texas. A sharp contrast from the adjacent prairie, this thick timber was a travel obstacle as well as a natural dividing line of hunting grounds for the plains and East Texas Indians. The Cross Timbers entered Texas through present Cooke County, located west of Clarksville, and continued southwesterly between the present Dallas and Fort Worth areas.[28]

Rusk's powerful new force found and destroyed some Caddo villages before marching across a dead, barren prairie to the Brazos River. "The villages were deserted and evidently with precipitation," Colonel Hugh McLeod wrote. "Buffalo skins, a few blankets, [and] some guns were left behind."[29]

McLeod had been thrown from his horse at the first of the month and had been left behind to recover. The adjutant general and several others did manage to catch up with Rusk's troops late in the December expedition. By the time McLeod rejoined General Rusk, the Texan expedition had already turned to head home, as their supplies were dwindling. Likely alerted by Tejano allies, the Indians along the upper Trinity had retreated west into the Brazos valley.

Upon returning to the baggage wagons, the exhausted troops found that Captain Tarrant's men had not arrived with the promised cattle and that supplies there were exhausted. Rusk's men abandoned the wagons and had to subsist on the oxen. Throughout the entire expedition "the weather was very cold and disagreeable and the men suffered much."[30]

Although his forces had not fought any Indians, Rusk considered his venture successful.

> Our march was from the upper settlement of Red River, across to the Red Fork of the Brazos and back, crossing the Three Forks of the Trinity some twenty miles above their junction. From there, to the heads of the Neches and Sabine and into the settlement, we met no hostile Indians and in fact no Indians but Kickapoos. I ascertained that the main body of the enemy were located high up on the Brazos and had not our provisions given out, we should have been able to reach them.

> I feel great anxiety to hear from Congress. I fear if a decisive blow is not struck against the Indians before spring, we shall be much troubled with them.[31]

Rusk and Dyer's forces had swept through the present areas of Fort Worth and Dallas, driving the Caddos toward Louisiana. The weather had been brutally cold and the march was, stated McLeod, "in my opinion unparalleled since DeSoto's." Despite such trying conditions, Colonel Mix's companies suffered surprisingly few desertions. Five men from Captain Birdwell's company absented themselves without leave before the close of the expedition in January.

During the return from their expedition, the men noted large droves of buffalo and wild horses. By early January 1839, Rusk's Fourth Brigade volunteers had reached a point in Red River County sixty miles below Clarksville. The men were given their discharges and McLeod and Rusk turned back for Nacogdoches.

General Rusk's Three Forks Expedition
December 5, 1838–January 7, 1839

General's Staff, 4th Brigade Texas Militia: Sept. 6, 1838–Jan. 7, 1839

Brigadier General:	John Lewis *	*Chaplain:*
John H. Dyer	*Surgeon:*	John B. Denton *
Brigadier Major:	John F. Smith	*Color Bearer:*
Clement Reed Johns	*Judge Advocate:*	H. A. Allen *
Aides:	Andrew J. Fowler *	
Lemuel Peters	*Paymaster:*	* Joined Nov. 18, 1838.
Richard Peters *	James W. Luper *	

Field and Staff, 1st Regiment, 4th Brigade of Mounted Gunmen
September 6, 1838–January 7, 1839

Colonel:	*Quartermaster:*	*Sergeant Major:*
Samuel W. Sims [1]	Edward West	James W. Sims [5]
Joseph R. Mix [2]	*Surgeons:*	George Clark [6]
Lieutenant Colonel:	Joseph Haslett [3]	
Lindley Johnston	John S. Davis [4]	[1] Resigned Nov. 28, 1838.
Major:	*Assistant Surgeon:*	[2] Appointed Nov. 28.
Stephen Peters	George Gordon	[3] Died Oct. 18, 1838.
Adjutant:	*Judge Advocate:*	[4] Appointed Dec. 1, 1838.
Albert H. Latimore	Thomas F. Smith	[5] Through Nov. 28, 1838.
		[6] Appointed Nov. 28.

Captain Pollitt's Company of Guards: October 12, 1838–Jan. 12, 1839

Captain:
George Pollitt
First Lieutenant:
George M. Casey [1]
Privates:
William Colberson [1]
John Lambert [2]
Ransom Langham [2]
Henry Meers [2]
James Pollock [2]
Mitchell Snyder [1]

[1] Discharged Nov. 22
[2] Discharged Nov. 2
Muster roll signed on January 12, 1839 in Nacogdoches by Captain Pollitt and Thomas Rusk. Company served as baggage guards for baggage wagons under command of General T. J. Rusk.

Captain Edmondson' Company A: Sept. 6, 1838–January 7, 1839
1st Regiment, 4th Brigade of Mounted Riflemen under Col. Mix

Captain:
William Edmondson
First Lieutenant:
John Snider
Ignatius L. Aud [1]
Second Lieutenant:
Samuel A. Miller
First Sergeant:
J. P. Dunlap
Privates:
David P. Alexander
Charles L. Askins
Thomas Askins [2]
Wesley Askins
Samuel Bank [2]
Henry Bingham [2]
Israel Boren
James Bourland
John D. Bruton [2]
William H. Burton [2]
James Campbell
P. B. Chapin
Smith R. Cherry
Claiborne Chisum
Daniel M. Cole
George W. Cox
Mansel Crisp
Jacob M. Crook [2]
Lewis J. Crook [2]
Richard Dandridge [2]
Benjamin B. Davis
Joel Davis
John L. Davis
John Eastwood [2]
William C. Fently
Ambrose D. Foster
Felix R. Foster [2]
William F. Frampton[2]
Robert Glass
James Graham
John Griffey
W. R. Harland
James S. Johnson [2]
Jacob Lyday
Zachariah B. Miller
Seaver V. Moore
Whitfield Moore [2]
Walter Murray [3]
Wesley Netherly [2]
Jesse Pace [2]
Larkin Rattan [2]
Sherod Riland
Reddin Russell
Henry Shackley
John Simmons
Alexander Stevenson [4]
Henry Trimble [2]
David Waggoner [2]
Madison Ward
Joel D. Webb
James Wheat [2]
John Wheat
W. Wheat [2]
Warren Williams
Jason Wilson [5]
Caleb Wood

[1] Served till November 2, 1838.
[2] Enlisted November 27, 1838.
[3] Discharged on November 16, 1838.
[4] Transferred to Company B on December 2, 1838.
[5] Enlisted November 18, 1838.

Captain Craddock's Company B: Sept. 6, 1838–January 7, 1839
1st Regiment, 4th Brigade of Mounted Riflemen under Col. Mix

Captain:
John R. Craddock
First Lieutenant:
John Dennis
Second Lieutenant:
Robert Price
First Sergeant:
William D. Morgan[1]
Second Sergeant:
John C. Bates [2]
Third Sergeant:
Thomas Dennis
First Corporal:
Mathias Click [4]
Privates:
Elijah Benton [3]
Jesse M. Boyd [6]
Thomas Brumley [4]
William M. Burton [5]
Andrew J. Click
Rufus K. Click
James Dalton
Samuel M. Dalton [6]
John Davis Jr. [1]
Ralph Davis [6]
William T. Dillingham
John E. Doss [1]
John Emberson
James Ferril [7]
Silas Ferril [7]
George Kennedy
Thomas King [8]
William Lawless
Thomas Lofton
Bennett T. Logan [6]
William Mason [9]
Abram Mittover [10]
Greenville M. Nicholsen
Matthew R. O'Brien
John Oliver
John S. Porter
John Roberts [1]
Alexander E. Rofs [1]
Charles W. Sadler
Hiram Sadler
James C. Sadler
Thomas R. Sadler [6]
William S. Sadler [6]
Andrew J. Sage [9]
Gordon Sage [11]
Eli Smyers [12]
John D. Spears [6]
Littleton Stephens [14]
Alexander Stephenson[13]
John D. Thomas [1]
Andrew Viser [1]
Henry F. Viser [1]
Hezekial Walters [6]
Rufus Ward [16]
Edward Wileman [3]
William M. Williams[15]

1 Absent without leave as of November 13, 1838.
2 Acted as orderly sergeant from Nov. 13–Dec. 5, 1838.
3 Joined Nov. 24.
4 Joined Dec. 5.
5 Joined December 2. Transferred to Company A on Dec. 6.
6 Joined Nov. 13.
7 Joined Nov. 22.
8 Left home sick but later joined Capt. Tarrant's company.
9 Absent sick from Nov. 13.
10 Voluntary physician for company.
11 Served as teamster from Nov. 13.
12 Joined Nov. 27 from Company C.
13 Joined Dec. 2 from Company A.
14 Joined Dec. 4 from Company C.
15 Joined Nov. 13. Promoted to orderly sergeant on December 5.
16 Joined November 27.

Captain Scurlock's Company C: Sept. 6, 1838–January 7, 1839
1st Regiment, 4th Brigade of Mounted Riflemen under Col. Mix

Captain:
Joseph R. Mix [1]
William Scurlock [2]
First Lieutenant:
Henry J. Harmen [2]
Second Lieutenant:
Samuel S. Harry [2]
First Sergeant:
Eli M. Smith [3]
Second Sergeant:
Gilbert Ausley
Third Sergeant:
William Moran
First Corporal:
James Reily
Second Corporal:
George Fletcher [3]
Third Corporal:
Richard McLamore [3]
Privates:
James Adkinson
John Askey
Aaron Bailey [13]
George Basin [4]
Joseph Briggs [13]
Harrison Brunet [8]
Lorenzo Bryan
Thomas Burns
John Campbell [3]
John Carter [3]
George Clark
William Cox [8]
William Crissup [8]
James Curry [3]
John S. Davis [5]
Harmon C. Day [7]
Benjamin H. Dop [8]
Lewis Duvall [11]
Amos Elliott
Elias P. Fort
James Fort [8]
James M. Garner
William Geyton [8]
Mark Griffin [3]
John M. Hann [8]
Lewis Harmon [8]
Josiah Hart
Daniel Hartz
Joseph H. Haslett [6]
Robert Hill [3]
Peter B. Johnson
James King [3]
Pharoah Kitchens [8]
James Lakin [3]
Smith Largin [8]
Henry Lucky
Hugh Lucky [14]
William McClenan [3]
John McMin [8]
Peter Mooney [8]
Lawson Moore [8]
Zach Moore [14]
William Murry
William S. Osborn
William A. Park [3]
Daniel Perkins [8]
Samuel Perkins [12]
Charles Ragsdale [8]
Thomas Ragsdale [8]
Joseph Savage [8]
John T. Scott
Clark Simmons [8]
Elijah Simmons [3]
Canan Smith [3]
John Smith
Samuel S. Smith [3]
Thomas F. Smith
Eli Smyers [10]
Littleton Stephens [9]
William F. Wetherly
A. M. Williams
Richard N. Williams
Sylvester Williams [3]
James Wimberly
Wiley Witherspoon
Alexander Wright
Travis G. Wright [8]

[1] Promoted to colonel on November 28, 1838.
[2] Promoted on Dec. 1, 1838.
[3] Joined November 22, 1838.
[4] Company surgeon. Furloughed Sept. 23, 1838.
[5] Joined Nov. 22. Promoted to surgeon on Nov. 29.
[6] Company surgeon. Died on Oct. 18, 1838.
[7] Discharged Sept. 19.
[8] Discharged Sept. 23.
[9] Transferred to Company B December 4.
[10] Transfer to Company B November 27.
[11] Joined Nov. 22. Deserted Dec. 2.
[12] Joined Nov. 22. Deserted Dec. 11.
[13] Deserted Nov. 20.
[14] Discharged Sept. 25.

Captain Hopkins' Company: Sept. 6, 1838–January 7, 1839
1st Regiment, 4th Brigade of Mounted Riflemen under Col. Mix

Captain:
James E. Hopkins
First Lieutenant:
James D. Alley
Second Lieutenant:
Josiah F. Wheat
First Sergeant:
Edward Hunter
Second Sergeant:
Daniel Shook [1]
Third Sergeant:
Alfred Allyn [1]
Fourth Sergeant:
John D. Bloodworth
First Corporal:
David Clark
Second Corporal:
William H. Hopkins
Third Corporal:
Robert Wheat
Fourth Corporal:
Jacob Gregg
Privates:
William Allison
Eli Barrett [2]
W. G. Benton [1]
Benjamin Bland
John W. Bland
Preston J. Bland [2]
Benjamin Blanton [2]
Jacob Blanton [2]
Needham Boon [1]
B. F. Brewster [1]
W. Brinton
George A. Brown [5]
Isaac Bruton [9]
A. Buchanan
J. W. Buchanan
Henry Buckler [1]
Wash B. Carroll
Benjamin Clack [2]
C. P. Collier
Philip Cornelius [2]
Ed M. Dean [6]
John H. Duke [1]
A. D. Duncan
Jefferson Duty [1]
Philip Duty [1]
James H. Elliott
James W. Elliott
Joseph Fields
Isaac H. Fishback
Thomas C. Forbes [1]
Andrew J. Fowler [2]
Alexander Graham
Elijah Green
William Gregg [1]
A. Hampton [2]
Samuel W. Hillis [1]
William Holland [6]
R. M. Hopkins [1]
John Humphries
William Humphries
William C. Ingram [2]
John Jackson [7]
John S. Kennedy
R. Lane [1]
James Levins [3]
John Levins [1]
Nicholas Levins
C. J. Lyons
Allen McClendan [2]
John McCowen [1]
William McCutcheon [1]
L. G. McGaughey
Charles K. Miller [1]
Thomas Montcriff [1]
Martin G. Nall [5]
Samuel B. Orton [10]
Bushrow Osborn
Redrick Overton
Ephraim Peebles [1]
J. P. G. Pickle [1]
H. A. Reed
John S. Reed [1]
Joseph Reed [2]
Cyrus Richey [1]
John M. Richey [1]
Samuel Richey [1]
Thomas J. Richey
William Richey [1]
John Robbins [5]
Daniel Sample [1]
John Sandler [4]
James W. Scott [1]
Martin Setzer
William Stalcup [2]
William Stenham [3]
Samuel Stewart [1]
Henry B. Stout [2]
James S. Stout [2]
William B. Stout [8]
John J. Vinning [1]
William W. Vinning
J. H. Wallis [2]
James J. Ward [1]
Samuel Wheat
Thomas Wilson [1]
James Woods [2]

[1] Joined November 17.
[2] Discharged November 17.
[3] Joined spy company on December 3.
[4] Joined November 17. Drummed out of company December 4 for stealing shoes.
[5] Furloughed, lost horse on December 6, 1838.
[6] Joined November 17. Furloughed, lost horse on December 6.
[7] Joined November 17. Discharged November 29.
[8] Discharged November 14.
[9] Discharged November 27.
[10] Served special duty as waggoner.

Captain Hamilton's Company: Sept. 6, 1838–January 7, 1839
1st Regiment, 4th Brigade of Mounted Riflemen under Col. Mix

Captain:
Robert S. Hamilton
First Lieutenant:
George Milligan
Second Lieutenant:
James M. Hamilton
First Sergeant:
Benjamin F. Lynn
Second Sergeant:
Robert W. Madden
Third Sergeant:
James Moore
First Corporal:
Richard F. Giddins
Second Corporal:
Richard C. Allen
Privates:
William S. Andrews [2]
George W. Bagby[1]
James Bankston [1]
Andrew S. Beard [2]
James Chute [2]
William Clapp
Thomas L. Crier
Josiah Davidson [8]
Asa Dean
Levi Dean
Wiley W. Giddens
George Gray [8]
Adam Hamilton [2]
James Hamilton [2]
William J. Hamilton [2]
Leander Hancock [1]
Dennis Harty [8]
John Hasty
David Holbrook [2]
Isaac Hudson
John Hudson [1]
Edward Hughart
David R. Jamison [2]
Thomas Jouett [4]
Isiah Lawson [1]
John L. Lovejoy [3]
George W. McCurley
Cyrus Moore
Samuel F. Moore
Abraham Murphy [1]
Mathias Murry [2]
James S. Pace [5]
Leonard W. Perry [1]
Samuel Pew
Ira S. Poor [2]
John M. Rhouse [6]
William D. Richards [1]
Thomas Salathiel
Felix Scarborough [2]
Middleton Scarborough[7]
William Scarborough[1]
Benjamin F. Sherlock
Samuel W. Sims [3]
Caleb Smith
Samuel W. Sowell [8]
Oliver Spencer [1]
Benjamin F. Stewart[1]
John Stiles
William Walker [2]
John Ward
Morris G. Ward [1]
William C. Ward
Samuel Wilson
James Wyatt
George S. Young

[1] Joined November 17, 1838.

[2] Absent without leave December 19 or thereafter.
[3] Joined November 27, 1838.
[4] Joined December 1, 1838.
[5] Absent without leave December 1.
[6] Left without leave January 4, 1839.
[7] Discharged November 25.

[8] Discharged November 17.

Notes: John M. Bourland, James B. Cassedy, James G. Hamilton, and Ezekiel P. Wallace appear on muster roll but saw no service with unit. Samuel Sowell lost horse in service valued at $100.

Captain Gillian/Dyer's Company: Sept. 6, 1838–January 7, 1839
1st Regiment, 4th Brigade of Mounted Riflemen under Col. Mix

Captain:
James Gillian [1]
First Lieutenant:
Dickerson Dyer [2]
Second Lieutenant:
David M. Chisholm [3]
First Sergeant:
James F. Dixon [4]
Second Sergeant:
David P. Key [5]
Third Sergeant:
R. C. Harris
Fourth Sergeant:
R. M. Richardson
First Corporal:
Calvin C. Breeding
Second Corporal:
H. P. Bermingfield
Third Corporal:
D. B. Thomas
Fourth Corporal:
James Graham
Privates:
H. A. Allen [6]
A. S. Bacon
John Ball [6]
Robert Ballin [6]
John M. Bennett
James Blair
William Blythe [6]
John A. Booth
Josiah Bountly
Jesse Brothers
W. D. Browning
Charles Collin
Jacob Collin
William Criger
L. M. Dewent [6]
M. E. Dukes [6]
George W. Dyer
William D. Ellis [6]
John Escue [6]
Jesse B. Everette
Calvin Farris
George Farris
George Fletcher [6]
George Fletcher (Jr.) [7]
Martin Glover [4]
O. S. Haygood [6]
Frederick Jordan [6]
John P. Key
Benjamin D. Kimbell [6]
Edward Kimbell [6]
Thomas Kimbell [6]
John Kittrell [6]
James W. Leeper
J. M. Lewis [6]
Thomas Lewis [6]
John Magby [8]
Thomas Mahon [6]
H. D. Mason
J. M. Matlock
P. Maulding
R. E. McGee
Aslys McKinney
Daniel McKinney
G. Y. McKinney
H. C. McKinney
T. S. McKinney
William McKinney
Stephen McLeary [6]
John Milligan [10]
Richard Mulligan
Pallas Neely [12]
George Patterson [6]
W. J. Paxton
Lemuel Peters [11]
Martin A. Poor
George Reed [9]
Levi M. Rice
J. M. Smith [6]
W. C. Thomas [6]
T. F. Titus
Wright Titus
Amos Ury [6]
Jeremiah Walker [6]
Samuel Walker [6]
T. J. Watson
Peyton S. Wyatt [6]

1 Resigned December 5.
2 Elected to captain on December 5.
3 Elected first lieutenant December 5.
4 Absent without leave from November 18, 1838.
5 Served as first sergeant from Sept. 12 till Dec. 5; then as second lieutenant until discharged.
6 Enlisted November 18.
7 Enlisted November 17.
8 Discharged December 5.
9 Orderly sergeant from December 5.
10 Discharged November 27.
11 Discharged November 17.
12 Deserted November 26.

Captain Birdwell's Company: November 17, 1838–January 7, 1839
1st Regiment, 4th Brigade of Mounted Riflemen under Col. Mix

Captain:	James Basham	Robert Maxwell [1]
George Birdwell	Thomas G. Birdwell	William Morris [1]
First Lieutenant:	Elijah Blanton	William H. Raney
James Patton	Joab Bruton	John Reed
First Sergeant:	J. G. Chandler	Jacob Spears
John Beckwell	James Cooksy	Julius Tedmore
Second Sergeant:	William B. Crowder	Thomas Trent
Jonas Bruton	Isam Ferris	
First Corporal:	John Ferris	
Isaac Smithers	Loyd M. Garrison	
Second Corporal:	Thomas Hill [1]	
Monroe Shell	Balden C. Johnson [1]	
Privates:	William Jones [2]	
Elias Barrell	Thomas Luckwell [1]	

1 Absent without leave by January 7.
2 Enlisted November 28.

Source: All muster rolls presented for this expedition are transcribed from copies from the Texas State Archives.

The expedition had not been cheap. One military estimate submitted to the Fourth Congress in 1839 shows that General Dyer and his First Regiment of the Fourth Brigade were owed $49,940 for their service in the field.[32]

Upon wrapping up the campaign, Rusk sent a letter to President Lamar on January 9, 1839, from his headquarters in Red River County. "I have just returned from the campaign very much worn down and exhausted," he wrote. He promised to send his full report to the secretary of war within days, once he arrived back in Nacogdoches. Once he did reach Nacogdoches, Rusk was criticized by some for his intrusion upon U.S. soil in pursuit of the Indians.

By the time Colonel McLeod reached Nacogdoches on January 18, he had received information from captives of the Caddos who had recently escaped. He was told that Rusk's expedition has been "misled on the prairies by the Kickapoo Indians," leading them on to the Brazos River while the Caddos were actually camped out on the Trinity River. McLeod was skeptical of the reliability of this information and felt that Rusk's recent mission had served a purpose.

> This campaign, however, has had one great effect which amply compensates for its expense. The Indians never knew

they had an enemy beyond this neighborhood [Nacogdoches], no did they believe a white man could go to the prairies–and when they find a wide road made from Clarksville to the Brazos and learn from the Kickapoos that five hundred men made that road, they will perceive the hopelessness of such a contest.[33]

Chapter 6
Morgan Massacre and Bryant's Defeat

January 1–January 16, 1839

The new year of 1839 would prove to be a busy and bloody year on the frontiers of the Republic of Texas. Indian depredations, battles, and campaigns were more frequent than in any other year since Austin had colonized Texas.

In the Third Militia Brigade, word soon reached General Douglass that Rusk and Dyer's Three Forks expedition had been concluded. Secretary of War Johnston wrote to President Lamar on January 9 of his latest offensive plans. He explained that Douglass had been authorized to raise 800 volunteers, half to serve as infantry and half as mounted men. These men were to join one militia company and about 150 friendly Indians under Douglass who were already in the field.

> I deem this force with that in the field under Gen. Rusk, together with the regiment to be raised under the command of Col. Karnes, sufficient to prosecute the war with the Indians to a speedy termination.[1]

If General Douglass' force was brought into active service, Johnston informed Lamar that appropriations for six months of service should be made to cover these men's pay, subsistence, clothing, arms, and accoutrements.

In the favor of its settlers, the Third Congress of Texas worked diligently during the early weeks of January on revamping the military. Foremost among these changes was a fresh approach to stationing Texas Rangers as required by various counties.

The first county ranging company authorized was done so on January 1, 1839, by an "Act for the Protection of a Portion of the

Frontier." The sum of $5,000 was

> appropriated for the purpose of raising and supporting a company of fifty-six Rangers for three months, to be commanded by Captain John Wortham, whose duty it shall be to range on the frontier of Houston, or any frontier counties, and to protect the settlements.[2]

Wortham, of course, was already in command of a ranger company since shortly after the Kickapoo battle of October 1838. His rangers now came under orders of the government and Wortham was to advise Brigadier General Douglass of his movements at least every two weeks.

In addition to Houston County, the Third Congress authorized fifty-six-man local ranger companies in seven other frontier counties: Bastrop, Gonzales, Goliad, Milam, Refugio, Robertson, and San Patricio. The term "mounted volunteers" became synonymous with "ranging service" in these subsequent congressional acts.

The act for the company for Gonzales County was passed on January 15 and called for "the raising of a company of fifty-six men for the ranging service." The captain of the company was to be chosen by President Lamar, and he was required to enlist his men for three months "to range on the frontier of Gonzales County and protect the settlements." Another $5,000 was appropriated for this company. Its captain was required to report to the secretary of war and to the brigadier general of the First Militia Brigade, keeping them advised of movements.[3]

Mathew Caldwell, a ranger recruiter during the Texas Revolution, was selected by the people of Gonzales County to be captain of their county's ranging company. A bill was sent forth to Congress in Houston, asking President Lamar to confirm Caldwell as captain. Congress recommended that this nomination be vetoed, which Lamar did because he felt "the example is both dangerous and unconstitutional." The laws of Texas stated that the President "shall commission all the officers of the Republic." As for Caldwell, Lamar had "not the slightest objection" with his remaining commander of the Gonzales County rangers, but "only with mode of his appointment." To prevent other companies from selecting their own commanders Lamar apparently properly named Caldwell as commander of this company. Records do not show this, but Caldwell did take command. It would be two months, however, before he raised enough men to commission his company into service.[4]

The next three counties provided for were those of Bastrop, Robertson, and Milam, all in one joint act of January 23, 1839, that provided for "the raising of three companies of mounted volunteers for frontier service against the hostile Indians." These units were to serve for six months, as opposed to three-month-terms for the companies previously authorized in Houston and Gonzales counties. Also of note, the captains of these three companies were not appointed by President Lamar, but instead "the men composing each company will elect the officers of the company." The three companies in Bastrop, Robertson and Milam would elect a major to command them.[5]

San Patricio, Goliad, and Refugio counties were provided for on January 26, 1839. Their ranger companies were to be voluntarily enrolled for six months with the president appointing the officers. The individuals were to furnish their own horses, arms, and other equipage. Payment for privates and non-commissioned officers was to be twenty-five dollars per month. The sum of $15,000 was set aside by Congress to cover the costs of these companies.[6]

During 1839, the Indian fights would be carried out by these new ranger companies, by hastily organized volunteer parties, and by the new Frontier Regiment. The population growth in Texas brought hostile encounters closer to the settlements as the pioneers pushed further out into the frontiers. From only 30,000 white settlers in 1836, the white population of Texas had grown to almost 45,000 by the beginning of 1839.[7]

The constant campaigning of the militia during late 1838 helped to incite the Indians to strike against some of the pioneer families. The first major depredation of 1839 occurred on the first day of the year. This attack was particularly violent and it set the pace for the course of Indian actions for the year.

★ ★ ★ ★ ★

Morgan Massacre: January 1, 1839

New Year's Day 1839 was relatively peaceful for the settlers of the upper Brazos River. The night hours, however, brought a disturbing new round of violence from the Indians. This evening found several related families gathered together at the home of George Morgan.

His little settlement was known as Morgan's Point, located about six miles above the town of Marlin. At George Morgan's home this night were: his family; his relative Mrs. James Marlin and her children Isaac and Stacy Ann Marlin; the Morgan's daughter-in-law, Mrs. Jones and her sons Jackson and Wesley Jones; and the family of

Jackson Morgan. The other relatives of the Morgan and Marlin families had retired for the night at the home of John Marlin, a brother of James Marlin, seven miles lower down the river.[8]

The Morgan home was located on the east side of the Brazos River, near the falls. Shortly after dark on January 1, his home was surrounded and attacked by Indians who rushed in without warning and left little opportunity for the families to defend themselves.

These Indians included Caddos, Ionies, Anadarkos, and Kichais led by Chief José María. Born around 1800, he had led his Caddoan-speaking Anadarkos from their home north of Nacogdoches to settle in present Young County. By the mid-1840s, José María would become principal chief of all Caddo groups and had become a proponent of peace with Anglo-Texan settlers. It is unknown what provoked his Indians to go on the offensive in 1839, but their first victims were the settlers of Morgan's Point. The assault was vicious and bloody, as the Indians hacked their victims with tomahawks and scalping knives. Within minutes of the first alarm being shouted out, at least five settlers had been murdered.

George Morgan and his wife, both older citizens, were killed quickly, as was their grandson Jackson Jones. The oldest boy in the house, Jones had been reading to the family from a song book when the door burst open and the Indians rushed in. He was shot through the head. Sixteen-year-old Adeline Marlin and Mrs. Jackson Morgan were also quickly tomahawked and scalped by the Indians. Stacey Ann Marlin was left for dead, her wounds being severe.[9]

Three children were playing in the Morgan's yard when the attack commenced. Ten-year-old Isaac Marlin quickly hid under the fence and remained there throughout the assault on his family. Little Wesley Jones ran into the house as the attack started. Upon seeing the adults being tomahawked by the Indians, the scared boy ran out unobserved by the attackers. He was followed by young Mary Marlin and both children escaped unhurt.

Stacy Ann Marlin had regained consciousness during the final minutes of the massacre and saved her own life by playing dead. By some stroke of good luck, she was not scalped although all six other victims were. The Indians ransacked the Morgan home, stealing all contents of value, and then departed.

In the silence after the Indians' departure, young Isaac Marlin crept out from his hiding place and entered the horrific scene of the household. He examined the bodies, including that of his sister Stacy Ann, who continued to play dead as this person she supposed was an Indian entered the house. After he left, the wounded girl crawled out of the house and toward safety.

Young Isaac Marlin was thus unsure that anyone at all had survived the bloody depredation. The other two surviving children, Wesley Jones and Mary Marlin, had fled on their own toward the nearest settlement. Little Isaac ran the entire seven miles down the path through the night hours toward his Uncle John Marlin's house. The two other children to escape did not arrive at this house until daybreak the following morning. Stacy Ann Marlin, severely wounded, made her way to John Marlin's home around noon the following day.[10]

When the first terrified little boy arrived, he stammered out his pathetic story to the men at this home. They were John Marlin, his brother James Marlin, William N. P. Marlin, Wilson Marlin, Jackson Morgan, George W. Morgan, and Albert G. Gholson, all veteran frontiersmen and rangers. These men hastened to the scene and found the slaughter to be just as the child had related. More relief arrived on the scene the next morning. The victims were buried "amid the wailings of their grief-stricken relatives and friends."[11]

The January 9, 1838, issue of the *Telegraph and Texas Register* reported that the George Morgan home had been attacked by a party of about fifteen Indians. The newspaper reported, perhaps incorrectly, that Morgan and his son William Morgan were killed and that three women were captured.

★ ★ ★ ★ ★

Milam Guards Ordered Out to Help

As word spread of the Morgan Massacre, Captain Joseph Daniels' Milam Guards in Houston were immediately ordered out to protect. Daniels and his company had only just arrived in Houston on January 8 when the orders came to proceed back to the Falls of the Brazos. General Moseley Baker, in command of the Second Militia Brigade, sent orders to Daniels on January 9 for these rangers to "march forthwith to the Falls of the Brazos and there station yourself, for the purpose of giving protection to the frontier against Indian depredations." Baker advised Daniels to keep flankers out to the right and left of his position to watch for Indians en route.[12]

After hearing of the Morgan Massacre, Captain Daniels was not pleased that his men had been unable to help these citizens. When Major Bonnell had ordered his men back to Houston, Daniels felt that "the country had not been sufficiently scoured." He had proposed to remain and continue the operations into January. Daniels later wrote:

> Bonnell, however, ordered a retreat home, and it so happened the murder of the Morgan's family took place within an hour of the time this discussion was held—and it was this very murder that occasioned [my] return to the Falls.[13]

The Milam Guards suffered an accidental death of one of their own while moving to protect the Brazos area residents. On January 14, Sergeant Robert Hamet Breedin, a native of Mobile, Alabama, died of a gunshot wound. Captain Daniels detailed First Sergeant Joseph C. Eldridge to conduct a formal inquiry into the matter. Eldridge, serving as clerk, appointed twelve members of the Milam Guards to act as a jury: John Chenoweth, Timothy O'Neill, William G. Evans, Lewis Way, Lyman Tarbox, Best, James Duncan, Alfred Lee, Joseph Wells, Thomas Waters, Joseph Little, and John E. Jones.[14]

It is interesting to note the process by which such an early ranger company formally investigated its own misfortunes. Witnesses from the company were called forth. Private William T. Carter related:

> I, together with Patrick D. Cunningham, was in charge of the packmules, and at the time of the accident was in advance of the company, and had stopped at the roadside to let our horses graze and to light a pipe. We dismounted, and I asked Mr. Cunningham twice if his gun was loaded; he replied that it was not. He then laid his rifle in the hollow of his right arm, and primed it. I had a piece of rag rubbed with powder in my hand ready to light. I was facing Mr. Cunningham with my back to the road when the explosion took place. I turned around and saw Sergt. Breedin in the act of falling from his horse. I ran up and caught him in my arms, and called him twice by name, but he did not speak. His face was from me, so that I could not see whether he made an attempt to do so. I laid him on the ground, and in less than five minutes he was dead.

Carter deemed Robert Breedin's death "to have been purely accidental." Musician Francis Bettinger was also in advance of the company and about sixty yards behind Carter, Cunningham, and Breedin. He heard Carter ask Cunningham if his gun was loaded, but did not hear a reply. "Immediately after I heard the explosion, I turned and saw Carter catch Breedin as he was falling from his horse," stated Bettinger.

Private Cunningham pleaded that he had no disputes with Sergeant Breedin and that his misfire was a true accident. When

Carter had asked if his gun was loaded, Cunningham had stated that it was not.

> [I] since recollect that I fired it off last evening and loaded it again this morning to shoot some game, but before I had primed it the game flew, and I was ordered to assist in packing mules, laid down my rifle and so forgot about its being loaded. Sergeant Breedin rode up a few minutes before the rifle went off. I was holding it in the hollow of my left arm, having just primed, snapped it for the purpose of lighting a rag held by Mr. Carter, when it went off, and I saw Sergt. Breedin falling from his horse.

After hearing the testimony of those involved, jury foreman John Chenoweth read the verdict that Breedin had come "to his death by the accidental discharge of rifle in the hands of Patrick D. Cunningham." It was a tragic lesson learned, but an operational hazard of the trade that has claimed many a serviceman in the many decades since.

Captain Daniels sent a detail party fifteen miles to Washington for a coffin to be brought to the scene. At the Navasota River residence of Mr. Arnold, considered "Camp Arnold" by the company, Daniels had Sergeant Breedin buried with honors in a lonely grave on the banks of the river.[15]

Daniels was already upset that the Morgan Massacre had happened after his company had been ordered back to Houston. The loss of one of his men to an accident certainly did not lighten his spirits. To make matters worse, he soon found that his company's return to the Brazos River area would prove to be too late to aid in another desperate fight waged by these settlers.

★ ★ ★ ★ ★

Attack on John Marlin Household: January 14, 1839

The grieving families of the Marlins and Morgans had not yet recovered from the tragedy of losing loved ones on New Year's Day when they were dealt another assault by the Indians.

Varying accounts state that an attack on the home of John Marlin occurred between January 3 and January 14. The *Telegraph and Texas Register* of January 20 stated that the Marlin attack occurred on January 3. The account of historian James DeShields, however, states that Marlin's home was attacked about ten days after the Morgan attack. Due to the course of events which immediately followed this depredation, it appears that January 14 was the date that Marlin's home was attacked.[16]

At the time of the attack, there were three other men in Marlin's fortified home on the Brazos River, his son Benjamin Marlin, relative Jarrett Menefee, and Jarrett's son Thomas Sutherland Menefee. A party of perhaps seventy Indians appeared and made an assault against the fort, but they soon found that these Texans were armed and ready to fight back.

The Indians charged but suffered seven killed and several others wounded without the whites receiving any injury to themselves. Not anticipating such strong resistance, the Indians soon retired, carrying off their dead and wounded.

Jarrett Menefee's slave "Hinchey" was a short distance from the house when the assault commenced, but failed to join them in time. He quickly raced for the neighboring settlements below, running some twenty-five miles reportedly in the time a good horse would have covered the same distance. Hinchey reported the attack at Menefee and Marlin's homes, and his word caused an armed party to be immediately organized to fight the Indians.

The local settlers decided that these Indians must be pursued and attacked or the upper settlements themselves would have to be abandoned. Fifty-two men who lived in and near the settlement of Bryant's Station organized themselves as a volunteer company and elected Captain Benjamin Franklin Bryant, a veteran officer of the battle of San Jacinto, to command them. As many as a dozen of these volunteers had previously served as rangers during 1836 and 1837.

The morning after the Marlin-Menefee attack, January 15, Captain Bryant's volunteers started in pursuit, crossing the Brazos River near Morgan's Point. Traveling up the west side of the river, they soon discovered a deserted camp with fresh signs. About a mile away, they located a fresh trail of Indians leading into the settlements. Where the trail reached the river, the men determined that there were sixty-four fresh horse tracks and another trail of Indians on foot, which all crossed the river.[17]

Bryant's volunteers followed the tracks until night, at which time they discovered a fire in the neighborhood of John Marlin's home. The men left the trail and went in the direction of the fire, believing the Indians might have attacked their houses in their absence. They found, to their relief, that the fire was nothing more than the burning of a prairie.

★ ★ ★ ★ ★

Captain Bryant's Defeat: January 16, 1839

The next day, January 16, they started for Morgan's place. They soon found that the Indians were still in the area and had been at the deserted houses two miles above, plundering them. Captain Bryant's party proceeded six miles to Morgan's Point. Within a half mile of his home, they met an advance guard of the Indians in the open timber near a dry creek.

The Anadarko leader who was riding in front of the group, Chief José María, made the first move. In a seemingly casual effort, he halted his horse, slipped off his gloves, took deliberate aim and fired a shot at one of Bryant's advance guards. The rifle ball ripped through the coat sleeve of Joseph Boren, who was riding ahead of the others. José María then gave the signal for his men to fire and the battle commenced.[18]

Captain Bryant ordered his men to charge and they rushed forward against the Indians. In this opening charge, Bryant was shot through the arm. He turned the command of the volunteers over to his lieutenant, fifty-one-year-old Ethan A. Stroud. In response to the Texan charge, Chief José María's Indians fell back into a ravine near the Morgan house. During this initial charge, veteran ranger David Campbell shot José María in the chest, with the rifle ball striking him squarely in the breastbone. The tough chief managed to stay on his horse until Albert Gholson, another veteran Texas Ranger, shot the chief's horse, which died in the ravine.

Stroud's men charged up to the bend of the ravine and fired. The Indians commenced retreating down the bed of the ravine towards a densely timbered bottom. A portion of the Texans, realizing this effort, charged ahead to cut them off from the timber. This forced the Indians to move back to their first position in the gully and renew their defensive fire. By that time, some of the volunteers had already decided that the Indians had been defeated and had eased up on their tight formation.

As a result, the Indians were able to wound several of the lax Texans when they charged back and renewed their offensive. Confusion ensued at once. Lieutenant Stroud had tried ordering some of the men on horseback to dismount, but not all had done so in the time when they first had the Indians on the run. Now a portion of the volunteers were on horseback and approximately fifteen or more men were on foot. As the Indian gunfire suddenly erupted heavily over the unorganized men, Stroud gave the order for the men to retreat to another point about two hundred yards distant. His intent in so doing was to draw the Indians from their ravine. This command, unfortunately, was understood by some of the men to be an unqualified retreat.

Panic swept over a few of the men and this opportunity was quickly seized by the wily Chief José María. He led his Indians in a charge forward on the retreating Texans. As the war whoops rang out, several of the volunteers fell to the gunfire of the charging Indians. This completed the panic and the remainder of the volunteers scattered in the ultimate confusion. Those on horseback took their own safety first and left those on foot to be slaughtered by the Indians.

Captain Joseph Daniels and his Milam Guards arrived in the area in the immediate wake of this battle. He was not impressed with how the Texans had handled their fight.

> The fire of the Indians still increasing, and Stroud finding but little disposition in his men to attack the Indians in the position they occupied, ordered them to retreat to a point of timber which was too promptly obeyed. They retreated accordingly, with great precipitancy, leaving the fifteen men on foot to their fate–who being too tightly pursued by the Indians, could not

Bryant's Fight Volunteers: January 16, 1839

Captain:
Benjamin F. Bryant [1]
First Lieutenant:
Ethan A. Stroud
Volunteers:
Armstrong Barton
Hale Barton [2]
Joseph Boren
David W. Campbell
Nathaniel Campbell
Walter Campbell
Wiley Carter
Michael D. Castleman
Eli Chandler
Clay Cobb
David Cobb
Britton Dawson
L. Dorsey [2]
____ Doss
Thomas Duncan
Alfred P. Eaton [2]
William Fullerton [2]
Albert G. Gholson
Henry Haigwood [2]
Hugh A. Henry [2]
Hugh Henry
John R. Henry
William Henry
Chadison Jones [1]
Enoch M. Jones [1]
John Marlin
William N. P. Marlin [3]
Wilson Marlin
Robert H. Mathews
Joseph McCandless
Jeremiah McDaniel
Washington McGrew[2]
William A. McGrew
Andrew M. McMillan
George W. Morgan [1]
Jacob Plummer [2]
A. Jackson Powers [2]
Lewis B. Powers [1,4]
William C. Powers [4]
Wilson Reed
Charles Sauls [3]
Major Smith
Richard S. Teal
John Tucker
Cyrus L. Ward [2]
A. Jackson Webb [2]
John Welsh
(3 other names unknown)

[1] Wounded
[2] Killed outright
[3] Mortally wounded
[4] Erroneously listed as killed on Melton letter.

Source: Ethan Melton letter of January 16, 1839. Gulick, *The Papers of Mirabeau Buonaparte Lamar*, II: # 1016, 420.

> regain their horses, and ten were killed. None was killed in the action; they were all killed in the retreat.[19]

The Indians spared no mercy on the foot soldiers they overtook. A young man named Andrew Jackson Powers was one of those who had dismounted according to Stroud's early orders. He had suffered a broken arm in the battle but was able to jump onto the pony of William McGrew. His brother, William C. Powers, rode up on a larger horse in order to take the burden off McGrew's pony. He yelled for his brother to jump on behind him. Jackson Powers had great difficulty with his broken arm. As he struggled to swing onto the back of his brother's horse, the Indians rushed upon them with tomahawks. Jackson Powers perished. Hugh Henry and William Fullerton fought back-to-back with guns and knives until they both perished.[20]

David Campbell, who had fired the shot which struck Chief José María, was another of those caught on foot in the mass retreat. He was so preoccupied with fighting, in fact, that he did not at first observe the retreat. As the Indians suddenly rushed forward all around him, Campbell was narrowly spared his life by fellow volunteer Eli Chandler, who later served as a captain of rangers. Racing in on horseback, Chandler took Campbell on the back of his horse and raced away from the battleground.

In the fighting before the retreat was ordered, William N. P. Marlin was severely wounded in the hip. Unable to mount his horse, he was momentarily left behind until David Cobb raced up to throw him onto his horse, all amid a shower of rifle balls and arrows. Another man with a close escape was Wilson Reed, who was knocked from his horse during the retreat by a protruding tree limb. He was fortunate in that another fleeing Texan slowed long enough to carry him safely off.

Captain Bryant's volunteer party suffered eleven men killed, two more mortally wounded during the retreat and another five men wounded in the day's battle. The Indians were believed to have suffered about equal casualties. They were greatly elated with their victory over the whites. Chief José María later acknowledged that his men had been whipped and were retreating until he observed the confusion among the Texans. Many years later, José María visited the Bryant's Station community and offered Captain Bryant to smoke his pipe. Bryant insisted that the Indian chief smoke first since his Indians had won the battle. The old chief proudly accepted this offer. By the mid-1840s, José María's Andarkos were small in number and lived under the constant threat of attack from the Wacos and

The Bryant's Defeat battlefield is noted by this centennial marker along State Highway 6, located 4.5 miles south of Marlin in present Falls County. *Author's photo.*

Tawakonis. The chief and other Caddoan bands turned to Anglo authorities for protection and he became a proponent of peaceful relations with Anglo-Texans.

The battle between Bryant and Chief José María's men, labeled by some as "Bryant's Defeat," took place in present Falls County south of Perry and north of Marlin. A Texas historical marker identifies an "Indian Battlefield" on State Highway 6, four-and-a-half miles north of Marlin.[21]

The survivors of this poorly handled fight returned to their settlements and quickly sent out the word for more help. From Stroud's in Robertson County, Ethan Melton wrote a circular letter that was carried to other settlements. His express was dated January 16, 1839.

> This morning at 9 o'clock a battle was fought by 52 men principally of this county and as many or more Indians near the Falls of the Brazos. The whites had 13 killed and 5

wounded, 2 of them mortally. The greater part of the company are at Mr. Marlin's near the battle grounds guarding some women and children and have sent an express for from 50 to 100 recruits to assist in getting them away, also to bury the dead. There are many more Indians near them than were in the battle, beyond a doubt. If you can help us, come quickly—as many as can. The situation of these men is critical."[22]

Fortunately, Captain Daniels' Milam Guards were already en route from Houston. When Captain Bryant's surviving volunteers returned from their battle, the families near the Little River area began packing. At least five families had decided to fall back down to Stout's settlement, located about thirty-five miles below the area of George Morgan's home and the Bryant fight. They had only proceeded about a half mile on their way when they were met by the Milam Guards.

Captain Daniels found that their "settlement had been broken up by the Indians." He was able to convince the settlers to return to their homes. The condition was that his company would build a proper fort and provide protection to them for six weeks.[23]

Daniels and his company agreed and constructed a fort that Daniels noted was still standing in 1843. "The fort (the first and only one built by volunteers), was about 150 feet square, built of cedar pickets double banked, eleven feet high with bastions at each angle," he wrote.

Throughout January and into early February, the Milam Guards worked on the fort and performed daily patrols for the Little River citizens. They named this outpost Fort Milam, the second such establishment in the area to carry that name. Both stood in present Falls County, but the first had been on the west side of the Brazos closer to the falls.

They headed back for Houston about mid-February, once the settlers were content with the protection offered by their new fort. By February 12, Captain Daniels' company was still at Fort Milam at the Falls of the Brazos, where it took on 109 bushels of corn from Bryant's Fight veteran Albert Gholson. Another receipt of the Milam Guards shows them to be back in Houston as of February 21, 1839. On that date, Lieutenant John W. White turned over sixteen public horses, two mules, six saddles, and bridles and two blankets to Quartermaster Pinckney Caldwell.[24]

Captain Daniels was appointed as a captain in the First Regiment of Infantry on February 24, 1839, by Secretary of War Johnston. He was to dissolve his current duties and would receive his proper commission as soon as it was ratified by the Senate of Texas in their next session. This process apparently never occurred, for Daniels does not appear on the army's officer rolls during 1839 or 1840. An ordnance department note of October 7, 1839, from Colonel Hockley showed that "Captain Daniels of the Milam Guards will deliver to the order of Capt. Holliday twenty muskets belonging to the government."[25]

The work of Captain Daniels' company for the Little River citizens was in line with the thinking of President Lamar. He, of course, had proposed a line of frontier forts and a military road to be constructed through the remote Texas settlements. The recruiting for his new First Regiment had been slow thus far. Defense of the frontiers was largely handled by ranger companies and, in times of crisis, by hastily assembled volunteers.

The lessons learned from Bryant's Defeat would help the western settlements to be better prepared for their next Indian confrontations.

Chapter 7

Moore's Comanche Raid and the Battle of Brushy Creek

January 17–February 1839

Captain John Wortham's rangers mounted up and departed Fort Houston on January 22, expecting a confrontation with Indians. They had received reports that the Indians were on the move near Hall's trading post, which was located about twelve miles away on the Trinity River.

Wortham's frontiersmen had not reached the Trinity, however, when a courier raced up on horseback with a message from Lieutenant Colonel Jacob Snively. North of Fort Houston on the Neches River at the Neches Saline, Snively was still stationed with his Texas Ranger battalion. With him were the companies of captains James Timmins, James Cleveland, and Lewis Sánchez. In addition, he had two Indian companies, the largely Cherokee ranger company of Captain James Durst and Captain Panther's Mounted Shawnees. From camp on the fringe of the Cherokees' territory, Snively stated in his express that he fully expected to be attacked by a band of Indians the following morning.[1]

He thus requested help from the other two companies based out of Fort Houston. When the messenger arrived at the fort on the afternoon of January 22, Wortham's company had already departed for the Trinity. The strange tribe threatening to attack Snively's rangers was reported by the courier to be a division of the Creeks and Seminoles. A second courier was immediately dispatched by Captain James Box, commanding Fort Houston, to chase down Captain Wortham.

The news caused Wortham to immediately wheel his company around and ride back toward the Neches Saline. Since being designated as Houston County's rangers three week prior by the Texas Congress, Wortham's company continued to support the Third Militia Brigade. His company and Captain Box's Fort Houston rangers still ultimately reported to General Kelsey Douglass. Aside from these units and those stationed with Lieutenant Colonel Snively at the Saline, Colonel Willis Landrum still supervised three Third Regiment, Third Brigade mounted gunmen companies as of late January 1839. The companies of captains William P. Wyche, Joseph Ferguson, and John B. Gaines operated under Landrum's command without any known brushes with Indian forces.

Captain Wortham's men reached Fort Houston by 3:00 a.m. on January 23. By 9:00 a.m., they had departed with Captain Box's company to join Jacob Snively at the Neches Saline. That afternoon, some of the citizens of the Fort Houston settlement discovered the tracks of horses leading in two different directions near the fort. One of these sets of tracks would soon prove to be that of a party of Indians moving through the area. While the Houston County rangers were in the field near the Neches on January 23, the Indians committed a depredation against a family whose home was less than a mile from the fort.

★ ★ ★ ★ ★

Campbell Massacre: January 23, 1839

The family of Charles C. Campbell had settled near Fort Houston in 1837 on Town Creek, three miles east of present Palestine. Campbell passed away during mid-January 1839, leaving his wife, five children, and two slaves to work the fields.

On the night of January 23, a group of approximately fifteen Indians attacked the widow Campbell's home around 9:00 p.m. The neighing of the family's horses alerted them that strangers were approaching on this bright moonlit night. The attackers rushed the pioneer home while Mrs. Campbell and several of the children attempted to lock themselves in. The Indians furiously assaulted the wooden door with their tomahawks.[2]

Mrs. Campbell ripped up two of the puncheon boards from the floor and ordered her seventeen-year-old daughter Pamelia under the house with her four-year-old son George. The eldest son, twenty-year-old Malathiel Campbell, vainly attempted to ward off the attackers with the family's old rifle, only to find that it had a defective flint lock. As two of the children escaped under the floorboards, one of the Indians began forcing the door open far enough to reach in. He chopped almost through Mrs. Campbell's arm with a tomahawk and then the others burst into the room. They quickly slaughtered the widow, fourteen-year-old Hulda Campbell, and eleven-year-old Fountain Campbell.[3]

Malathiel Campbell made it from the house into the yard with only a knife with which to defend himself. He was shot down and killed by the Indians outside. The family's servants were allowed to escape unharmed and the older male slave ran for Fort Houston to alert others. During the commotion, Pamelia Campbell and her young brother George crawled out from under the house and tried to sneak away. The Indians spotted her and opened fire with bows and arrows. One arrow sliced across Pamelia's forehead, but fortunately did not penetrate her skull. Bleeding profusely, she fled through the thicket with her little brother for Fort Houston. They arrived in a panic and reported the slaughter of their family. Pamelia Campbell would sport the arrow wound on her forehead for the rest of her life.

The Campbell home was ransacked by the Indians, who ripped open the feather beds and scattered the feathers. They stole a keg of gunpowder, some bedding, clothing, paper money, and a trunk containing $400 worth of silver.

The servant reached the rangers at Fort Houston about 10:00 p.m. on January 23 and he relayed the distressing news. The Fort Houston postmaster, William S. McDonald, wrote that Pamelia Campbell and her brother reached the fort before midnight.

> The eldest daughter and youngest son of Mrs. Campbell have reached this place without any serious injury, except a slight wound the young lady received from an arrow on her forehead in attempting to make her escape. There are yet four of the family missing. The negro man gives an account of one of the women that is missing, being shot and falling and suppose he heard her agonizing and struggling. He thinks the remainder of the family that are missing were killed.[4]

Captain Wortham's ranger company, which had departed Fort Houston that morning, did not make contact with the Indian party. Another armed pursuit party, likely headed by Captain Box, was assembled and departed from the fort for the Campbell residence. These men found the Campbells' trunk, paper money, and the empty powder keg discarded about a mile from the home. The trail of the Indians was followed some eight miles to the Trinity River, but the chase was given up at this point. The lands on the west side of the Trinity were more heavily populated with hostile Indians and such a small band of men could not effectively wage a battle against them.[5]

Postmaster William McDonald had accompanied this party to the Campbell home. He noted on January 24 that the family members had been "all killed in the house or near. I saw them myself, and such a scene I never saw before." He quickly penned a letter to Captain William Sadler, the postmaster and regular army officer posted at Fort Brown just farther south. McDonald addressed his plea to the "people of Houston County" and asked for "as much assistance as can be afforded us." Calling the Campbell depredation an "awful massacre," McDonald asked Sadler to spread the word. "You will please forward this or a copy of it to Nacogdoches and one to Crockett and if possible one in the direction of the city of Houston."

The Campbell Massacre helped to ensure that the militia maintained a strong presence in Houston County during 1839. Congress passed a supplementary militia act on January 24, 1839, which enabled President Lamar to appoint such persons as might be necessary to enforce militia laws. Those trying to avoid militia service could now be punished with a $500 fine, to be assessed by court martial.[6] By the first supplementary militia act of December 18, 1837, every county was charged with participating in its own protection.

Each county was to have been broken up into militia districts with a fifty-six-man or more company created in each district. On February 15, 1839, President Lamar issued a proclamation ordering the completion of the organization of the militia. This work was to be directed by the chief justice of each county, with the sheriff assisting if necessary. In the absence of a chief justice, the duty of organizing the militia fell upon the county's sheriff.

In the case of Houston County, three militia districts were created in early 1839 to better protect its citizens. In addition to the ranging companies in the area, a militia company under Captain Balis Edens is known to have been in operation during the early part of the year. His company was under orders of Third Brigade General Kelsey Douglass and was stationed at Brown's Fort near San Pedro Creek.

Evidence of Edens' company can be found in a promissory note issued to George W. Wilson on February 28, 1839, for supplying thirty bushels of corn to men in the field. This note was signed at Brown's Fort by William Miller, commissary, and approved by Captain Edens, General Douglass, and Quartermaster John S. Roberts. Armstead Bennett and Thomas Lagow were later compensated by Texas for providing corn to the militia. One of their receipts was signed "Brown's Fort, Feb. 28, 1839."[7]

It does not appear that Captain Edens' company remained in operation for more than a couple months, as the San Pedro area soon fell under direction of Captain Benjamin W. Davis. The new three-district militia for the county included Davis supervising the San Pedro and

Neches settlement areas. Captain John Crist, one of the original Fort Houston settlers, controlled the militia district of Crockett and Mustang Prairie. Captain William Sadler was superintendent of the district which included Fort Houston, where Captain Box's rangers remained on duty.

In the days after the Campbell Massacre, Captain Box tried to enlist more men into the ranging service to protect the Fort Houston settlement. One quartermaster correspondence note shows that he had sent William Wilkinson of his company to Nacogdoches via Crockett to recruit.[8]

Lieutenant Colonel Snively's Third Militia Brigade ranger battalion only served a short time after the Campbell Massacre. The Indian companies of captains Durst and Panther were disbanded on January 25. Captain Sánchez's rangers returned to Nacogdoches and were discharged on January 27. Snively's staff was paid through February 2, 1839. Captain Cleveland and Captain Timmins' men had returned home and disbanded by February 5 and 6, respectively. After this time, the ranging duties in East Texas were left up to the county companies and to the rangers under Major Baley Walters. Payroll records show that Major Walters' Mounted Texas Rangers Staff went into service on February 14, 1839.

On February 8, Captain John Wortham was promoted to major within the Third Brigade and he continued to serve as the regional supervisor of the Houston County ranging companies. He oversaw Captain Box's company and that of Captain Solomon Adams, who took over Major Wortham's old company.

President Lamar on February 14, 1839, appointed Martin Lacy as an "agent, to act as the organ of communication between the government and the Cherokees, Shawnees, and other Indian tribes." His special appointment was designed to "cultivate and preserve the friendly relations existing between the frontier inhabitants of Texas and the Indian tribes." He was particularly charged with dealing with those tribes such as the Shawnees and Cherokees who had emigrated to Texas soil from the United States whose occupation of their soil was not yet recognized by the Republic of Texas. In fact, their territorial rights were a "grave deliberation on the part of the Texian Government."[9]

Any aggressive movements by the Indians were to be reported by Lacy to the government. Lamar regarded the prairie Indians as possessing "atrocious conduct" that was still being dealt with. Lacy was to encourage Cherokees and other "friendly tribes" to show their own good intentions by "prohibiting any intercourse" with the hostile tribes. Lamar appointed Lacy to this position because of his "extensive knowledge of the Indian character."

★ ★ ★ ★ ★

Frontier Regiment's New Officers

On January 24, 1839, President Lamar was authorized and required by Congress to discharge all officers and soldiers in service of Texas who did not fall under the use of the new Frontier Regiment or its required ordnance department. Thus, by February 1839, Texas was serviced by four government-recognized military forces: 1) the new Frontier Regiment; 2) the eight-company mounted rifleman brigade to be recruited by Colonel Henry Karnes; 3) the county ranger companies specifically approved by congress during January 1839; and 4) the Texas Militia, whose enlistees were required to perform service in their respective counties.

The militia would shortly come under close scrutiny during 1839 as Lamar forced the issue of mandatory enlistments. In addition to these forces, Texas pioneer settlements would continue to be protected by local citizen groups, who generally formed in a hurry to combat some Indian menace.

The legislation of January 24 also revised the Texas Militia, whose brigade generals had been designated by congress in December 1837. A provision had been included that these key positions and that of the major general should be re-elected by the people during 1839. President Lamar would delay making his proclamation for the required voting until September 11. The elections, held on the second Monday in November, were used to select the new senior militia officers. Due to delays in counties reporting their votes, the new major general of the Texas Militia and the respective brigadier generals were not announced until March 7, 1840. They would be Major General Felix Huston and Alexander Somervell, Edwin Morehouse, James Smith, and Edward H. Tarrant being elected as brigadier generals for the First, Second, Third, and Fourth Brigades, respectively.[10]

To help pay for the expanding military expenditures in Texas, President Lamar approved a new congressional plan to issue large quantities of non-interest bearing notes which would be discounted almost .63 on the dollar when first issued. The paper currency issued by President Houston had been backed by the value of public land and the Republic's credit, but this was soon considered shaky.[11]

The Third Congress appropriated a budget of $1,520,455 for military expenditures in 1839. Army expenditures comprised $1,140,000 of the total, up from the Texas government's total 1838 fiscal year army expenses of $831,401.

Most of the officers of Lamar's new Frontier Regiment were appointed by congress on January 23, 1839. Another group of army officers was appointed on January 30 and others were added as needed throughout the year. Colonel Edward Burleson, a popular leader who had previously commanded militia, army, and ranger regiments, was elected to command the First Regiment of Infantry. William S. Fisher, who had commanded a company at San Jacinto and later served as secretary of war, became his lieutenant colonel and Peyton S. Wyatt was selected as major of infantry.

Colonel Lysander Wells, a cavalry commander under Henry Karnes previously, became the senior officer of the First Regiment of Cavalry. President Lamar reinstated Colonel Hugh McLeod as his adjutant general of the army, a post he had held during his 1838 campaigns with General Rusk. Many of the other new army officers were veterans of the Texas Revolution who had been active in the army. Others, such as Isaac Burton, William Sadler, William Moore, and Timothy O'Neill, were experienced leaders of the ranging service.

Recruiting for the Frontier Regiment began earnestly in January, with major recruiting posts staffed in Houston, Galveston, and Matagorda. Additional recruiting was done in Velasco and Clarksville during the early part of the year. Later in the year, officers were stationed in New Orleans to forward new recruits from the United States to Galveston for enlistment. Several of these recruiting captains later took command of their own companies as enlistment grew in late 1839 and early 1840.[12]

The enlisted soldiers of Lamar's new army were generally paid sixteen dollars per month. The company commanders were paid forty dollars per month, which was supplemented by eight dollars per month for clothing, $2.50 for forage for his horse, plus thirty dollars per month for food rations.

Colonel Burleson made his First Regiment of Infantry headquarters close to home in Bastrop. Recruits received from west of the Brazos River fell under his First Battalion of the First Regiment. Those recruited east of the Brazos fell under the Second Battalion, which was superintended by Lieutenant Colonel Fisher and Major Wyatt. Enlistments into the First Regiment increased dramatically following the summer of 1839, likely spurred by news of the Texas Indian wars.

Original Officer Appointments Of The Frontier Regiment
(Appointed January 23, 1839, unless otherwise noted)

Colonel, First Regiment Infantry:
Edward Burleson
Colonel, First Regiment Cavalry:
Lysander Wells [1]
Adjutant General:
Hugh McLeod [1]
Quartermaster General:
Isaac Watts Burton [1]
Commissary General of Subsistence:
William Gordon Cooke [1]
Inspector General:
Peter Hansbrough Bell [1]
Lt. Colonel, First Regiment Infantry:
William S. Fisher
Lt. Colonel, First Regiment Cavalry:
Peter Bartelle Dexter [1]
Major, First Regiment Infantry:
Peyton S. Wyatt
Major, First Regiment Cavalry:
William Jefferson Jones [1]
Quartermaster:
Pinckney C. Caldwell [1]
Assistant Adjutant General:
Benjamin H. Johnson [1]
Paymaster General:
Benjamin B. Sturgess [1]
Jacob Snively [2]
Major, Commissary of Subsistence:
John Forbes [1]
Hillequist Landers [1]
William Leslie Cazneau [3]
Colonel, Commissary of Purchases:
William Henry Dangerfield
Col., Commissary General of Ordnance:
George Washington Hockley [2]
Surgeon General:
William R. Smith [4]
Surgeons:
Ezra Read [1]
Thomas P. Anderson [1]
Shields Booker [1]
Edmund Tucker [5]
Assistant Surgeon:
Richard Cochran [5]
Captain, First Regiment Infantry:
William Davis Redd
Adam Clendenin
Samuel W. Jordan
George Thomas Howard
H. W. Davis
John J. Holliday
Benjamin Y. Gillen [1]
Martin Kingsley Snell [1]
Robert Oliver [1]
Mark Blake Skerrett [1]
George F. Laurence [1]
George Washington Morgan [1]
William H. Moore [1]
William Turner Sadler [1]
James Belvarde Pope January [1]
First Lieut., First Regiment Infantry:
James C. P. Kennymore
Palmer Job Pillans
William Green Kerley
James Goodall
O. P. Kelton [1]
Samuel Price Carson [1]
Duncan Campbell Ogden [1]
Edward Adams Thompson [1]
William N. Dunnington [1]
Joseph M. Wiehl [1]
Robert Simpson Neighbors [1]
Martin Moran [1]
Davis Verplank Ackermann [1]
Alenson T. Miles [1]
William H. Crutchir [1]
Second Lieut., First Regiment Infantry:
George N. Palmer
William D. Houghton
John Schuyler Sutton
William Redfield
John Brown
Henry L. Grush [1]
Daniel Lacry [1]
Collier C. Hornsby [1]
Timothy O'Neil [1]
W. Hufton [1]
Daniel Lewis [1]
Abram H. Scott [2]
James M. Alexander [6]
Matthew McGovern [7]

[1] Appointed January 30, 1839.
[2] Appointed March 23, 1839.
[3] Appointed October 25, 1839.
[4] Appointed July 20, 1839.
[5] Appointed April 6, 1839.
[6] Appointed February 20, 1839.
[7] Appointed November 15, 1839.

★ ★ ★ ★ ★

Red River Rangers of Early 1839

During the early months of 1839, several ranger companies remained in service to patrol the areas of the Fourth Militia Brigade. In spite of the rangers' presence, the Indians continued to commit depredations.

On January 29, two sons of the McIntire family on Choctaw Bayou in Fannin County were killed in an Indian attack. At this time, Captain William Stout's rangers had taken station at Fort Sherman, which they had helped construct in December. This post was located near present Farm Road 21's crossing over Cypress Creek in Titus County, about thirteen miles southwest of Mount Pleasant. Stout's company had been left on duty by General Rusk to combat Indians and to range "from the Cross Timbers down to Lake Soda."[13]

According to Stout, it was February 8 or 9 when Indians killed at least three more settlers in Fannin County. Two men, named George Garner and Camp, were ambushed and killed in Fannin County while another man by the name of Keithley from Arkansas was killed at his residence the same morning. Captain Stout later related that these were the only five known murders committed during the winter or summer of 1839 in that section of the country. "Their deaths went unrevenged," he wrote. "The Indians could not be caught and were not retaliated upon."

Another ranger company in operation in Red River County at the time of these depredations was that of Captain Mark R. Roberts, whose unit had been mustered into service just a week after General Dyer's winter expedition to the Three Forks closed out. Roberts had previously served under Captain Robert Sloan through January 14, 1839, on which date he assumed command of his own twelve-man unit. Three other men previously under Sloan extended their service for another three months. Captain Roberts gave a written report of the Red River area murders, which he numbered as seven, to the secretary of war.

> In the month of Decr last, Genl Rusk promoted me from the grade of first lieut in a ranging company to the grade of Captain with orders to raise a company of rangers to continue on the frontiers of this county and at the same time continued Capt N. T. Journey's company in the service until the 14th March.

> In the month of Feby there was seven persons murdered by the Indians near Journey's Camp and the Indians made their retreat across Red River. We then believed them to be Caddo or Kickapoo, but lately we have been visited by a band of Cherokee Indians from Arkansas, who stole 20 head of horses. They were pursued to the nation and the horses found, and also one of the horses of the murdered men in February last seen among them, which is a convincing proof that the murder was done by the same Indians.
>
> I was ranging on the waters of the Trinity when the murders were committed and then was not able to ascertain any information as to the route the enemy had come from that struck the blow, as there was no trace of their trails to be found in the direction that we expected an enemy from. Those murders was committed in the very bosom of the country, and on the banks of Red River where no rangers are ranging, and unless the United States can compel her Indians to remain peaceable, we will be compelled to keep a company on the river to range up and down to prevent similar depredations.[14]

Captain Roberts further related that Captain Journey's company had gone after the Cherokees who had stolen American horses during February. The party was only able to recover three horses, but received the promise of General Armstrong, an agent for the United States for the western Indians, that he would "try to recover the property of our citizens." Journey's men found the Indians too strong to fight and left General Armstrong to try his luck.

Journey's company was disbanded in March, while Roberts remained on duty through April 13, 1839. After disbanding his own company, Roberts wrote to Secretary of War Albert Sidney Johnston on May 28 in hopes of organizing another unit.

> I discharged my company on the 14th April at which time there was a company raised to range on the south of this county, where I had ranged for the 7 months previous. I have been requested to ask of the government 20 men to range up and down the Red River for the purpose of defending the settlements against the depredations of the United States Indians, and if the government should think proper to raise such a company and order me to raise it, I will take a pleasure in obeying the summons to the defense of the country, and such a company can be raised in a very short notice.

The ranging company Mark Roberts made reference to was that of Captain John Emberson, an early settler of Red River who had mustered in his volunteers from Red River and Fannin counties on March 16, 1839. Both Roberts and Emberson's rangers operated under the direction of Lieutenant Colonel Montague's Second Regiment of the Fourth Militia Brigade.

After the rangers of captains Journey and Roberts completed service, the next company to muster out was that of Captain Stout, whose men had been on duty since November 1838. During his company's six-month service, he said that they were "active and vigilant but not able to accomplish much, owing to the scanty supply of subsistence and other hindrances."[15] Stout's rangers, although unsuccessful in finding a fight with the Indians, had constructed Fort Sherman, Fort Rusk, and Fort DeKalb and also assisted at Inglish's, Montague's, and at Coffin's station.

Captain Stout had some difficulty in keeping his men on duty at their regular Fort Sherman station. Since many of them had only enlisted for a three-month period, about seven of his men resolved to go back home when their three months began to expire in late February. When Stout forbade this, a difficulty ensued.

Lieutenant John M. Watson and two others had to restrain their furious commander. In the end, the rebellious soldiers were forced to serve three months longer, as Stout later wrote.

> The ringleader was kept confined for some time until he manifested repentance. Captain Stout acted in this matter under the act which said that men enlisted for one tour (which is three months) may be compelled to extend their service to two tours (six months) if the exigencies of the country required it. He also had an order from General Dyer to pursue the course he did.

During the last days of their service, Stout's rangers brought in the five provision wagons that had been abandoned during the luckless Rusk/Dyer expedition the previous December. The wagons "had been much damaged by the Indians, who had taken off many of the irons and had abused the woodwork by chopping it with their hatchets."

Stout's company was disbanded on May 26, 1839, leaving Captain Emberson's company as the only militia or ranger unit in active service in the Red River area. His men ranged in the upper frontier of Fannin County and reportedly killed three Indians in a skirmish during July.

★ ★ ★ ★ ★

Col. Moore's Comanche Raid: February 15, 1839

During the Republic years, the Comanche and Lipan Indians were bitter enemies. The Lipans were a branch of the Apache tribe, but an old feud had caused rival Chief Lipan to branch off and start his own band in another part of the country. These Indians adopted the name Lipan for their tribe. Chiefs Flaco and Castro were very cooperative with ranger and army forces in the areas of present Austin. Flaco hated the Comanches and cherished the opportunity to fight against them.[16]

The Colorado River area settlers were much disturbed by the violent depredations carried out in January and were still stinging from the bitter defeat of Captain Bryant's volunteers. By January 21, veteran Indian fighter John Henry Moore was organizing a ranger company in La Grange in present Fayette County for service as frontier protectors. Moore, of course, had led the first ranger expedition during the summer of 1835 and had organized the Gonzales fight that opened the Texas Revolution. The company elected Captain William Eastland, a former ranger captain, as its leader and mustered in on January 21, 1839, as the "La Grange Company Volunteers."[17]

In neighboring Bastrop County, the citizens were also organizing their own ranger company, as authorized by congress on January 23. Approximately thirty men enlisted and they elected their senior officers on January 24 to be Captain Noah Smithwick and First Lieutenant Noel M. Bain. Smithwick had been involved with many of the early ranger companies of Texas since the revolution. He had served in the same battalion as Eastland for most of 1837. Serving as adjutant of Moore's new expedition was William Bugg, a veteran of Captain Daniel Monroe's 1837 rangers.

The organization of such county ranging companies was timely, for Lipan Indian scouts discovered that a band of their rival Comanches was camping on the San Gabriel River. The Lipans alerted John Moore in La Grange and they offered to help drive off the Comanches. Captain Smithwick's Bastrop rangers joined Captain Eastland's La Grange volunteers on January 25. Colonel Moore assumed overall command of the two Texan units and the friendly Lipans.

The muster rolls for the companies of Eastland and Smithwick no longer exist, but Colonel Moore reportedly commanded 109 total volunteers. This number included fifty-five whites, forty-two Lipans, and twelve Tonkawa Indians. The Lipans were commanded by Chief

Castro, whose company included his son Juan Castro, young Chief Flaco, and lieutenant Juan Seis (Quansise).[18]

Moore's expedition departed La Grange on January 26 with the intent of driving the Comanches from the area before they had the opportunity to raid the settlements. One of Captain Eastland's rangers was poor Andrew Lockhart of the Guadalupe area, whose beautiful daughter Matilda had been taken captive by the Indians several months prior, along with the four Putman children.

When the Texans in early February reached the point on the San Gabriel River where the Comanches had been reported, they found that their enemy had moved. The Indians left an easy trail to follow, which led up this stream. The expedition encountered severe winter weather about February 10, however, as Captain Smithwick later recalled.

> We followed on up to the head of the San Gabriel, where we were overtaken by a storm of snow and sleet which was so severe that we were obliged to seek shelter. We made for a grove of post oaks on the divide between the San Gabriel and Colorado, in the shelter of which we struck camp. The storm continued with increasing cold. Some of the horses froze to death, and the Indians, loth to see so much good meat go to waste, ate the flesh. Three days and nights we remained there.[19]

While camped out during the heavy storm, the men suffered from lack of food as well as the bitter cold. The expedition had started out with little more than coffee, salt, and some bacon, as the poor weather had not been anticipated. While battling the cold, scouts Joe Anderson and Felix McCluskey went out to hunt game. They returned to camp and reported to Moore that they had sighted a large band of Indians marching through the country toward home. Perhaps due to the extreme winter conditions, their alarm went unheeded for the time being.[20]

There was also a tragedy in camp as the men weathered the storm. Campfires were maintained throughout the day and night for the men and the horses to survive. One of the Lipans, while carrying firewood, accidentally bumped a gun which had been propped against a tree. The loaded gun fell down and discharged, shooting through the body of Private George Wilson of Captain Eastland's company.

Some of the men became discouraged by this accident and the severe weather and wanted to turn back. Colonel Moore finally decided to move his camp over to the Colorado River, where game had been driven by the storm. Here, the men were able to kill wild cattle and begin constructing a boat of hides in which to transport the severely wounded Wilson down the river to the lower settlements.[21]

Another of Eastland's soldiers was seventeen-year-old Private Rufus Perry, who had previously fought with Captain William Hill's rangers in an Indian battle on the Yegua in 1836. Perry later wrote his recollections of this expedition.

> It was snowing at the time and for two days we had nothing to eat or drink except coffee. The third day I killed 11 deer and 2 buffalo. We carried the wounded man to the Colorado.[22]

The storm died off on the fourth day, February 13, at which time Captain Smithwick took a Lipan scout out in search of the Comanches, whose trail had been obliterated by the snow. They followed the Colorado to the mouth of the San Saba River. Upon climbing a hill overlooking the valley, they saw smoke rising from a camp some miles up on the San Saba. They turned back for Moore's camp, traveling through the night. They made it back to camp after daybreak the next morning.[23]

In their absence, Captain Eastland's men finished constructing a boat of buffalo hides for George Wilson. Two others from his company piloted the boat and set out to take him to seek medical help in Austin. The wounded soldier died en route, however, on the second day. His comrades used the blade bone of a buffalo to dig his grave and he was buried in the sand along the river's banks.[24]

Camp was broken on the morning of February 14 as the men saddled up and started on their way up the Colorado for the Indian camp. Colonel Moore wrote a detailed report of this expedition several weeks later.

> We marched about an hour under cover of the timber of the Colorado bottom. We then deposited our packs and baggage in a place of security, and proceeded onward, still seeking the cover of timber and valley, to a place about 10 miles from the village.[25]

Moore halted his men and sent forward his spies again, two Lipans in company with Malcolm Hornsby and Joe Martin from Smithwick's company. Upon returning, they reported that the Comanche camp was much larger than previously reported.

"Disconcerted by the unexpected intelligence, Colonel Moore was rather demurred to attacking," wrote Smithwick, "but we had come out to hunt a fight and were willing to take the responsibility." One intrepid volunteer declared that he didn't care if there "were a thousand of them, if there were horses enough to justify the fight."[26]

The Texans remained in place until after sunset, after which time they proceeded to within a mile of the village, halting in the cover of a ravine. "We dismounted and tied our horses in a valley," recorded Moore, "and having put eight Lipans on horseback, with orders to stampede the enemy's *caballardo*, proceeded on foot to within 300 yards of the town, still keeping our spies in advance."

The Comanche camp was located on a small stream called Spring Creek in the valley of the San Saba River. The morning of February 15 was clear and frosty and the Texans were in a favorable position for surprising their foe, totally undiscovered. The Texan horses remained tied in a cedar brake while the rangers and their Indian scouts waited silently for sunrise. At a given signal, every man understood his duty. Chief Castro, with a portion of his Indians, was to stampede the horses grazing in the valley and rush with them beyond recovery. The whites and remaining Indians were to charge into the Comanche village.[27]

According to Colonel Moore, Captain Eastland's La Grange company formed the right wing of the advance. Captain Smithwick's Bastrop company took the center and Chief Castro's Lipans took the left. As light sufficiently distinguished friend from foe, the signal was given. With thirty of his people, young Juan Castro soon had a thousand or more loose horses thundering over hill and dale toward the south. His father, Chief Castro, and Flaco remained with about twelve Lipans and twelve Tonkawas to attack with Moore's forces. Moore stated that the number of men involved in the battle was sixty-three whites and sixteen Indians, totaling seventy-nine fighters.

Moore wrote that Eastland's company marched

> in advance, down between the timber and the village, whose skirts run parallel to each other, for the purpose of having the timber in our rear, and driving the enemy towards the prairie. When opposite the center of the town, we were discovered by the enemy, at which moment I ordered a charge, which was promptly obeyed and carried to near the center of the village, the men throwing open the doors of the wigwams or pulling them down and slaughtering the enemy in their beds. It was now discovered that the opposite side, which had been supposed to

> have opened to the level prairie, was bordered by a meander of the bayou, which formed a deep and a secure place of retreat into which the savages had fled, and in which they had already rallied and formed for defense.[28]

The first light of morning had been enough for Moore's men to begin their attack. The ensuing volume of rifle shots filled the air about the camp with smoke which added to the confusion and hampered distance vision. As the Texans fired into the buffalo skin tents and wigwams, the entire campground soon became filled with warriors yelling and women and children crying.

The Comanches lost their war chief, Quinaseico, early in the slaughter and this threw them into distress for a time. During the first charge, DeWitt Lyons called loudly for his brother Warren, who had previously been taken captive by the Comanches.[29]

During the height of the assault, the Indian women and children wildly fled the scene to the bottomlands and the neighboring thickets. It was in this instant, amid the screams and war whoops, that Andrew Lockhart ran ahead of his comrades, screaming out for his daughter Matilda to "run to me!" The poor child had already been lashed into a run with the retreating Indian women, although she heard her father's pitiful cries for her. When she was recovered in 1840, she claimed to have screamed as loudly as she could, but her cries for help had been lost in the gunfire and commotion.[30]

The Texans soon became mixed up in the tents among the Indians and were in danger of shooting one another in the ensuing madness. Colonel Moore noted the confusion and the fact that the Comanche Indians far outnumbered his little force. He therefore ordered his men to retreat back to a nearby ravine, where they took up a defensive position for the expected retaliation.[31] Moore's men reloaded their weapons as the scattered Comanches regrouped in the deep meander of the bayou along Spring Creek. The only casualty thus far for the Texans had been Captain Eastland, who suffered a slash from an arrow that cut his nose.

The Indians accompanying Moore's forces formed in line and advanced an attack on the thoroughly aroused Comanches. One of the enemy warriors, under cover of his shield, advanced in front of his comrades and flourished his bow, delivering a challenge to the whites. Jim Manor of Bastrop took careful aim and dropped this Comanche to the ground. The other Comanches then made a charge to retrieve their downed warrior, but a fierce fusillade from the Texans drove them back.

Colonel Moore's Comanche Campaign: January–February 1839

Colonel John Henry Moore — William Bugg, Adjutant

Capt. Eastland's La Grange Volunteers: Jan. 21–Feb. 26, 1839

Captain:
William M. Eastland [1]
First Lieutenant:
Nicholas M. Dawson
Privates:
Garrett E. Boome
John H. Burnam
Isaac D. Coulter
John Y. Criswell
Socrates Darling
Smallwood S. B. Fields[1]
Beriah Grover
James S. Houston
Zadock Hubbard
Jacob Humphreys
Theodore S. Lee
Andrew Lockhart
DeWitt C. Lyons
William B. Meriwether
Jesse C. Pendleton
John W. Pendleton
Cicero Rufus Perry
Benjamin Phillips
Samuel S. Pipes
James Price
John Rabb
Albert Redfield
Henry P. Redfield
M. C. Rountree
Lyman M. Stewart
Martin Felix Taylor [1]
George Wilson [2]
E. S. Woolley

[1] Wounded in battle.
[2] Accidentally killed.

Capt. Smithwick's Bastrop Rangers: January 24–February 25, 1839

Captain:
Noah Smithwick
First Lieutenant:
Noel M. Bain
Privates:
Joseph Anderson
Arnold Bird
John Bryan
Ross Byars
Alexander M. Cameron
William A. Clopton
James M. Dickson
Samuel Fowler
Cyrus K. Gleason
Wm. P. Hardeman
Abel Harness
Milton Hicks
Malcolm M. Hornsby
Ira Leffingwell [1]
James Manor
Joseph S. Martin [2]
Felix McCluskey
Thomas McKernon
Patrick Moore
William Newcomb
Francis Ward
Henry Gonzalvo Woods
Jacob Zengerle

[1] Wounded in battle.
[2] Mortally wounded.

Captain Castro's Mounted Lipan Volunteers

Captain:
Castro
1st Lieutenant:
Quansise
Privates:
Casa
John Castro
Charcia
Conpah
Coshatee
Eisashlishta
Ellorttes
Fernando
Flaco
Ganto
Gosly
Hawneeky
Helliama
Hoesky
Hosey (Jose)
Jack
Joshua
Manuel
Moccasin
Muess
Mundoisi
Musconttish
Neckinina
Nehelki
Neuhantis
Nuchl
Pecar
Pehenial
Platta
Saeonkell
Satella
Sechi
Sentika
Shilkoe
Shindial
Slarshal
P. Sockersiss
Sockins
Tazazanto
Tohotoliny

Captain Placido's Mounted Tonkawa Volunteers

Twelve Indian volunteers. No muster roll available.

Sources: Captain Castro muster roll courtesy of Texas State Archives. Eastland and Smithwick muster rolls represent author's research of Republic of Texas audited military claims.

Captain Smithwick later recalled the young Lipan Flaco's desire to finish off this enemy.

> That Indian then lay there flat on his back and shot arrows upward so that they fell point foremost among our men, till young Flaco ran out in the midst of a perfect rain of arrows and dispatched him with his lance.[32]

Flaco took the Comanche's shield, but was unable to retrieve the ceremonious scalp due to heavy fire. The Comanches were driven back again. Lipan First Lieutenant Juan Seis, listed on the Indian company's muster roll as "Quansise," then decided he would advance and retrieve the coveted scalp from the downed enemy. Since the Texans could not fire against the enemy without endangering him, Seis was not allowed to make his advance.

Some of the men later recalled a light moment when a little Irishman named Pat Moore crawled to the edge of the bluff and tauntingly presented his cocked gun to the Indians. "What are you doing, Pat?" some called. "Your gun is not loaded!" Undaunted, he retorted, "Hush! Bejabers, they don't know it!"[33]

The Comanches continued to try to drive Moore's forces from their ravine. After two charges failed to dislodge the rangers, longer range firing continued for some time. At 10:00 a.m., Colonel Moore dispatched ten spies "by the way of the bayou, to reconnoiter, who returned soon after and reported the enemy very numerous."[34]

Moore's force stayed in their position for more than another hour, at which time the Comanches had ceased firing. Ranger Rufus Perry stated that the fighting continued near the gully until about 2:00 p.m. "Having abandoned the hope of being able with so few men to force them from the strong position they occupied in the rear," Moore wrote, "I ordered litters to be prepared for our wounded, and soon after retired to the place at which we had left our horses."

The cedar brake in which the horses were tied was about a mile away. The Texans had by this time suffered four men wounded but none killed. Moore continues:

> In fifteen or twenty moments after our arrival at this place, we were surrounded by a large body of the enemy, who, I believe, were between three and five hundred in number, who immediately opened a fire upon us, which was soon silenced, and a white flag (the same presented to them last summer at the seat of government by the President, Sam Houston)

approached, carried by a woman, accompanied by a man.

A parley ensued, in which she stated that they had five white prisoners, one a woman about middle age; understood to have been captured on the Brazos River; a girl about fifteen years of age, supposed to be the daughter of one of our company, Andrew Lockhart, captured on the Guadalupe; the other three were children, captured at the same place a short time since. This information, I believe, was given because they were under the impression that we had some of their prisoners, which they wished to exchange for, as some prisoners had been taken by the Lipans, which they killed or otherwise disposed of without advice from me. They also made some statements relative to their great numbers, which were constantly increasing, and the cooperation of the Shawnees, who were near. To which was replied, our numbers are small, come on!

Lieutenant Juan Seis (Quansise) of the Lipans served as the translator for this parley. He bluffed to the Comanches that the Texans had not suffered one man wounded in the fighting thus far. The Comanches had apparently suffered enough losses for one day, including Chief Quinaseico. They elected at this point to allow Moore's small forces to withdraw without further fight.

The attack was not resumed again after this point. Realizing how badly outnumbered his men were, Moore ordered his men to fall back to their horses. The more seriously wounded men were carried in the hastily-constructed litters. Those in the worst shape were Martin Felix Taylor of Eastland's company and Joe Martin of Smithwick's. Taylor had been shot in the knee, while Martin had taken a bullet in the back which paralyzed his legs.

Martin implored Captain Smithwick to shoot him dead and leave him behind, in order not to slow the others' retreat. Smithwick refused, and Martin begged, "Then give me your pistol and I will shoot myself." Martin and Taylor were instead hauled on their litters onward. The others wounded in varying degrees had been Captain Eastland, Jim Manor, Ira Leffingwell, and Smallwood S. B. Fields, the latter a lawyer from La Grange. One Lipan was also wounded, bringing the total number to seven volunteers wounded in action, one mortally.[35]

The situation looked worse for the Texans when they found that the Comanches had managed to steal all their horses during the time that the Lipans under Juan Castro had been stealing the Comanches' own herd.

The audited military papers of Captain Smithwick show that he lost his horse while "on the campaign against the Comanche Indians under the command of Colonel John H. Moore." Two of his rangers, James Manor and William Newcomb, decided the value of their captain's horse to be two hundred dollars. They affirmed the fact that it had been "captured by the Comanches on the San Saba on the 14th day of February, 1839."[36]

Moore reported that during his expedition, his men lost a total of forty-six horses, "including those which had previously died from various causes." As for the number of enemy Comanches they had killed, he wrote:

> The number killed on the part of the enemy, it was impossible to know, but must have been very considerable. Our men were furnished with about three shots each, which, during the first attack upon the village, were discharged with great accuracy, at only a few feet distance, and in many instances, by placing the muzzle against the object; add to this, their exposed condition in their repeated attacks upon us, and the unerring accuracy of our riflemen, justifies the belief that their loss must have been very great. In supposing their loss to have been thirty or forty killed, and fifty or sixty wounded, I make an estimate much below what I believe to be correct.[37]

Ranger Rufus Perry later stated that "Forty-eight Comanches were also killed and many more wounded."[38] Less conservative estimates of those directly killed and those who would die of their wounds put Comanches losses at more than one hundred. Moore's battle report gave credit to some, but not all, of his senior officers for their conduct on the field. It is interesting to note that he gave no praise to Captain Smithwick nor to Captain Castro for their roles.

> Much credit is due to Capt. Wm. M. Eastland and Lieut. N. W. Dawson, also to Lieut. N. M. Bain, of the Bastrop company, and Adj't Wm. Bugg, for the strict and prompt obedience to orders, and their general officer-like conduct, and to the men and officers in general for their bravery on the field of battle, and their subordination and good conduct.

Following the battle, the Texan volunteers found themselves in a sad predicament. The Comanches had captured their horses. The disillusioned Lipans under Chief Castro had left the battlefield and proceeded homeward ahead of Moore's forces, taking with them all of the captured mules and horses.

According to the memoirs of Smithwick, Chief Castro became so disgusted when Colonel Moore was forced to order his troops to retreat that he took his Lipan band with him and departed. Rufus Perry wrote that the Indians maintained a strong presence near the Texans during late afternoon but did not attack again.

> We fell back to where we had left our horses. We found no horses, blankets, or saddles worth taking. Comanches had gotten away with everything we had, including provisions. Five hundred scoundrels surrounded us and kept us at bay until dark, when we started for home with our wounded carried on litters. It was very cold and we built rows of fires and slept between them.

According to Noah Smithwick, his Indian fighters were forced to trudge many miles homeward on foot, aided only by a few pack horses they had secreted away in an area farther from their horses.

> We carried Martin and Taylor ten miles back to the river, where, fortunately, we had left our pack horses. Taylor was able to ride and we rigged a horse litter in which we carried Joe Martin home. He stood the torture of that terrible journey with heroic fortitude, never uttering a complaint. We had two doctors with us, but they were unable to find the bullet, it having lodged in his spinal column. That poor fellow lived several weeks after reaching home. So ended our disastrous expedition.[39]

When Colonel Moore and his men were able to catch up with the Lipans near home, he recorded that Chief Castro's Indians had captured some ninety-three horses and mules from the Comanches. Forty-six of these were received by the whites, but not everyone was able to replace his loss. Captain Smithwick, for one, had lost a fine horse and received nothing in return. He felt that the "Lipans got away with the lion's share of the spoils." He was not reimbursed for the loss of his horse for more than a year.

Colonel Moore discharged his two volunteer companies from service. Smithwick's men disbanded on February 25 and Eastland's were discharged during their return to La Grange on February 26, 1839.[40]

Despite having lost only one man killed and six wounded against superior odds, Colonel Moore expedition was considered by some to have been a defeat. It would be 1840 before this veteran Indian fighter could make good on this campaign, when he led another expedition that year against the Comanches.

Moore's expedition was the beginning of a more offensive push against the hostile Indian tribes of Texas. The people of the frontier communities were growing less content with defending themselves and more eager to actively chase away potential threats to their livelihoods.

Some of the men of President Lamar's new Frontier Regiment were equally eager to go on the offensive. One such man was Captain William Sadler of the First Regiment of Infantry. Stationed in Houston County, he wrote to his old companion Lamar on the state of Indian affairs in his area on February 22, during the time that Moore's men were returning from their Comanche expedition.

Sadler explained to Lamar how he had lost his own wife and child to Indians the previous October. He was also critical of the volunteer groups which were hastily assembled to go against the Indians in times of crisis. Without "better discipline and more subordination" such volunteers only served as long as they felt was proper before returning home. Such brief expeditions did "nothing toward cowing the enemy." Sadler thus proposed to Lamar a more hostile course of action.

> All say that something must be done and I say so too, but it is with great diffidence that I attempt to hint, your Excellency, what I think should be done. We cannot check the Indians unless we follow them to their place of rendezvous or where they have their families and visit them with the same kind of warfare that they give us. We should spare neither age, sect nor condition, for they do not. I know it will be said this is barbarous and too much like the savage. And it certainly is harsh, but it is the only means in my view that will put them down and as such should be resorted to.
>
> The plan of calling on the country for volunteers to go against the Indians will not do unless they are kept under better discipline and more subordination than they have been heretofore, for they only go so far as they think proper and swear they will go no farther.[41]

★ ★ ★ ★ ★

Comanche Vengeance: Coleman Attack

After mourning their losses for one week, the Comanches rode south on a raid in order to exact the revenge that their culture demanded. In attempting to head off a large Indian raid, Colonel Moore's attack had only given the Comanches more reason to fight.

Colonel Burleson was informed on February 22 that a large force of Indians had been spotted in a prairie about halfway between Bastrop and Waterloo, the settlement which soon became Austin. He had just returned to his home at Mount Pleasant upon receiving this news.[42]

On Monday, February 24, these Indians attacked the home of widow Elizabeth Coleman, whose late husband Robert Coleman had served on Sam Houston's staff at San Jacinto and had commanded his own ranger battalion in 1836. The Coleman cabin stood near the Colorado River in what was called Wells' Prairie, at the lower end of Webber's Prairie, some twelve miles above Bastrop. The nearest neighbors were George W. Davis and Dr. Joseph W. Robertson.[43]

Burleson reported to Secretary of War Johnston that a group of northern Indians comprising Caddos, Wacos, and Kichais attacked the Coleman house on Monday, February 24 at about 10:00 a.m. It is likely the Comanches enlisted Indians from other tribes to join their raid. The combined force of Indians first came upon James Rogers and James Coleman. These two were out plowing in the field when the Indians attempted to cut them off from the house. At first sight of them, Rogers and Coleman broke for an adjoining thicket and made their escape. Powerless to help their family members, they moved through the woods to secure help for the others.[44]

A large body of two to three hundred Indians appeared a short distance from the Coleman cabin while Elizabeth Coleman and her other four children were out working. Their garden was only about fifty paces from the cabin. They fled for their cabin, although the Indians overtook and captured five-year-old Thomas Coleman, who was never to see his mother again.

Elizabeth Coleman, her three small children and older son Albert V. Coleman, who was about twelve years of age, made it into their cabin. Mrs. Coleman paused long enough to look for her missing son Thomas, but received an arrow through the throat while so doing. She and Albert managed to bar the door with the children safely inside.

Young Albert Coleman boldly fought the Indian attackers with the two or three guns stashed in his family's cabin. The Indians "forced the door open wide enough to admit a man; they were fired upon by the boy, who killed one dead on the spot" and reportedly wounded another. Albert raised a puncheon board in the floor under the bed and hid his younger siblings below the cabin. He strictly ordered them not to make a noise until they were sure that white men called for them. Albert soon thereafter received a fatal wound. As he lay dying, he instructed his little sisters to remain hidden. His body was later found collapsed against that of his deceased mother.

For some reason, the gunfire of young Albert must have led the Indians to believe that there were other males in the Coleman cabin. They withdrew with their one young captive, Thomas Coleman, leaving two dead and two in hiding. After attacking the Coleman house, the Indians attacked Dr. Joseph Robertson's residence, only a couple hundred yards from Mrs. Coleman's. There were no whites available to defend the place, so the Indians carried away "one negro woman and four children, one old man, and [a] boy." These seven were slaves owned by Robertson.

The Indians then proceeded to what was known as Wells' Fort, where three families resided, those of Martin Wells, John Walters, and George W. Davis. These families were spared by luck and a force of about fourteen men hastily put together just before their arrival.

Gideon White, an Alabama native who had recently brought his family to settle near present Austin, and a few neighbors had gone out that day to hunt buffalo near Wilbarger Creek. They instead found many fresh Indian signs and rushed back into town to report it. A volunteer squad of fourteen men was assembled and placed under charge of Captain John J. Grumbles. The men headed out in pursuit of the Indians and arrived at Wells' Fort as the Indians appeared.[45]

Several men wanted to fight them, but Captain Grumbles noted that the Indians appeared to number at least one hundred. He instead decided to send out runners to call for more volunteers to Wells' Fort. The men had momentarily spared these families at the fort, but the Indians did not leave the area. It was obvious that they were not afraid of a fight.

At twilight, a youth named John D. Anderson who lived a few miles from the Colemans rode to the cabin. He called out to the children by name. The girls recognized his voice and answered. Anderson raised a puncheon, rescued them and loaded them on his horse, one in front and one behind. With the terrified Coleman girls, he rode to Wells' Fort, where former ranger superintendent George Davis provided a guard for these children and other women and children.[46]

★ ★ ★ ★ ★

Battle of Brushy Creek: February 25, 1839

The early Bastrop area citizens were warned of the Indian danger by a signal system established by Colonel Edward Burleson. The blowing of a horn followed by two gunshots was a sign that hostile Indians were on the attack. Anyone hearing the signal was to repeat it, thus passing the alarm throughout the section. In the town of Bastrop, an old cannon was fired to signal the able-bodied men to quickly gather.[47]

More volunteers soon arrived at Wells' Fort in preparation to take on the Comanches. Joining those already gathered under John Grumbles, the number of volunteers climbed to twenty-five. The men elected Jacob Burleson, brother of Colonel Edward Burleson, to take command. Three other Burleson brothers were among this company: Jonathan, John, and Aaron.[48]

Captain Jacob Burleson's volunteer company began reconnoitering the area for the Indians. By mid-afternoon of February 24, they were joined by another volunteer company under Captain James Rogers, a brother-in-law of Edward Burleson. This company had been formed at Josiah Wilbarger's fort. The two companies totaled fifty-two men, all so eager to pursue the chase that they decided to head out immediately without electing any further company officers. They decided to march in double file, with captains Rogers and Burleson each riding at the head of one file.

One of the volunteers was Allen J. "Ad" Adkisson, who had previously served as a ranger under Captain John Lynch. Adkisson later gave his recollections of this battle to historian J. W. Wilbarger.

> About ten o'clock the next day, we descended a long prairie slope leading down to a dry run, a little above and opposite Post Oak Island, and when about three miles north of Brushy, we came in sight of the enemy.[49]

Post Oak Island was located about four miles north of Brushy Creek and east of Waterloo. The ensuing skirmish took place about twenty-five miles north of the Colorado River on February 25. When the Indians realized that they had been sighted, they commenced racing toward a thicket ahead of them. The Texan volunteers under captains Burleson and Rogers were about half a mile behind. They immediately charged up, open file, flanking to the right and to the left to cut the Indians off from the thicket.

Captain Burleson tried several times to find a suitable ground for his company to dismount and take up the fight. The Indians did not halt and take up their own defensive positions, making this effort difficult at best. Burleson finally ordered his men to dismount and hitch their horses for the fight. Almost immediately, the Texans were at a disadvantage.

The Indians, remaining on horseback, suddenly charged this dismounted Texan company and created a panic. Burleson called for a retreat, but some had a difficult time regaining their horses. A. J. Adkisson relates the near-fatal plight of his fellow volunteer William Simpson Wallace.

> The horse of W. [S.] Wallace became frightened, pulled away from him and ran among the Indians, leaving the gallant Texan on foot in the midst of the conflict. His horse was soon mounted by one of the Indian warriors, who appropriated him for his own use. Just at this time Captain Jack Haynie, observing the perilous situation of Wallace, made a dash for him, pulled him up behind him on his horse, and both made good their retreat.

For this brave rescue, Wallace's father later presented a handsome rifle to John "Jack" Haynie, a fifty-three-year-old Methodist preacher who had settled in Bastrop after arriving in Texas only one month prior to the Brushy Creek battle. Haynie was not a captain during this battle, as indicated by Adkisson's account.

As the Indians charged, Jacob Burleson and two of his men, Winslow Turner and Benjamin Franklin Highsmith, were caught on foot as their own squad retreated. Highsmith, twenty-two, was a veteran of the 1832 battle of Velasco and son of a man who served as a scout during the War of 1812. The trio fired at the rapidly approaching Indians and then jumped upon their horses to flee. Captain Burleson was about to mount his horse when he spotted young Turner, a boy of about fourteen years, leap onto his horse without untying it. Burleson ran back and untied the boy's horse. Racing to his own horse, he was just mounting the saddle when he was shot in the back of the head.

The Indians had fired a volley from close range at the three Texans. Ben Highsmith "felt the wind of a ball close to his ear." At the same instant, he saw Burleson struck in the head at the base of his hat. As Captain Burleson reeled and fell from his saddle, Turner and Highsmith raced for safety.[50]

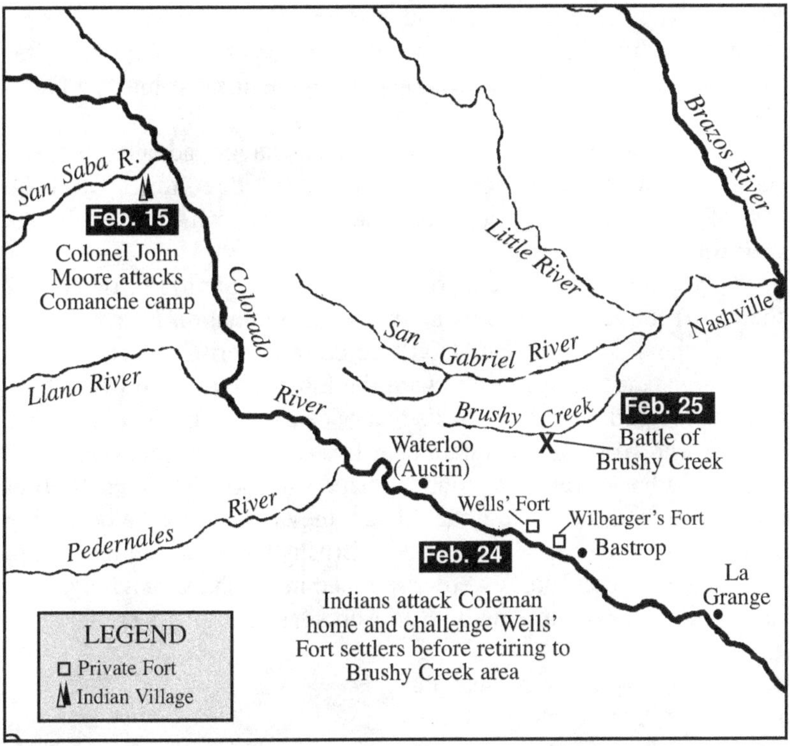

This map shows the February 1839 battle areas of Colonel Moore's Comanche Raid and the Battle of Brushy Creek.

Burleson was killed in the front of the battle and his body fell into temporary possession of the Indians. The Indians fell upon him with a vengeance, mistakenly believing they had downed their hated Colonel Edward Burleson. They cut off his right hand and right foot, scalped him and even cut out his heart, which they took with them.[51]

The remainder of Burleson's company and that of Captain Rogers retreated three miles from the battlefield before resting their horses.Adkisson later summed up the frustration of his fellow volunteers.

> Unwilling and ashamed to return to the settlements without a fight, and being loath to leave the dead body of the gallant captain upon the field, we halted at Brushy, not knowing what to do.[52]

In the meantime, another party of volunteers had been organized by Colonel Edward Burleson, who made his headquarters for the

Frontier Regiment on his farm near Bastrop. The Texas Army commander-in-chief arrived on the scene after noon on February 25 after the first fight. With him were another thirty mounted volunteers under Captain Jesse Billingsley.

Colonel Burleson found that the "Indians having advantage of the position, caused the whites to fall back about three miles, with the loss of one man."[53] This one man lost, of course, was his own brother Jacob.

The combined volunteer forces held a consultation to determine their next moves. There was a general determination to avenge the loss of the first fight. Burleson's force, numbering approximately eighty-four men, moved on toward the Indians again. Unfortunately, time has erased any muster rolls that once existed for the companies of men who so valiantly fought near Brushy Creek on February 25.

The Indians were not found where Burleson expected to find them. Instead of occupying the thicket, they had selected a defensive position at a toe-shaped plateau near Brushy Creek which had steep, rising banks. Their forces were assembled in the shape of a horseshoe and when first encountered by Burleson's rangers, they were ready to fight.

Advance spies were sent out to reconnoiter the enemy forces and several of them exchanged shots near the plateau with some of the Indians. As Burleson's forces approached, he split them up. Captain Billingsley would lead half the men in approaching directly below the Indians. The other party under Captain Rogers went above and gained possession of a small ravine which emptied into the main one above the Indians. By Burleson's report, it was about 1:00 p.m. when his forces attacked.

Rogers' men were to drive down the ravine and move the enemy before them, while Billingsley's men worked their way up the little ravine they occupied before the Indians. The lead-

Benajmin Franklin Highsmith (1817–1905), was born in Mississippi and came to Texas in 1823 with his father. At the battle of Brushy Creek, Highsmith narrowly escaped with his life as Captain Jacob Burleson was shot down in front of him.
Photo originally published in Sowell's *Early Settlers and Indian Fighters of Southwest Texas*, 1900.

ers hoped to secure a complete rout in this manner. The Comanches lay massed behind high banks on either side, however. The ravines occupied by Rogers and Billingsley's men opened out into an open stretch of some fifty yards before reaching the Indians' stronghold. It would be extremely dangerous for the Texans to cross these open expanses to carry out their plan.[54]

"We were forced to select safe positions, watch our opportunities, and whenever an Indian showed himself, to draw down on him and send the messenger of death to dispatch him," related battle veteran A. J. Adkisson.

According to Ben Highsmith, the Texans suffered losses at the hand of a determined Indian sharpshooter. The Comanche managed to crawl from a creekbed to a patch of prickly pears, where he lay flat on the ground and well concealed. He waited for clear shots against settlers who unwittingly exposed themselves. When the smoke from his firing gun was finally spotted, young Winslow Turner reportedly braved the danger to scale a small tree. He obtained a bead on his adversary, fired successfully, and scrambled back down to safety. Turner's shot struck the Comanche solidly and thus ended this deadly sniping.[55]

The two-pronged Comanche and Texan sniping contest continued until sunset, after which time the Indians retreated under cover of darkness. In addition to the loss of Captain Burleson earlier in the day, three more men were lost and several others wounded in the afternoon fight at Brushy Creek.

Two Texans were killed outright. John B. Walters, a twenty-four-year-old who had come to Texas from Missouri in 1825, had worked as a carpenter, gunsmith, and ranger in Texas. At Brushy Creek, he was fatally shot in the head. Edward Blakey was another veteran frontiersman who was shot down this day. The fourth casualty of the day was Reverend James Gilleland, forty years old and the organizer of the first Methodist Church in Austin's Little Colony in 1834. He was shot in the neck, the ball going down through his lungs. He would survive more than a week before dying from his wounds.[56]

The Comanches lost a number of warriors this day, as well. As they retreated in the darkness they put up "the most distressing cries and bitter lamentations ever uttered by mortal lips or heard by mortal ears." Adkisson felt that their "bitter wails indicated that their loss was great, either in quantity or quality, perhaps both."[57]

Colonel Burleson's report summarizes the afternoon fight at Brushy Creek.

> I continued to pick them off at every opportunity until dark. They retreated from their strong hold under cover of the night, and, from their superior numbers, were enabled to carry off their dead and wounded, as appears from the statements of the negro who was found on the battle ground after night, with nine arrows shot into him, supposed to have been left for dead. He says he saw several killed and wounded, say thirty. From the appearance of blood seen on the ground, I am induced to believe the above number is not overrated.

Burleson's men made camp for the night on the battlefield. Early the next morning, February 26, the men constructed litters for the dead and wounded. The slow march back to the settlements then began.

The battle took place in Williamson County near Brushy, Cottonwood, and Boggy creeks, a few miles from present Taylor. A red granite marker was erected at the battle site in 1925, located on private land 1.4 miles south of Taylor on the west side of Highway 95. The State of Texas added an historical marker commemorating the "Battle of Brushy Creek" on State Highway 95, four miles south of Taylor.[58]

While Colonel Burleson's men fought at Brushy Creek, another group of volunteers was en route to assist them. Captain William Hancock was in charge of a small force of men who had been organized by the city council of Bastrop to scout daily and to protect nightly the town of Bastrop. Each member of this twenty-man company was to be paid twenty dollars a month. According to the Minutes of the Corporation of Bastrop for January 6, 1839, he was to furnish his own horse and firearm.[59]

One of Captain Hancock's men was sixteen-year-old John Holland Jenkins. He had come to Texas with his family as members of Stephen F. Austin's Third (or Little) Colony. His family first lived with that of William Barton on Barton Creek while his father assisted with surveying work. The family received their own league of land on the west bank of the Colorado River about thirty-five miles below Austin. John's father Edward Jenkins had been killed by Indians in 1833 while working in his field. His widow Sarah was forced to sell half her land and move her three young children into the town of Bastrop to live with friends.

Sarah Jenkins remarried, but lost her second husband James Northcross when he perished in the Alamo in 1836. Young John Jenkins became the man of the house and helped provide for his family by working the field. His involvement with the Bastrop town rangers was only natural, considering his family's turbulent past. John Jenkins and Captain Hancock's small force did not make it to the Brushy Creek fight in time.

> We were just behind Burleson's force, and were making all possible speed to overtake them. About sundown, as we were riding along in couples, considerably scattered, we saw to our left a band of men moving about, and thinking they were Burleson's force we turned aside to join them, not dreaming of danger until they charged upon us and we saw that we had approached a band of Indians.
>
> We retreated to a mot of timber where we awaited an attack for some time, but for some reason they gave up the charge and we waited in vain. In the meantime, we were much perplexed as to the whereabouts of Burleson's force. Finally, after a short deliberation, deciding it to be dangerous for so small a party to be riding about in the face of such odds, we returned to the settlements.

In Bastrop, the men stood guard that night for Indians, posting themselves in and around the town. After neither hearing nor seeing danger by late in the night hours, the men retired into town for the night. Shortly after they had gone in, an older man named Stephen V. R. Eggleston, who had built the first two-story home in Bastrop, heard an unusual noise and went outside to check on it. An Indian shot him through the bowels with an arrow, a painful wound which caused Eggleston to die the next day.[60]

Edward Burleson wrote to Secretary of War Johnston from Bastrop several days later. He related the actions of his men following the battle at Brushy Creek.

> I remained encamped on the ground until next morning, and found the Indians had left several guns, bows, and arrows, all their camp equipage, and one mule tied, and several horses and mules killed. I ordered, without delay, Captain Billingsley, with 30 men, to follow on their trail, which he did three miles, and found they had dispersed to avoid more depredations committed on this frontier, with the exception of some thieving parties. It is confidently believed that the Indians will renew hostilities on this part of the frontier early this spring.[61]

Burleson's forces returned to Fort Wilbarger with their casualties in tow in their litters. On arriving there, the bodies were laid out in a room in the fort, preparatory to their funeral. Nancy Blakey insisted on seeing the disfigured body of her son Edward, who had been shot through the forehead.

After resting her head on his chest, Mrs. Blakey exclaimed that her husband, John Blakey, and only other son had already given their lives defending their new country. Lemuel Stockton Blakey had been killed at San Jacinto, ironically also under command of Captain Billingsley at that time.

In spite of her losses, the grieving mother reportedly uttered, "But if I had a thousand sons, and my country needed them, I would cheerfully give them up."[62]

Chapter 8
The Córdova and Flores Fights

March 1–May 18, 1839

Ben McCulloch's Peach Creek Fight: March 1839

The winter of early 1839 was brutal in southwest Texas, with hard freezes and ice that snapped tree limbs and even many trees. The severe cold lasted about two weeks and cloudy days prevented ice and snow from melting. This cold snap occurred during mid to late February 1839. It was during this harsh weather that an expedition was organized against the Indians by a soon to be famous Texan.[1]

Benjamin McCulloch, a veteran of San Jacinto, was twenty-eight years old at this time and a resident of Gonzales, where his younger brother Henry Eustace McCulloch had joined him during 1837. During this period, the Tonkawa tribe of Indians was camped at the junction of Peach and Sandies creeks, about fifteen miles northeast of Gonzales.

Prior to the great sleet storm, Ben McCulloch had made an agreement with a portion of the Tonkawas to join him and other white volunteers in a winter expedition against the neighboring hostile Indians. The heavy sleet postponed their little expedition, and when the weather did fair off, McCulloch found it difficult to enlist anyone to join him. All were fearful of a return of such a winter storm. To follow up on Colonel Moore's San Saba venture and in hopes of yet recovering Matilda Lockhart and the Putman children, McCulloch felt that his expedition was still very necessary.

Thus, about March 1, McCulloch left the Tonkawa village for the mountains in search of hostile Indians. His party consisted of five whites: himself, Wilson Randall, John D. Wolfin, David Henson, and his brother Henry McCulloch. To this was added some thirty-five Tonkawa warriors commanded by their well-known old chief, "Captain Jim Kerr." This chief had assumed this name in 1826 as evidence of his

Benjamin McCulloch (1811–1862) and, to right, his younger brother Henry Eustace McCulloch (1816–1895) originally worked as surveyors in Gonzales. In March 1839, Ben McCulloch led a small force of volunteers in an attack against hostile Indians near Peach Creek. Both men would become famed ranger captains and congressmen during their long service to Texas.
Texas State Library and Archives Commission.

friendship with the first settler of Gonzales, after the original Kerr had been assaulted by Indians in July 1826. Included on this foray with Captain Jim's Tonkawas was Chico, the tribe's medicine man.

Hoping to locate the winter camp of the Comanches, and possibly rescue some of the captive women and children, McCulloch's party moved up beyond the headwaters of Peach Creek. About twenty-five miles from the Tonkawa village on the second day out, they found a fresh trail of foot Indians who were bearing straight for Gonzales. This immediately changed their plans. McCulloch decided to follow this path and disrupt any hostilities that might be in the makings for the settlers.

The trail was followed rapidly for several hours, after which time they came within sight of what they perceived as thirteen Wacos and Comanches. The Indians promptly entered a very dense thicket which bordered a branch in post oak terrain. The Indians, concealed from view, had the clear advantage, and every attempt to reach a point from which they could be seen or fired upon was found to expose McCulloch's party to the fire of the unseen enemy. Several hours passed, in which time several shots were fired.

From the first, Captain Jim refused to enter the thicket or allow his men to enter, saying that the danger was too great and his Tonkawas were too scarce to sacrifice. One of his men was killed behind the only tree well situated for defense, the only loss suffered by the attacking party. Finally, impatient of delay and dreading the approach of night, McCulloch got a promise from Captain Jim to place his men about the lower end of the thicket so as to kill any one who tried to escape. McCulloch then opted to lead his brother Henry, Randall, and Henson in crawling through the impenetrable thicket from the upper end. Wolfin declined this dangerous venture.

Slowly, McCulloch and his three volunteers moved into the thicket, observing every possible precaution. Steadily, one by one, each of these four managed to shoot and kill an Indian, while wounding two or three others. The assailed Indians responded by firing many shots and arrows, but without success. The Texan rifles proved more effective in the thicket. Finally, the survivors of the enemy, numbered at nine of an original thirteen, emerged into the branch at the lower end of the thicket. They were allowed by Captain Jim to escape. While the whites made an exit from the thicket, the Indians were quick enough to reach the next large thicket beyond and escape.

Thus ended McCulloch's little campaign. The Tonkawas proceeded to scalp the four dead Indians, and then returned home to celebrate their victory. They sliced off portions of the thighs and breasts of the dead and severed the victims' hands, feet, arms, and legs. Shortly thereafter, they commenced a mystic war ritual, complete with a dance and wailing to commemorate their own fallen comrade. Ben McCulloch and his comrades left this grisly celebrating to the Tonkawas and proceeded on home to Gonzales, where they were welcomed by the people who had been spared a night attack from this hostile band.

★ ★ ★ ★ ★

Lamar Calls for More Volunteers

Responding to the rise of frontier violence, President Lamar in Houston issued an appeal on February 28 for volunteers to aid "the suffering conditions" of the "brave and energetic" Texans who were becoming overwhelmed by the increasing numbers of hostile Indians.[2]

Colonel Burleson's Frontier Regiment was far below its planned strength by early March. Of fifteen infantry companies slated to man frontier outposts, there were no more than four in operation at any time during the first half of 1839. West of the Brazos, Burleson's First Battalion included Captain John Kennymore's Company C (later commanded by Captain Samuel Jordan) at Post Béxar in San Antonio, and Company D under Captain George Howard at Gonzales. The First Regiment's Second Battalion, under Lieutenant Colonel William Fisher, included new recruits in Captain Sadler's Company A in Houston County and Captain Adam Clendenin's Company B in Houston.

Due to the undersized army, Lamar put out a new requisition in March 1839 on the counties of Harrisburg, Brazoria, Matagorda, Colorado, Liberty, and Galveston to furnish six companies of volunteers to serve for a six-month period on the Texas frontiers. The major responsibility for recruiting these men was placed upon Colonel Henry Karnes, Lieutenant Colonel Devereaux Woodlief, and Major William Jones. These three officers had been instated by Congress on January 9 to form a new mounted rifleman battalion.[3]

Karnes and his companions began a vigorous recruiting campaign to raise the requested companies. As with the ranging service, his mounted riflemen would be paid by the government and issued land grants upon completion of service. Three companies would soon be recruited around the Houston area.

Another company organized during this time was that of Lieutenant William G. Evans, recently of Captain Daniels' Milam Guards. Evans took command of thirty-four Houston volunteers who called themselves the "Travis Spies" on March 20. His men were well provisioned, as evidenced by the papers of Orderly Sergeant William H. Weaver. He received from the quartermaster's department one horse, one bridle, one saddle, two blankets, one pair of shoes, one shirt, one roundabout (coat), and one pair of pants.[4] The Travis Spies were soon given orders to take up station at Fort Milam.

Captain John Bird raised thirty-five men from Fort Bend and Austin counties on April 24. Bird had been born in Tennessee in 1795 and served under Andrew Jackson in the War of 1812. He came to Texas with his family in 1829 as one of Austin's early settlers and obtained a league of land in present Burleson County. Bird had led volunteers against Comanches on the Brazos River in 1832 and in November 1835 he engaged Mexican cavalrymen near San Antonio. On March 6, 1836, in San Felipe, he formed a volunteer company which served under General Sam Houston during the San Jacinto campaign and protected settlers during the Runaway Scrape. Captain Bird's new ranger company would soon be stationed at Fort Milam with that of Lieutenant Evans.[5]

During March, some of the county ranging companies that had been authorized by Lamar's congress in January were still forming. Bastrop, Robertson, and Milam counties had been authorized in one joint act of January 23, 1839, for "the raising of three companies of mounted volunteers for frontier service against the hostile Indians." These companies were to serve for six months, as opposed to the three-month terms for the companies previously authorized in Houston and Gonzales counties.

Also of note, the captains of these three companies were not appointed by Lamar, but instead "the men composing each company will elect the officers of the company."[6] In addition, the three companies in Bastrop, Robertson, and Milam would elect a major to command them.

Many men who formed these companies were already seasoned veterans of the Texas Rangers. Some were former captains, such as Ripley Wheelock and Calvin Boales, plus Ethan Stroud, who had assumed command of the volunteers during Bryant's Fight in January. Captains Nimrod Doyle and James Mathews commanded the two Robertson County ranger companies. Among their men were at least eleven survivors of January's ill-fated Bryant's Defeat.

The Milam County Rangers were mustered into service on March 8 under Captain George Erath. He had served as a ranger on campaigns from 1835 through 1837 and had commanded the small ranger unit which fought at Elm Creek the previous year. Erath later wrote of these new companies.

> The Indians in the spring of 1838 and summer committed continual depredations, stole a great many horses [and] killed many men without scarcely any resistance—no force being on the frontier—and continued to do so till the spring of 1839. Three companies were organized by the order of President Lamar on the 8[th of] March in Robertson and Milam. I commanded the Milam Company. Those three companies in a manner checked the proceedings of the Indians and although nothing very notorious took place, the frontier was in some manner defended and began to gain ground.[7]

While Erath's company did not see battle, some of the other companies did in early 1839. Captain Micah Andrews, another veteran ranger leader, mustered in the La Grange County Rangers on March 10. His company would quickly be involved in frontier action with both Indians and Mexican rebels.

Robertson County/Milam County Ranger Brigade

Captain Doyle's Robertson County Rangers: March 8–June 10, 1839

Captain:
Nimrod Doyle
First Lieutenant:
Enoch M. Jones
Second Lieutenant:
Albert G. Gholson
First Sergeant:
Jackson Doyle
Second Sergeant:
Melton J. Tidwell
Third Sergeant:
John Welch
Fourth Sergeant:
John D. Smith
First Corporal:
Henry J. Hill
Second Corporal:
Jesse J. Webb
Third Corporal:
Charles Smith
Fourth Corporal:
William J. Morgan
Privates:
William H. Anderson
Nathaniel Campbell
Michael D. Castleman
Wright Cooley
Winchester Doyle
Samuel Gholson
George Grafton
Jonathan R. Hardin
Isiah Harlin
Joseph Harlin
William Harlin
Edward Howard
James Lane
Hugh Lockney
Noah McChristian
Jeremiah McDonald
Elias Mackey
G. H. Maness
Bailey Martin
Flood McGrew
Hardin McGrew
Buckner Melton
Ethan Melton
Andrew J. Morgan
Samuel Nelson
Sian Smith
William Smith
James M. Springfield
Ethan Stroud
Beadon Stroud
John Touchstone
John Treadwell
William J. Treadwell
Jesse Webb
Joseph Webb
Thomas R. Webb
Wesley C. Webb
William M. Webb
Charles Welch
John West

Captain Erath's Milam County Rangers: March 8–June 8, 1839

Captain:
George Bernard Erath
First Lieutenant:
Richard Ellis
Second Lieutenant:
Samuel Chance
First Sergeant:
Neill McLennan
Second Sergeant:
Phillip Scott
Third Sergeant:
William F. Thompson
Fourth Sergeant:
Jasper N. M. Thompson
First Corporal:
John S. Jones
Second Corporal:
James Shaw
Privates:
T. T. Addison
John Beal
E. T. Bell
Stephen Bell
William W. Bell
Calvin Boales
Gideon Bowen
Samuel Bowers
Daniel Cullins
Ansel Darniell
C. M. Dickson
W. S. Dobbins
James Fulcher
Thomas A. Graves
Berry L. Ham
James H. Harvey
Samuel Harvey
John H. Hobson
James Howlett
William Isaacs
Peter Jackson
Samuel Johns
Wiley Jones
J. Y. Jones
Henry Kattenhorn
Solomon Long
David Maford
John B. Miliken
A. W. Moore
Lewis Moore
Frederick Neibling
John Pool
John W. Porter
Daniel Robinson
James W. Scott
Montgomery Shackleford
James W. Smith
S. D. Smith
Isaac Standefer
Joseph Tivey
John Treal
W. H. Whitton
E. T. Wortham

Capt. Mathews' Robertson County Rangers: March 8–June 8, 1839

Captain:
James D. Mathews
First Lieutenant:
Benjamin Sewell
Second Lieutenant:
Thomas N. B. Greer
First Sergeant:
Henry Reed
Second Sergeant:
Harrison York
Third Sergeant:
Stephen Eaton
Fourth Sergeant:
James W. Hill
First Corporal:
James Scofield
Second Corporal:
William B. Hill
Third Corporal:
Andrew D. Stephens
Fourth Corporal:
A. W. Cooke
Privates:
James Allen
Cavit Armstrong
John Armstrong
David Bartlett
James Boone
Mordicia Boone Jr.
Mordicia Boone Sr.
Thomas Bosman
Isaac Burns
James Burns
William Butrell
Wiley Carter
John Casey
R. W. Cavitt
John Chalmers
Eli Chandler
John Copeland
Joseph Copeland
Laurence Copeland
Martin Copeland
Richard Copeland
George W. Cox
William Cox
John Douglass
Charles Duncan
Thomas Duncan
Samuel M. Eaton
Edward Estes
Forest Fifer
David P. Flint
Sandford P. Flint
William T. Flint
Philip Golden
John Graham
Moses Griffin
Williamson Griffin
David Hagerty
John R. Henry
George Higgs
William James
John Kennedy
Robert R. Lingbottom
Andrew Mathews
Robert H. Mathews
Benone Middleton
Thomas Middleton
William B. Middleton
Andres Millican
James Mitchell
Mannon Mitchell
W. D. Moore
William L. Moss
W. C. Nanny
Harrison Owen
John P. Philips
Lewis B. Powers
William C. Powers
James Riley
John L. Robinson
Albert Rogers
Joseph Rogers
Robert Rogers Jr.
Robert Rogers Sr.
Stephen Rogers Jr.
Stephen Rogers Sr.
Francis Slauter
James J. Swaney
Jeremiah Tinnon
John F. Underhill
James B. Ware
E. L. Ripley Wheelock
George Ripley Wheelock
Philip Wippler
Thomas Young

Source: Compiled from original muster rolls, courtesy of the Texas State Archives.

Captain Mathew Caldwell mustered the Gonzales County Rangers into service on March 16, two months after he had been appointed to raise this frontier unit. Among his men were John Wolfin, Henry McCulloch, and David Henson, three of the small group of men who had fought Comanches the previous week with surveyor Ben McCulloch.

Captain Caldwell's company would range over the country between Gonzales and San Antonio over the next three months. The main camp for these rangers was established some fourteen miles above Gonzales on the Guadalupe River near present Luling in Caldwell County.[8] The service of this company was impressive enough that President Lamar selected Caldwell several months later to fill an officer opening in his First Regiment of Infantry.

The development of Lamar's county ranging system would prove beneficial in the months to follow.

★ ★ ★ ★ ★

Córdova Fight at Mill Creek: March 29, 1839

Two veteran frontier fighters, George W. Davis and Reuben Hornsby, were out riding on the morning of March 25 when they stumbled upon the rebel camp of Vicente Córdova. His forces were near the foot of the mountains just north of present Austin. Believing they had discovered the trail of a large party of Indians, they quickly sent the word back to the Waterloo settlement.

The efforts of Vicente Córdova's Mexican rebels had been beaten down in East Texas in 1838 by the battle of Kickapoo, but their efforts to stir the local Indians continued. Córdova had written a letter to Mexican agent Manuel Flores in Matamoros, and these two instigators set a meeting to discuss their plans and future movements.

Desiring to meet directly with Flores and General Valentin Canalizo, who had succeeded General Filisola as commander at Matamoros, Córdova decided to go in person to Matamoros. He left his temporary place on the Upper Trinity in March 1839 with an escort of about fifty-three Mexicans, six Biloxi Indians and a chief, and five runaway slaves.[9]

General Canalizo had sent documents dated February 27, 1839, to the chiefs of several tribes via Flores. The letters advised the chiefs "to prevent any adventurers again destroying the repose of your families, or again treading the soil where repose the bones of your forefathers," they should pay heed to Flores' instructions. These letters were addressed to Captain Ignacio of the Guapanagues, Captain Coyote of the Caddos, the chief of the Seminoles, Chief Big Mush of the Cherokees, Captain Benito of the Kickapoos, to the chief of the Brazos, and to Lieutenant Colonel Bowles of the Cherokees.[10]

News of the sighting of Córdova's rebel force by Hornsby and Davis on March 25 soon reached Colonel Edward Burleson. In a report to Secretary of War Johnston published in the *Telegraph and Texas Register* on April 17, Burleson stated that he received intelligence on March 27 of a large body of Indians encamped at the foot of the mountains on the Colorado. As leader of the Texas Army, Burleson was also commander of all Texas Ranger companies. He quickly organized a volunteer party of seventy-nine men. These men were organized at the town of Waterloo (present Austin) on the afternoon of March 27.

Burleson organized the men into two companies under his most experienced ranger leaders. Captain Jesse Billingsley took command of one unit and Captain Micah Andrews, who had just formed his own ranger company on March 10, took the other. A muster roll of those serving under Colonel Burleson shows that only half of Andrews' twenty-four man company would march out to fight, indicating that he must have left half of his men on detached duty guarding the settlements. At least a half dozen of Burleson's volunteers had recently completed Colonel John Moore's February campaign against the Comanches under Captain Noah Smithwick.

While the men were forming, spies were sent out. They returned with information that the unknown party had crossed the Colorado River between the falls and the settlement, seemingly heading in the direction of Seguin.[11]

Burleson marched out with his seventy-nine-man ranger and volunteer force, camping that night on Bear Creek, ten miles southwest of the Waterloo settlement, in the area of present Manchaca in Travis County. Camp was broken early on the morning of March 28, and as this was happening a runner arrived from the Hornsby's Bend settlement with news that a large Indian trail had been discovered nearby. Burleson's party turned back to protect their families and the Waterloo settlement, only to soon find that the whole alert was a false alarm.

The "Indian" trail was actually that of Córdova, which they had been following in the first place. The volunteer party camped again on Bear Creek, after losing a whole day in their pursuit. Worse yet, some of the volunteers refused to go on any further for fear of their families' safety.

About ten o'clock that evening, Tom Moore, known as "Black Tom," and William M. Robison appeared in the camp and informed Colonel Burleson of the composition of the force he was pursuing. Robison was an escaped member of the Córdova force, whom Córdova had come to distrust and ordered court-martialed. Sentenced by Córdova to be shot the next day, Robison escaped. Although he was hunted all day, he had made his way to Moore's house, whereupon the two had set out to warn Burleson's men. Córdova's mission, as they explained to Burleson, was to proceed to Mexico to secure munitions of war with which to equip the Indians for their planned attack on the Texan settlers.

Robison joined Burleson's party for the remainder of the expedition, but the colonel ordered him monitored at all times for suspicious activity. The force set out again the next morning, March 29, and soon found the trail to be only a few hours old by afternoon. Pushing their horses as fast as they could travel, they were soon within close distance of Córdova's men. About half an hour before sundown, the Texas scouts came within sight of Córdova at a place on Mill Creek near the Guadalupe that came to be known as Battle Ground Prairie.

Córdova's men were lying about carelessly on the grass while their horses grazed with saddles on. It appeared they had been caught unaware. Subsequent information from prisoners would show Burleson that Córdova's own spies were out ahead scouting the situation at Seguin, five miles to the west. They were apparently planning on raiding the town that night. Seguin was then a small settlement of about twenty-five households which had formerly been known as Walnut Springs.

Upon receiving the news from his scouts, Burleson decided to move immediately and ordered his men to spur their horses on. They came within sight of their enemy late on March 29 in an open grove of oaks through which ran a small ravine. Burleson split his men in preparation for attack, sending Captain Andrew's company to the right and Billingsley's to the left. Córdova at this time first became aware of the impending danger, and formed his men to meet the attack.

The line of battle assumed the form of an inverted "V" as the Texans advanced. The fight began at the head of a ravine around which the Seguin road later ran near the old Handley place. Dr. James Fentress boasted that he intended to kill Córdova himself, if someone would only point him out. Córdova's men fought persistently from behind the cover of trees, at which point some of the Texans also dismounted to fight from behind trees. Seeing the enemy wavering as the Texans edged closer, Burleson's Colorado volunteers burst into the open and charged them. Faced with this first full-scale charge, Córdova's men broke and ran, with the Texans in hot pursuit.[12]

As twilight approached, the rebels were entering the Guadalupe bottom two miles from the battlefield. As Córdova wheeled to flee, he was pointed out, and Dr. Fentress fired at him. He felt certain that he had struck his opponent in the arm, and one of the Texan participants agreed that Córdova was seen to be reeling in his saddle as he fled. His sword and hat were found about four miles from the battlefield. Those who doubted Fentress' aim would no more when the body of Córdova was examined after his death at the Battle of Salado three years later. One of his arms was found to sport an old and severe wound.[13]

During the battle, one of the Biloxi Indians lost his horse and charged back with his gun drawn to fire. Coming face to face with a half dozen Texans, he fired a shot at Doctor Fentress which missed. The doctor immediately returned fire and dropped him dead. Fentress then proceeded to cut off the Indian's head and carry it away with him for medical examination.

Muster of Burleson's Volunteers Against Cordova's Rebels
Mill Creek Fight: March 29, 1839

Allen J. Adkisson *	John Dancer	Thomas McKernon *
Henry Alderson *	John G. Durst	James P. Miller
John D. Alexander	John J. Eakin *	R. W. Miller
George Allen	Lewis Engelhart	Richard M. Mills *
John D. Anderson	Dr. James Fentress	John Moore
Micah Andrews, Capt*	Nelson Flesher	Thomas A. Moore
Joseph Henry Barnhard	John L. Foster	H. S. Morgan
Wayne Barton	Samuel S. Gillet	William Newcomb *
Spirus C. Bennett	D. C. Gilmore	Isaac Norris *
Jesse Billingsley, Capt.	George W. Glasscock	John W. Pendleton
Allen E. Brown *	James P. Gorman	James Ogden Rice *
John William Brown *	Owen P. Hardeman	John B. Robinson
Edward Burleson, Col.	William P. Hardeman	J. N. Robison
John Burleson *	Dr. Samuel G. Haynie	William M. Robison
Jonathan Burleson	Cornelius M. Hemphill	Thomas Sanders
Ross Byers	William A. Hemphill	George W. Scott
John Caldwell	Milton Hicks	G. W. Sharp
B. A. Campbell	Samuel Highsmith	Daniel C. Shelp
William Carter	William Holmes	John W. Smith
William Caruthers	Malcolm M. Hornsby	Winslow Turner
Hugh M. Childress	William W. Hornsby	Logan Vandever
William A. Clopton	Enoch S. Johnson	Martin Walker
Samuel Colver	Josiah S. Lester	F. P. Whiting
Preston Conley	Richard J. Lloyd	George Wilson
Napoleon Conn	John L. Lynch	Henry Gonzalvo Woods
Henry Crockeron	James L. Mabry	* Member of Captain Andrews' rangers.
John R. Cunningham	Isaac McGary	

Original volunteer list published in *Telegraph and Texas Register* of April 17, 1839.

During the course of the fight, the burning paper wads from the Texans' shotguns started fires in the tall grass. With the fall of night, further pursuit was useless and Colonel Burleson led his men up the Guadalupe valley six miles to Seguin to protect the locals there. Bodies of some of the victims were found the next morning.

Some early accounts list Córdova losing as many as twenty-five killed but others seem to agree upon eighteen killed. The previous captive, William Robison, identified one of Córdova's dead as Canze. Burleson's forces captured several prisoners after the battle and eventually rounded up a total of nineteen, including a number of slaves.

Among them was a husky French black named Raphael, about thirty-five years of age, and he confirmed Robison's story of Córdova's forces. Noting that Raphael weighed approximately two hundred pounds, Burleson placed him under the custody of Irishman Tom McKernon for safeguarding. When Burleson returned from his pursuit of the fleeing rebels, he had found that McKernon had securely bound Raphael's hands behind his back and then had tied his horse's stake rope to his hands.

Two other blacks were captured. One was a youth of about "sixteen summers" and the other was "an old gray haired man something near sixty years old." The youth had suffered at least three gunshot wounds from the rangers and was knifed by another ranger's bowie knife. When he was found to be still alive, the rangers decided not to kill him.[14]

Burleson's men lost none killed in the Mill Creek battle, although at least three were wounded. The citizens of Seguin were relieved that the ranger/volunteer forces had intercepted Córdova, thus foiling his planned raid on their town. The Texans captured several papers belonging to Córdova and these were turned over by Burleson to Secretary of War Johnston. The battle with Córdova took place in Guadalupe County on Mill Creek about five miles east of the town of Seguin. "Battleground Prairie" is marked with a Texas historical marker on U.S. 90-A, five miles east of Seguin.[15]

★ ★ ★ ★ ★

From a ridge near Mill Creek, the rangers suddenly spotted a large swarm of buzzards all moving south.

"Boys, what does that mean?" asked nineteen-year-old James Wilson Nichols, the leader of the four-man scout patrol.[16]

Two of the other rangers, John Sowell and James B. Roberts, each offered his own thought on the buzzards. Andrew Jackson Sowell, a

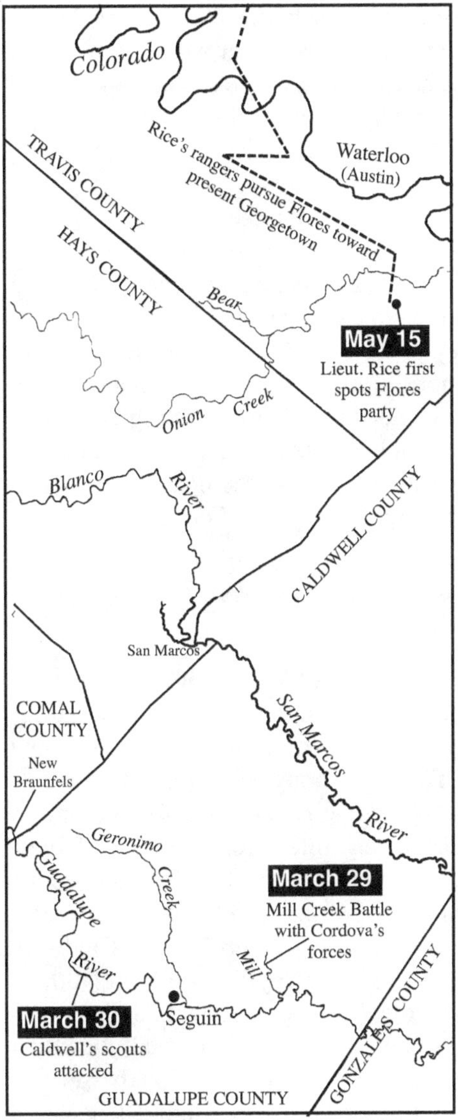

Area map showing locations of key events of the Córdova and Flores fights. Colonel Burleson's forces fought Córdova's rebels near Seguin on March 29. The rangers of Captain Micah Andrews and Lieutenant James Rice began pursuit of Flores' forces on May 15.

veteran of the Texas Revolution and the 1835 Indian fight on the Rio Blanco, said, "I will tell you what I think they mean."

Sowell ventured that the buzzards were following a large band of Indians hauling meat who were moving directly for Seguin. Sowell and company were members of Captain Mathew Caldwell's Gonzales County ranger company, which had been mustered into service on March 16, two weeks prior to Burleson's Mill Creek fight. They had been sent on a scouting patrol up San Geronimo Creek and were returning to join their company.

The rangers' horses were heavily laden with venison from deer they had killed on York's Creek earlier in the day. Jim Nichols decided that they should ride for Seguin and warn Captain Caldwell that a body of Indians was moving through the area. Nichols:

> They all agreed and we started for home. We rode as fast as we could with our heavy packs and when we arrived we learned that two of Burleson's men had come in and reported that Burleson had attacked Córdova that evening and had a running fight and had killed and wounded over half his number.
>
> The citizens was in considerable excitement.

Andrew Sowell later told his nephew that he and one of the other rangers scouted on ahead further to the head of Mill Creek before turning for Seguin. There, they came upon the fire-consumed battlefield. In a deep hollow, they noticed two dead Mexicans and further out in the open ground were two dead ex-slaves close together, their clothing burned off by the fire that had spread. Further up on the rising ground, near some lone mesquite trees, lay the body of the Biloxi Indian whose head had been removed by Doctor Fentress.

★ ★ ★ ★ ★

Rangers Attacked on the Guadalupe: March 30, 1839

Jim Nichols' scouts rode into Seguin on the evening of March 29. A portion of their company was stationed in town under First Lieutenant James Campbell. The main body of Captain Caldwell's company was camped on the Guadalupe River some fourteen miles west of Gonzales and about eighteen miles from Seguin. Mathew Caldwell had actually gone into Gonzales on this day, leaving Second Lieutenant Canah C. Colley in charge of the Guadalupe River camp. Colley dispatched a messenger to Gonzales to alert Captain Caldwell, who received the news of the battle before daylight on March 30.[18]

Caldwell sent word amongst the sleeping citizens to call for volunteers to depart at daylight. A good number volunteered, including Benjamin McCulloch, whose brother Henry was already serving under Caldwell. With these extra men, Captain Caldwell departed rapidly and they reached Lieutenant Colley's camp on the Guadalupe. The rangers and additional volunteers then lost no time in reuniting with Lieutenant Campbell's other detachment in Seguin on March 30.

Within thirty-six hours of Burleson's fight in the Guadalupe river bottom, Caldwell would have reunited his company, added citizen volunteers, sought, found, and followed the trail of Córdova. He took with him the volunteer citizens and left behind only a few men to guard their own camp.

Before Caldwell's party reunited with Lieutenant Campbell's Seguin detachment, a small group of the company's spies ran into trouble with Córdova. In the wake of the battle, Córdova's men had retreated but found the Guadalupe River too dangerous to cross. During the night, they detoured to the uplands east of Seguin and reached the river six miles above that town. There, just before daylight on March 30, Córdova's party accidentally happened upon five of Campbell's men who were retiring from a scouting mission. Privates James Milford Day, Thomas R. Nichols, John W. Nichols, Daniel Noyes Poore, and David Reynolds had stopped to camp near Young's Ford and were thereupon attacked by Córdova's rebels.

The rangers were sound asleep near the river when a group of Córdova's men slipped into camp and stole their horses. In the ensuing gunfight, Milford Day was seriously wounded. Jim Nichols, fellow Caldwell ranger and brother of two of those present for this March 30 early morning attack, later wrote of it in his journal.

Captain Caldwell's Gonzales Co. Rangers: March 16–June 16, 1839

Captain:	James Forrester	William Putman
Mathew Caldwell	Daniel Gray	David Reynolds
First Lieutenant:	John G. Gray	Abram Roberts
James Campbell	Thomas Grubbs	Alexander Roberts
Second Lieutenant:	Frederick W. Happle	James B. Roberts
Canah C. Colley	Everett H. Harris	Jeremiah Roberts
First Sergeant:	Vaughter Henderson	D. W. Russell
George D. Miller	David Henson	John H. Russell
Second Sergeant:	John S. Hodges	Ezekiel Smith Sr.
John R. King	Maury Irvin	French Smith
Third Sergeant:	Ebenezer R. Jones	William Smith
William N. Henry	Wiliam H. Killen	Andrew Jackson Sowell
Fourth Sergeant:	Henry B. King	Asa J. Lee Sowell
John Archer	Henry McCulloch	John N. Sowell
Privates:	T. N. Minter	John S. Stump
M. L. Baber	George H. Nichols	James A. Swift
Seth Baldridge	George W. Nichols Sr.	T. W. Symonds
Nathan Burgett	James W. Nichols	Nathan Wadkins
Curtis Caldwell	John W. Nichols	Isaac Wallace
William Clinton	Solomon G. Nichols	John D. Wolfin
James M. Day	William S. Osborn	
Miles G. Dikes	James Pinchback	*Source:*
A. S. Emmett	Daniel Noyes Poore	*Texas State Archives.*

> After Córdova had been defeated by Burleson, he changed his course to a ford on the river near six miles above Seguin where Milford and his men were camped. Córdova was not aware that anyone was near the ford, but some of them being afoot, having lost their horses in the fight, and seeing the boys' horses staked out, made for them. The horses commenced snorting and awoke Milford just as one of them was untying his horse. Milford supposed that the Indians had followed them in to steal their horses, snatched up his gun, and fired at the one that was untying his horse and he fell. That raised the other boys and the firing became general on both sides and lasted several minutes.
>
> After Milford discharged his gun, he was standing on his knees reloading when the ball struck him just back of the hip, going in his back and down by his left kidney and out his right hip. Brother Thomas [Nichols] fired about then at the same man that shot Milford. There was twenty or thirty of them Indians and Mexicans.[19]

The five rangers were able to keep Córdova's men in check well enough to secure their own safety in a nearby thicket, although two had been wounded. Dave Reynolds was hit with a large rifle ball just below the collarbone. In the process of escaping they lost all of their horses and equipment, save their firearms. The men were later reimbursed for the loss of their horses, as evidenced by Private Poore's audited claim, written by Captain Caldwell on July 11 in Seguin.[20]

> Daniel N. Poore had a certain American mare valued into the service of the Republic of Texas Gonzales Ranging Company at one hundred and fifty dollars. Said mare was taken by Córdova and his company in an engagement between a party of spies (sent out by the commander of said company of Gonzales Rangers) and Córdova's company in which several guns were fired and two of the Gonzales Rangers wounded. Said fight occurred the morning after the fight between General Burleson and Córdova on the Guadalupe River near Seguin.

John Nichols became separated from his companions during the battle and was forced to make his own way back to Seguin without any bullets for his gun.

The Indians and Mexicans were on the run and thus did not stick

James Milford Day, one of Guadalupe County's earliest settlers, was seriously wounded in a gun battle with Cordova's rebels on March 30, 1839. (Originally published in A. J. Sowell's *Early Settlers and Indian Fighters of Southwest Texas.)*

James Wilson Nichols (1820–1887), another of Captain Mathew Caldwell's Gonzales Rangers, left details of the early Indian fights in his journals. (Jim Nichols portrait, circa 1870s.)

around to continue the firefight with Caldwell's rangers. The five Texans listened to the clatter of horse hooves crossing the river and stayed in hiding until they were convinced that they were safe. Milford Day was in the most serious shape. He asked Tom Nichols to drag him down to the banks of the Guadalupe and hide him under a bluff.

Dave Reynolds was elected to run back for Seguin for help, leaving Poore and Tom Nichols to assist Day in his suffering. Reynolds stuffed a piece of his shirt into his own chest wound and set out on foot for Seguin. John Nichols arrived in town ahead of him after daybreak, bulletless and unaware of his companions' fates. Nichols reported "killing an Indian" and that he did not think that the other rangers were all dead.

Upon hearing this news, John's brother Jim Nichols and Seguin citizen John Box quickly mounted their horses and prepared to ride out to assist the wounded. As they were harnessing their horses, the wounded Dave Reynolds soon appeared. He "reported none kilt but that Milford was badly wounded."

A party was quickly dispatched to Young's Ford on the Guadalupe to help the wounded ranger scouts. There they found Tom Nichols,

Daniel Poore, and Milford Day. The latter was loaded into a cart and brought back into Seguin, where he would survive but remain crippled. One of the rescue party, ranger Jim Nichols, wrote of Day's suffering.

> We taken them home but Milford had a lingering hard and painful time before he recovered, and after he was thought to be well his hip rose and several pieces of bone worked out. Then for many years he had to undergo the same pain and suffering from his hip rising and pieces of slivered bones working out. He finally recovered after years of pain and suffering, but it made a cripple of him for life. But he is still living at this writing and limping around on one short leg and has seen as many ups and downs since that time as any man of his age.[21]

Although crippled, Milford Day would fight in 1840's battle of Plum Creek and continue to serve in ranger units for years.

★ ★ ★ ★ ★

Prisoner Execution in Seguin

By the time Captain Caldwell arrived back at Seguin from Gonzales, he was aware that Córdova's rebels were retreating back upriver toward the Waterloo area.[22]

While the wounded rangers were being escorted back to Seguin, eight of Edward Burleson's men from the Mill Creek fight also arrived in town with their prisoners. The youngest of these three, the former slave boy of about sixteen years' age, had been wounded several times but had been sewn up by Doctor Fentress. Their captors planned to bring these rebels of Córdova into town and auction them off to the highest bidder.

Once in Seguin, the former slaves soon learned that they would be sold back into captivity again. This thought compelled Raphael, the older gray-haired ex-slave, to protest. He reportedly told John Box, the sergeant of the guard, "You had better kill us now, for we will fight till we die before we will be slaves again."[23]

Raphael then bragged that he had killed many women and children in his time. To gain his freedom, he had also once killed his master and his master's whole family. Once this word was spread to Colonel Burleson, a court martial was ordered for these Córdova force prisoners. Burleson called Seguin rangers Mathew Caldwell, George Washington Nichols, John G. Gray, Paris Smith, French

Smith, and Abraham Roberts to sit on the court-martial board. Ranger Jim Nichols recorded:

> The prisoners were brought before this court martial and they interrogated the old negro first. He stated the same thing to the court that he had stated to Box with the addition that he would fight till he died before [he would be a slave again to any] master. The court passed sentence [that he] suffer the penalty of death by being shot until dead.
>
> The middle aged negro was then brought forward and interrogated. He said he had never kilt anybody but would if necessary to gain his freedom if he was put back in slavery.
>
> "Now," said he, "If you will turn us loose we will go to Mexico and promise to never bother white folks again, but won't be a slave again. We have been free too long."
>
> The court gave him the same sentence and to be executed with the old one. The boy was brought before the court and interrogated. He said he was willing to be sold into slavery again, that he had not been free very long and the first time he ran away he was caught and had to take five hundred lashes on his bare back, and now the second time I ran away I have been shot in four places and captured again, and I am tired of such a life as them colored men, pointing to the two negroes that had been sentenced, calls freedom. The court sentenced him to be sold as a slave to the highest bidder.[24]

At the conclusion of the court-martial, a runner from Bastrop arrived stating that a member of Colonel Burleson's family was ill. Burleson departed with several guards, turning the business of carrying out sentence to Captain Caldwell. The executions were ordered for the next morning and a double guard was kept on the three slaves overnight.

The next morning, March 31, Caldwell had the prisoners marched up the slope west of Seguin. They were halted under a clump of live oaks about a half mile from town, where the two men to be executed were forced to first dig their own graves. According to Jim Nichols, Caldwell "then ordered 8 of Burleson's men to march past the tree and each one to take a gun."

The two condemned prisoners were then made to kneel over their graves and were blindfolded. Upon the order, the shooters fired and the bodies of the men dropped into the graves. Lieutenant James Rice of Captain Andrew's rangers reportedly paid five dollars to take the place of one of the shooters, but was frustrated to have his gun jam at the moment he was to fire, thus missing out on the execution.[25]

The younger slave had been marched to the site to witness the executions. He was eventually sold to the highest bidder, the money being split between the men who had fought the battle at Mill Creek.

★ ★ ★ ★ ★

Caldwell's Pursuit of Córdova

Captain Caldwell's rangers and the Gonzales volunteers were joined by several Seguin resident volunteers before they started after Córdova's forces. The Seguin men volunteering included Ezekiel Smith Sr., Peter D. Anderson, William Clinton, Hugh G. Henderson, Doctor William N. Henry, Frederick Happle, George H. Gray, and two or three others. The total force now numbered about fifty men.

Caldwell's men crossed the Guadalupe where New Braunfels stands, pursuing Córdova through the highlands north of and around San Antonio. He was there joined by Colonel Henry Karnes' cavalry company and the two followed Córdova until his trail divided. His men then proceeded west-northwest to the Old Presidio de Rio Grande Road, where it crosses the Rio Frio, and then followed that road to the Nueces River. Karnes' company took the other trail.

Signs showed Caldwell that he had gained nothing in distance on the retreating Córdova, who appeared to have a comfortable thirty or forty miles lead on them to Mexico.

Deciding that further chase was futile, Captain Caldwell turned his party around and followed the road back to San Antonio. The point at which Caldwell turned his pursuit party around was known as Prickly Pear Prairie, near the Nueces River. There was very little undergrowth about this prairie, save the ever-present cactus, which grew very thick in this area. One of these rangers, Andrew Sowell, later told his nephew that these prickly pear growths made a perfect den for rattlesnakes. From the time the rangers began crossing this prairie until they were well clear of it, Sowell remembered that there was almost constantly the sound of rattlesnakes and the men and their horses had to take great care to avoid being bitten.[26]

Having started without any provisions, his men relied upon wild game. After a winding route of some one hundred and sixty miles through the Texas hills, the men were in need of food and water. Upon arriving back in town, Caldwell found the town welcomed them warmly. Ranger Henry McCulloch, a private under Caldwell, later wrote:

> The hospitable people of that blood-stained old town, gave us a warm reception and the best dinner possible in their then condition, over which the heroic and ever-lamented Col. Henry W. Karnes presided. They also furnished supplies to meet our wants until we reached our respective encampments.[27]

On the way out, Caldwell passed at different places wounded horses abandoned by Córdova's men. One such severely wounded horse was found in the mountains and attracted the attention of Private McCulloch. Upon leaving San Antonio for home with Captain Caldwell's permission, McCulloch and another man sought out and found this horse of chestnut color. Given good attention, the horse recovered entirely and later became well known with McCulloch as "Old Pike."

Although Caldwell's rangers had not engaged Córdova's rebels, they were successful in their pursuit and their actions certainly kept them on the move and without time for further depredations. During the summer of 1839, Captain Caldwell also furnished and commanded an escort for his former private Benjamin McCulloch. McCulloch was involved in surveying and opening a wagon road from Gonzales to the proposed capital of Texas being laid out in Austin. From the courthouse in Gonzales, the road ran fifty-five and one-fourth miles to Austin.

Mathew Caldwell's rangers returned to Seguin, where they were disbanded on June 16 due to expiration of their terms of enlistments.

As for Córdova, he and about twenty of his rebels were last seen on April 5 by a party of Mexican traders from the Rio Grande. The beaten party was by that time about fifty miles below Bexár and apparently making their way for Matamoros.[28]

★ ★ ★ ★ ★

Major Jones' Gunmen Stationed at Austin

The First Regiment of Infantry struggled to enlist new men during the spring of 1839. Captain James January manned a new recruiting station at Post Velasco, located on the Gulf Coast on the east bank of the Brazos River. January's station failed to draw many new recruits, however, and was closed on July 3, 1839.[29]

Captain George Howard's company at Post Gonzales received new soldiers in the early spring who had been enlisted at Galveston, Houston, and Brazoria. In San Antonio, Captain Samuel Jordan's company was composed almost exclusively of cavalrymen who had joined the army during 1838. He had enough men, in fact, that he sent Lieutenant John Brown to La Grange on April 6 with additional men he had received from Colonel Henry Karnes.[30]

Stationed at Post Béxar, Jordan's men were ever aware of the presence of the raiding Comanches. Just as the Colorado River rangers of 1837 had suffered stampeding, the Alamo infantrymen lost their mounts to the Comanches, as noted by Captain Jordan on April 22, 1839.

> Yesterday morning what five public horses and mules I had in camp were stampeded and driven off by the Indians. All the horses belonging to the officers of this post were taken with them.
>
> J[uan] A. Zambrano has some forty or fifty horses ready to deliver, but it will be impossible for me to use them until I receive saddles and bridles. I cannot mount even one man and was consequently obliged to hire men in town to drive the horses to La Grange. Col. Karnes has a number of good horses on hand he will sell the government at the sum rate heretoforth paid.

Henry Karnes remained stationed in the San Antonio area while the first of his new mounted gunmen companies moved up from the Houston area. Major William Jones held supervising command of the first two ranger companies. Captains Mark B. Lewis, who had commanded a company during the 1835 Béxar siege, and James P. Ownby, a San Jacinto veteran, had each mustered in his new volunteer company on March 2. One of Lewis' gunmen was Francisco "Frank" Becerra, who had fought for Santa Anna's Mexican army at San Jacinto. Wounded and then taken prisoner, Becerra had taken residence and been employed by Texans since the revolution.

After gearing up, Lewis and Ownby's companies set out up the Colorado River for the Austin area, where the government was surveying and building the new capital city. The work party under general contractor Edwin Waller was offered protection on this most exposed frontier by Major Jones' gunmen.[31]

On April 9, Jones' men had already moved through Bastrop. By April 14, Major Jones' ranger battalion had made camp at Webber's on the Colorado River. James S. Jones, second lieutenant of Captain Lewis' company, wrote of their expedition on this date.

> We are now upon the borders of the extreme northern settlements and we have not yet heard or seen anything of the enemy. Our little army of volunteers are greatly disappointed in not meeting them and seem delighted with the idea of pursuing them over the mountains.
>
> We shall take up the line of march tomorrow for Waterloo, a small village at the foot of the mountains, where it is probable we shall remain in camp—protecting the frontier when necessary until ordered to form a junction with the residue of men designed for the Santa Fe expedition. We are marching through a beautiful country. Its face presents a scene of grandeur and magnificence rarely, if ever, witnessed in any other part of the American continent.[32]

Due to past Indian raids, this area of Texas was only sparsely settled. Jones' troops found many houses in the area deserted and property rapidly falling to destruction. Major Jones visited the town of Waterloo on April 15 in company with Colonel Edward Burleson. He found the townsite for the republic's new capital to be a beautiful scene of springtime glory.

"The frontier is now quiet and perfectly safe," Jones assured President Lamar. "All fears of an Indian invasion are dissipated and the people are actively employed in planting and landing their crops." He also found that Burleson had recently "acted like a hero and skillful officer" in defeating the Indians and routing the Mexican rebels, all without cost to the Texas government.

As for the men under his command, Major Jones did not think highly of his subordinate officers' ability to control their volunteers. Keeping these men in line while on march was largely done by his own cursing and making examples of men to "make soldiers of them. I hope I have succeeded in part."

Jones' companies were at "Camp Austin, near the mountains" by April 24. Lewis and Ownby's men would remain in the Austin area during the next month, during which time the Indians did not attack the capital workers.[33]

The third company recruited under Colonel Karnes' mounted gunmen battalion was that of Captain John Garrett. Muster roll records show that Captain Garrett's company was mustered into service on April 8, 1839, in Houston. His men were issued much of their provisions by the government, including jackets, pants, shirts, shoes, socks, and blankets.

Known as the "Houston Yagers," Captain Garrett's rangers marched up the Colorado and were also stationed in Austin by May. The work continued on the capital city with little Indian activity to bother the men. Major Jones would soon be called to depart Austin for East Texas with two of his three gunmen companies to quell other hostilities, leaving Garrett's men to defend the Austin area during the summer months.

★ ★ ★ ★ ★

Rice/Flores Fight at the San Gabriel: May 17, 1839

Ignorant of the struggles endured by Córdova to reach Matamoros during March and April, Mexican Indian agent Manuel Flores still desired to meet with Córdova. During the latter days of April 1839, Flores departed Matamoros to meet with Córdova and the Indian

Captain Garrett's "Houston Yagers": April 8–August 8, 1839

Captain:
John Garrett [1]
First Lieutenant:
John A. Creery [2]
Second Lieutenant:
Robert L. Brane [1]
Orderly Sergeant:
Abel A. Chapman
Second Sergeant:
Archibald Ellis
Third Sergeant:
Samuel Lincoln
First Corporal:
Patrick Cushing
Second Corporal:
Charles M. Blackwell
Third Corporal:
Nathaniel Mix
Fourth Corporal:
John Workman
Privates:
John Addy
Peter Baxter
Christopher Brimer [4]
Samuel D. Conaway
Samuel Crawford
William C. Dalrymple
B. P. Duncan [3]
Cuthbert Edwards
John Footman
Charles Gallagher
Thomas F. Graves
John D. Hair
Edward Hall
Henry R. Head
Thomas Headley
John A. Hitzelberger [6]
E. B. Hotchkiss
Henry T. Jones
Francis Kelley
Francis Kelley (Jr.)
John Kelley
Joseph Kelley
Moses Kuykendall [4]
Thomas Martin
Joseph Mary
Hugh McColm
John McCorn
Robert Morris
G. D. Oneale
John M. Perdue [5]
James L. Randolph
Carl C. Rhodes [5]
W. L. Shackley
M. M. Stewart
William P. Stickney
John Swusey
William Thomas
William Thompson

Note: Garrett's company enlisted into Colonel Karnes' mounted gunman regiment.

[1] Resigned June 10.
[2] Assumed command of company June 11.
[3] Enlisted June 4.
[4] Enlisted May 5.
[5] Enlisted May 24.
[6] Enlisted May 17.

Source:
Texas State Archives.

tribes wherever he might find them. Second in command of Flores' party was ensign Juan de la Garza. He also took with him Juan Bautista Sota, plus an escort of about thirty Mexicans and Indians, supplies of ammunition for his allies and all the official papers from Filisola and Canalizo. These papers gave him power to treat with the Indians to secure their friendship with Mexico and combined hostility toward Texas.[34]

Flores' march was slow, as he only crossed the road between Seguin and San Antonio on May 14. On and near this route, his party committed several depredations. One attack was made against a portion of a surveying party which included former ranger captain Louis B. Franks, John James, Ephraim Bollinger, George Lord, George Edwards, William Bracken, and Miles Squier Bennett.

The surveyors had learned to be careful. "Ephraim Bollinger was one of our best frontiersmen," wrote Bennett, "a first rate shot, whose daily practice it was to shoot at a mark, wipe out and reload his rifle carefully."[35]

On Tuesday, May 14, Bollinger was left as the camp guard along with three San Antonio Mexicans. The other surveyors were approaching camp that evening when they heard screams, gunshots, and the war whooping of Indians attacking their camp. By the time the other surveyors reached their camp, it had been overrun, as Miles Bennett recorded.

> Among fragments of camp equipage thrown around we soon came upon the dead bodies of our cook and Manuel [Maria]. Then Flores [a Tejano not to be confused with Manuel Flores], who was mortally wounded, attracted our attention by his groans. Giving him some water, we learned from him that the savages were looking for us; he entreated us to leave the place immediately, for we might expect to be attacked at any moment.
>
> He also said that then the Indians had succeeded in capturing Mr. Bollinger. They stripped him and tied his hands behind him and made him run while they pricked him with their lances.

Captain Franks' surveying party soon found Ephraim Bollinger's naked, scalped body. They moved the body and covered it, tended briefly to the dying Mr. Flores, and then headed back to San Antonio. A relief party was quickly dispatched to offer proper burials to the dead.

These Indians were working in conjunction with Flores' men and were well armed. With knowledge from William Robison that Córdova planned to return to East Texas after visiting with Mexican authorities in Matamoros, Texas leaders kept a ranging company of about twenty men from Bastrop under Captain Micah Andrews out on scouting duty to the west. These men were instrumental in uncovering the Manuel Flores party.

In Béxar, the news of the May 14 killing of Louis Franks' four surveyors quickly spread. Cornelius Van Ness and Franks left at once to carry the word to Colonel Burleson at Bastrop, reaching that settlement on May 17. Burleson immediately raised about two hundred volunteers and started in hot pursuit on the morning of May 18.[36]

In the meantime, Flores' party crossed the Guadalupe at the old Nacogdoches ford on May 15 at the spot where the city of New Braunfels now stands. While on patrol south of Austin on May 15, Captain Andrews' company, among whom were six civilians, discovered the Flores party.[37]

While reconnoitering on Onion Creek near where the Old San Antonio Road crossed the creek, Lieutenant James Rice and ranger B. B. Castleberry had ridden over a hill south of the creek to kill a deer for supper late in the afternoon of May 15. Rice was a veteran ranger who had survived the deadly 1837 Stone Houses fight and most recently had participated in Burleson's Mill Creek fight.

Rice and Castleberry galloped back to Andrews' company and reported that they had observed a large drove of horses in the distance, many of which appeared to be mounted. Captain Andrews decided that he would intercept the party at the crossing of Onion Creek. Taking advantage of a range of hills south of the creek which obscured the unknown party from the rangers, the patrol pushed forward as rapidly as the terrain would permit. When the rangers arrived at the foot of the range of hills, they found that the party they sought had crossed the creek and had entered the thick post oak and cedar thicket on the north side.

The rangers took up the trail and followed it a few miles, but were forced to halt with the onset of darkness. They left their own horses saddled, sleeping on their arms. At daylight on May 16, they renewed the pursuit. Captain Andrews was becoming more confident that this was the Córdova-Flores party returning from Mexico. After pursuing the trail about two miles and just as they were entering a large cedar brake, Andrews' rangers met their enemy face to face. The two parties suddenly came to a halt within forty or fifty yards of one another. It was apparent that Flores' party had been rambling around in the cedar brake all night, tired and worn out. They were apparently trying to back track out when they ran into Andrews' men.

At the time the Texans confronted Flores' party, they were not convinced of how many opponents they were facing. Andrews' men were divided on whether to attack or not. Although close at hand, the Mexicans were well concealed by brush and timber. Their exact number could not be determined. Perceiving a hesitation on the part of the Texans, the Mexicans put up a bold front by cursing and daring the rangers to charge them. Several of the Texans who spoke Spanish shouted back in that language.

One of the volunteers who had gone along with Captain Andrews, Wayne Barton, was opposed to giving battle. Turning to Andrews, Barton informed Andrews that if he led his men into the thicket, "it will be the equivalent of leading them into a slaughter pen." He stated that all would be killed.

Captain Andrews and some of those men contemplating making the assault were taken by this statement. While the Texans discussed their next move, the enemy moved into the heart of the cedar brake. In the end, Andrews decided to withdraw his men and turned them toward home.

Most of his men were still ready to fight, however, and they were disgusted with their captain for not fighting. The farther they rode from the enemy, the more vocal they became. After heading about three miles toward home, one of the party, A. J. "Ad" Adkisson, told those dissatisfied to hold up a little. He would ride up and ask Captain Andrews to give those who desired so the permission to return and follow the enemy. These men dropped back while Adkisson informed Andrews of some of his men's desires.

Adkisson assured Andrews that these men did not ask for Andrews' assumption of responsibility for them, but simply to grant them permission to withdraw from his immediate command. The captain hesitated a moment, and then said, "Yes, and I'll go back, too."

This news was good to all but six of the patrol, who chose to go ahead and return home. Only about twenty Texans remained in pursuit of Flores at this point. They headed out in a westerly direction with the intention of intercepting the Mexican force as it came from the cedar brake. Upon arriving at the spot where they expected them to exit, the rangers found that the enemy was already ahead of them.

It was nine in the morning when the Texans started in a fast gallop after the enemy's trail. They soon realized that the enemy was also moving at a fast gallop and were unable to overtake them during the day. With the nightfall's approach, Andrews' party camped near the mountains about a mile to the north of the Colorado River. During the night a heavy rain fell, rendering travel very difficult the next morning. Soon after resuming the line of pursuit early on May 17, Captain Andrews' horse became quite lame, and since he was a large man of about two hundred pounds it became necessary for him to turn back for home. According to a report of Colonel Burleson, "Capt. Andrews being very heavy, his horse failed." Two men with horses more lame than the others were detailed to accompany their commander.

The Texan force was now reduced to seventeen men, falling under command of Lieutenant Rice. They pushed on in pursuit, although many of their horses were equally worn. By traveling slowly and closely examining every sign, the rangers succeeded in following the dim, water-logged trail through the mountains out into the prairie towards the San Gabriel River. There, the Mexicans had camped the previous night. From this point, their trail was fresh and could be followed at a gallop.

About 2:00 p.m. on May 17, Rice's men reached the south fork of the San Gabriel at a point near a spring, not far from the residence of William Johnson. Here, the enemy had taken a noon break and cut down a bee tree. The bees had not yet settled when the Texans arrived, and four camp fires still burned. Perceiving only four fires to mean a small number of enemy, the Texans pushed ahead enthusiastically, hoping to quickly meet their foes.

About a quarter mile in advance of the main body rode spies Felix McCluskey and B. B. Castleberry. When the main body was about a

Captain Andrews' Rangers: March 10–June 10, 1839

Captain:	John William Brown	Thomas McKernon
Micah Andrews	John Burleson	Nelson Merrill
First Lieutenant:	B. B. Castleberry	Richard M. Mills
James Ogden Rice	R. T. Chandler	William Newcomb
Orderly Sergeant:	Allen J. Davis	Isaac Norris
John J. Eakin	Francis Duncan	Milton Parker
Privates:	Samuel Fowler	C. S. Parrish
Allen J. Adkisson	Abel Harness	R. T. Smith
Henry Alderson	David Hudson	
Mathew Anderson	Ira Leffingwell	*Substitute for G. Glover.
B. D. Bassford	Winfield Lowe*	
Allen E. Brown	Felix McCluskey	*Source: Texas State Archives.*

mile past the camp, they signaled for the others to hold up, dismount and cut switches. These orders were followed, and the other rangers then remounted and advanced with their switches. Upon catching up to the spies, they were informed that the enemy had just passed over a hill immediately ahead.

Rice's rangers now headed out at a steady gallop, and within another quarter of a mile came within sight of their enemy. The Mexicans now spotted them, and whipped their own horses to flee. The Mexicans occasionally turned as if to prepare to fight, but quickly renewed their retreat when the advancing Texans continued to advance. As the distance narrowed, the Texans sounded their own battle yells, each time sending the Mexicans fleeing again.

Each time the Mexicans stopped, a leader presumed by the Texians to be Flores could be seen riding up and down their ranks with sword drawn, shouting at his men to bolster their courage. Each time, however, he and his men would renew their flight. The Texians continued their chase until they had driven the enemy onto a steep bluff on the banks of the North San Gabriel about twenty-five miles from the newly selected capital site of Austin. This bluff was so steep that the enemy could not descend it.

The Mexican commandant now found himself in a tight spot. In an effort for some of his men to be able to find a crossing spot, he and a few of his companions now turned and charged the Texans. Rice's men quickly took cover in a live oak grove nearby. With eight or ten men, the Mexican leader desperately charged to within fifteen or twenty paces of the Texans and fired a volley without effect. Having just dismounted, the Texans had not hitched their horses and were ill-prepared to return fire.

William Wallace, already a hero of the Brushy Creek battle in February, was quicker than the rest this day and was ready for action. Just as the rebel leader believed to be Flores wheeled his horse to retreat, Wallace took good aim and fired. At the crack of his gun, the commandant rolled from his horse and fell dead from a shot through the heart. Two of his companions were also killed. The rest of the charging Mexicans fled to join their comrades, who had in the meantime succeeded in finding a crossing point on the river.

Abandoning all their extra horses, the Flores party hastily left their mules, baggage, ammunition, and other belongings behind. The Mexicans fled rapidly toward the mountains beyond the San Gabriel, presumably towards the Falls of the Brazos area.

Too tired to pursue any further, and feeling victorious in their brief fight, Rice's men collected the discarded goods. They gathered 114 horses and mules, some three hundred pounds of powder, plus a similar quantity of shots, balls, and some bar lead. From the Mexican leader's body—believed to be that of Manuel Flores—they took a quantity of important papers, including several land certificates taken from the surveyors killed near San Antonio. Most historical accounts have Flores being killed in this encounter, but he would continue to be a factor in the Texas Indian wars into 1842. The March 28, 1840, issue of the *Colorado Gazette*, in fact, clarifies that the body of "the person supposed to have been Flores was only the commander of a small party who had the papers and baggage of Flores in charge."[38]

There was also a letter written at Matamoros by General Canalizo to Córdova, to the chiefs of the Caddos and Seminoles and to Big Mush and Bowles of the Cherokees. Also among the papers was a letter dated April 20 from Córdova that informed Flores of Córdova's inability to accompany him on his way east on account of a wound he had received en route from Burleson's men. In a report to the secretary of war on May 22, Burleson stated that he had lost this particular letter.

Two Texas historical markers stand in tribute to the fight in which Flores was killed. One is located on State Highway 29, four miles east of Liberty Hill and eleven miles west of Georgetown in Williamson County. Another commemorates James Rice and the Battle of San Gabriels. It stands at the intersection of FM 973 and 1660, eight miles south of Taylor.[39]

Those of Rice's men who had participated in this fight are known to include A. J. Adkisson, Jonathan Davis, S. G. Harness, William P. Hardeman, and B. B. Castleberry.

Everything thus collected, Rice's party struck out for home, arriving at the spring on the South San Gabriel in time to camp for the night at the same spot where the Mexicans had camped the previous night. While en route to the South San Gabriel, Rice's men were met by Captain James Ownby, who was in command of about thirty cavalrymen recently employed by the new act of December 1838. Ownby's men were well provisioned and were followed by Colonel Burleson with another party of men. Burleson's men had started in relief of the Andrews-Rice party when word was received in Austin and Bastrop of the events from the men who had abandoned Andrews' command after the cedar brake episode.

When Captain Ownby's men at first discovered a large *caballada* of horses being driven by men in Mexican sombreros (taken from their enemy), they felt that they were intercepting the Flores party. Ownby ordered his men to dismount and prepare to fire, but one of his more alert men saved Rice's rangers from harm by announcing that he thought these were Texans. These two parties met at a point between the battleground where Flores was defeated and the South Fork of the San Gabriel. As Rice's men came up and salutations were exchanged, some of Ownby's men commenced talking about a division of the spoils.

What started as a joke was taken seriously. Those who had fought the Mexicans and captured the spoils thought Ownby's men were serious about wanting half the spoils. They were informed that they would receive nothing, having not fought for it. Ownby's men then chose not to share any food or provisions with Rice's men, who had been without for two days. Rice's men were not even allowed to camp with the others, and these fatigued men had to post their own guards during the night to ensure that their spoils were not pilfered by their "relief" party.[40]

Early the next morning, May 18, Rice and his men started for Austin. As they were ascending Pilot Knob, near present Round Rock on Brushy Creek, they were met by Colonel Burleson with another relief group. This party generously furnished Rice's men with food and provisions without requesting part of the booty. After dinner, Burleson and Rice's forces returned to Austin, where Colonel Burleson, Samuel Highsmith, and Logan Vandever were selected as arbitrators to determine the division of the spoils.

They quickly decided to give the horses and other goods to Rice's men. Rice's men then proceeded to Hornsby's Bend, nine miles below Austin, where all the captured horses were put in a corral and divided into seventeen lots by disinterested parties. Each man drew for his choice. After dividing the horses, each man began opening the captured leather bags. One of these contained the papers of Córdova, Flores, and the Mexican officials in Matamoros. A Mexican on hand by the name of Francisco was able to translate some of the documents on the spot, roughly enough to tell that they were important. These papers were then turned over to Burleson, who transmitted them to the Texas government at Houston and to Secretary of War Sidney Johnston.

The letters proved Flores and Córdova had been commissioned by Mexican authorities to "harass the Texans persistently, burn their habitations, lay waste their fields, steal their horses." They had also been commissioned to "pursue and punish all Indians friendly to the Texans and all Mexicans who traded with them."[41]

Burleson and Johnston found evidence that Flores had contacted chiefs of the Caddos, Kickapoos, Shawnees, and other tribes. He also carried with him letters for Big Mush and Chief Bowles of the Cherokees. These captured papers were enough to convince President Lamar and his cabinet that the Cherokees were in correspondence with the Mexicans, even though there were no reply letters from Cherokee leaders to justify this conclusion.

In fairness to the Cherokees, they may have actually done little more than just listen to the warlike proposals being shoved at them by Mexican agents. Whether justified or not, this perceived conspiracy of the Cherokees against Texas settlers would soon lead forces to push them into the bloody Cherokee War.

CHAPTER 9

Bird's Creek Fight

May 19–Early June 1839

Walters Ordered Away From Cherokees' Saline

President Lamar, having decided that the Cherokees were conspiring with Mexico to forge another assault on his young republic, authorized Major Baley Walters to raise two companies to be stationed at the Neches Saline. Walters, a veteran of the 1838 Kickapoo battle, was to occupy the saline, located in present Smith County just inside the Cherokees' claim.

The village of Chief Bowles was located near the Saline, just east of the Neches River. His village had moved several times since the Cherokees had first entered Texas. His three hundred to four hundred tribesmen had made their home on the Sabine River in northeastern Texas in 1828. In 1836, Bowles had been in the village that was about fifteen miles southwest of present Henderson. As many as six other Cherokee villages existed north of Nacogdoches during the late 1830s, including that of Chief Big Mush south of the present town of Rusk.[1]

By 1838, the large tribe of Cherokees under Chief Bowles had moved their village to a location near the Neches Saline. In the course of operating his salt business at the Saline, Bowles entered into partnership with Dr. Elisha DeBard, who had been wounded at nearby Kickapoo and thereafter lived near the Saline. The Cherokees considered this Great Saline their tribe's business source and were therefore aggressive defenders of this natural commodity.

Lamar asked Major Walters to employ his two companies for six months' service in occupying the Saline. Secretary of War Johnston explained the reasoning behind Lamar's move.

> At this point it was thought that all intercourse might be cut off between the Cherokees, and the Indians of the Prairies

> who were known to be hostile; and that the adoption of this measure would give protection to that portion of the frontier, and leave no pretext for attributing any depredations committed to the Indians of the prairies, while it would be no inconvenience to the Cherokees.[2]

Walters was only able to raise one company, Captain Henry Madison Smith's Nacogdoches County Rangers, who mustered in on March 1. Captain Smith's men marched to the Neches Saline, where they set up a working camp that became known as Fort Saline in present Henderson County. Upon their arrival, Walters was informed by Chief Bowles through agent Martin Lacy that "any attempt to establish the post in obedience of his orders would be repelled by force." Taking advice from Lacy, Walters decided it prudent to move his small force to the west bank of the Neches and there establish a post. Camp was established in the old Kickapoo village, near the site of the previous year's battle. Walters' rangers established Fort Kickapoo, which would soon became a major assembling point for Texan troops.[3]

Private Peter F. Rodden, who had just arrived in Nacogdoches from Mississippi at the time Captain Smith's ranger company was organizing, wrote of his experiences.

> No sooner did our little handful of men march into the Cherokee Nation before we was ordered by the Chief of the tribe to return back to the settlements.
>
> "Forward" was the watch word and forward we did go beyond the bounds of their nation and commenced to build a fort wherever we could shelter ourselves against the attacks of more hostile tribes.[4]

During the time that Walter's men were establishing Fort Kickapoo, Major John Wortham still commanded two companies of the Third Militia Brigade's volunteer rangers in the Houston County area. The men under his command included Captain James Box's Fort Houston company and Captain Solomon Adams' Crockett-area company.

Major Wortham issued an appeal on April 27 for more Houston County citizens to enroll as members of his "Battalion of Rangers." His battalion was furnished by the government, as evidenced by quartermaster correspondence between Major Hillequist Landers, Commander of Subsistence, and the army's Quartermaster General

William G. Cooke. Letters from Landers dated May 21 and May 22, 1839, show that Wortham's men were issued a thirty-day supply of corn and beef. Another note shows that the Houston County Rangers were to be furnished with pork, rice, three barrels of flour, thirty-two pounds of soap, twelve pounds of candles, fifty pairs of pants and shoes, twenty boxes of percussion caps, and twenty pounds of lead.[5]

The supplies were stored in cribs built in Crockett and at Fort Houston for the rangers' use. The supplies in Crockett were overseen by the Honorable Isaac Parker "to be issued under orders of Majr. Wortham."

The buildup of such troops in this area would soon become significant as peace between Bowles' Cherokees and the whites slowly deteriorated. Chief Bowles wrote a letter to General Rusk in Nacogdoches, complaining that his people were alarmed by the presence of Major Walters' troops at the Kickapoo village.[6]

In response to Walters being ordered away from the Neches Saline, President Lamar wrote an ultimatum for Bowles which he had hand-delivered to the Indian chief. This letter was delivered to the Cherokee village by Indian agent Martin Lacy, twenty-one-year-old Private John Henninger Reagan, Dr. William George Washington Jowers, a surgeon attached to Walters' ranging company, and a half-breed interpreter named Cordray, who all went to meet with the Indians. This foursome ventured from Fort Kickapoo in late May with Lamar's letter.

According to Reagan, Bowles's main village was located south of the Saline at this time. This second village was located about four miles northwest of the present town of Alto, about five miles north of the Old San Antonio Road and about three miles north of Fort Lacy. The Cherokee camp was located 150 feet from a spring now called Bowles Creek and about five hundred yards northwest of the small community of Red Lawn, several miles northwest of present Alto along Highway 69.[7]

Lamar stated that six men would place a value on all the property of the Indians that was immovable and that a fair compensation would be paid to them for their move. Lamar's communication to Chief Bowles on May 26 warned him about ordering Major Walters away from the Saline, saying that "In this, you have committed an error." He warned Bowles that he and his people had been deceived by "the forked tongue of the Mexicans" into rising against the white settlers. These enemies of Texas had coerced the Cherokees to run "into dangerous paths" which Lamar felt would only lead to "our injury and your ruin."[8]

The president of Texas pulled no punches. He informed Bowles "that the Cherokee will never be permitted to establish a permanent and independent jurisdiction within the inhabited limits of this government." They were only being allowed to remain where they were in East Texas until the government could make peaceful arrangements for their removal, "without the necessity of shedding blood."

Lamar told Bowles that he was only being painfully truthful about the intentions of the Texas government. Bowles denied that his tribe had had any responsibility for the recent depredations in the area. He stated that "the wild Indians had done the killing and stealing, and not his people."[9]

John Reagan, one of the four who delivered the message to Bowles, later described this meeting.

> When we reached the residence of Bowles, he invited the agent, the interpreter, Jowers, and myself to a fine spring near his house, where he and others seated themselves on a fallen tree. The President's message was then read and interpreted by one Cordray, a half-breed Mexican. In the conversation which followed, Bowles stated that he could not make a definite answer as to abandoning the country until he could consult his chiefs and head men; so it was agreed that he might have time for such a consultation. If I remember correctly, about ten days was the limit set.[10]

Lacy's party departed Cherokee Nation with an agreement that both sides would meet about the end of the first week in June. President Lamar used this time to begin mobilizing troops.

He had already ordered Colonel Edward Burleson's regular army to march from Camp Burleson to East Texas to join the other forces being gathered. On May 27, two of the volunteer mounted ranging companies under the direction of Lieutenant Colonel Devereaux Woodlief and Major William Jones departed Bastrop to join with Burleson.

★ ★ ★ ★ ★

Rangers Take Station at Fort Milam

By the spring of 1839, the frontier service was operating at its strongest level since the fall of 1836. Lamar's call for three hundred new volunteers from heavily populated coastal and interior counties to help bear the burden of frontier defense had boosted the number of companies previously authorized by Congress in December and January.

One of the newer ranger companies organized in Houston during March was a thirty-four-man unit placed under command of First Lieutenant William G. Evans. Evans had served during late 1838 and early 1839 under Major Bonnell's Second Militia Brigade in the companies of captains George Briscoe and Joseph Daniels. First Sergeant William H. Weaver and bugler Francis Bettinger of Evans' new company had also served in Daniels' Milam Guards through February 1839.

Lieutenant Evans' company, known as the Travis Spies, was organized on March 20 and ordered several days later to report to Fort Milam. They departed Houston and reached their designated station on April 3, 1839, where they were directed to protect the local settlers.[11] Fort Milam was situated two miles above present Marlin and had been built by Captain Daniels' Milam Guards.

While at Fort Milam, Evan's company, and later that of Captain John Bird, made use of the residents of Fort Marlin for supplies and subsistence. These residents were not paid and later filed for what they were owed. They asked in 1856 to be paid twenty dollars per ranger and his horse per month who stationed themselves at Marlin's Fort, for a total of $3,520. John Marlin and Jarrett Menefee were the

Lt. Evans' Rangers (The "Travis Spies"): March 20–Sept. 20, 1839

First Lt., Commanding	Joseph Flippen [1]	Washington Rhodes [1]
William G. Evans [1]	Abner Frost [1]	Jarrett Ridgway [1]
First Sergeant:	Thomas Gay	James M. Robinett
William H. Weaver	Charles M. Gevin	Thomas Robinett
Second Sergeant:	W. W. Hanman	John Romann
James O. Butler [1]	James Hickey [1]	John St. Clair [1]
First Corporal:	Hezekiah Joner [1]	John Weston [1]
Thomas Brown [1]	John Kirk [1]	William Winkler
Second Corporal:	Joseph Mayor [2]	
Samuel A. Blain	Jarrett Menefee [1]	
Musician:	Laban Menefee [1]	
Francis Bettinger [1]	Thomas A. Menefee [1]	
Privates:	Thomas S. Menefee	
Charles Ball [1]	Thomas J. Miller [1]	
Grafton H. Boatler [1]	Robert Mills	
Littleton Brown [1]	Frederick Pool [1]	
David W. Collins [1]	Hiram A. Powers	

[1] Left at Fort Milam during May 1839.

[2] Crippled; left behind at Houston.

Source: Brown, *Indian Wars and Pioneers of Texas*, 72-73.

men who supplied the goods, but the claim was filed by their children and heirs. This petition described in part Marlin and Menefee's services to the rangers.

> The said John Marlin and Jarrett Menefee emigrated to the Republic of Texas in the year A.D. 1834 and settled in what was then known as Robertson County, near the Great Falls of the river Brazos, where they resided until their death, and when so living there, which at the time of their settlement was the very extreme border of the frontier in that section of the country, they suffered great hardships and privations necessarily attendant upon a frontier life in a savage country . . .
>
> For five months and a half, from the third day of April to the twelfth day of September in the year A.D. 1839, there was a company of Rangers raised at the instance of the then existing government, to protect the frontier from the ravages of the Indians–which said company was commanded by Captain John Bird and Lieutenant Wm G. Evans . . . Thirty two men with their horses belonging to the same company were quartered upon the said John Marlin and Jarrett Menefee, and for the time specified above, they had to feed and take care of the said number of men and horses.[12]

These families were not paid by Texas for their troubles at the time. Corporal Samuel A. Blain of Lieutenant Evans' company later testified that Menefee and Marlin had indeed furnished such goods as corn and wheat to the rangers. He added that

> Marlin served often in said company as a pilot [guide] in Indian expeditions without ever having his name placed upon the muster roll. His services were important to us because he was well acquainted with the country and none of us were.

On May 6, Lieutenant Evans' company was joined at Fort Milam by the company of Captain John Bird. Bird was in command of fifty-nine rangers who had been mustered into service on April 21, 1839, from Fort Bend and Austin counties for a three-month enlistment. Bird, born in Tennessee in 1795, had brought his family to Texas in 1829 and received title to a league of land in present Burleson County on October 14, 1831. He had commanded a company of volunteers in General Sam Houston's army during the San Jacinto campaign, but had missed the main battle.[13]

As senior officer, Captain Bird took command of Fort Milam, although he actually took up quarters in some deserted houses on the spot where Marlin now stands. Lieutenant Evans and his men actually resided in the fort.[14]

The men under Bird and Evans had nothing of any action during May, and their provisions completely ran out. The men were forced to survive on wild game meat alone. This caused some grumblings and five men became mutinous to the point that Bird felt a court-martial

Captain Bird's Rangers (Austin Volunteers): April 24–July 24, 1839

Captain:
John Bird[1]
First Lieutenant:
James Ervine[2]
Second Lieutenant:
William R. Allen
Second Sergeant:
William P. Sharp
First Corporal:
William P. Bird
Second Corporal:
William B. Blair[2]
Privates:
Anderson Alkenson[9]
George Allen[2]
John Atkinson[3]
William Ayres
William Badgett
Joseph H. Barnard[2]
C. Beisner[3]
Joshua O. Blair
Andrew J. Bond
Milton Bradford
Thomas Bradford
Daniel Bradley
James Brookshire
Nathaniel Brookshire[4]
James Bunch[5]
Jackson E. Burdick[3]
Elijah Foreman
Tillman C. Fort
Ezekiel George[6]
Stephen Goodman[3]
George W. Grimes
H. M. C. Hall
M. J. Hannon[3]
Warren Hastings
George W. Hensel
James Hensley
William Hensley
Wiley Hickerson[2]
William J. Hodge[3]
John H. Hughes
Lewis L. Hunter[2]
A. J. Ivey
Edward Jocelyn
A. J. Joy
Lewis Kleberg
Benjamin G. Kuyger
T. W. Lightfoot
Green B. Lynch
Joseph S. Marsh
J. D. Marshall[2]
John Marshall[8]
Robert Marshall[8]
James H. Martin[2]
Archibald McCorkle[8]
Neil McCrarey[3]
Joseph McGuines[3]
James M. Moreton[3]
Jesse E. Nash
Argalus G. Parker
George W. Pentacost
Jonathan Peters
Oliver Peters[2]
William Peters
William R. Randall[8]
John E. Rector
Charles B. Shepherd
Joseph H. Slack
William Smith[7]
Thomas Stephens[7]
James Stephenson
Jesse W. Stoddard[2]
James H. Thompson[8]
John D. Thompson[2]
Henry Vern[2]
Bela Vickery
Charles Waller[3]
Lewis M. H. Washington[2]
F. G. Woodward

[1] Killed May 26, 1839.
[2] Absent from fight. Joined company June 9.
[3] Absent from fight.
[4] Became captain on May 26, 1839.
[5] Joined June 27.
[6] Joined June 9.
[7] Joined June 18.
[8] Joined June 9.
[9] Discharged June 21.

Source: Muster roll from Texas State Archives; Brown, *Indian Wars*, 72-73.

was due. Without proper officers present to conduct such a tribunal, he determined to send these men under guard to Colonel Burleson in Bastrop. For this purpose, twelve men were detailed under First Lieutenant James Ervine.[15]

Captain Bird decided that he would proceed a portion of the way to Bastrop with his own company. To bolster the loss of these rebellious soldiers and the dozen who had been pulled to guard them, Bird pulled a dozen men from the ranks of Lieutenant Evans' company to strengthen his own. Sergeant William Weaver was in charge of the detachment from Evan's company that joined Bird's. Evans remained at Fort Milam with a few of Bird's rangers and twenty-two of his own men.

Before leaving Fort Milam, Captain Bird wrote to the quartermaster general's office in Houston on Monday, May 20. Frustrated by his lack of supplies, he requested stores without taking time to fill out a proper requisition.[16]

Captain Bird's party of fifty-odd men departed Fort Milam on May 20 and headed for Fort Smith on the Little River. This frontier post had been built in November 1836 by Colonel Coleman's rangers and had been largely abandoned for two years, since the Indian battles of May 1837. Bird's men reached Fort Smith, later known as Fort Griffin, on Friday morning and made camp.

★ ★ ★ ★ ★

Captain Bird's Last Fight: May 26, 1839

On Sunday morning, May 26, Lieutenant James Ervine and his twelve guards were dispatched by Bird to take the five deserters to Colonel Burleson in Bastrop. Leaving his next most senior officer, Second Lieutenant William R. Allen, in charge of camp, Captain Bird rode along with the guards for part of their journey. Bird was accompanied by Private Nathaniel "Nathan" Brookshire.

Bird and Brookshire accompanied the prisoners for a few miles. Thereafter, they turned, sending the other party of men on toward Bastrop as they retraced their path back to Fort Smith. During their return, they came across three Indians who were skinning a buffalo. They "routed" them, and captured one of their horses laden with meat.

During Bird's absence, the men left at Little River Fort also sighted Indians. Around 9:00 a.m., a small party of Indians busily chasing buffalo ran a gang of the creatures very close to the fort. Upon sighting the rangers at the supposedly abandoned fort, the Indians made a hasty retreat north over the rolling prairie. Sergeant Weaver was eager to pursue them, but Lieutenant Allen refused, fearing that an attack would expose Bird and Brookshire to certain death.

As soon as Bird and his companion returned, they were informed of the excitement. Bird directed an examination into the condition of his men's armament and then ordered, "To horse." A rapid march in the direction of the fleeing Indians was undertaken. "At one o'clock p.m., Captain Bird marched against them with a command of 35, rank and file," wrote Nathan Brookshire five days later.

Various figures exist as to the exact number of men who fought in the impending battle, but most differ only slightly. Nathan Brookshire's accounting of the men who fought in the battle was taken only five days after the action and is the most likely. His report shows that thirty-five men departed to fight the Indians, twenty-three from Bird's company and twelve from Evans'. Twenty-two men remained under Lieutenant Evans at Fort Milam from his company, plus several men of Captain Bird's company.

After moving about five miles out from the fort, Bird's rangers came in sight of a group of Indians. The Texans counted twenty-seven of the Indians and decided to give chase. They were unable to overtake them. The Indians were well mounted on horseback and could easily evade the Texans, but appeared to stay only just out of gunshot distance. The Indians continued at a moderate, deliberate pace through the broken prairie. Occasionally, a single Indian would dart off in advance of his comrades and disappear. After pursuing some four or five miles, small parties of well mounted Indians would frequently appear and join the first body. Still the retreat and pursuit was maintained.

Private Brookshire figured that the complete pursuit of these Indians carried Bird's rangers a distance of more than eleven miles from Fort Smith. One charge was ordered when the Texans reached a distance of as close as 175 yards, but it had no effect, due to the speed of the Indians' horses. Brookshire wrote:

> Finding the pursuit in vain, a retreat was ordered. After retreating about one-half mile, we found ourselves surrounded by about forty Indians, hurling their arrows upon us from every direction. We discovered in our front, about 600 yards, a ravine; between our lines and the ravine were the main body of the Indians, who made a desperate effort to keep us out, but in vain; we routed them and gained a favorable position.

The fight was even more desperate than Brookshire's account makes it sound. When the Indians charged down from their vantage point on a nearby ridgeline, the Texans were immediately surrounded and taken under heavy fire. It was Sergeant William Weaver who directed Captain Bird's attention to the welcome ravine, afterwards named Bird's Creek, in the distance. The spot of this battle is located about seven miles northeast of present Belton. Located at the base of the hill, the ravine offered the thirty-five Texans the most advantageous position in the area. Bird showed the utmost composure amid the shower of bullets and arrows, directing his men to dismount their horses.

Leading their horses in solid column, Bird's men made their way to the ravine and made a lodgment for both men and horses. One man, H. M. C. Hall, persisted in remaining on horseback and he was mortally wounded while dismounting on the bank. The ravine was in the open prairie with a ridge gradually ascending from its head and on either side, reaching the principal elevations at from two hundred and fifty to three hundred yards. For about eighty yards the ravine had

Participants of Bird's Creek Battle: May 26, 1839

Captain Bird's Company: 23 men

Officers:

John Bird, Capt.[1]
William R. Allen, 2nd Lieut.[2]
William P. Sharp, 2nd Sergeant
William P. Bird, 1st. Corporal

Privates:

William P. Ayres
William Badgett
James Brookshire
Nathaniel Brookshire
Tillman C. Fort
George W. Grimes
H. M. C. Hall [1]
Warren Hastings
George W. Hensel [2]
John H. Hughes
A. J. Ivey
Lewis Kleberg
Benjamin G. Kuyger
Joseph S. Marsh
Jesse E. Nash [1]
William Peters
Joseph H. Slack
James Stephenson
Bela Vickery

Lieut. Evans' Company: 12 men

Officers:

William H. Weaver, 1st Sgt. [1]
Samuel A. Blain, 2nd Corporal

Privates:

Thomas Gay [1]
Charles M. Gevin
W. W. Hanman
Thomas Sutherland Menefee
Robert Mills
Hiram A. Powers
James M. Robinett
Thomas Robinett
John Romann
William Winkler

[1] Killed. [2] Wounded.

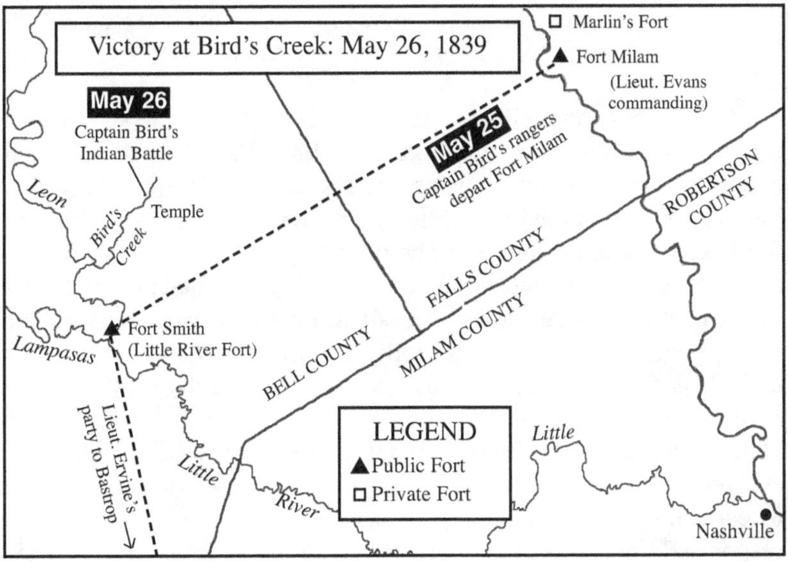

washed out into a channel, and then expanded into a flat surface. The Texans, having secured this only defensible point within reach, took cover.

As the rangers took cover in the ravine, the Indians retired to the top of the nearby hill, which was a distance of about three hundred yards away. They appeared to be holding a council of war and smoke signals were sent to other Indians in the distance. The Indians were Caddo, Kickapoo, and Comanche. To the dismay of all watching, these signals attracted more Indians, who began appearing atop the ridge over the passing minutes.

The senior warrior among them was noted to be Buffalo Hump, a Comanche war chief. According to Texan accounts, he was "bedecked with his immense and grotesque buffalo hide war bonnet surmounted with horns." Some of his other warriors were seen to strip for battle and one warrior hoisted a beautiful flag of blue and red, likely the trophy of some previous victory.

One of Bird's men, Nathan Brookshire, recalled:

> In about half an hour, a reinforcement of about two hundred Indians came up in full view, making about two hundred and forty or fifty strong. After drawing up their lines, the war-whoop from one end of their line to the other was heard, which shrieked in the ears of our gallant little band, which was soon followed by a desperate charge from every point; but our

> boys gave them such a warm reception they were handsomely repulsed, though the charge continued one-half hour.

At the signal, the Indians rode down the hill at gentle and beautiful gallops, making a regular single file line. They then commenced encircling Bird's rangers, using their shields with great dexterity. Passing in front of the head of the ravine, they then turned in front of the Texan line at a distance of about thirty yards. This was viewed as a trial of sorts for the men being attacked. This created among Bird's men a deathly silence and doubtlessly tested every man's nerves. The lead Indian saluted the Texans with, "How do you do? How do you do?" This chant was repeated by a number of his followers.[17]

Just as the Indian repeated his chant for the third time, a Dutchman named William Winkler presented his rifle with great composure and took stance as if he were aiming at a deer. According to early historian John Henry Brown, Winkler cried out angrily in response, "I dosh tolerably well! How dosh you do, God tam you!" He fired, striking the chief, and yelled at him, "Now, how dosh you do, you tam red rascal!"

Not another word had been uttered to this point, but the impromptu action of Winkler served as a stimulus for the rest of his fellow Texans, who now opened fire with their rifles and shouted hurrahs. The first shots from Bird's rangers, however, dropped very few Indians. In return, ranger Thomas Gay fell dead in the ditch from a rifle ball.

Recoiling under the fire, the Indians again formed on the hill and remained there about twenty minutes. A second charge was then made in the same fashion, but this time they made a complete circle around the Texans while dealing out a heavy fire among them. The Texans' early fears had been replaced by adrenaline, anger, and courage. Their shots this time dropped a good number of the Indian warriors. Captain Bird's own losses were high during this charge, however. Jesse Nash was killed by an arrow. Lieutenant Allen and George Hensel were severely wounded and disabled.

Also killed was fearless Sergeant Weaver, who received a fatal rifle ball to the head. Weaver had joined the Travis Spies during the company's formation on March 20 and was elected orderly sergeant. Lieutenant Evans recorded that Weaver "was killed in a battle with Comanche and other Indians." The late sergeant's public debt papers described him as five feet seven inches tall, with "dark hair, eyes, and complexion, twenty-one years of age, a native of Mississippi, and was by occupation a clerk."[18]

As the Indians fell back a second time, Captain Bird jumped up on the bank to encourage his men, but it proved to be a fatal move. He was shot through the heart by an arrow launched by an Indian at the extraordinary distance of two hundred yards, a feat considered incredible to anyone who had ever used a bow and arrow. It was certainly one of the best, or luckiest, arrow shots in the annals of Indian warfare.

The rangers were now left with three of six officers uninjured. Bird and Weaver were dead and Lieutenant Allen lay severely wounded. Command fell to the oldest man in the company, forty-six-year-old Nathan Brookshire, a veteran who had served in the Creek Indian War and the War of 1812 under Andrew Jackson. Brookshire had been a member of Captain John Bird's 1836 company during the San Jacinto campaign, for which he had received a bounty certificate for 640 acres. At the suggestion of Second Corporal Samuel Blain, Brookshire was unanimously called upon to take command.[19]

After a brief delay, the Indians came charging down from the ridge for a third time in full force amidst terrible war yells. They appeared to be ready to become triumphant in their slaughter or die trying. They charged right on to the brink of the ditch, recoiling only under a fierce fire from the Texans. The Indians rallied themselves again and again and charged with great firmness. Dozens of the warriors fell within twenty or thirty yards of the Texans. They were so close that almost every rifle fired killed or wounded an Indian every time. According to those present, Brookshire's voice could be heard through the Texan lines as he shouted words of inspiration.

It was now close to night, and the Texans were worn out from a full day's fight. They decided it would not be wise to cheer or cause commotion any more, as they had before, for fear of bringing another charge upon themselves. They would only become vocal if they were charged yet again.

The Indians withdrew into a compact mass on the ridge above and were vehemently addressed by their principal chief, Buffalo Hump, who was seen to be mounted on a beautiful horse and wearing on his head a buffalo skin cap, with the horns attached. It was apparent from his manner and gesticulations that he was urging his men to a final attempt for victory, but it would not do. His crowd was defeated.

Chief Buffalo Hump was not defeated, however. Failing to nerve his men for another try, he resolved to lead those few who might follow him. With no more than twelve warriors as his only hope, he proudly waved defiance at his own people and then made one of the more daring assaults in Texas Indian wars history. The stubbornly proud chief rode down the hill with his few comrades, charging straight for the Texas line. Within a few paces, he fired his gun and wheeled his horse, throwing his shield at the same instant over his shoulders for protection, leaving only his head and neck exposed.

At this moment, a young German ranger named James W. Robinett fired a rifle ball straight through the Indian's neck, causing instant death. Robinett was a veteran of Captain Thomas Robbins' 1836 cavalry company who had lost a relative in an Indian scrape in August 1836. This time, however, he shouted with joy as Chief Buffalo Hump fell and a tremendous hurrah was echoed by his fellows. The other Indians on the hill were spectators to this killing. Seeing their great war chief fall dead within thirty feet of Brookshire's men, they were instantly possessed with a reckless frenzy to retrieve the body. They rushed headlong and surrounded their dead chief, oblivious to their own danger.

The Texans poured shots into the warriors, wreaking awful havoc. The struggle was short but deadly. The martyred chief was borne away, but many more bodies were left in the process. The Texas Comanches had a leader known as Chief Buffalo Hump in subsequent years. Perhaps this title passed to the chief who wore the ornamental buffalo skin cap and horns.

It had now reached sunset. Only one horse of the Texans had been killed. The Indians were still far superior in number, but chose to move off and leave the white men. Texan leader Brookshire estimated that his men had killed thirty to forty Indians, and wounded at least that same number more in the day's fight. Others would later conclude that the Indians had lost at least fifty killed. The Indians withdrew slowly and sullenly, uttering peculiar guttural howls that veteran Texan frontiersmen could not mistake for any other creature. [20]

Brookshire relates the closing act of the Bird Creek battle:

> We snugly kept our places. The Indians then separated into two bodies and marched off, throwing up into the air a composition of something that had the appearance of lightning, which we supposed to be a signal for retreat. About nine o'clock, we secreted our dead in the ravine, as well as possible, and took up a line of march down the ravine, in order to gain the timber, a distance of three miles, carrying off our wounded with us.
>
> This body of Indians was composed of Caddoes, Kickapoos and Comanches; the Kickapoos and Caddoes we supposed to be with them from the great quantity of guns they fought with; several of them also spoke the English language to us while fighting.[21]

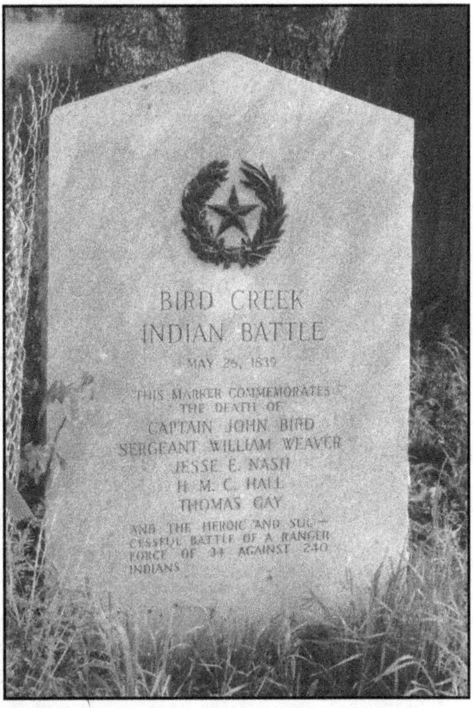

This marker in Bell County lists the ranger casualties of the May 26, 1839, Bird's Creek Fight with Chief Buffalo Hump's Comanches. *Author's photo.*

Brookshire's rangers reached Fort Smith about 2:00 a.m. on March 27. They were exhausted and without any provisions. Hall, Allen, and Hensell were carried in, but Hall died soon after reaching the fort. Some accounts state that the Texans carried the bodies of Captain Bird and the others with them. Nathan Brookshire and Corporal William Bird both later verified, however, that the dead were left on the field for several days and that only the three wounded were carried back to the fort.[22]

The next day, Brookshire sent a runner to Fort Milam near Nashville, some fifty miles away. By that night, when supplies completely ran out, Captain Brookshire elected to move his company on to Nashville on the Brazos to get medical help for his wounded. William D. Thompson received them and offered the best feast he could for the men.

Brookshire wrote his brief report of the action from Camp Nashville on May 31, noting that

> We will leave this place tomorrow morning, together with a hundred of the citizens, for the battle ground, to inter the dead and see what other discoveries we can make.

The party returned with a crude coffin which had been prepared for the victims. Captain Bird and the other casualties were placed in this huge coffin and carried back to the fort by a detachment for burial. The victims were buried on the banks of the Little River near the site of old Fort Smith.[23]

The remainder of the pursuit party took up the trail of the Indians and followed in hot pursuit as far as Stampede Creek. There, having halted for a short rest, their horses were stampeded about midnight. Left therefore on foot, the stream they had camped near thus became known as Stampede Creek.[24]

Brookshire offered the best report he could to the government, and was retained in command until the company's three months' service term expired. Wounded Lieutenant William Allen "of the Austin Volunteers" was boarded for twenty-one days by William Thompson of Nashville. Corporal William Bird remained behind to help tend to Allen until both could rejoin Captain Brookshire's company on June 21. Private George Hensel, more seriously wounded at Bird's Creek, was boarded by John Beal of Nashville through July 15.[25]

Brookshire's men soon received much needed supplies. William Green Kerley's quartermaster department in Houston responded on May 29 to Captain Bird's May 20 request for supplies. In addition to basic foodstocks, the quartermaster also sent one hundred pounds of coffee, 200 pounds of sugar, one hundred pounds of soap, and a bushel of salt. At the time Kerley authorized the provisions, he was unaware that the gallant captain had been killed.[26]

They had no further actions with the Indians. This battle became known to Anglo-Texians as "Bird's Victory" and it was believed to have spread a message to the Indians. It was the first serious repulse of wild tribes that they had suffered in some time and its effect was much noted.[27]

Historian John Henry Brown obtained copies of the muster rolls of Bird and Evans' companies. His rolls did not show who composed the prisoners or the guards, except for the names of two of the guards, Lieutenant Ervine and Lewis Washington. The original muster rolls burned in the Adjutant General's office fire decades later, leaving only Brown's annotation of these to survive. Brown notes that those in the fight were based on a survivor's recollections.

There is a surviving muster roll of Nathaniel Brookshire in the collections of the Texas State Archives. This roll was given at the end of the company's service, after Brookshire had assumed command of Captain Bird's company. By comparing this list and that of Brown, it is possible to construct a complete muster roll of Bird's company (see page 217). This list includes those who deserted and were sent as guards with them, although determining which of these men were the deserters is not possible with any accuracy.

Today, a Texas Centennial marker stands one mile northwest of Temple on State Highway 36. It states

> One mile north to Bird Creek Battlefield
>
> Named in honor of Captain John Bird who lost his life here May 26, 1839.
>
> With only 34 Texas Rangers he met 240 Indians at this point, and routed them.[28]

★ ★ ★ ★ ★

Karnes Campaign and Surveyor Skirmishes: June 1839

In San Antonio during 1839, frontiersman Jack Hays occupied himself alternately working as a surveyor, frontier scout, or as a ranger. He reportedly commanded a small group of volunteer rangers formed about February, likely in response to President Lamar's appeal for frontier volunteers. Unfortunately, there is no extant muster roll to show the service of Jack Hays and his volunteers. One of those joining his company was Charles Wilkins Webber, who wrote later of his experiences in 1852 in a book called *Tales of the Southern Border*.

Webber joined in February 1839 and found Captain Hays to be "a slight, raw-boned figure, with a lean Roman face, and an expression of modest simplicity." He was somewhat surprised that

> so unsophisticated, easy, good-natured looking a personage should be treated with so much respect by men necessarily of hardy cast as those around.[29]

Jack Hays' frontiersmen were certainly the rough image of the West. Those who used tobacco smoked Mexican cigarettes. Their attire was often buckskin suits adorned with multi-colored serapes thrown over their shoulders and a Mexican sombrero on their heads. From their waistlines gleamed braces of pistols and knives tucked into their belts. Charles Webber felt that he and his fellow rangers "made up a very picturesque costume."

In June, Hays and his fellow frontiersmen were involved in an expedition against the Comanches led by Colonel Karnes. The expedition was in response to the May 14 killing of four Béxar surveyors under Louis Franks and to a number of other killings around the area during the early days of June which had much alarmed the local citizens. Among these had been the killing of William P. Delmour, the clerk of the San Antonio court, who had been murdered and scalped on May 28 at the Mission Concepcion.[30]

Colonel Henry Karnes began organizing two volunteer companies in San Antonio on June 6. One of these volunteers, Frank L. Paschal, stated in a sworn oath that President Lamar had ordered Karnes to raise the men to "fight the hostile Comanche Indians then committing great depredations on the frontiers."[31]

Another Karnes volunteer was John James. In military claims filed May 27, 1861, James provided details of this small campaign.

> I reside in San Antonio, have continued to do so since the spring of 1838. I was a private in Capt. L. B. Franks' Co. under command of Col. Henry W. Karnes in a campaign against the Indians made from San Antonio in the summer of 1839. We were out about three weeks. There were in service two companies of 54 or 55 men each, under command of Capt. L. B. Franks and John N. Seguin.

Captain Louis Franks had fought in the 1835 siege of Béxar and later commanded rangers during the Texas Revolution. His surveying company had, of course, suffered four casualties by Indian attack just three weeks prior.

Captain Juan Seguin had served in the Alamo until days before its fall. He fought at San Jacinto and commanded various cavalry units in 1836 and 1837. Through March 1838, he had served as Karnes' lieutenant colonel of cavalry. As with Captain Franks' company, no muster roll survived, as the officers were apparently under the impression that they would never be paid for this expedition. Fortunately, Captain Seguin and others later dictated his Tejano company's muster roll from memory.[32]

Frank Paschal wrote that this "expedition went west and northwest from San Antonio on the headwaters of the Medina and Hondo Seco rivers and the Canyon de Uvalde."

Fortunately, more details of the little-known summer 1839 Karnes expedition can be found in the diary of Miles Squier Bennett and in a compilation of his notes entitled "Experiences on the Western Frontier." He gives the other officers of Captain Franks' company as First Lieutenant George M. Dolson, Second Lieutenant John King, and Orderly Sergeant Horatio Alex Alsbury. Bennett wrote in his notes that he shared a camp mess with Roderick T. Higginbotham, William M. Small, Thomas H. Spooner, Stephen Dinkins, George Edwards, John James, and Samuel Augustus Maverick.[33]

John Coffee Hays (1817–1883) in the earliest known portrait of the famed Texas Ranger. During his early years in Texas he was a soldier, surveyor, and scout on various expeditions, including several led by Colonel Henry Karnes. *UT Institute of Texan Cultures at San Antonio.*

Juan Nepomuceno Seguin (1806–1889), born in present San Antonio, was captain of a company on Karnes' expedition. One of the last to leave the Alamo, Seguin is depicted here in the uniform he wore in 1837–1838 as lieutenant colonel of the Texas Cavalry. *Texas State Library and Archives Commission.*

While the companies under Juan Seguin and Louis Franks were organizing, camp was made at San Pedro Springs. Small stores of salt, coffee, rice, dried beef, and corn meal, ground at William Small's mill, were prepared. "The roster showed 100 men, forty-five of whom were Americans," wrote Bennett. The expedition departed camp on June 10 resolved to make "such a demonstration against the hostiles as would tend to keep them at a more respectful distance from the settlements."

The narrative diary of Miles Bennett provides the best details on the movements of Karnes' volunteers.

> In the expedition were men who wanted to explore the country and make selections of land that at that time was mostly unsurveyed. Some wished to penetrate the rough hill country and the beautiful valleys near the far-famed "Can[y]on de Uvalde," about which were romantic legend of ancient mining and rich silver ore. Others only wanted to have a real good hunt where bear, deer, and wild horses were plenty, and perhaps see an Indian or two.

June 1839 Comanche Expedition
Col. Henry Wax Karnes, commanding

Capt. Louis Franks' Mounted Volunteers: June 6–23, 1839

Captain:
Louis B. Franks
First Lieutenant:
George M. Dolson
Second Lieutenant:
John R. King
Orderly Sergeant:
Horatio Alex Alsbury
Adjutant:
Andrew Neill
Privates:
Hendrick Arnold
Miles Squier Bennett
Valentine Bennett
William Chrysler
Eli Clapp
Henry Clay Davis
N. J. Devenny
Stephen Dinkins
George Edwards
Cyrus W. Egery
William H. Ewing
Joseph Gresham
Berry Lewis Ham
John Coffee Hays
Roderick T. Higginbotham
John James
Samuel A. Maverick
Franklin L. Paschal
William H. Patton
Wilson J. Riddle
Jeremiah Roberts
William Small
Thomas H. Spooner
Thomas A. Thomson
Samuel S. Tucker
Edmund Weideman
Daniel Winchell
William O. Winston

Sources: Incomplete roster based on author's research of audited military claims and diary of Miles S. Bennett, the Center for American History, Valentine Bennett Scrapbook.

Capt. Juan Seguin's Mounted Volunteers: June 6–23, 1839

Captain:
Juan N. Seguin
First Lieutenant:
Salvador Flores
Second Lieutenant:
Leandro Arriola
Privates:
Eusebio Almaguez
Miguel Arsiniega Jr.
Antonio Benites
Pedro Camarillo
Jose Luis Carabajal
Ignacio Castillo
Nemecio de la Cerda
Augustin Chavez
Trinidad Coy
Nicolas Delgado
Polonio Dias
Ignacio Espinosa
Antonio Estrada
Manuel Estrada
Nepomuceno Flores
Damacio Galbán
Leandro Garza
Vicente Garza
Manuel Hernandez
Felipe Jaimes
Xavier Lazo
Manuel Leal
Cayetano Lerema
Manuel Lopez
Gabriel Martinez
Manuel Martinez
Manuel Montalvo
Francisco Flores Morales
Pedro Flores Morales *
Antonio G. Navarro
Luciano Navarro
Jose Maria Rios
Cayetano Rives
Ambrosio Rodriguez
Francisco Rodriguez
Juan Rodriguez
Mariano Romano
Cristobal Rubio
Antonio Ruiz
Francisco Ruiz
Francisco Antonio Ruiz
Nicolas de los Santos
Agapito Servantes
Antonio Sombraño
Juan Sombraña
Gregorio Soto
Ramon Treviño
Jose Maria Valdez
Marcos A. Veramendi
Antonio Hernandez Zavala
Jesus Zavala

* Died during campaign.

Sources: John James PD, R164, F349-62; *A Revolution Remembered*, 184–86.

> A march was made through the circuitous trails of Pasa del Bandera—some of them narrow and on the edge of steep places, where there was only room for passing in single file. On the first day or two out, bear and deer were killed in abundance, as many as twenty bears being seen during one day's march.
>
> Some of the men by change of fare and habit became ill. Rain set in, Mr. [William] Chrysler was accidentally shot, and the progress of the march was somewhat retarded. Indian scouts were reported on the head waters of Arroya Leon, but were not overtaken.

While passing one of the valleys, the men spotted a small bunch of wild horses and a chase was made. Irish merchantman Wilson Riddle, riding a fleet horse, managed to rope "a beautiful mustang." The feisty horse made a run and ripped the rope from Riddle, "severely blistering the hands of his captor."

Soon after Riddle lost his lariat, Indian lodges were spotted. The Texan scouts under Jack Hays were constantly out, directing the route of Colonel Karnes' expedition. Indian signs were abundant, but it soon became clear that any Indians in the area were fleeing westward ahead of the Texans.

The expedition scouted high up above the forks of the Medina River. Miles Bennett and Daniel Winchell were ordered "to go back on our trail five or six miles and look for Indian signs." Secure that he was not being trailed, Karnes pushed on for the Rio Frio, where others scouts reported Indians.

On June 18, one of the volunteers of Captain Seguin's unit, Private Pedro Flores Morales, was accidentally shot and mortally wounded. Captain Seguin listed him as "killed on the campaign" in papers filed in Béxar County in 1860. The expedition camped without fire that night and made a tent for Morales. A strong guard was left with him and the larger part of the provisions was left at this cold camp.

The following morning, June 19, Colonel Karnes led out the remainder of Seguin and Franks' men. Miles Bennett was among this group.

> We pushed on after the enemy and soon found recent encampments of the hostiles, their tent poles still standing, and large trails leading out into the dusty roads, where their caballado had been driven and their numerous tent poles dragged

> along. At one of their camps as we entered the Canon de Uvalde there were the remains of a human body, which had been suspended from the limb of a tree, under which were dead embers and charred bones lying scattered around. Evidently, some unfortunate had been roasted there.

Pushing forward, Karnes found that the Indians were driving their herds out of the area ahead of the Texan expedition. His men were obviously being watched. The Indians were not of the mood to fight unless it was absolutely necessary.

Karnes ultimately decided to break up his expedition, as the Indians did not appear disposed to fight him. N. J. Devenny also sent a courier from the camp of the fatally wounded Private Morales who stated that the guards were returning to San Antonio. Colonel Karnes advised his men that they should turn back for San Antonio also, although some were reluctant to do so.

He therefore split his men into three squads, one passing back through Camp Flores to see if any of the expedition stores had been left behind. The other two parties slowly continued to hunt Indians and "pursued different routes to town." Miles Bennett's squad saw no action with Indians. Nonetheless, he felt the Béxar men had "doubtless intimidated the Indians somewhat."

Jack Hays led one of the three squads during the final days of the expedition's return. Scouting back around Canyon de Uvalde, he and his men destroyed deserted Indian villages that they encountered and claimed to have killed a few Indians in brief encounters. Several stolen horses were also recovered. Mary Ann Maverick wrote that her husband Samuel rode with Hays' scouts on this expedition. "Our men had killed only a few savages and returned with some Indian ponies, dreadfully ragged, dirty, and hungry."[34]

Henry Karnes' expedition returned to San Antonio on June 23, 1839, where the companies of captains Franks and Seguin were honorably discharged. In celebration of their service, Karnes invited his men "to partake of refreshments at Black & King's coffee house" in San Antonio.[35] Perhaps due to the majority of the army and its paymasters being in East Texas for the Cherokee War, these men were not paid for their services at the time they disbanded.

There were other Indian encounters during the late spring and early summer of 1839 in the Guadalupe River area. James Campbell, who had laid out the town of Walnut Springs in 1838 and had fought Córdova under Edward Burleson, took five or six men from Bastrop and went surveying on the Guadalupe, but did not return.[36]

Another large surveying team set out behind them shortly thereafter. This party was under William Simpson Wallace, who had been elected Bastrop County's surveyor in 1837 and had killed a man believed at that time to be Manuel Flores during the Córdova Rebellion in May 1839. Wallace's men came upon some of Campbell's first survey area and continued, intending to move out further ahead of them. They instead found all of Campbell's men dead further up the river. They had made a camp and cut a hollowed-out bee tree. With nothing else to use, Wallace's men used this hollow bee tree as a crude coffin for the surveyors.

Wallace and his eighteen men ignored the dangers of Indian signs and even the occasional sighting of Indians to continue their surveying. They stayed out more than another week until prowling Indians near their camp became enough of a concern to send them back to Bastrop. Upon their return, enough time had passed that a serious effort to mount a party to pursue these Indians was not made.

John Harvey, a twenty-nine-year-old San Jacinto veteran who worked as a surveyor, raised a party of surveyors in Bastrop in June 1839 and set out to work claims on the Colorado River. His party consisted of ten men. After more than a week of work, his men became concerned enough of fresh Indian signs to post nightly guards. On one particular night, a sentinel named Mr. Burnet stood near a steep hollow. A mule staked near the steep bank began snorting at something it could sense down in the hollow. When Burnet went to the edge of the bluff and peered down into the hollow, several hidden Indians fired at him. Burnet's arm was ripped to pieces by rifle shot, breaking his arm above the shoulder.

Another group of Indians instantly opened fire on the sleeping Texan party from the opposite side of camp. The whites returned the fire quickly, although three of the freshly awakened men ran for their lives. One took to his horse and rode, while two others, Ira Leffingwell and Shadrach W. Pipkin, fled on foot. Twenty-one-year-old New York native Leffingwell was a veteran of John Moore's February Comanche fight, where he had been wounded.

John Harvey and the other six men in camp fought off the Indians. When the attack began, they took cover and even climbed up into the trees around camp to successfully defend themselves.

In 1874, Captain Harvey wrote an account of the Indian attack on his surveying party.

> Such yelling I thought that I had never heard in all my life —thought that they were all there. Such jumping and snorting

Captain John Harvey, born in 1810 in Tennessee, commanded a ten-man surveying party in a fight against Indians near Bastrop in June 1839.
Photo originally published in DeShields' *Border Wars of Texas*.

of horses–well, it beat anything I ever met up with. I told my boys, 8 or 9 in number, to reserve their fire, get behind trees, and not shoot without a good chance.

There was only three guns fired from my party, all at one Indian, who was killed immediately. The old Chief commanded a retreat and left us. When daylight came, we found 4 head horses gone and three men. Looked around for the bodies of our men; could not find them. Found 2 of their guns and all of their shot pouches. Were satisfied that they had run. I called aloud several times, and one of our boys answered me across the river. He came over alone.[37]

The other two Texans had fled on foot until the gunfire behind them ceased. Deciding that the Indians had been beaten, Pipkin and Leffingwell retraced their steps back toward camp. En route, they met a party of Indians carrying the body of the slain warrior. The Indians immediately dropped their comrade's body and took after the Texan surveyors. These two men fled through the rough terrain and would spend some ten days in the wilderness without food or water and only one gun to protect them. They survived on buds, berries, and other wild edibles.

Harvey's men returned to Bastrop with the badly wounded Mr. Burnet a week after the assault, assuming that Pipkin and Leffingwell had been killed. By the time the two badly fatigued and hungry surveyors staggered into Bastrop on foot ten days later, no effort was made to strike back against these Indians.

CHAPTER 10

The Cherokee War

June–July 16, 1839

About ten days after receiving Lamar's ultimatum, Chief Bowles finally reported in mid-June that he and Chief Big Mush were unable to reach a peaceful agreement. From Fort Lacy, agent Martin Lacy, Dr. Jowers, John Reagan, and their interpreter Cordray again visited the Cherokee leader near present Alto.

Reagan was impressed with how the Indians and his little negotiating party managed to carry on the talks.

> These conferences produced a strong impression on my mind for two reasons. The first was that neither the agent nor the chief could read or write, except that Mr. Lacy could sign his name mechanically; and neither could speak the language of the other. The second was the frankness and dignity with which the negotiations were carried on—neither tried to disguise his purpose nor to mislead the other.[1]

Bowles told the negotiators that the younger men of his tribe were ready for war, although he and Big Mush wished to avoid it. According to Reagan, Bowles said that the young braves "believed they could whip the whites; that he knew the whites could ultimately whip them, but it would cost them ten years of bloody frontier war." The Cherokee leader said that he had no choice but to stand by his people's wishes, for "if he fought, the whites would kill him; and if he refused to fight, his own people would kill him."

Bowles explained the plight of his people. He had led this band of the Texas Cherokees since they had first split from the main band of Cherokees in Arkansas. He and his people had tried to settle near pre-

Dr. William George Washington Jowers (1812–1892) tended to the wounded during both the Kickapoo War and the Cherokee War. Later a Texas statesman and a judge, Jowers was among the negotiating party sent to Chief Bowles' village for peace talks during the Cherokee War.
Originally printed in Hohes, *A Centennial History of Anderson County, Texas*.

John Henninger Reagan (1818–1905), another Cherokee negotiator, fought bravely in both subsequent battles. He would later serve as a judge, legislator, and as postmaster general of the Confederacy. Reagan's home in present Anderson County was built on the site of the original Fort Houston.
Texas State Library and Archives Commission.

sent Dallas at the Three Forks of the Trinity River, but other Indian tribes fought them for this land. Bowles had moved his tribe near Nacogdoches with the consent of Mexico and, later, a treaty approved by Sam Houston. Now, at age eighty-three, he was willing to follow the will of his other head men and fight for their land.

Although negotiations would be resumed again soon, both the Texans and the Indians were quietly preparing for conflict from this point forward. After this meeting in June, Bowles hurriedly conferred with his fellow chiefs and began to gather forces, including Shawnees and Delawares, in Cherokee Nation east of the Neches River in present Smith County. It appears that after this last conference on Bowles Creek, the elder Cherokee leader ceased to use his village near Fort Lacy and began to operate from his village near the Neches Saline.[2]

Mirabeau Lamar wasted no time in making his intentions known and the publishers of the *Telegraph* in Houston agreed with his thinking. In an editorial printed on June 19, the newspaper stated that the Cherokees were "unwelcome intruders among us." The *Telegraph* also stated that the Cherokees' connections with Mexican rebels "have already cost us much blood and suffering" and time had come to put "an end to these things."

To this end, a large number of forces began converging on East Texas to stand up to the Cherokee threat. President Lamar had previously ordered Colonel Burleson on May 27 to collect his First Regiment troops and move east. Due to some rebellion among new recruits, Burleson had to ride to Gonzales and settle the matter. Therefore, it was not until late June that his forces were completely collected at his headquarters in Bastrop and ready to move out.

When Colonel Burleson finally departed his Mount Pleasant plantation on June 27 to move northeastward, his force numbered more than 260 men. From the regular army, he traveled with his First Battalion—Company C under Captain Samuel Jordan and Captain George Howard's Company D. The regular forces were augmented by Lieutenant Colonel Devereaux Woodlief's two volunteer ranging companies under captains Mark Lewis and James Ownby. In addition, Burleson's close friend Chief Placido would lead twenty-four of his Tonkawa braves as a small scouting company.

While Woodlief was in the field in charge of two of the ranger companies, Colonel Henry Karnes was still actively recruiting for his mounted rifleman battalion during late June. In San Antonio on June 24, he advertised for more volunteers, stating that he had been authorized by the president to raise four to six companies.

Another company raised by Karnes under the mounted gunmen act of December 1838 was placed under command of Captain Greenberry Horace Harrison on June 28, 1839. These men were self-armed and self-provided, unlike the government-equipped companies mustered in months earlier under Ownby and Lewis. Captain Harrison signed a document for Peterson Lloyd that he had served as a "private in my company of mounted gunmen for the Cherokee Campaign" and was paid at a rate of twenty-five dollars per month.[3]

After Burleson's forces departed the central Texas area, Colonel Karnes left the mounted ranger company of Captain John Garrett in Austin to protect those who were constructing the new capital city. Lieutenant Colonel William Fisher, second-in-command of the regular army's infantry, was originally ordered to remain at the Brazos

River with a detachment of men to guard against possible Indian attacks on this frontier while Burleson's troops were east of the Brazos. Fisher was later allowed to join Colonel Burleson for the Cherokee campaign. In his place, Captain John C. Neill of Houston commanded a volunteer company charged with patrolling the frontiers between the Brazos and Colorado rivers during the Cherokee campaign.[4]

In the absence of the First Infantry to protect the Brazos and Little River settlements during the Cherokee crisis, Captain Nathan Brookshire's Austin County Rangers were also assigned to protect this area. They served in this area during June and July and as of July 16, 1839, were headquartered out of Camp Brazos on the river in present Falls County.[5]

On June 27, President Lamar appointed five men to a special commission to deal with the Cherokee crisis. They were Major General Thomas Rusk, Vice President David Burnet, Secretary of War Albert Sidney Johnston, Isaac Watts Burton, and James S. Mayfield. Lamar advised these men that he felt a "necessity of the immediate removal of the Cherokee Indians and the ultimate removal of all other emigrant tribes now residing in Texas." He authorized the group to make liberal compensations for the Indians' improvements, but to pay them no more than one-fourth the agreed value in cash. This sum was not to exceed $25,000 and was to be advanced by the merchants of Nacogdoches and San Augustine on credit from the government.[6]

President Lamar also cautioned the commissioners to not allow the Cherokees to remain in Texas any longer than it took them to make preparations to move.

> Unless they consent at once to receive a fair compensation for their improvements and other property and remove out of this country, nothing short of the entire destruction of all they possess and the extermination of their tribe will appease the indignation of the white people against them.

In Nacogdoches, two new militia companies were hurriedly organized from the numerous volunteers. Captains Bob Smith and Jack Todd, already veteran leaders in the Third Militia Brigade, headed up the units formed on June 28. It is interesting to note that Thomas Rusk, major general of the Texas Militia, was enrolled into Captain Todd's company as a private. This was perhaps due to his new appointment as a commissioner for the Cherokee removal meetings.

The companies under Smith and Todd would join two others which had recently formed under captains Lewis Sanchez and Alexander Jordan, both men veterans of previous Rusk campaigns. The company of Captain Sanchez included a mixture of some white citizens but was comprised almost entirely of Tejanos who resided in Nacogdoches County. His company payroll shows that two of his men were provided with gun locks and that several others were outfitted with butcher knives.

The Indian commissioners and the new "Nacogdoches Regiment" assembled at Fort Kickapoo, where Major Walters had remained with the forces who had been in talks with the Cherokee Indian leaders. At the old Kickapoo village, the Texan companies were more formally organized into regiments over the next weeks.[7]

In the Houston County area, Major John Wortham was serving General Kelsey Douglass' Third Militia Brigade by mid-June in the role of quartermaster, to provide for the troops marching into the area. Supervision of ranger companies under captains James Box and Solomon Adams passed from Wortham to Major Baley Walters. The army's Company A of First Infantry, commanded by Captain William Sadler and also stationed in the Houston County area, joined the movement of troops toward the Cherokee Nation.

The First Regiment of the Third Militia Brigade would be directly commanded by General Kelsey Douglass, the senior regional commander of the militia between the Trinity and Sabine rivers. He would supervise Major Walters' ranger companies of captains Box, Adams, and Henry Smith. To this would be added Captain Harrison's mounted gunmen and another mounted volunteer company formed July 1 under Captain Benjamin Vansickle.

Colonel Willis Landrum organized his Third Regiment of the Third Militia Brigade staff on June 28. Over the course of the next two weeks, he would raise four companies of volunteers from the counties of Harrison, Sabine, San Augustine, and Shelby. His regiment would soon make its way from the east toward the staging area at Fort Kickapoo.

Indian commissioner Tom Rusk and the Nacogdoches militia companies reached camp during the first days of July and were joined by General Douglass' regiment. From Fort Kickapoo, Rusk and the other commissioners immediately resumed the negotiations with Chief Bowles and his Cherokee leaders. The additional forces under Landrum and Burleson were still en route as of early July. This mass assembly of army, militia, and ranger forces that would gather at Fort Kickapoo had not been equalled since Sam Houston's forces had gathered at San Jacinto.

As the passing days brought swelling numbers of volunteers, the troops were formally organized into regiments. On July 9, elections were held to organize the "Nacogdoches Regiment." As commander of the Texas Militia, Rusk was a natural selection as colonel commanding this regiment. His staff would include Adjutant Major William N. Dunnington, Sergeant Major Ira Munson, Surgeon Lemuel B. Brown, Quartermaster Edward B. Noble, and Captain James Carter, commander of a special mounted spy company organized in camp from existing units.

In Nacogdoches, William Hart received news of this regiment's organization from a courier, First Corporal Robert Watkins of Captain Bob Smith's company. Hart learned of the election of Colonel Rusk's two senior officers.

> Watkins informed me that they had an election in the camp on Monday last for one colonel and one Lieut. Col. and one Major. Genl. Rusk was unanimously elected Col.
>
> Jim Smith and Jacob Snively were candidates for Lieut. Col. Smith was elected. D. S. Kaufman (ex Aide de camp), John M. Hansford, ex Speaker of the House, and Capt. [Elisha] Clapp, tavern keeper in Cincinnati [Houston County], were all three candidates for major. Clapp got more votes than both the others and of course was elected.[8]

Colonel Rusk and Lieutenant Colonel Smith's Nacogdoches Regiment would be organized as the Second Regiment of the Third Militia Brigade.

★ ★ ★ ★ ★

Cherokee Peace Talks: July 9–14, 1839

Colonel Hugh McLeod and several officers rode north from the Texan camp on July 9 with a message for the Cherokees from militia commander Tom Rusk. Aware that Chief Bowles had already cautioned that any large group would be considered hostile, McLeod's small party carried a white flag of peace as they cautiously entered the Indian village. Chief Bowles was informed that Rusk and others were part of a presidential commission appointed specifically to "arrange for the removal of the Cherokees" from Texas.[9]

Another of the commissioners, Secretary of War Albert Sidney Johnston, wrote that he and his companions were under orders of President Lamar to attempt to negotiate

> the peaceable removal of the Cherokees. We had been instructed to allow a fair compensation for their improvements, to be ascertained by appraisement, and to be paid for in silver and goods before their removal. The Commissioners, in several talks held with them, essayed every means to effect a friendly negotiation, but without success.[10]

Hugh McLeod's party met briefly with Chief Bowles. He and Big Mush were invited to join Tom Rusk and the Texas commissioners the following day, July 10, for peace talks. The designated rendezvous spot was "Council Creek," a location near Saline Creek just off the Neches River. McLeod's party returned to camp and reported that Bowles had agreed to this meeting.

The Texan camp had swelled to roughly 550 men with Rusk and Douglass' regiments. In expectation of the commissioners' meeting, the troops moved from Fort Kickapoo on the west side of the Neches River to Council Creek on the east side. They established Camp Johnston in honor of the secretary of war at a spot about six miles south of Chief Bowles' camp.

True to his word, Chief Bowles arrived at Council Creek on July 10 with twenty-one Indians, including Chief Key of the Cherokees and interpreter Spy Buck representing Chief Linney of the Shawnees. The Texas commissioners attempted to begin the negotiations, but the Cherokees refused to speak until they could summon Chief Big Mush to join them.[11]

While the Cherokees stalled, more Texan forces marched in. George G. Alford, a member of Captain Bob Smith's company, returned to Nacogdoches with express rider Robert Watkins on July 10 on one of the courier runs. "Col. Landrum is here with about 160 men, leaves for Kickapoo Town tomorrow," Alford wrote. "The Indians have left the Saline."[12]

Nacogdoches citizen William Hart noted that he "had sixty in the field before [Captain Mitchell Garrison's Shelby County volunteers], which make 260 from Landrum's Regiment." A count of Landrum's field and staff and four companies shows a total of 262 volunteers of the Third Regiment, Third Militia Brigade. From the Texan camp couriers, Hart passed the latest news along to Secretary of Treasury James Starr in Houston.

> Landrum is ordered to go through the Williams Settlement to the Saline. Robert Watkins has just arrived from camp. He says that they have found four Indians at [Chief] Sam Benge's old place who informed them that the Indians were encamped about 25 miles from the Saline.[13]

Judge Charles Taylor was "recovering from a severe attack of fever" in Nacogdoches as of July 11. He also heard the news from the Cherokee Nation couriers.

> The Indians have all recamped and their place of retreat (about 25 miles from the Saline) was not discovered till a day or two ago and only then through some Indians that were taken by our spies.[14]

Colonel Rusk's commissioners and the Indian leaders met again briefly on July 11 at Council Creek. Chief Harris of the Delawares had also joined. Rusk carried out most of the talks for the Texans. He took this chance to remind Chief Bowles of his peaceful visit to the Cherokee Nation in August 1838 during his pursuit of Córdova's rebels. "We do not wish to injure you now unless you force us to do it," he advised. Rusk then cautioned Bowles that if his people persisted in being friendly with "the wild Indians and Mexicans, we will be forced to kill your people in defense of our frontier."[15]

Rusk flatly stated that Bowles and his people were "between two fires" and that if he chose to remain, "you will be destroyed."

The elder Cherokee chief answered only that he "had not much to say today." He promised that he would have more to say the following day, when Big Mush would join the peace talks. After this latest delay in direct negotiations, the Texans could only guess that Bowles was quietly mustering his own forces for battle.

The Indians leaders and the Texan commissioners met for the fourth consecutive day on July 12. Bowles stated that his tribe intended to leave peacefully and that he would "go to my people whence we came." His young men would need some time, however, to kill game for provisions due to their lack of ammunition. Spy Buck, representing the Shawnee's Chief Linney, said that his people would need three moons' time, or about two months, to prepare to move.[16]

Chief John Bowles (1756–1839), leader of the Texas Cherokees. Long avoiding confrontation with Texan forces, Bowles ultimately respected the wishes of his people to fight to the end against their removal from East Texas in 1839. Known in the Cherokee tongue as "Duwali," Chief Bowles was among at least one hundred Indians killed in the Cherokee War.
Texas State Library and Archives Commission.

The commissioners advised the Indians that they would not get the three moons' time to prepare for removal, but that ample time would be allowed. Rusk concluded by stating, "I believe the Great Spirit will look down with satisfaction upon the arrangements." All parties agreed to meet again in two days, at which time it was hoped that the Delaware chief and the Cherokee's Chief Big Mush would be present to sign a treaty.

Colonel Rusk would not sit idly by during those two days. He immediately dispatched a rider back to Nacogdoches for more troops. One of the volunteers joining a hastily formed new unit was William Hart.

> On Friday the 12th Inst., an express arrived from Rusk calling for more men. On the morning of Saturday the 13th, a company was made up of fifty-three men; was made up from Walling's and Sparks' settlements and the town of Nacogdoches. From town, there was [Charles S.] Taylor, [Nicholas Adolphus] Sterne, [R. H.] Pinney, [Richard]

> Parmalee, [Rinaldo] Hotchkiss, [William] Crutchir, [Charles] Chevallier, Dr. [Henry] Rogers, [Bennett] Blake, and myself. This was the last effort, leaving only a few men in town and they could not get horses. We elected Peter Tipps Capt. and A. Sterne Orderly Sergeant.
>
> We left Saturday and made a forced march and arrived at Camp Johnston, six miles northwest of DeBard's plantation near the Saline.[17]

On July 14, the final meeting at Council Creek was held between Rusk, Johnston, Burnet, Burton, and Mayfield for Texas and Bowles and twenty Indians. Bowles and Chief Key at first refused to sit on blankets on the ground in traditional Cherokee fashion, although Bowles did give in finally. Rusk noted with apprehension that the Indian leaders had painted their faces "as black as the devil" for this meeting and they carried war clubs in their hands.[18]

David Burnet read the agreement to the Indian leaders while Cordray interpreted. The Cherokees and their associated bands, the Delawares and Shawnees, were to leave in peace. Texas would pay them "just compensation" for their improvements, crops, and properties and would help the less fortunate Indians. In return, the Cherokees must leave the locks from their guns with Texas troops until they had crossed into the United States.

The commissioners demanded a signed treaty, reminding Bowles that he had previously corresponded with Mexican General Cos in 1835 and that he had sent Cherokees to Mexico in 1836 to hold talks with the Mexican Army. They also told Bowles that a Mexican officer had visited his village in 1838 and that Córdova's rebels had previously sought refuge in the Cherokee Nation from Rusk's militia. Bowles ignored the accusations and steadfastly refused to sign the agreement. He said that he would call a council to present the articles to the other chiefs, promising their answer to Mayfield the following morning.

A significant happening on July 14, and one that may have served to further discourage the Indians from negotiating, was the arrival of the rest of the Texan troops. Colonel Burleson's companies of regulars and volunteers had marched steadily, stopping briefly at Fort Milam on the Brazos in early July before pushing across the Neches River for Rusk's camp. His men had arrived in Houston County and stopped at Fort Houston on July 13 before pushing on. Captain Adam Clendenin, who had commanded Fort Houston for the previous two weeks, and his Company B of the First Regiment, joined Burleson at this time for the march to Camp Johnston. The large force under Burleson arrived at Camp Johnston in Cherokee country on the afternoon of July 14, shortly behind Colonel Landrum's four-company militia regiment.[19]

With the arrival of Landrum's men, the number in camp had surpassed eleven hundred, more troops than had engaged the Mexican army at San Jacinto. Disagreements arose as to who would command the vast force which had been gathered to fight the Cherokees. There were many different sentiments, but the volunteers generally wanted Rusk to lead, while the regulars demanded Burleson.

Refusing to oppose each other, Rusk and Burleson made a common agreement to let General Kelsey Douglass, the regional commander of the Third Militia Brigade, take overall command. Douglass' own general staff included Brigadier Major Jacob Snively and James Mayfield, Samuel Davis, Palmer Job Pillans, James H. Millroy, Benjamin Sturgess, and Leonard Mabbitt as his volunteer aides.

In a letter written the following day from "Headquarters, Camp 6 miles from Saline," General Douglass acknowledged his new role. "I am in command of the Army. The Army is 1,000 strong. Burleson has come up with the regulars."[20]

On July 15, Colonel Mayfield rode to the Indian campgrounds in company with Colonel McLeod, John Thorn, James Durst, and Leonard Williams in hopes of having the treaty signed. Williams understood the Cherokee language because his wife Nancy Isaacs Williams was a half breed Indian from Chief Bowles' own tribe. Her father was a Scotch trader and her mother was a sister of Cherokee War Chief Richard Fields. This party met with Bowles and about eighty warriors. Although Mayfield urged the Indians to give up their gunlocks and sign the treaty, Bowles told him the young men were frightened that they would be killed as soon as they were unarmed.[21]

Mayfield advised the old Cherokee chief that the Texas Army would march against them this day if they refused. Bowles contemplated an offer to go with Mayfield's party for a final peace talk, but decided that he would not ride with the Texans to Camp Johnston. Before noon that day, the commissioners arrived back at the Texas camp and announced that they had failed to reach a settlement in the peace talks with Chief Bowles. Apparently, the Indian warriors were prepared to put their fates in the hands of the Great Spirit and fight to their deaths for the land they had claimed in Texas.

★ ★ ★ ★ ★

First Blood On Battle Creek: July 15, 1839

Captain Peter Tipps' company of Nacogdoches volunteers arrived at Camp Johnston at 10:00 a.m. on July 15, the last of the hastily assembled militia companies to join General Douglass' forces. These late-comers were quickly informed by fellow Texans that there would not be any battle. Private William Hart wrote that as his company rode into camp, they were met by

> some noisy fools who told us we had come "a day after the fair." That a treaty had been made and that there was no fighting to be done. At this intelligence, I and a majority of our company were well pleased. We did not wish for blood, but if war must come we were ready.
>
> We were ordered to dismount and as soon as I could dispose of my horse, I went down and saw Genl. Johnston and Judge Burnet. We then heard that a demand had been made for the gunlocks and that Bowles was to give an answer that day.[22]

While the negotiations proceeded on July 15, General Douglass dispatched Captain William Kimbro's seventy-man company of San Augustine volunteers to the village of the Shawnees to enforce neutrality by demanding the surrender of their gunlocks. When they arrived the following afternoon, Kimbro and William C. Duffield explained to them the orders of the government and received from them their gun locks. Private "Rip" Ford of Kimbro's company, however, believed that interpreter Spy Buck had just returned from battle and that the Shawnees had removed the locks from only their "ordinary pieces, and kept the best concealed."[23]

Shortly after the Texas negotiators reached camp again around noon on July 15, Chief Bowles sent his son John and a prominent half-breed Cherokee named Fox Fields to Camp Johnston under a truce flag. True to his word, the old chief was honoring the agreement that both sides keep each other notified on moves. These messengers informed Sidney Johnston that the Cherokees would break camp this day and move to the west of the Neches River. John Reagan recalled that both John Bowles and Fox Fields "spoke English very well." Johnston "told the messenger that his father had acted honorably in giving the notice according to agreement."[24]

Johnston thanked the son of the Cherokee leader, and informed him that the Texas Army would break camp and follow the Cherokees. When approached by Texas forces, the Indians were to display a white flag and surrender their gun locks or be attacked. Bowles and Fields were then accompanied half a mile beyond the Texas picket lines.[25]

Following the departure of the Cherokee messengers, Secretary of War Johnston ordered the Texans to break camp. General Douglass wrote that his "whole force was put in motion towards the encampment of Bowles on the Neches." The troops of Colonel Landrum's Third Regiment were ordered to cross to the east side of the Neches and move upriver. Landrum's men were under orders "to reunite with the main body as soon as he could ascertain that the Indians had not crossed over."[26]

The separation of Landrum's volunteers left General Douglass with roughly 900 men. The Texas troops had orders to proceed to the Cherokee village but to not, however, fire upon the Indians until the warriors had been summoned for a chance to accept the terms of the government. Douglass' men moved out from Camp Johnston around 1:30 p.m. "We were ordered to saddle in quick time and pursuit was made," wrote Private Hart.[27]

The Texans advanced quickly over the sixteen-mile distance toward Chief Harris' Delaware village, where it was believed that the Cherokees had retreated only hours before. Upon reaching the Indians' most recent campground on the west bank of the Neches, Hart wrote that they found it "entirely abandoned. We made the quickest kind of a move. In fact, we went four or five miles in a gallop."

The retreating Cherokees were easy to follow by the trail of their horses and cattle. The spy company of Captain James Carter raced out ahead to scout the enemy's position.

Two of Douglass' volunteers, James D. Long and Jeff Wallace, later reported that the Indians retreated west of the Neches on July 15 to a spot about one-hundred yards south of where a small creek named Indian Creek empties into the Neches River. Carter's men spotted the Indians near the Delaware village at the head of a prairie on the point of a hill. They were at this time west of the Neches near another small creek later named Battle Creek, located about 3.5 miles northwest of present Chandler in Henderson County.[28]

Chief Bowles had sent the women and children on farther ahead of the battle area, while leaving his men behind to fight. After discovering these warriors around 5:00 p.m., Captain Carter quickly sent a rider back to alert the command. The remainder of Captain Jack Todd's company, from which Carter's spies were largely pulled, was ordered from General Tom Rusk's regiment to move forward rapidly to support the spy company. (An account of the Cherokee War in the August 7, 1839, *Telegraph and Texas Register* mistakenly identifies this company as that of a "Captain Ford.") Colonel Burleson also rushed ahead to support the spy company, taking two of his regular army companies and Lieutenant Colonel Woodlief's two mounted gunman units.

The Indians initially occupied a hut and a corn field near Battle Creek. In the first draft of General Douglass' campaign report, written the following morning, James Mayfield recorded that Carter's spies, Major General Rusk and "about twenty five from Capt. Todd's company" were the first to bring these Indians to battle. Rusk motioned for the Cherokees to "come on."[29]

The Indians obliged and "fired four or five times" on the advance Texan forces. Bowles' warriors then quickly entrenched themselves behind a high creek bank. Behind them lay thick woods to provide them a safe retreat or a good secondary line of defense. The Texans found before them an open prairie with only a thicket of gum bushes to their right which paralleled the creek from which to advance. The Indians clearly had the upper hand in terms of positioning.[30]

Following the first firing upon Carter and Todd's men, the action soon became heated. Rusk advanced with his men, while Lieutenant Colonel Woodlief led two companies of Colonel Burleson's regiment. With Captain Samuel Jordan's regular infantrymen and Captain Mark Lewis' mounted rangers, Woodlief charged toward the enemy in the ravine. The Indians taking shelter in the ravine were instantly charged and flanked on the left by Colonel Burleson and the first portion of his regiment, which included the companies of captains George Howard, James Ownby, and Chief Placido.

The *Telegraph and Texas Register* of August 7 captures the intensity of this first clash with the Cherokees on July 15.

> The hideous yells of the savages, instead of startling our soldiers, excited their spirit for the combat, and they rushed to it pell-mell, determined to drive the enemy from the cover of the timber and brushwood.

The rest of Tom Rusk's troops took a position on a point of a hill to the right of the main prairie. They drove a party of Indians which attempted to flank General Douglass' main body of troops on the field from that quarter. By splitting their men, the Texans were able to quickly drive the Indian forces from their ravine and thicket. The engagement near Battle Creek commenced about half an hour before sundown.

"You would have thought our men were mad," wrote William Hart, who rode into the action with Captain Tipps' company. "I believe I shouted as loud as any" of the whooping Indians.[31]

In the heat of the early action, Major David Kaufman and Private John Reagan from Captain Bob Smith's Nacogdoches company had a close brush with death. They charged on horseback toward an Indian who was firing at them from a creekbed. As they neared the creek, they were suddenly taken under heavy fire by other Indians who had been lying in wait in the creek. Reagan and Kaufman wheeled their horses and rode back through a flurry of enemy fire to escape. They rejoined a portion of their regiment which included Chief Placido's Tonkawas. Reagan recalled the other Texans fighting near him to be Bob Smith, First Sergeant Andrew Caddell, his sons John and Jeremiah Caddell, Indian agent Martin Lacy, Ambrose H. Crain, and David Rusk of Captain Carter's company.[32]

General Douglass' forces suffered four men fatally wounded and eight others wounded in varying degrees. Three of those wounded were Texas Rangers, including George T. Slaughter of Captain Box's Houston County rangers and John A. Harper of Captain Henry Madison Smith's Nacogdoches County rangers. Peter Rodden, one of Captain Smith's rangers, recalled the intensity of the action. "We sustained a heavy fire from the enemy while crossing upon them through a prairie. We at length drove them from their concealment." The third ranger wounded was Private John S. Anderson of Lieutenant Colonel Woodlief's regiment, which was part of Colonel Henry Karnes' "corps of rangers."[33]

Captain Harrison's mounted riflemen, also recruited by Karnes for his ranging corps, suffered two men killed. One, Henry P. Crowson, was severely wounded and died shortly after the battle. The other was John Crane, a captain during the storming of Béxar in December 1835, who was mortally wounded as his horse reared up on him. At that instant, a rifle ball struck him just under his heart. Realizing that he was dying, Crane cried out for his brother-in-law, Lieutenant John Robbins. John Reagan, fighting nearby with another company, noticed.

> Robbins came promptly, and Colonel Crane rode by him for two or three rods, telling him what messages to bear his family, and then fell from his horse, quite dead.[34]

Crane's body and that of another man were later buried on the battlefield by John Robbins and Benjamin Highsmith. Dr. Albert Woldert, author of a detailed 1920s article on the Cherokee War, later had large iron pins placed in the ground where Dr. Henry M. Rogers and John Crane were buried, about two hundred yards due west of a bend in Battle Creek.[35]

Captain George Howard's Company D suffered casualties while with Edward Burleson in the main charge. Private John Day was fatally shot in the head and Private James Ball received a rifle shot through the eye.

The heavy firing of the Indians claimed its other casualties from the volunteer companies of captains Bob Smith, Ben Vansickle, Greenberry Harrison, and Peter Tipps. Dr. Henry Rogers of Tipps' Nacogdoches company was riddled with three shots and "was killed on the spot. He did not live 10 minutes," wrote another from his company. James McAnulty of Tipps' company was wounded when his mount was shot out from under him. Colonel Hugh McLeod gave up his own horse to the injured Private McAnulty and continued the battle on foot.[36]

Many of the Texans dismounted their horses and proceeded on foot as they drove the Cherokees from their defensive thicket and ravine positions. The Indians escaped the battlefield as darkness fell over the Battle Creek area. They had suffered their share of wounded and killed. General Douglass' report states that the Indians fled, leaving "eighteen dead on the field that have been found and carrying off, as usual, their wounded, as was seen by many of our men."

With the fall of darkness, the Indians moved into the woods and the fighting ended for July 15. The heated engagement on Battle Creek had lasted just over fifteen minutes. The Texans gathered a sizable quantity of goods left behind by the fleeing Indians, including horses, cattle, corn, 250 pounds of lead, and five kegs of gunpowder.

Colonel Landrum's regiment missed the fight while on the opposite side of the Neches. A messenger was sent the following morning with orders for him to rejoin Douglass' main body.

Edward Burleson later considered General Douglass' report of the July 15 battle to be biased toward the Third Brigade's militiamen. He wrote a letter to the *Telegraph and Texas Register* which was pub-

Texan Casualties of July 15, 1839
First Engagement on Battle Creek

GENERAL DOUGLASS' FIRST REGIMENT (THIRD MILITIA BRIGADE)

Name	Company	Remarks:
Solomon Allbright, Pvt.	Capt. Vansickle	Wounded.
John Crane, Pvt.	Capt. Harrison	Killed.
Henry P. Crowson, Pvt.	Capt. Harrison	Mortally wounded.
John A. Harper, Pvt.	Capt. H. M. Smith	Wounded.
George T. Slaughter, Pvt.	Capt. Box	Slightly wounded.

COLONEL RUSK'S SECOND REGIMENT (THIRD MILITIA BRIGADE)

Name	Company	Remarks:
James McAnulty, Pvt.	Capt. Tipps	Wounded.
Dr. Henry M. Rogers, Pvt.	Capt. Tipps	Killed.
John B. Thacker, Pvt.	Capt. Bob Smith	Wounded.
James R. Wilehart, Pvt.	Capt. Tipps	Wounded.

COLONEL BURLESON'S INFANTRY (TEXAS ARMY)

Name	Company	Remarks:
James Ball, Pvt.	Capt. Howard	Shot in the eye.
John Day, Pvt.	Capt. Howard	Fatally shot in head.

LIEUTENANT COLONEL WOODLIEF'S REGIMENT (RANGERS)

Name	Company	Remarks:
Joseph S. Anderson, Pvt.	Capt. Lewis	Wounded.

lished on October 23, 1839, in which he gave credit largely to his and Woodlief's four companies for driving the Indians from the ravine. They were joined, Burleson wrote, by Captain Carter's spies, a portion of Captain Todd's company, and "some few scattering volunteers from other companies."[37]

The Texan forces made camp for the night near the battleground. The camp was named Camp Carter in honor of Jim Carter, whose spy company was first to find and engage the Indians this day. Guards kept a watchful eye for enemy counterattacks after darkness while the camp doctors worked through the night caring for the wounded.

★ ★ ★ ★ ★

Battle Of The Neches: July 16, 1839

Chief Bowles and his Cherokees retreated up the Neches River in the predawn hours of July 16. They moved up to Chief Harris' Delaware village, located west of the Neches. This village was north-

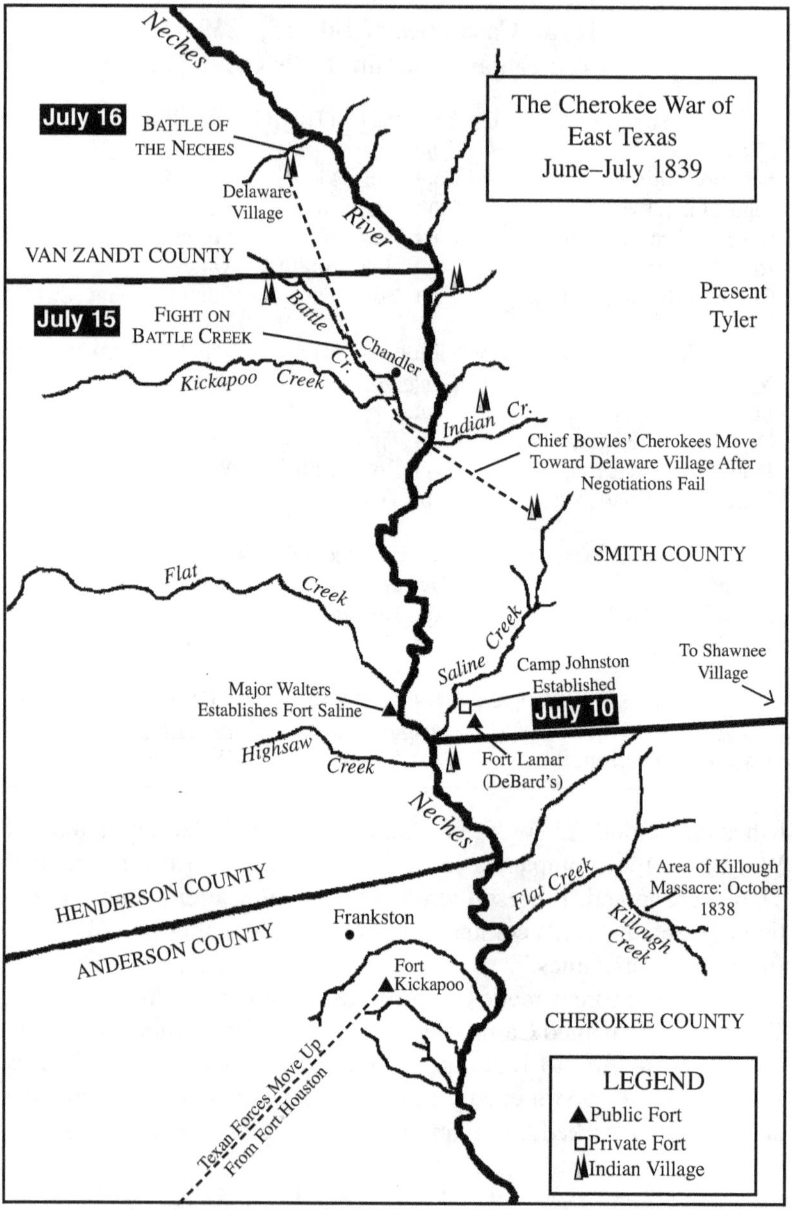

west of present Chandler, situated in the extreme southeastern corner of present Van Zandt County, west of Tyler.

The first light of day gave the Texans at Camp Carter a chance to look over the previous evening's battlefield. William Hart of Captain

Tipps' Nacogdoches company noted:

> In the morning we buried our dead and attended to our wounded. We also examined the battleground and I found 10 dead Indians, 5 kegs of powder, and 8 or 10 rifles.[38]

While the dead were tended to, General Douglass detached infantry guards to Fort Lamar with the wounded. Fort Lamar was actually the home of Dr. Elisha DeBard, who had recently been in the salt-making business near the Neches with the Cherokees. Captain Adam Clendenin's Company B of the First Regiment of Infantry had been detached on July 15 to construct a more durable fort. Colonel Burleson obviously expected the Cherokee War to carry on for some time and knew that a less-disciplined volunteer company would not allow itself to miss the fight to work on a military structure.

Clendenin's company began building several cabins around DeBard's house and salt-producing warehouse. A stockade fence was eventually built around the perimeter and the structure was named Fort Lamar in honor of the new Texas president. The army's surgeons set up a field hospital on this site following the first battle of July 15.[39]

General Douglass' main body of troops dwindled down to about 500 men in the morning hours of July 16 as units of men were given duties. In addition to the guard detail sent to Fort Lamar, Douglass sent "many others upon detached service."[40]

The remaining troops were ordered to saddle up. Camp was broken at 10:00 a.m. and the Texans renewed their march toward the Delaware village of Chief Harris. The spies under Captain Carter had been sent out early once again to contact the Indians. Douglass sent orders to Colonel Landrum "to continue his march up the east side of the Neches" until such time as he could join "the main body on its march in the direction of Harris."

Carter's spies soon spotted the Cherokees near the Delaware village, which was perched on a small hilltop overlooking the Neches River in the distance below. William Nobbitt was sent on horseback to carry the word to Kelsey Douglass and the main body of Texas troops. He caught them about five miles north of Camp Carter around 11:00 a.m.

Douglass had been marching with Colonel Burleson's regiment to the right and Major General Rusk's men to the left. His battle report describes the arrangement of his troops for battle.

> To provide against every contingency, and not have the march of our forces impeded by the body of the enemy, the following order of battle was immediately adapted. Burleson with one battalion of his command was ordered to move forward and sustain the spy company, in the event the enemy made a stand, and Rusk, with one battalion of his regiment to move up and sustain in a like manner Burleson and the spy company if the enemy engaged and made a stand against them. One battalion of each regiment [was] to be kept in reserve to act as occasions might require.

Colonel Burleson quickly moved forward with Chief Placido's Tonkawas and the two blue-uniformed regular army companies of his regiment, Captain George Howard's Company D and Captain Samuel Jordan's Company C. Jim Carter's spies had discovered the advance forces of Chief Bowles' Cherokees. It soon became evident, however, that the main body of the Indians had taken up concealment around the hill upon which the Delaware village known as "Delaware Town" sat.

The second battalion of Burleson's regiment included the two mounted volunteer companies commanded by Lieutenant Colonel Woodlief and Major William Jones. Arriving on the scene shortly behind Burleson's advance forces, Jones later described the setup.

> It soon became apparent that the reinforcements looked for by Bowles had not reached him and that he was falling back to meet them. This he succeeded in accomplishing next morning, at the Delaware village . . . occupying an eminence in the open post oaks, with the heavily timbered bottom of the Neches in their immediate rear. When our forces overtook them, the main body of the enemy were in full sight occupying the eminence where the village was located, while a detachment was posted in a ravine, tortuous in its course, and was intended to conceal their movements towards our rear, with a view to throw themselves between our men and their horses.[41]

Burleson's battalion rode to the Delaware village and reached the brow of the hill. The Indians were in their defensive position on the lower slopes of the hill that spread down toward the Neches River. As his men prepared to dismount, the cracking of rifle fire could be heard as Captain Carter's men were taken under fire by the Cherokees.

Before Burleson's men even had time to dismount, Indians opened fire on them as well. Seven horses were shot and Private Martin Tutts of Captain Jordan's company was fatally wounded in this opening exchange. The Texans fought back, joining Carter's spies in driving the aggressive detachment of Indians back into the ravine below for better shelter.

Arriving at the Delaware village just behind Burleson was Major General Rusk with captains Peter Tipps and Jack Todd's companies. They rushed to join the action. General Douglass wrote that the Indians' position "was a very favorable one for defense, they occupying a ravine and thicket." The Texans were forced to "advance upon them through open woods and down a considerable hill."

William Hart was among Captain Tipps' company "in the front of Rusk's command" as they rode into Delaware Town. Hart noted that the first firing on Captain Carter's spies had

> wounded David Rusk in the leg, who was just ahead of us.
>
> We were ordered to dismount and form, which we did promptly and ran until we came on the brow of a hill. The Indians occupied a deep gully below us and were covered by trees and brush.[42]

The Delaware village was burned as the Texan troops moved on through to prevent the structures from being used for cover. The black clouds of smoke and towering flames quickly added to the misery of the noontime East Texas July heat.

The Indians were well entrenched in the dry creekbed below the burning village. This ravine ran a crooked course from north to south downhill, eventually turning east and running out to the Neches River. Just above the bend in the creek was a large prairie about a half mile in length. Near the lower end of the prairie running parallel with the creek was a thicket of hackberry bushes and rattan vines of about three hundred yards in length.[43]

Tom Rusk's lead battalion quickly occupied the point of the hill on both sides of the road leading toward the ravine where the heaviest fire was concentrated. General Douglass' troops arrived at the Delaware village in good time. From these men, Douglass ordered that every sixth man was to remain behind and guard the horses while the rest of the soldiers advanced on foot into the fight.[44] The Texans had become wise to the popular Indian battle tactic of sending a detachment to capture their enemy's horses during the heat of battle.

Lieutenant Colonel Jim Smith, commander of the East Texas ranger regiment in 1836, advanced from the village with the remainder of Rusk's regiment. He was followed in by more troops of Burleson's regiment under Lieutenant Colonel Woodlief and Major Jones, as described in General Douglass' campaign report.

> Lt. Col. James Smith arrived upon the ground, with the 1st Battalion of Rusk's regiment, Capt. R. W. Smith on the right, and Capt. Madison Smith on the left; and formed in good order on the left. Col. Burleson in the meantime having obliqued to the left and engaged the extreme right of the Indians; Lt. Col. Woodlief, with the two volunteer companies under Captains Lewis and Ownby had been ordered to deploy and form upon the extreme right, which order was promptly obeyed. The men were brought up in good order, and formed directly on the right. Rusk occupying the center, in which a brisk fire was kept up for about an hour and a half and returned with spirit and animation by our men, who continued to advance upon the enemy.[45]

Douglass was later convinced that the Indians his men were facing numbered "not less than" 700 to 800 warriors. Private Hart of the Nacogdoches Regiment felt that "there could not have been less than 600 Indians on the battlefield of the second battle." These Indians were known to have included the Cherokees of Chief Bowles and Big Mush, plus a number of Delawares, Shawnees, Kickapoos, Quapaws, Choctaw, Biloxi, Ionies, Alabamas, Coushattas, and others.[46]

General Douglass stated that the volunteers under Rusk made a "general" charge to support Burleson's two regular companies and those of Carter, Tipps, and Todd. Army commander Edward Burleson, who had been assured of speedy reinforcement by Secretary of War Johnston, found that Douglass' militiamen did not charge together in force quickly enough. Burleson's men were quickly overwhelmed by the number of Indians and he found

> that I would be compelled to rely for success upon the bravery of those then in the action. The tardy advance of the main body of Col. Rusk's Regiment (who did himself admit and lament the fact in the strongest terms of reprobation) rendered my movements extremely critical, and I was compelled to make the charge upon the right flank of the enemy, alone and unaid-

> ed, save by the gallant few who came to my succor early in the struggle. Delay was dangerous, and exposed my men to be slaughtered by the Indians.[47]

Several of those in the forefront of the battle were wounded during the early part of the battle. From Captain Carter's spies, David Rusk was wounded in the leg and Captain Samuel Jordan of the First Regiment was badly wounded in the hip.

Burleson later named some of the men whom he considered to have fought most valiantly in this engagement, including David Rusk, David Kaufman, Henry Augustine, Captain John Lynch, and Thomas Bates. Bates and Lynch, he noted "were not attached to any company, but volunteered in the west and accompanied me through the whole expedition." An existing army muster roll shows that Lynch commanded a six-man mounted spy unit for three months under Burleson's direction.

Pinkney Caldwell, quartermaster of Colonel Burleson's Frontier Regiment, was equally critical of the time it took Rusk's militia to respond during the second Cherokee engagement.

> Our last battle was a hard fought battle for one and a half hour[s]. At least one half of our men could not be brought to a charge. The charge had to be made by about three hundred men. Eastern Texians can fight Mexicans but can't stand Cherokees.[48]

This criticism of Rusk's volunteer companies was not completely merited and would cause some heated debate among veterans of the Cherokee War in later months. Burleson gave little credit at all to Rusk's militiamen, while General Douglass' report was felt to unfairly credit Burleson and Woodlief's troops. Newspaper accounts published in the *Telegraph and Texas Register* gave credit only to portions of Captain Carter's spies and Captain Todd's men from Rusk's regiment. Adjutant General McLeod tried to explain that Douglass' report had mistakenly confused Woodlief's volunteer division (under Burleson) and Rusk's second division.

McLeod stated that he had a high opinion of Rusk's men, but felt that it was proper to point out the Douglass had erred in not mentioning Burleson's men and their aggressive leadership in the midst of conflict. McLeod only further stirred the anger in some East Texans who felt they had been neglected for praise.[49]

William Hart of Captain Tipps' company happened to observe a letter that McLeod wrote for President Lamar after the battle which claimed that "Genl. Rusk could not get his regiment to charge and that he cursed them on the field." Hart bitterly swore that Colonel McLeod was a "damned hell fire infernal god damned liar." He strongly felt that "Rusk's men did charge. They did fight. They done their duty." Hart claimed to be standing over the adjutant general's shoulder when he wrote the letter to Lamar. He wrote that McLeod was "half drunk at the time" he penned this letter.[50]

Casualty reports of the Neches battle on July 16 show that the rangers and militiamen suffered just as many casualties as did Burleson's men. From Rusk's regiment, Captain Tipps' company was in the heat of the Indian action, as recorded by Hart.

> Our company was right before and in reach of their guns. The best evidence of that fact is that 5 were wounded. Mr. [John Rutherford] Hubert's apprentice was shot right by my side. [Nacogdoches Justice of the Peace R. H.] Pinney was in the hottest and behaved well.

Tipps' unit was fighting in tandem with Jack Todd's Nacogdoches company. Todd's company actually suffered the five wounded, plus another mortally wounded, which Hart referred to. Private Willis Bruce recalled some companions who were wounded in the battle.

> I remember George Rogers as he jumped in the gulley before me. George Martin, Lemmons, and William Bell I remember were wounded, besides several others whose names I do not recollect. Was paid $30 dollars Texas money for my services in this expedition. David S. Kaufman was wounded in the face. I was in Todd's company.[51]

Charging into the midst of the fight with Captain Bob Smith's Nacogdoches company was young John Reagan. As he passed over the top of the ridge from the burning Delaware village, he spotted Indians entrenched in the ravine below. A rifle ball struck his friend David Kaufman in the face and knocked him down. Reagan checked his buddy's heavy bleeding, decided the wound was not severe and continued into the battle.[52]

The heavily entrenched Cherokees were not easily driven from their ravine. The Texans charged them several times but were forced to withdraw back up the slope and to nearby woods each time due to heavy counterfire. The mid-July Texas heat was relentless. Many men without water braved their thirst to keep up firing and charging.

Chief Bowles and his warriors stood strong throughout the early fighting. Private Reagan recalled that the Indians managed to put a fright in some of the Texans during one of the rallies.

> Word ran along our line that the Indians were in our rear getting our horses. This came near producing a panic. Len Williams and Ben A. Vansickle, who were with us, and who understood and could speak the Cherokee language, told us that at that time they could hear Bowles, who was urging his warriors to charge, and telling them that the whites were whipped if they would charge."[53]

Private Peter Rodden of Captain Smith's ranger company agreed with the momentary mayhem on the Neches battlefield.

> Under a scorching meridian sun we again met a rallied enemy. The captain of my company was shot down on the first onset. Confusion spread among the ranks, the Indians on three sides of us. The contest was general.

During these charges, Captain Samuel Jordan of the army's Company C remained on the battlefield. Shot in the hip during the commencement of the action, he continued to yell orders to his men. Dr. Shields Booker, who had cared for the wounded at San Jacinto three years prior, tended to Jordan and the other wounded men of Burleson's regiment. General Douglass later praised doctors Booker, Lemuel Brown, and William Jowers for treating men "with their respective regiments throughout the hottest of the action."

Private Hart wrote that the Indians "tried to outflank us but did not succeed. They also at one time attempted to make a charge and came out of the gully or ravine." Chief Bowles hoped to unnerve the Texans, "but in place of retreating before them we fired and gave them such a peppering that they yelled and ran."[54]

Douglass finally ordered an all-out charge upon the ravine from all regiments. Burleson was critical of much of Rusk's regiment for not charging immediately during the initial part of the battle. In a letter written shortly after the battle, he acknowledged the fact that "Col. Rusk's entire Regiment came up to the charge" this time.[55]

Texan Casualties of July 16, 1839
Battle of the Neches

GENERAL DOUGLASS' FIRST REGIMENT (THIRD BRIGADE: RANGERS)

Name	Company	Remarks:
John Ewing, Pvt.	Capt. Harrison	Mortally wounded.
Henry Madison Smith, Capt.	Capt. H. M. Smith	Wounded.
M. Tansell, Pvt.	Capt. H. M. Smith	Wounded.
John S. Thompson, Pvt.	Capt. H. M. Smith	Mortally wounded.

COLONEL RUSK'S SECOND REGIMENT (THIRD MILITIA BRIGADE)

Name	Company	Remarks:
Henry W. Augustine, Pvt.	Capt. Todd	Seriously wounded.
William Bell, Pvt.	Capt. Todd	Wounded.
John Newton Brimberry, Pvt.	Capt. Todd	Wounded.
James Elijah Gilliland, Pvt.	Capt. Todd	Wounded.
David S. Kaufman, Major	Capt. Bob Smith	Wounded in face.
Felix Grundy Lemmon, Pvt.	Capt. Todd	Slightly wounded.
George F. Martin, Pvt.	Capt. Todd	Mortally wounded.
Hugh McLeod, Colonel	Douglass' Staff	Slightly wounded.
David Rusk, Pvt.	Capt. Carter	Wounded in the leg.

COLONEL BURLESON'S INFANTRY (TEXAS ARMY)

Name	Company	Remarks:
Ferdinand Booker, Cpl.	Capt. Howard	Shot in the arm.
Wm. Joseph Campbell, Pvt.	Capt. Howard	Wounded.
William Clements, Cpl.	Capt. S. W. Jordan	Shot in shoulder.
Samuel W. Jordan, Capt.	Capt. S. W. Jordan	Shot in the hip.
Millard M. Parkerson, Sgt.	Capt. Howard	Shot in leg and thigh.
Martin Tutts, Pvt.	Capt. S. W. Jordan	Fatally shot in chest.
Joseph B. Young, Pvt.	Capt. S. W. Jordan	Slightly grazed.

LIEUTENANT COLONEL WOODLIEF'S REGIMENT (RANGERS)

Name	Company	Remarks:
James J. Caskey, Pvt.	Capt. Lewis	Shot in the shoulder.
Thomas McLaughlin, Pvt.	Capt. Lewis	Shot in the arm.
Edward S. Ratcliffe, Pvt.	Capt. Lewis	Shot in the arm.
J. M. Smith, Pvt.	Capt. Lewis	Shot in the side.
George Willman	Capt. Ownby	Intermittent fever.

Sources: July 16 Medical Report of Surgeon Shields Booker of the First Infantry for Colonel Edward Burleson's troops, July 16 Medical Report of Surgeon Lemuel B. Brown of the Texas Militia, and company roster research by author.

Rusk's regiment swept in from the left side of the battlefield while Colonel Burleson's forces took the right. General Douglass' campaign report shows that the other battalion leaders moved in quickly.

> The second battalion of Rusk's regiment under the command of Lieut. Col. James Smith speedily reinforced the left wing and behaved handsomely. The right under Burleson was in like manner sustained by the detachment from his command under Lieut. Col. Woodlief, when the enemy were charged and driven from their strong hold.[56]

During this major charge, Captain Madison Smith, son of Lieutenant Colonel Smith, was badly wounded. He was forced to turn command of his Nacogdoches County Rangers over to First Lieutenant Albert G. Corbin.

The strong advance succeeded in forcing the Indians to break from their defensive area. "After an hour's fighting we charged and took possession of the gully," wrote Private Hart. "They had in their rear a large cornfield into which they retreated."[57] Apparently whipped, the Indians fled in every direction from their advancing assailants without fighting. Major William Jones, sweeping in with Woodlief's mounted gunmen, later wrote that this charge drove the Indians from the ravine towards the Neches River.

> When they retreated upon the main body, their entire force was terrorized and fell back in great disorder upon the cornfields, then in full bearing, and the dense timber of the river bottom. It was here that Bowles evinced the most desperate intrepidity, and made several unavailing efforts to rally his trusted warriors.[58]

★ ★ ★ ★ ★

The Killing of Chief Bowles

Throughout the entire battle on July 16, Chief Bowles was noted to have displayed the utmost in courage. The eighty-three-year-old leader of the Texas Cherokees remained on horseback in full view throughout the engagement. Bowles was decked out in silk vest, a military hat, a magnificent sword, and a sash presented to him years earlier by Sam Houston.

"He was a magnificent picture of barbaric manhood and was very conspicuous during the whole battle," wrote militiaman John Reagan.[59] Even as his younger Indians fled during this final Texan charge, Chief Bowles was the last to ride from the field. He tried valiantly to restore order to the broken ranks of his men.

Perched atop his fine sorrel horse with its blaze face and four white feet, the old chief was a prime target. His horse was shot seven times and Bowles himself was wounded as his forces retreated. According to Major Jones, the chief soon thereafter "was shot in the back, near the spine, with a musket ball and three buckshot."[60]

Exactly what man delivered the crippling shot to the old chief may be argued for eternity. Historian John Henry Brown wrote in 1885, "I well remember in those days, however, that the names of half a dozen men were paraded as the champions, who, under as many different circumstances, had killed Bowles."

One such man was Private Henry C. Conner of Captain Madison Smith's ranger unit. Having seen his own captain shot down with a serious wound, Conner reportedly settled the score by dropping Chief Bowles with "buck and ball." John Reagan later recorded that Bowles' horse had already been wounded numerous times and that the chief was suffering from a bullet shot through the thigh.

> His horse was disabled and could go no further, and he dismounted and started to walk off. He was shot in the back by Henry Conner, afterwards Major Conner; walked forward a little and fell, and then rose to a sitting position facing us, and immediately in front of the company to which I belonged.

Another man less often credited with shooting Bowles was the Frontier Regiment's Captain William T. Sadler, whose family had been slaughtered by Indians the previous year during the Edens-Madden Massacre. As related to his children, he was among those on the Neches battlefield who fired a musket shot which struck the old chief. An East Texas newspaper later stated in an historical sketch, "There is evidence that Sadler fought with great bravery, [and] he may have fired the shot that killed Chief Bowles."[61]

His horse shot out from under him and suffering from at least two shots himself, Chief Bowles was approached by several Texans from Rusk's regiment. According to Second Sergeant Charles N. Bell of Captain Tipps' company, Captain Bob Smith finished off the wounded chief. Smith was reportedly motivated to avenge the murder of his father-in-law, Jesse Jernigan Watkins, who had been killed by Indians in 1838. Sergeant Bell was among many witnesses.

> He was sitting in the edge of a little prairie on the Neches River. The chief asked for no quarter. He had a holster of pistols, a sword and a bowie knife. Under the circumstances, the captain was compelled to shoot him, as the chief did not surrender nor ask for quarter. Smith put his pistol right to his head and shot him dead.[62]

Sergeant Bell also noted that Smith took this opportunity to remove the prized sword which Chief Bowles now "of course had no use for." Private John Reagan would later write that he and Smith approached Bowles as he was struggling to sit up from the wound to his back. He hoped that his commander would take the key Cherokee prisoner. "Captain, don't shoot him," Reagan said as Smith approached the Cherokee with his pistol drawn.

> But as I spoke he fired, shooting the chief in the head, which caused instant death. It ought to be said for Captain Smith that he had known of the many murders and thefts by the Indians, and possibly did, in the heat of battle, what, under other circumstances, he would not have done, for he was esteemed as a most worthy man and citizen.[63]

Eyewitness William Hart of Tipp's unit was as inspired by the courage of Chief Bowles as John Reagan. In a letter written one week after the Neches battle, Hart described the end of the Cherokee leader.

> Bowles was on his horse until the last. He behaved as well in the battle as it was possible for a Genl. to do. He waved his sword and urged his men to charge.
>
> As he was the last to leave, the Indians had no time to take him off. His horse had 3 or 4 balls in him. He (Bowles) was shot in the thigh and in the back. He was on his hands and knees and Bob Smith shot him above the eye with a pistol. Smith has his Houston sword and Genl. Rusk took off him the red military jacket that Houston gave him. I have got his saddle, all stained with his blood and his scalp is sent to Augustine for Sam Houston's constituents to keep till he returns.

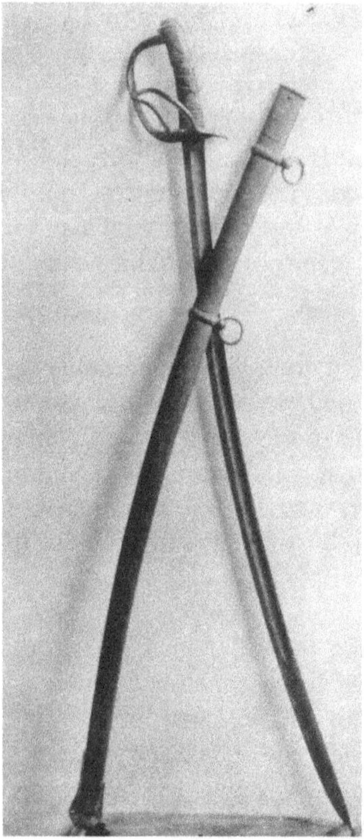

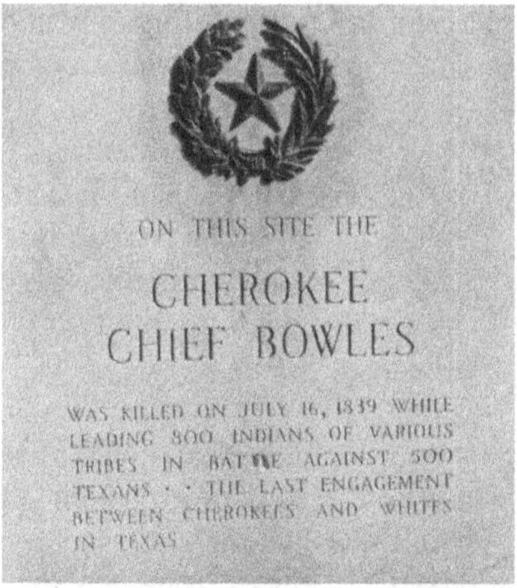

The steel military sword of Chief Bowles (left), presented to him by President Sam Houston, now resides in the Cherokee Nation archives in Tahlequah, Oklahoma. *Texas State Library and Archives Commission.*

This Texas centennial marker (above) indicates the area where Bowles perished on the Neches battlefield. It is located at the base of the hill (see below) which descended from the Delaware village and near a little wooded ravine which runs toward the Neches River. *Author's photos.*

> During the battle my horse had got loose and lost my saddle and bridle . . . When we had pursued the Indians some distance, we were ordered to fall back and charge on horseback. I mounted my horse without a saddle and Judge Taylor reminded me of Bowles' saddle and I took possession of it and mounted it while it was still wet with his blood. Major Reily wants it. I will keep it, for old I am, as a momento of his own dear Cherokees.[64]

The Indians were in full retreat at the point that Chief Bowles was killed. Colonel Burleson noted that the Cherokees were driven to the rear of the cornfield beyond the large ravine. "The Indians made no stand," he wrote, "and retreated rapidly towards the river, firing a few random shots, near the body of Bowles, their head chief."[65]

Chief Big Mush, the other principal Cherokee, was also killed. An estimated one hundred other Indians were also left dead on the Neches battlefield. Many of these were slaughtered as they fled in squads into the thickets near the marshy river bottomlands. Despite previous claims to have been short of arms and ammunition, the Indians had held off two charges by the Texans before finally being overrun during the final charge.[66]

The Indians fled across the Neches River as some of the Texans retrieved their horses. "As soon as we were mounted, we were ordered to charge on horseback," wrote Private Hart. "That order was countermanded."[67] Seeing that the enemy was beaten, General Kelsey Douglass decided to call a halt. His men were exhausted from their long march and more than ninety minutes of fighting in the July heat. The Indians were on the run and Douglass felt it more important to reform on higher ground and tend to the wounded men.

Edward Burleson, commander of the Texas Army, had of course relinquished overall command during this campaign to the Third Militia Brigade's General Douglass, as had Colonel Tom Rusk. Having participated in and led many an Indian fight in his years, Burleson was not happy when the "close chase" of the Indians on July 16 was called off.

> I regret that the decided advantage which we had then gained was not promptly followed up. I was fully impressed with the opinion that it was a military move to continue the pursuit of the Indians, who had retreated to the opposite bank of the Neches to secure a safe encampment for the night and so

> expressed myself. The country on the opposite side of the river was extremely favorable for pursuit, being thinly covered with post oak timber. The Indians were evidently heavily encumbered and greatly fatigued from the early stand they made, and another dislodgment would have placed them completely in our power. Of the success of another attack I could not doubt for a moment, as the troops, flushed with their past victories, were eager to be led on to the charge.[68]

Perhaps Douglass did not see the need that Burleson saw to completely annihilate his enemies once the battle had been won. In any event, the task at hand quickly turned to tending to the wounded Texans. Four men had been killed outright during the Neches battle on July 16. Private Martin Tutts of Burleson's army had been killed early on. John S. Thompson, John Ewing, and George F. Martin, were killed while fighting under captains Madison Smith, Greenberry Harrison, and Jack Todd, respectively. Twenty other Texans suffered wounds of varying degrees. Among the wounded, none severely, were Vice President Burnet, Secretary of War Johnston, and Adjutant General McLeod.

Most wounded men suffered gunshot wounds, but a few suffered arrow wounds. Henry Augustine, who had been a major of General Rusk's field staff during a previous 1838 Indian campaign, suffered an arrow through the leg while fighting with Captain Todd's company. Augustine's wound required his leg to be amputated at the knee. The Republic of Texas rewarded him with a special wooden leg.[69]

Colonel Hugh McLeod was also hit by an arrow which lodged in his thighbone during the closing minutes of the Neches battle. A newspaper account from eyewitnesses stated that throughout the fight he was "seen alternately in every part of the field dashing from rank to rank." McLeod was "heedless of the balls that were flying around him as if it were the mere pattering of rain." Although bleeding profusely after being struck by the arrow, McLeod continued to engage the Indians until the firing ceased. The arrowhead would remain in his thigh for life and plague him with fevers. Following medical attention in Nacogdoches, however, McLeod would return to Austin and resume his duties as adjutant general.[70]

In his campaign report, General Douglass wrote that he could not "invoke too earnestly the thanks of the country to those officers and men who participated in this action, for the bravery and determination they displayed." He commended Burleson, Rusk, Woodlief, and

James Smith for leading their respective regiments and battalions in the victory on July 16. He made special mention of his own staff officers, namely Colonel McLeod, Major Snively, and volunteer aides Samuel Davis, Leonard Mabbitt, Benjamin Sturgess, James Millroy, and Palmer Pillans.

Following the death of chiefs Bowles and Big Mush, many of the surviving Cherokees fled to the old camp of Bowles. Under cover of darkness, Indians returned to the area of the battle to retrieve the bodies of some of their slain and wounded. The eerie sounds of mourning continued through the night from the Indian camp. The sounds ceased by dawn on July 17, at which time the Indians had already vacated their camp to begin their retreat toward United States territory.[71]

Private Hart felt that it was fortunate the Texans did not pursue the Cherokees across the Neches on the evening of July 16. He wrote that the Texans later found that the Indians had "placed breastworks along on [the] east side with forked sticks placed to rest their rifles on." The Indians made their camp about "300 yards beyond the river" near the open road which led beyond the Neches. Hart felt that as the Texans would have crossed the river onto the open road, "they would have flanked us on every side."[72]

Whether the surviving Cherokees were as well prepared for another attack as Hart believed is debatable. In any event, General Douglass had ordered the pursuit abandoned for the evening. Hart and his fellow Texans made camp on the spot.

> We camped that night on the west side of the Neches within a few hundred yards of the battleground and within 300 yards of the Indians, who were on the east bank of the river.

A study of battle reports and muster rolls shows that the two main battles of the Cherokee War had cost the Texans eight men killed and at least twenty-nine wounded. William Hart's estimate written on July 24 was that "There is in all 6 dead and 33 wounded." Two of those he counted as being wounded soon died and he likely counts another militiaman who was accidentally shot in camp on July 17.

The campaign later known as the Cherokee War was viewed at the time as an important victory for the Texans in that it largely ended the Indian depredations in eastern Texas that had caused the settlers to live under such terror. The Neches battle was unquestionably a turning point in the Indian wars of Texas. For many Native Americans

Among the Texans wounded at the Neches battle were, left, Vice President David Gouverneur Burnet (1788–1870) and Secretary of War Albert Sidney Johnston (1803–1862). Burnet had served as President *ad interim* of the Republic of Texas in 1836. Johnston would later serve as a general for the Confederate Army during the Civil War. *Texas State Library and Archives Commission.*

living in Texas, it was a clear warning that their only chance of living peacefully near Anglo settlers would have to be on the other side of the Red River. The conflict has been described as the second most important fought on Texas soil after San Jacinto.[73] Indian advocates such as Sam Houston, however, were openly critical of Tom Rusk and other leaders of the Cherokee campaign.

The battle sword of Chief Bowles stayed in the possession of Captain Bob Smith until he later donated it to Clinton Lodge No. 23, A.F and A.M., of Henderson, Texas. Colonel James H. Jones of Henderson carried Bowles' sword with him through the Civil War before returning it to the Clinton Lodge.

The brass-hilted, steel-bladed single-edge sword was presented to Judge Will H. Barker of Oklahoma in about 1891. Barker, speaker of the lower house of the Cherokee legislative council, formally presented the weapon to the Cherokee Nation with a speech that was printed in both English and Cherokee. The trophy of the Texas Cherokee War now stands in the archives of the Cherokee Nation in Tahlequah, Oklahoma.[74]

The Cherokee War of East Texas
Roster Of Known Participants As Of July 15, 1839

Sources: Each of the following company rosters was compiled from available pay roll and muster roll records, furnished courtesy of the Archives and Information Services Division of the Texas State Library. For companies without an available muster roll, a partial roster is given from the best information available. Specific notes on sources accompany these partial rosters.

Author has attempted to record names as accurately as possible, but these documents were often handwritten with poor penmanship and frequently misspelled names. Where possible, a cross-reference of audited military claims and census information was used to fill in names and correct spellings. The service dates for each company indicate the particular muster and pay rolls referenced.

Brigadier General Kelsey Douglass' Third Militia Brigade Staff
June 29–August 5, 1839

Brigadier General:
Kelsey Harris Douglass
Adjutant General:
Hugh McLeod, Colonel
Major:
David Spangler Kaufman
Brigadier Major:
Jacob Snively
Indian Commissioners:
David Gouverneur Burnet
Isaac Watts Burton
Albert Sidney Johnston
James S. Mayfield

Aides de Camp:
Samuel Davis
Leonard H. Mabbitt
James H. Millroy
Palmer Job Pillans
Benjamin B. Sturgess
Quartermaster:
John Wortham, Major
Indian Agent:
Martin Lacy
Surgeon:
William George Washington Jowers

FIRST REGIMENT, THIRD MILITIA BRIGADE

Major Baley C. Walters

Captain Box's Mounted Rangers: March 26–October 18, 1839

Captain:
James Edward Box
First Lieutenant:
Daniel LaMora Crist
Second Lieutenant:
Elijah B. Reneau
Orderly Sergeant:
Gibson Gastin
Privates:
Thomas Berry
Jeremiah Blackwell
Benjamin Cannon
Stephen Crist
Richard C. Dixon
Arnold Evans
Harrison Farmer
Eli Faulkenberry
William M. Frost
Devereaux Gatewood
Spencer Hobbs
Levi Hopkins
Solomon Hopkins
Samuel Huffer
William Killian
Levi Martin
Daniel McKenzie
Lacy McKenzie
Jacob C. Morrow
John M. Morton
Peyton Parker
William B. Perry
Mark Roberts
George T. Slaughter
John Smith
William Smith
Humphries Ussery

Captain Adams' Houston County Rangers: May 8–August 9, 1839

Captain:
Solomon Adams
First Lieutenant:
Ira P. Ellis
Second Lieutenant:
Henry Masters
First Sergeant:
William J. B. Ford
Second Sergeant:
William D. F. Adams
Third Sergeant:
John Walker
Privates:
Cephus Adams
John Adams
Edward Allbright
Jacob Allbright
John P. Barnett
Alfred Benge
James W. Brent
Joel Clapp
John E. Clapp
Miles I. Eason
Benjamin B. Ellis
Charles Ellis
Charles Erwin
John Erwin
Elijah Gossett
Lee C. Gossett
James M. Hall
John B. Hall
William V. Hall
Daniel Hand
Samuel Harrison
William D. Harrison
John Hartgrave
William Harvey
Thomas Hayes
James B. Horten
Alfred M. Liles
Jose de Marteres Maria
Simon Matthews
Edry McCoy
Marshall B. McIver
John McLaughlin
Albert A. Nelson
Avery Nolan
Henry Ovender
Greenberry Pate
John Powers
William Riley
James R. Russell
George L. Short
Ira Shute
George M. Stewart
Abraham Stroud
Philip Walker
William White
William W. Wilkinson
George Wolverton

Captain Vansickle's Mounted Volunteers: July 1–August 5, 1839

Captain:
Benjamin A. Vansickle
First Lieutenant:
Hiram C. Vansickle
Second Lieutenant:
Green B. Hardwick
Orderly Sergeant:
John D. Miller
Privates:
Solomon Allbright
William Allison
Lewis Borkerdah
Samuel Charles Box
James W. Brown
William Butler
Wiley Caldwell
William Caldwell
Bird Carr
Charles Chevallier
William Connor
David Cook
William Crawson
Balis Edens
Darius H. Edens
John N. Elliott
Abraham Frizly
John Garceo
Samuel Gililland
John Gregg
John Griffin
John Crawford Grigsby
Daniel Harrison
Stephen Hatter
James Hill
Abel Hodges
George Isaacs
Leon Jones
James Kuykendahl
John Lennix
Robert Lennix
John Little
Micham Main
Jacob Masters
James McLean
Daniel Meredith
Samuel Miller
Joseph R. Moore
John Parker
James Patton
Samuel Patton
E. J. Pinkett
Edgar Pollitt
Clinton A. Rice
Ransom Rucker
Reuben R. Russell
Edwin P. Sims
Luther Smith
Charles Taylor
Peter Towns
Robert Walters
Alexander White
Leonard Houston Williams
Robert Williams
Thomas Williams

Captain Harrison's Mounted Gunmen: June 28–August 10, 1839

Captain:
Greenberry H. Harrison
First Lieutenant:
John Robbins
Privates:
Abram Anglin *
Asa Brigham
Anderson Buffington *
John Crane
Henry P. Crowson
Nicholas Henry Darnell*
John Ewing
Michael Hale
John W. Harrison
Samuel Harrison
Benjamin F. Highsmith *
George E. Hunter
Joseph Jordan
Peterson Lloyd
William M. Love
Oliver Lund
Jacob Mays
James Ross
Wesley Selman *
A. J. Stephens
Jeff Wallace *
George W. Wilson

* Known participant not in service with First Regiment of Infantry. No complete roster is available for Captain Harrison's company. Partial roster from author's research of Audited and Unpaid Claims of Republic of Texas. Harrison's volunteer company was recruited by Colonel Henry W. Karnes.

Captain Henry Smith's Volunteer Rangers: March 1–Sept. 1, 1839

Captain:
Henry Madison Smith
First Lieutenant:
Albert G. Corbin
Second Lieutenant:
Jackson Ward
First Sergeant:
William W. Wade
Second Sergeant:
John F. Grigsby
Third Sergeant:
John C. Snow
Fourth Sergeant:
Jeremiah Ball
First Corporal:
Elijah H. Moore
Second Corporal:
William Mayfield
Third Corporal:
James W. Robertson
Fourth Corporal:
John B. McDonald
Privates:
John Anderson
Durham Avant
William Avant
Samuel Baker
T. C. Barnes
William M. Berryhill
George A. Box
M. L. Boyd
Alfred Bright
Charles Brimmingham
Andrew J. Click
Henry C. Conner
William T. Davis
Morgan Egleson
Peter Elliott
Daniel Eskens
Elisha A. Evans
John A. Evans
G. W. Floyd
Henry Geough
Thomas Gower
John A. Harper
Benjamin C. Harrill
Samuel Huffer
John Hunter
John Jacobs
George Kimbro
Thomas Larkins
Mapers Lennix
Jesse H. Looney
William Loyd
Joseph Martin
John H. Matthis
W. H. Matthis
David F. O'Kelly
George W. Payne
Z. F. Petty
Richard Pollard
John Pollitt
William A. Ravy
John Ridens
Peter F. Rodden
John Rome
Samuel D. Sansom
William Saper
John Shepherd
John Smith
Conrad Snider
Thomas Spears
John Stokely
M. Tansell
John S. Thompson
James Triplett
Elisha Tubbs
William H. Vardeman
S. W. Vardeman
G. Xavier

SECOND REGIMENT, THIRD MILITIA BRIGADE

Colonel Thomas Rusk's Field and Staff: July 9–August 8, 1839

Colonel:
Thomas Jefferson Rusk
Lieutenant Colonel:
James Smith
Major:
Elisha Clapp
Adjutant Major:
William N. Dunnington
Sergeant Major:
Ira Munson
Quartermaster:
Edward B. Noble

Commissary:
Alexander McIver
Surgeons:
Lemuel B. Brown
Levi Martin
Captain of Spy Company:
James Carter

Note: Captain Carter's company was formed after Rusk's regiment departed Nacogdoches. The majority of his men were pulled from the ranks of Captain Todd's company.

Capt. Alexander Jordan's Mounted Rangers: June 21–August 5, 1839

Captain:
Alexander Jordan
First Lieutenant:
F. C. Haynie
Second Lieutenant:
Russell Kelley
Orderly Sergeant:
David Gage
Privates:
Edward Abshire
Elijah Allred
Henry Awalt
Thomas Berryhill
William Bruce
Joseph Buffington
Hesituah Charty
R. Chisum
A. Dill
Augustin Duncan
Alston Ferguson
Elijah Ferguson
John Ferguson
John Grace
Jackson Grayson
Henry Hilton
James Hutton
Thomas Jones
Andrew Jordan
Armstead Jordan
Samuel Jordan
Isaac Lemans
John Lollar
Thomas Maxwell
Matthew Mays
James McWilliams
Farris Montgomery
William Reagan
S. J. Sims
William T. Smith
H. J. Stackman
Hardy F. Stackman
Henry Stackman
G. W. Starr
Samuel R. Stephenson
Corbin Tansell
William W. Umsted
David Vanwinkle
William Vardeman
William Washburn
Francis Williams
William Williams
James Woodworth

Captain Sánchez's Mounted Gunmen: June 16–August 5, 1839

Captain:
Lewis Sánchez
First Lieutenant:
Juan Monsola
Orderly Sergeant:
Santiago Rabia
Privates:
Francisco Accosta
Watkene Adomades
Lusino Anandas
Howard Bailey
Thomas Berryhill
Candelario
Santiago Carro
Henry Chapman
Santiago Comarche
Manuel Garcia
Manuel Gouteras
Incarnacion Juarez
Francisco Lacerine
Cornelias Lopez
Feliciano Lopez
Sylvester Luna
Delores Martinez
Juan Matto
Jose Maria Mendez
Jacinto Miganio
Jose Maria Monsola
Poular Monsola
Jose Maria Montes
Anastacio Mora
Maximo Salazar
David Sánchez
Pedro Sanchez
Ygnacio Sanchez
Secusmunda Sepulvado
Berry Smith
William Smith
James Solar

Capt. Robert Smith's Mounted Volunteers: June 28–August 5, 1839

Captain:
Robert W. Smith
First Lieutenant:
Stephen F. Sparks
Second Lieutenant:
Daniel Weeks
First Sergeant:
Andrew Caddell
Second Sergeant:
Henry C. Cook
Third Sergeant:
W. L. Song
Fourth Sergeant:
S. A. Askew
First Corporal:
Robert W. Watkins
Second Corporal:
Eli G. Sparks
Third Corporal:
Henry Rogers
Bugleman:
Benjamin F. Sills
Privates:
George G. Alford
Elijah Anderson
W. Barton
John Bascus
Isaac T. Bean
Robert Bean
Samuel M. Bean
Samuel L. Burns
William W. Burrows [1]
Jeremiah D. Caddell
John Caddell
George W. Click
Ambrose Hulen Crain
Colby W. Crawford
Asa Dorsett
Calvin Eaton
Jesse F. Ellington
Malcolm Givin
Archabald C. Graham
John F. Graham
Vincent Hamilton
Thomas Hawkins
David Spangler Kaufman
Daniel Lacy
Joshua Leach
James D. Long
William Manor
George Martin
Alexander McIver
William McKaughn
Francis C. McKnight
James McKnight
Samuel A. McNutt
Penson Miles
Elijah Mosley
Kindred Henry Muse
William Nelson
J. G. Parker
Moses L. Patton
George Pollitt
John Henninger Reagan
Dimer W. Reaves
John Roark
Russell Roark
R. M. Roark
John Rowan
Martin Rugmupff
James S. Shanks
Henry Sibley
Alford G. Sims
Matthew F. Sims
Thomas Sims [1]
William Sims
David Skelton
James Hawkins Sparks
Hugh Stovall
John B. Thacker
Leander Erwin Tipps
John M. Watkins [3]
Benjamin F. Whitaker
Madison Guess Whitaker
Samuel W. Wilds
Pinson Wiles
Owen C. Williams
Maston Windsor
James S. Windsor
Zach F. Worley [2]

[1] Left July 15 due to sickness.
[2] Transferred July 11 to Capt. Tipps' company.
[3] Sub 7/13 for Robert Watkins.

Captain Tipps' Mounted Volunteers: July 13–August 5, 1839

Captain:
Peter Tipps
First Lieutenant:
George K. Black
Second Lieutenant:
James W. Cleveland
First Sergeant:
N. Adolphus Sterne
Second Sergeant:
Charles N. Bell
Third Sergeant:
Charles S. Taylor
Privates:
Henry P. Barron
Bennett Blake
J. M. Bradshaw
John Caddell
John Caruthers
Charles Chevaillier
John Chisum
William P. Chisum
William H. Crutchir
William Davis
Berry L. Dunkley
William Hart
John B. Holman
Henry Jacobs
James Jacobs
R. L. Lance
John C. Lane
Robert M. Long
John B. Martin
James McAnulty
Thomas T. McIver
John B. Murray
Richard Parmalee
Robert S. Patterson
Thomas Perry
R. H. Pinney
Charles L. Price
George Riddle
Samuel Rodgers
Dr. Henry M. Rogers
John Steward
William W. Taylor
Alfred G. Walling
Jesse Walling
James R. Wilehart
Jason Williams
William F. Williams
Zach F. Worley
John Wright
Archabald Yancy

Captain Todd's Mounted Volunteers: June 28–August 5, 1839

Captain:
Jackson Todd
First Lieutenant:
Isham Chisum
Second Lieutenant:
John C. Walling
First Sergeant:
Isham R. Chisum
Second Sergeant:
Presly M. Walling
Third Sergeant:
James R. Goodin
Fourth Sergeant:
Bradford Shorter
Privates:
Henry W. Augustine
William Bell
John Newton Brimberry
John F. Brown
Robert P. Brown
William M. Bruce
John C. Childers
Claiborne Chisum
Elijah Chisum
Madison Chisum
Benjamin Clark
Matthew Colewell
Samuel L. Davis
John Dorsett
James H. Durst
Gibson J. Dyer
Ephraim M. Eakin [1]
Robert Eubank
Ambrose B. Eubank
S. D. Fulton
James Elijah Gilliland
John Tunley Gilliland
Isaac Hamby
Joshua B. Hanks
Blackstone Hardeman
Henry R. Horn
Archibald Hotchkiss
Rinaldo Hotchkiss
William F. Humberson
Galland Jones
John Kryson
Felix Grundy Lemmons[3]
Jacob Lewis [2]
George Long
George F. Martin
Neil Martin
Alexander W. McAlpine
Thomas McClure
J. A. McFarland [1]
Henry M. McIntire [1]
Robert B. Merritt
Henderson Miller
George H. Millikin
Lorenzo M. Mills
John C. Morrison
David Muckelroy
Martin Murchison
Walter Murray
John Noblitt
Jose L. Padilla
Barnard Pantallion
Thomas Perry
Alfred Polk
James W. Richardson
L. L. Rogers
Louis Rose
John Rowan
Milton Rowan [4]
David Rusk
Thomas Jefferson Rusk [5]
James M. Sharp
Levi J. Shrader
James Simpson
John M. Sullivan
John S. Thorn
Leonard M. Thorn
W. M. Tigner
Asa Walling
Benjamin J. White
Elbert L. Williams
Jamail Wilson
William N. Wingfield
George H. Wright
John Wright
Louis L. Wright
John Swanson Yarbrough[6]

1 Joined July 18 after battle.
2 Taken sick and returned for home July 3.
3 Substitute for John Walling.
4 Substitute for Isaac Lee.
5 Elected colonel July 9.
6 Deserted July 7 with Barnard Pantallion's horse.

THIRD REGIMENT, THIRD MILITIA BRIGADE

Colonel Landrum's Regiment of Mounted Gunmen
Field and Staff: June 28–August 10, 1839

Colonel:
Willis H. Landrum
Lieutenant Colonel:
Moses L. Roberts
Major:
James M. Thompson
Adjutant Major:
George English
Sergeant Major:
Thomas Haugh
Quartermaster:
Robert O. Lusk
Surgeons:
John M. Hansford
J. R. Robertson

Note: Colonel Landrum's Regiment of Mounted Gunmen was detached by General Douglass to march up the west side of the Neches River and missed fighting the Indians on July 15–16, 1839.

Capt. Garrison's Shelby Co. Volunteers: June 28–August 10, 1839

Captain:
Mitchell Garrison
First Lieutenant:
Thomas Haley
Second Lieutenant:
Charles L. Haley
Orderly Sergeant:
William Cook
Privates:
Thomas G. Anderson
Joseph Ashton
John Boulden
Andstatia Carr
Arthur A. Clingman
John Crain
William J. Crain
Joseph Dial
W. G. Dial
George English *
Joshua D. English
T. M. Ewell
Allen Haley
John R. Haley
John R. Haley Jr.
Samuel N. Hall
John M. Hansford *
John Harden
Daniel Hasel
Zachus Hasel
Thomas Haugh *
Archibald W. O. Hicks
James M. Hooper
William M. Hooper
Thomas Jackson
William Jacobs
Thomas James
R. A. Jordan
Joseph King
C. L. Main
R. E. Mayfield
J. A. McFarland **
James S. W. Merchant
G. L. Moore
Robert Palmer
Dickerson Parker
John Parker
William Porter
J. E. Pugh
Stephen R. Richardson
Everett Ritter
Andres Roches
S. S. Runnels
William G. Runnels
John Shoemaker
Peter Stockman
William C. Vaun
J. W. Whitaker
Isaac Wisehart

* Promoted to Colonel Landrum's Staff. ** Transferred into Captain Todd's company.

Capt. Inman's Harrison/Shelby Co. Volunteers: July 9–August 10, 1839

Captain:
John Inman
First Lieutenant:
Richard B. English
Second Lieutenant:
Edward A. Merchant
Orderly Sergeant:
R. S. Biggers
Privates:
James Alford
William Arnold
George A. Ashabrane
Daniel Brown
James Brown
Joseph Butler
H. B. Cannon
John Choate
Levi Cole
James T. Denton
George H. Duncan
F. M. Fellows
Alfred A. George
Joseph G. Goodbread
George L. Graham
James M. Graham
Sherman Grosviner
William H. Hart
Samuel C. Heinight
Samuel C. Henderson
Elijah Hill
James Hinton
John Howard
Hiram Inman *
John H. Inman *
Thomas Jester
Thomas P. Kennedy
Charles Lawden
Aman Lewellen
Aaron Lowry
John Lowry
Andrew Martin
John Mason
Thomas P. Meers
Frederic H. Miller
M. B. Phillips
R. E. Price
Augustus Ryan
Evan Sanford
Snider Sanford
William T. Scott
Benjamin F. Smith
Jackson Smith
Bently Stewart
Leander Truett
William Turbin
James B. Tutt
L. D. Vance
Masan M. Vann
John Vanriper
James M. Vaughn
Zachariah C. Walker
Lee C. Wharton
W. T. White
William Winn
John Wood
Soloman Wood

* Transferred in from Capt. Garrison's company.

Capt. Kimbro's San Augustine County Volunteers: July 15–Aug. 10, 1839

Captain:
William Kimbro
First Lieutenant:
William D. Ratcliff
Second Lieutenant:
Joseph M. Burleson
Orderly Sergeant:
Lewellan A. Temple
Privates:
John Blair
Alan V. Braden
Hiram Brown
Samuel T. Burns
J. Cartwright
William H. Castleberry
Armstead Chumney
Robert Davidson
S. L. Davidson
H. Davies
George Davis
William C. Duffield
W. D. Ewing
William Fisher
John Salmon Ford
G. L. Foreman
John B. Foreman
Albert G. Frazier
Benjamin Fuller
David W. Gilbert
John A. Gilbreath
Davis G. Griggs
Calvin Hamilton
J. R. Hanks
Wiley Hanks
Amos Harris
J. M. Harris
Travis Harris
Demetrius Hays
Bird D. Hendrick
Thomas Hendrick
James Higgins
John Hunt
Samuel M. Hyde
Curtis Jesup
Samuel Jordan
W. B. Kelly
Isaac H. Kendrick
G. W. Lakey
William Lakey
Toles Landus
Walter Paye Lane
E. W. Lucas
James Madden
James Marshall
J. A. Martin
Mereda McCabe
Milton Moore
Henry Morgan
Thomas Payne
P. O. Pitman
R. Platt
Amos Roark
Solomon Rule
C. R. Sassamon
L. D. Simmons
William R. Scurry
B. Smith
William Thompson
J. B. Wafford
M. D. Wafford
A. L. Wilson
John A. Winn
Charles Worthington
Levi York

Captain McKim's Sabine County Company: July 9–August 10, 1839

Captain:
James McKim
First Lieutenant:
George W. Slaughter
Second Lieutenant:
William H. Ridgeway
First Sergeant:
Jonathan H. Ridgeway
Second Sergeant:
A. B. Capps
Third Sergeant:
William Payne
Privates:
P. W. Barber
T. M. Brown
J. Buchannon
William B. Burks
Phillip Burrow
J. B. Cameron
D. Carpenter
John D. Cathey
Frank F. Chaney
John R. Chatham
William R. Conner
James A. Currie
Richard Currie
David Damewood
H. B. Damewood
J. W. Damewood
William Donaho
John Easley
C. Fitzpatrick
Benjamin Foster
M. Goff
J. F. Gomer
William J. Gomley
O. P. Hains
E. R. Harris
William Harris
William D. Harris
W. R. Hester
James Horton
Stephen Horton
Jackson Hudson
David Huffman
Isaac Ivey
Curtis M. Jackson
H. A. Kendal
James Knight
Robert S. Love
John Marshall
Job Mason
F. McLamore
John H. McRey
G. W. Milton
Andrew Montgomery
Peter C. Ragsdale
George Reaves
Samuel M. Slaughter
John Sterling
H. A. Taylor
William P. Thompson
H. V. Towner
William H. Vories
Alfred A. Waite
Benjamin F. Weatherred
Francis M. Weatherred
James W. Williams

FIRST REGIMENT OF INFANTRY, TEXAS ARMY

Colonel Burleson's Field and Staff: June 28–August 10, 1839

Colonel:
Edward Burleson
Lieutenant Colonel:
William S. Fisher
Major:
Peyton S. Wyatt
Adjutant:
William D. Houghton *
Sergeant Major:
John R. Johnson

Quartermaster:
Benjamin B. Sturgess
Quartermaster Sergeant:
John P. Reavis
Surgeons:
Shields Booker
Richard Cochran

* Promoted from first lieutenant on July 7, 1839.

Source: *Defenders of the Republic of Texas*, 255.

Captain Lynch's Detachment of Spies: June 25–August 25, 1839

Captain:
John L. Lynch
Privates:
Thomas Bates
A. C. Carsen
Samuel Dubois
Samuel Fenters
___ Ross

Source: *Defenders of the Republic of Texas*, 288.

Chief Placido's Tonkawa Scouting Company

Twenty-four of Chief Placido's Tonkawa Indian braves formed a scouting company, riding and fighting with Colonel Burleson's regular army during the Cherokee War. No roster available.

Captain Sadler's Company A: First Regiment of Infantry

Captain:
William Turner Sadler
First Lieutenant:
Duncan C. Ogden [1]
Second Lieutenant:
Collier C. Hornsby [1]
First Sergeant:
Peter Flanley [2]
Second Sergeant:
Lewis Reaves [2]
First Corporal:
John Carroll [2]
Privates:
William Benson [3]
Thomas Casey [3]
John Cavitt [3]
Joseph Cecil [3]
Thomas D. Clark [3]
John Dennison [2,3]
William Dial [2,3]
John Hamrick [2]
Ross B. Jelkyl [2]
Henry Judd [2]
James Martin [2]
Alex McDonald [2]
Stephen A. McLeary [3]
Andrew Moore [3]
John P. Moseley [2]
Francis Rosendale [2]
Thomas Simpson [3]
Ephraim Stanberry [2,3]
Charles Stroud [3]
William Waterson [2]
James Wyatt [3]

This roster based on author's compilation.

[1] Known First Regiment participant of Cherokee War.
[2] Previously attached to Company C under Captain Kennymore until April 30, 1839. Not listed on any other existing company's muster roll at this time.
[3] Records show this man to have been enlisted in the First Regiment during this period and to have been part of Company A when it was temporarily commanded by Captain Adam Clendenin in late 1839.

Captain Clendenin's Company B: First Regiment of Infantry

Captain:
Adam Clendenin
First Lieutenant:
Edward A. Thompson
Second Lieutenant:
Timothy O'Neill *
James M. Alexander
First Sergeant:
Mathew McGovern
Second Sergeant:
James Alston
Third Sergeant:
William Walker
Fourth Sergeant:
Richard Nixon
First Corporal:
John James Johnson
Second Corporal:
Casper Lewiston
Third Corporal:
Robert Morris
Fourth Corporal:
William Berry
Privates:
Mathew Anderson
John Cassidy
Michael Daily
Henry S. Day
Cornelius Diggons
Joseph Dubignon
Oliver Farnsworth
William Gray
Thomas Harrison
Henry Hays
John Horan
Horace H. Houghton
John Humrich
M. Henry Judd
William Kelly
James H. Pollard
William Redfield
John Riley
John Shaw
Daniel Smith
Humphrey Sullivan
George Wilburton

* Killed by Indians July 26.

Note: Complete roster not available. This roster compiled from muster rolls in *Defenders of the Republic of Texas*, 67–80.

Captain Jordan's Company C: First Regiment of Infantry

Captain:
Samuel W. Jordan
First Lieutenant:
Wm. N. Dunnington
Second Lieutenant:
John Brown
Sergeants:
Washington Stephens
Henry Carhart
William Hill
Louis Neil
Corporals:
Washington Beatty
William Clements
Privates:
Charles S. Anderson
Alexander Bell
James Bird
Abraham Bradley
Alfred M. Cooper
Peter F. Craft
Michael Dunn
Louis Dunning
Michael Fanning
John Hare
John Harper
John Harris
Jacob Hoodle
Zephelin Islin
Augustus Kemper
James Kimberly
John Lewis
John Martin
John McDonald
David Miller
George W. Miller
Joseph W. Mott
William Oliver
John Robinson
Adolphus Rousette
William Scott
Harrison Simpson
Christopher Trouts
Martin Tutts
James Tweed
William Tyndall
James White
Mark Wilks
Joseph B. Young
Samuel Young

* Deserted June 24, 1839.

Source: *Defenders of the Republic of Texas*, 93–98.

Captain Howard's Company D: First Regiment of Infantry

Captain:
George Thomas Howard
First Lieutenant:
Samuel B. Carson
Second Lieutenant:
John Schuyler Sutton
First Sergeant:
William S. Johnson
Second Sergeant:
Eli Phillips
Third Sergeant:
Millard M. Parkerson
Fourth Sergeant:
Townsend Gardner
First Corporal:
Phillip Lyons
Second Corporal:
Ferdinand Booker
Privates:
James Ball
William Barker
James Burk
Daniel Burns
William Joseph Campbell

Captain Howard's Company D (Continued)

James Castillo
Stephen Cook
Martin Coyle
William C. N. Creed
John Day
John Downes
Horatio N. Eldridge
James Eldridge
John Garrett
Nehemiah Hauckenbury
Joshua Hudson
George Jenkins
Jesse Jones
Lewis Joseph
R. Knight
George Leonard
Robert P. Little
James M. McCormack
William McKain
Lewis C. Morrison
Charles Mossenton
Richard D. Newman
John O'Neal
James Parker
John R. Richardson
Francis Riley
John Taite Smith
John Snider
William Stewart
William Taylor
William Thompson
William Wallace
James Warmsley
John A. Wimble

Source: *Defenders of the Republic of Texas*, 125–136.

Captain Denton's Mounted Volunteers: July 15–August 15, 1839

Captain:
John Bunyan Denton
First Lieutenant:
Edward Hunter
Second Lieutenant:
John D. Bloodworth
First Sergeant:
Thomas R. Wilson
Second Sergeant:
Gilbert Reagan
Third Sergeant:
Edward West
Privates:
Samuel Borten
John Brewer
William Brinton
J. M. Buchannon
James Burn
William Crowder
Barshot Feguns
Andrew Jackson Fowler
Alex N. Graham
J. N. Gray
Robert Haley
William C. Hamilton
Joseph C. Hart
Henry Barlow Hutchins
John N. King
W. C. Lunney
John H. Matthis
James M. Patton
Andrew J. Price
H. S. Proctor
William B. Stout
J. J. Venning
Leory Venning
Benjamin Washburn

Note: Company shown on its muster roll to be First Regiment Infantry under Major Peyton S. Wyatt. It is unclear whether this company participated in the battles.

MOUNTED VOLUNTEER BATTALION (Burleson's Regiment)

Lieutenant Colonel Devereaux Jerome Woodlief
Major William Jefferson Jones

Capt. Lewis' Mounted Volunteers: March 2–September 9, 1839

Captain:
Mark B. Lewis
First Lieutenant:
A. L. McCoy
Second Lieutenant:
James S. Jones
First Sergeant:
J. Woodward
Second Sergeant:
Joseph Artoff
Third Sergeant:
H. H. Hazentine
Fourth Sergeant:
James Horie
First Corporal:
William Cockburn
Second Corporal:
John N. Webster
Privates:
A. Adams
J. L. Adams
W. M. Adams
Joseph S. Anderson
J. H. Baker
William Baker
Francisco "Frank" Becerra
William M. Bifset
M. Blood
Ambrose H. Boles
W. S. Brandenbush
John Bryan
J. Bryan
H. Cambray
A. Campbell
Pedro Cantrero
Simon Casbacon
James J. Caskey
R. W. Cecil
William Chambers

Capt. Lewis' Mounted Volunteers (Continued)

Charles H. Chevallier
J. S. Claiborne
William Coltron
Alton A. Crane
John Davis
Robert Deludy
James Doherty
Thomas Drumgold
Maria Durano
Jacob Ellis
Lawrence Erbil
Perry Fielson
John Flazer
Olmar Frederick
Harvey Garms
Emil Girard
Frank Girard
George Graddel
Daniel Harper
James Hawthorne
Jose Maria Hermes
Thomas Hernandez
Henry C. Holmes
Ratcliffe Hudson
D. G. Humblin
William Jergot
Charles Johnson
John Kerackner
George Kesnair
William Kresinka
Casper Leger
James Lowe
J. B. Marshall
Frederick Marter
J. P. Mayfield
R. S. Mayfield
William McKenzie
J. B. McKernen
Thomas McLaughlin
Francis Milheisler
William Oltman
James S. Phinneas
Ramon Piedas
C. J. F. Prales
Edward S. Ratcliffe
C. Reed
W. H. Reed
Carl C. Rhodes
James Rhohm
Montrevell C. Roundtree
John Schneider
Andrew Scott
George Scott
Abraham Smith
J. M. Smith
Robert Steel
Floyd Stillman
Berryman O. Stout
John Study
John Stumpskie
Wabria Taierte
Jeremiah Tarbon
Louis Thurman
Carlos Velasquez
A. Wade
W. D. Walk
John B. Williams
John H. Williams

Capt. Ownby's Mounted Volunteers: March 2–September 9, 1839

Captain:
James P. Ownby
First Lieutenant:
Matthew P. Woodhouse
Second Lieutenant:
Daniel Murphy
First Sergeant:
Hanibal A. Low
Second Sergeant:
Harvey Homan
Third Sergeant:
Kirkman Green
Fourth Sergeant:
Richard H. Waddell
First Corporal:
John Saunders
Second Corporal:
John Hilbert
Third Corporal:
James Lindsay
Fourth Corporal:
John Robinson
Privates:
Joseph Artoff
George Atkinson
J. G. Barrett
James Boyle
Isaac Brane
John F. Butler
E. S. Cochran
George Cooke
Richard Copeland
W. B. Craddock
Samuel Crogran
Samuel Crooks
Horatio Cunningham
Edward Daley
John Daniels
Henry Dibble
W. P. Dikeman
Richard Dillon
James Edgy
James M. Everett
Fidel Faholser
William Findley
Robert Follett
Alexander Frazer
W. Rhea Gillmer (surgeon)
Moses Hand
Benjamin C. P. Harrell
Samuel Haynes
James Hays
William Horsler
Francis Hughes (surgeon)
William Johnson
Francis Jones
William H. Kennedy
A. D. Kilker
James King
Francis Labrick
John Lafayette
John C. Lockhart
Ellis B. Lockridge
John Lysaught
W. Mail
Hugh Mathewson
M. McCartney
John C. McDermott
Daniel McKay
N. McRaney
James Moore
David Morrison
Charles A. Ogsbury
James H. Padget
William Rayhouse
Alexander Reiley
Henry Rinehart
Thomas Russell
Robert G. Saunders
John Talbot
Evan B. Thomas
T. J. Vitch
William D. Walker
F. Warnicke
J. D. Watkins
Thomas J. Watkins
T. K. Whaler
George Willman
Edward Woodruff

Chapter 11

Pursuit and Removal

July 17–October 22, 1839

The body of Chief Bowles remained on the battlefield as a grisly testament to the loss of the Cherokees. His lonely skull and skeleton were reportedly still visible on the spot for years. Some felt that his body was neglected by his followers due to a tribal custom which declared that Indians who had been scalped were not to be given funeral honors.[1]

A September 1, 1841, article in the *Telegraph and Texas Register* notes that "Some rude chaps scalped the poor chief after his death." Other Texans used their knives to cut away pieces of his body for personal charms and souvenirs.

Even those that had missed the fight were quick to mutilate the dead. Captain William Kimbro's company, which had been sent to Chief Linney's Shawnee village on July 15 to disarm the Indians, made its way back to the main battlefield by July 17. Lieutenant Joseph Burleson witnessed Alfred Polk, a private of Captain Todd's Nacogdoches company, "dismount to scalp a dead Indian" but was able to stop the act. The officer admonished his fellow soldier for what he considered behavior "too barbarious and uncivilized."[2]

Burleson's respect for the slain Indian is surprising, as his own brother, Captain Jacob Burleson, had been scalped and dismembered by Comanches on the Brushy Creek battlefield just five months prior.

Kimbro's company and all of Colonel Landrum's Third Regiment of the Third Militia Brigade had missed the battle on the Neches while marching up the opposite side of the river. They found much evidence of the battle and looked through the deserted huts of Chief Harris' largely burned village. One of Kimbro's men, Private John Ford, found a Bible which contained the birth records of an American family. He felt that the Indians' possession of this Bible "spoke of bloodshed and robbery."[3]

Still, Ford and his fellow militiamen could not help but feel respect for the courage of Chief Bowles when they stared upon his mutilated body as it lay in a small cornfield.

> We gazed silently upon his body as it lay unburied. He was dressed rather in the American style, had a red silk velvet vest said to have been a present from General Houston. It was not difficult to believe he sacrificed himself to save many of his people. Under other circumstances history would have classed him among heroes and martyrs.

★ ★ ★ ★ ★

Expulsion of Texas Indians

The Texan forces under Brigadier General Kelsey Douglass, Major General Thomas Rusk and Colonel Edward Burleson had made camp on the night of July 16 near the battlefield on the west side of the river. The next morning, litters were made to move the wounded men and the troops marched across to the east side of the Neches River.

The Texan spies were out early in the morning and found the Cherokee camp abandoned on the other side of the Neches. William Hart wrote that the spies found a second Indian camp that was

> some 2 or 3 miles beyond the river, where their wounded and children must have been. The Indians retreated in such a hurry that they left 3 wagons, 17 packs of old corn, feather beds, chickens, ducks, cooking utensils and, in fact, a little of everything and last not least about 600 head of cattle and 40 horses.
>
> On the morning of the 17th, just as we had saddled up and got ready to cross the river R.[ichard] Parmalee was standing next to me with his hand on the muzzle of his gun. [Second Lieutenant] James Cleveland's gun fell against the hammer of Parmalee's and discharged it. The ball passed through his right hand and his right shoulder. It is a very bad wound and if it does not kill him, I am afraid he will lose the use of his hand.[4]

Parmalee would survive. Captain Tipps noted on his muster roll that his man had been "wounded accidentally July 17th." He then selected several Nacogdoches County men—Hart, Rinaldo Hotchkiss, and Daniel Lacy—to carry Parmalee to Fort Lamar at the Neches Saline. Upon arriving there, Dr. Lemuel Brown detailed Hart and Corporal John Watkins "to go to Nacogdoches for medicine and bandages for the sick and wounded."

General Douglass ordered camp established at the site of the abandoned Indian camp. Named for the militia's senior commander, Camp Rusk was located in present Smith County just east of the Neches and just north of Highway 64. Camp aide James Mayfield penned the first draft of a battle report on July 17 at "Head Quarters, Camp Rusk on the Neches."

Captain Jack Todd was selected to lead a detachment of eighty men the following morning, July 18. They marched out with the wounded on litters for Fort Lamar, the fortification near the Neches Saline built three days prior by Captain Adam Clendenin's infantry company. In the meantime, Douglass moved his main army "forward two miles to good water and sent out scouts."[5]

The troops settled down to await the return of Captain Todd's detachment and the regiment of Colonel Landrum. Douglass' army remained camped on Prairie Creek in present Smith County for the next two days. Landrum's companies made their rendezvous on the evening of July 20 and Todd's forces were back at camp by the morning of July 21, at which time the men were organized to march after the retreating Indian forces.

The Texas scouts brought news that the main trail of the Indians lay back to the west and north near the headwaters of the Sabine River. Douglass, Rusk, Landrum, and Burleson moved their respective regiments up the Sabine in the general direction of present Lake Tawakoni. Secretary of War Albert Sidney Johnston reported that the retreating Indians had carried their wounded men off slung across horses. Many of these Indians had perished following the battle and their bodies were found dumped like discarded baggage along the trail for miles.[6]

By four o'clock in the afternoon, the Texas forces reached some cornfields and Indian huts. The troops burned several Indian villages and cut down all of the corn they encountered. Camp was made for the night at one of these villages. The trail of the Indians was picked up again the following morning, July 22. After covering a few miles, the army encountered several more Indian villages with more extensive cornfields and other improvements. General Douglass' campaign report details the actions of the Texas Army.

> Here we encamped, burnt the houses and cut down the corn.
>
> On the morning of the 23rd the army was again marched, pursuing on the retreat of the enemy. We passed and destroyed during the day on the march several villages and much corn. In the afternoon this day, the spies brought in intelligence that an Indian encampment with signs of a force being there was discovered in advance.
>
> The lines were thrown into battle order, and moved upon their encampment. It had been hastily abandoned. They left a yoke of oxen, some tools, peltries, and other plunder.[7]

Near the Sabine River on July 23, the retreating Cherokees reportedly killed a white settler named Blankenship.[8] Douglass and his troops were eager for further action and the discovery of the fresh camp charged their spirits even more. Collecting all the plunder from the Indian camp, the Texan army camped for the night on a lake. Scouts were sent out in various directions through the afternoon. Those sent back toward the vicinity of Chief Harris' village "reported much Indian sign to exist in that quarter." These men managed to kill one Indian and capture his horse.

Chief Placido's Tonkawa scouts reported to General Douglass that the Cherokee trails ahead were becoming widely scattered. Feeling secure that he had sufficiently laid waste to the Indian villages in his path, Douglass decided it was not wise to leave his own settlements too exposed. It was not uncommon for the Indians to stage a counterattack while the whites were out on an expedition.

On the morning of July 24, Douglass therefore ordered the Texas troops to countermarch back toward the July 16 battlefield near Chief Harris' Delaware village. En route to the Neches that day, the main body was rejoined by Captain Kimbro's San Augustine militia company, which had been trying to catch up for more than a week.

Two new companies also joined Douglass' army on July 24. Captain Andrew Jackson Berry had mustered in another company of San Augustine volunteers on July 19 and Captain Jacob E. Hamilton's men had formed in the same area on July 22. These men found that their services would not be needed, as General Douglass was planning to soon discharge most of his militiamen.

Walter Lane, a veteran of San Jacinto and the Surveyors' Fight, was among the San Augustine volunteers of Captain Hamilton's company. Among the battlefield trophies sported by the men who had fought the Cherokees, he noted one "festive cuss" who had cut a strip of skin from Chief Bowles' back. The man planned to use the dried flesh for a razor strap and good luck charm. Lane, feeling that the skin's previous owner "had remarkably bad luck," doubted the value of such a charm.[9]

Above Chief Harris' old Delaware village, the Texan forces found a beautiful lake which they called Lake Burleson. Camp was made for the night.

Quartermaster Pinckney Caldwell sent a note on July 24 from Camp Harris to the "Commander of the Station at Fort Houston." He advised that Colonel Burleson's Frontier Regiment would be moving to Fort Houston between the 8th and 12th of August. Caldwell detailed that Burleson would arrive

> with his command on his way to the Falls of the Brazos and wishes to have on hand for him two hundred bushels of corn and fifty bushels of meal. The corn can be ground at [Armstead] Bennett's Mill; also [need] rations of beef, salt, sugar, and coffee for two hundred and fifty men for twenty days.[10]

From Camp Harris, General Douglass sent out scouts in every direction the following morning, July 25, to determine if any Indian trails remained worthy of pursuit.

> All concurred in the general opinion that the enemy had outstripped us, more scattered and divided, and that further pursuit would be unavailing, so far as overtaking the enemy was concerned. Accordingly, on the evening of the 25th, orders were issued in conformity to the direction of the Secretary of War, to the commandants of the several volunteer regiments to march the troops under their command, by different routes home, and muster them out of the service.[11]

In his final report of the campaign, Kelsey Douglass noted that his forces had "marched over the greater part of the much talked of Indian Territory" of northeast Texas. His men had driven the Indians from the area and destroyed their crops and improvements. Douglass felt that these tribes had been plotting "with the Mexicans in a war against this country." He concluded by appealing to the war department for another expedition of one thousand Texans. He proposed that this force pass "up the Sabine and thence across to the Trinity and Brazos and destroy in their march the villages and corn of the Indians in that quarter" to prevent them from harboring further alliances with Mexican rebels.

On July 26, Lieutenant Timothy O'Neill of Captain Clendenin's company led a party of his First Infantry men out from their station at Fort Lamar near the Neches Saline to scout the territory west of the Neches. O'Neill, a veteran of Captain Joseph Daniels' Milam Guards, was killed this day when a party of Indians hiding in the Neches swamp surprised his men. His body was horribly mangled before it could be recovered. The Wednesday, August 14, issue of the *Telegraph and Texas Register* reveals of O'Neill:

> The deceased came to Texas in the fall of 1835, one of the volunteer corps raised in the city of New York by Col. E. H. Stanley. He was buried with the honors of war by his company at Fort Lamar.[12]

The Cherokee War of 1839 splintered the Texas Cherokees into small groups. Following the final battle, some of these Indians wandered for weeks without provisions. The majority crossed into the southeastern portion of Indian Territory, settling in present Oklahoma. Other small groups, including that of John Bowles, son of the slain chief, remained in Texas to encounter Texas forces again on a later date.[13]

While General Douglass was disbanding most of his volunteer forces, President Lamar was taking steps to force other Indians from Texas. He appointed Colonel Thomas Rusk and James Mayfield to serve as commissioners responsible for the removal of the Shawnees. They apparently decided not to force a fight such as the Cherokees had chosen to do. Secretary of War Johnston later summed up the removal agreement with the Shawnees.

> Stipulations on the same just basis as those made to the Cherokees were agreed upon, and they have received the compensation for their improvements and have been removed, in accordance with the agreement entered into between the Commissioners and their Chiefs.[14]

The treaty was made with the Shawnees in Nacogdoches on August 2, 1839. Representing the Shawnees were Elena, Pecan, and

Green-Grass, their chiefs and head-men. For the Anglo-Texans, Rusk and Mayfield served as commissioners, with James Hutton serving as interpreter and Joseph Ellis, Kelsey Douglass, and James Reily serving as witnesses.

The Shawnees agreed to depart in peace from Texas territory. In return, the government would pay them for their improvements, crops, and property that must be left behind. They were to be paid by Texas forces the agreed upon value in cash and goods. A small force of militiamen under Captain Alexander Jordan would escort and protect the more destitute Shawnee families in transporting their property. James Hutton would continue to act as their interpreter. When the time came to separate from their escorting militia party, the Shawnees would be provided their gunlocks once again.

The majority of the militia companies of the second and third divisions of the Third Brigade were en route home to disband at the time Douglass and Rusk were negotiating with the Shawnees. In Nacogdoches, the companies of Alexander Jordan, Lewis Sanchez, Bob Smith, Peter Tipps, and Jack Todd were mustered out of service on August 5. Captain Solomon Adams' Houston County Rangers were disbanded on August 9, but the rangers under Captain James Box remained in command of Fort Houston into October. Captain Henry Smith's volunteer ranging company remained in service through September 2.

The companies of Colonel Landrum's Regiment of Mounted Gunmen returned home and disbanded on August 10. Two of the volunteer companies organized for the Cherokee War, those of captains Greenberry Harrison and John Denton, were disbanded on August 10 and August 15, respectively. Private Peterson Lloyd's audited claims show that Captain Harrison's mounted gunmen, originally raised by Colonel Karnes, were mustered out after having served one month and 13 days.[15]

Another company recruited by Colonel Karnes, that of Captain Garrett in Houston, was also ordered to disband. Garrett's company was in Houston as of June 4, when a new recruit was added. Payroll records show that Garrett and Second Lieutenant Robert L. Brane both resigned on June 10. First Lieutenant John A. Creery assumed command of the volunteer company until August 8, on which date his men were discharged from service "by order of the Secretary of War."

As for Colonel Karnes, he was frustrated that the frontier battalion of mounted gunmen he was designated to command from San Antonio had never made it to him. The companies raised thus far had largely served in either the Austin area or in the Cherokee War in eastern Texas. Karnes resigned his commission as colonel on July 28, 1839.[16] Undaunted, he would soon manage to secure other troops for expeditions against the Comanches in his San Antonio area.

The Cherokee War was the greatest assembly of troops to deal with an Indian crisis in Texas history at that time. Paymaster General Jacob Snively later presented an estimate to Secretary of War Johnston of expenditures incurred during this expedition. The Third Militia Brigade under General Douglass was paid $21,000 for its service.[17] Snively listed the payments, splitting out some of the units individually, while grouping some of the others under their respective field and staff leaders, as follows:

General Douglass' Staff	$1,600
Field and Staff, Col. Rusk's command	3,110
Capt. Robert Smith's company	1,400
Capt. Lewis Sanchez's company	840
Capt. Benjamin Vansickle's company	1,850
Capt. Andrew Berry's company	1,250
Capt. Peter Tipps' company	800
Capt. Alexander Jordan's company	2,100
Capt. William Kimbro's company	1,710
Capt. Jackson Todd's company	2,100
Capt. George English's company	
Capt. James McKim's company	
Capt. John Inman's company	
Capt. Mitchell Garrison's company	
Col. Landrum's Field and Staff (total)	4,250
	$21,000

Colonel Edward Burleson's Frontier Regiment remained in Houston County for a few more days preparatory to returning to central Texas. Captain Adam Clendenin's Company B, which had lost its second lieutenant to Indians, departed Fort Lamar on August 12 and rejoined Burleson at Fort Houston on August 14.

On this date, a general court-martial was held for two men who had deserted from Captain Samuel Jordan's Company C. The army held its hearings at Fort Houston and its proceedings were published in the Wednesday, August 28, issue of the *Telegraph and Texas Register*.

> The court martial consisting of Capt. Clendenin, President; Capt. Howard, Lts. Carson, Ogden and Dunnington. Lt. Ackerman will act as special judge advocate. Private William Tyndell, of Company C, 1st Infantry Regt., found guilty of desertion on July 20, 1839, from Camp Harris, Cherokee Nation, sentenced to be shot to death. Private John Harris, of same company, found guilty of desertion on June 24 from Bastrop and sentenced to be shot to death; signed by 1st Lt. D. Verplank Ackerman, Judge Advocate, and Capt. Clendenin, President.[18]

These men were sentenced to death, but their sentences were later commuted to less severe punishments by President Lamar. Shortly after the court-martial, Burleson's army was ordered back toward the Austin area, where the Comanches remained a serious concern to frontier settlers. Around the San Antonio area, Colonel Karnes had found that in the west citizens had to deal now not only with violent bands of Indians and Mexicans, but also marauding parties of white Texas outlaws.[19]

Following the court martial proceedings, Colonel Burleson issued orders to Captain Clendenin on August 14 from camp near Fort Houston. Clendenin and his Company B of the First Regiment of Infantry was to proceed to Galveston "with as little delay as possible" to conduct recruiting. Captain William Sadler was also sent to recruit new men in Galveston, where he was paid on August 31.[20]

During the Frontier Regiment's return to Austin, Burleson's men stopped off at Fort Milam, located just east of the Brazos River in present Fall County. Part of Robertson County in 1839, the fort's location was close to the little community of Marlin and the Falls of the Brazos River. This second Fort Milam had been built earlier in the year by Captain Joseph Daniels' Milam Guards. Captain John Bird and Lieutenant William Evans had stationed their ranger companies there in May and Bird had been killed later that month in the Bird's Creek battle.

Lieutenant Evans' Travis Spies were still on duty when Colonel Burleson's army arrived in late August. Lieutenant Colonel William Fisher ordered the name of the post changed from Fort Milam to Fort Burleson on August 26 in honor of the regular army's commander.[21]

Evans' Travis Spies remained on duty through September 20, at which time they were discharged from duty after serving six months on the Brazos River frontier.

The army's chief recordkeeper, Adjutant General Hugh McLeod, handed over his duties temporarily to Paymaster General Jacob Snively. McLeod was recovering from the arrowhead that remained embedded in his thigh, a souvenir from the Cherokee War.[22]

From Houston, the Adjutant General's Office issued an updated list of officers of the Regular Army of Texas on August 29, 1839. Colonel Lysander Wells' cavalry regiment had two captains on the payroll, James H. Millroy and Samuel A. Plummer. Burleson's allotted fifteen captains of infantry were William Redd, Adam Clendenin, Samuel Jordan, George Howard, John Holliday, Benjamin Gillen, Mark Blake Skerrett, George H. Laurence, George Morgan, William H. Moore, William T. Sadler, James January, Mathew Caldwell, John Kennymore, and Palmer Pillans. Kennymore and Pillans had been promoted from first lieutenant. Caldwell had been commissioned as the third new captain to fill the shoes of three infantry captains who had already departed the service since being commissioned in January—H. W. Davis, Martin Snell, and Robert Oliver.[23]

The bulk of the Texas Army would remain stationed at the new Fort Burleson during September. Burleson's men had been mobile for the entire summer and some reorganization was in order before the Frontier Regiment was prepared to mount another campaign against Indian forces.

★ ★ ★ ★ ★

The Webster Massacre: August 27, 1839

The Cherokees and Shawnees were displaced from their villages as a result of the Cherokee War. Neither would be a serious threat to East Texas settlers again. Farther west, the aggressive Comanches remained an entirely different matter to early Texas settlers. Southwest of where the Texas Army was establishing its new Fort Burleson, the Comanches attacked a surveying party the following day. Various sources list this attack occurring anywhere from the summer of 1839 to October 1, 1839, although the date was later recorded as August 27, 1839.

The depredation occurred against a party centered around the family of John Webster, who had decided to move to his headright league lying on the North San Gabriel River. Webster was a lawyer who had owned land in Virginia and West Virginia before moving to Texas in the fall of 1835. He had served in the Texas Revolution and by 1839 was working as a land speculator. He set out from the

Colorado River for the San Gabriel in August with six provision-loaded wagons, guns, ammunition, one cannon, clothing, and twelve men plus one indentured servant.

Land surveyor John Harvey collected the men to accompany Webster on the surveying trip to lay off the adjacent land. Harvey's party would accompany Webster to his land north of present Austin and then board with his family while they completed their surveying work. Harvey was detained by other business at the last minute and he let his company of men and the Webster family depart from Hornsby's Station ahead of him.[24]

According to a report in the Wednesday, October 16, 1839, issue of *Telegraph and Texas Register*, the party included thirteen men, Mrs. Dolly Webster, and her two children, Virginia and Booker Webster. After traveling about thirty miles from Hornsby's, they encountered a large body of Comanche Indians. They were within six miles of the place where John Webster wanted to build his fort, but he decided to turn back and wait for more volunteers. He expected to meet the remainder of his company, which had been detained rounding up stampeded cattle.

Webster's party traveled until late in the night, when one of the wagons suffered a broken axle while crossing the San Gabriel River. The men worked for hours repairing the axle and completed this task by about 3:00 a.m. The party continued its retreat and reached Brushy Creek at sunrise.

The Comanches attacked the surveying party there during the early morning hours at a spot two miles east of Leander in Williamson County. From her home in California in 1912, Mrs. Virginia Webster Strickland Simmons recalled the horrible massacre she had survived some seventy years prior.

> The Indians were lying in wait. A short counsel was held by the men, some of them favoring going into the channel of Brushy Creek to fight the Indians, but they decided to corral the four wagons which was done and by this time the battle had begun between 14 men and 300 Indian warriors and the battle lasted from sunrise until 10 o'clock when the last man fell. By that time six hundred had come, making the Indians present about nine hundred.
>
> The Indians left the battlefield after dark. They broke up everything they could not carry off. The sacks of coffee were poured out on the ground. They smashed the crate that had

> mother's fine china and silverware. The devils broke the china, and took the silver and made trinkets to wear. They had it strung around their necks, arms, and ankles. They took my father's sword, [and] cut it all up in little pieces. The hilt of the sword they cut in three pieces, one piece for each one of the chiefs that were in the battle . . .
>
> It was an awful sight to see all those brave men fall at the hands of the savages. I remember well how I cried and how my brother fought the Indians after the battle was over, and how my mother suffered in mind and body too, to see all the men scalped and their clothing torn off their bodies and to see all her fine clothing torn into strips before her eyes. No tongue nor pen can describe those awful feelings of my dear old mother. My brother was eight years older than I and he was in his 11th year. I was three years old in April.[25]

By Virginia Webster's memory, her father and a dozen other men made their valiant fight from behind their circled wagons just before sunrise at Brushy Creek. Greatly outnumbered, they were all killed. The wagons, riddled with bullet holes and arrow spikes, bore testimony to the fury of the assault. As the Texans were steadily killed, the Indians rushed into the campground and massacred the remaining men. The remnants of broken gun stocks left evidence that some weapons were used as clubs in the desperate struggle.[26]

When the battle ended, John Webster and every man of the surveying party had been slain. From available records, the other men killed were: brothers William Parker Reese and Washington Perry Reese of Brazoria; John Stillwell and Wilson Flesher of Virginia; Martin Watson of Scotland; Mr. Bazley; Nicholas Baylor; Milton Hicks of Kentucky; William Rice of Virginia; Albert Silsbey of Kentucky; James Martin of Texas; Mr. Lensher, a Mexican; and a black man who was a servant of one of the surveyors.[27]

Due to the outcome of the attack, Virginia Webster's account is obviously the only recorded eyewitness account. She claimed the attack occurred on June 20, 1839, although the State of Texas later decided the actual date to have been August 27, 1839. Two commemorative markers erected in this area bear the date of August 27. One is located in Davis Cemetery, two miles east of Leander in Williamson County. The second marker was erected on State Highway 29 in Leander. It reads:

1 3/4 Miles East to the graves of the victims of the
WEBSTER MASSACRE
Which occurred August 27, 1839, when John Webster and a party of about thirty, en route to a land grant in Burnet County, were attacked by a band of Comanche Indians. After attempting to flee under cover of darkness, they were trapped on an open prairie. Mrs. Webster and her two children were made prisoners. All the others were killed. In death they rest together in one grave.[28]

The Indians carried Dolly Webster and her two children, Booker and Virginia Webster, into captivity. The three were separated at times but Mrs. Webster was determined to escape. She tried three times and was recaptured twice. She noted that of thirty-three white women and children prisoners held by the Comanches in late 1839 and early 1840, at least six were executed with tomahawks. Just prior to the Indian chiefs heading into San Antonio for the famed Council House meeting in March 1840, Mrs. Webster escaped for the third time with her daughter Virginia. After seven months of Indian captivity, they endured twelve days of hardships through the Texas wilderness before finding their way to San Antonio in late March 1840 weak, dehydrated, and nearly starved to death.

Virginia Webster later stated that the Indians who killed her father and held her captive were the Comanches. She listed the names of the chiefs as Yellow Wolf, Guadalupe, and Buffalo Hump. Rangers had killed a Chief "Buffalo Hump" in the Bird's Creek Fight three months prior, but the Comanches may have passed this name to another chief.

Dolly Webster's young son Booker was returned to San Antonio six days after his mother and sister arrived. Booker Webster later served in the Mexican War in Company F of Colonel Jack Hays' First Regiment of Texas Mounted Volunteers. He was mortally wounded in service and died in Mexico City on January 16, 1848, at eighteen years of age.

Surveyor John Harvey headed out to Webster's to join the company within a few days, suspecting nothing to be wrong. He instead found the gathered wagons surrounded by the bodies of the men he was to join. Doctor D. C. Gilmore was among a twenty-man surveying party which departed Austin October 5 to survey lands between the Brazos and San Gabriel rivers. He told the publishers of the *Telegraph and Texas Register* several days later that his party was the first to find the bodies of the Webster Massacre.

Harvey rushed back to the settlements and spread the alarm. From his nearby home in Bastrop, Colonel Edward Burleson quickly raised a volunteer force of some fifty-odd men and marched to the scene of the assault. One of the young men of his party was John Jenkins, who vividly recalled the scene at the Webster Massacre.

> A strange, unreal sight of horror met our eyes. Only fleshless bones scattered around remained of a brave and courageous band of men. In absence of coffin, box, or even plank, we collected them into an *old crate*, which was found nearby, and buried them. Only one skeleton could be recognized—that of one Mr. Hicks, who had his leg broken in the Battle of Anahuac in 1835.
>
> We supposed Mrs. Webster and her little girl had shared the terrible fate of the band, though we could find no skeletons which we could possible suppose were theirs, and we afterward learned that the Indians had carried them off into captivity.
>
> Having buried the bones of the slaughtered band, we followed the Indian trail some miles, and seeing nothing to encourage us in pursuit we finally came home, unsuccessful, *as usual*.[29]

★ ★ ★ ★ ★

State of the Ranger Service: Fall 1839

Companies of Texas Rangers remained in service throughout the entire year of 1839, although the number of units dropped significantly in the fall months. This was due largely to enhanced enlistments into Lamar's Frontier Regiment and the authorization of a new mounted gunman regiment.

In the days following the battle of the Neches, several new companies were formed to range the outlying settlements to prevent Indian counterattacks. Captain Joseph L. Bennett's company of mounted gunmen was organized on July 28 and served through September 3. Bennett's men were based out of Fort Houston and spent the summer months patrolling Houston and Robertson counties.[30]

On July 15, Captain John W. Middleton formed the Sabine County Rangers, the first ranging unit assembled in this county since Sabine County had been created in December 1837. He enlisted Joshua English, John May, J. B. Raines, John D. Raines, Rolley

Raines, William R. Wadle, Joseph White, Josiah White, Joshua White, William H. White, David Wilkerson, and William R. Warnell to patrol this county's frontiers. Captain Middleton's men saw no recorded action and disbanded a month later on August 14, 1839.

In Fannin County, another company that could be viewed as rangers operated during the month of August under Captain Joseph Sowell. Authorized by Lieutenant Colonel Daniel Montague, Sowell's unit was mustered into service of the Second Regiment of the Fourth Militia Brigade on August 1, 1839. The company served out of the camp of Warren, the home of Montague and the county seat of Fannin County.

Two weeks after Sowell's company was disbanded, Captain Mark R. Roberts formed a new company of Fannin County Mounted Rangers in Montague's area. He had previously commanded a ranger unit in Fannin County for three months in early 1839. The new company Roberts mustered in on September 16 would serve through December 31, 1839.

One other ranger company covered General John Dyer's First Regiment of the Fourth Militia Brigade during the fall of 1839. Captain James W. Sims commanded the Red River County Volunteer Mounted Riflemen from August 2 through November 2, 1839. Sims, the former sergeant major of Colonel Sam Sims' militia staff, was fortunate to enlist a company of Fourth Brigade veterans. His first lieutenant, John M. Watson, had previously served with Captain Stout's rangers in the same area. Many others had served on Dyer and Rusk's Three Forks Expedition. Each member of the company had one horse, one gun, one hundred rounds of ammunition, and ten days of rations ready on hand. Each man "mounted and equipped himself as the law directs for mounted riflemen," Captain Sims noted on his muster roll. He added that his company served "on the frontier of Red River County by order of Brig. Gen. John H. Dyer."

In the Third Militia Brigade controlled by General Douglass, only two ranger companies remained in service during September. Major Baley Walters' mounted ranger battalion, including the company of Captain Henry Madison Smith of Nacogdoches County, was mustered out of service on September 2. Captain James Box's Houston County rangers remained posted at Fort Houston through October 18 before disbanding after a full year of service in East Texas.

Captain Joseph Durst, founder of the town of Angelina, had organized another company of Third Militia Brigade Mounted Rangers on August 15. Durst's small settlement of Angelina (later named

Capt. Sims' Volunteer Mounted Riflemen: August 2–Nov. 2, 1839

Captain:	B. F. Bourland	William O. Mathis
James W. Sims	James M. Bourland	Washington McClure
First Lieutenant:	J. F. Box	Cyrus Moore
John M. Watson	James Brown	Samuel F. Moore
Second Lieutenant:	William S. Clifton	Mathias Mowry
John Wheat	Absolom Comer	John D. Nelson
Orderly Sergeant:	Alfonso Crowder	Samuel Pew
Benjamin F. Lynn	William B. Duncan	William D. Richards
Second Sergeant:	John C. Gahagan	Cyrus Richey
Robert S. Wheat	Richard F. Giddens	John M. Richey
Third Sergeant:	Joseph J. Guest	John R. Rodgers
Wiley W. Giddens	Joseph Guest	John Slites
Privates:	James G. Hamilton	Morris Stanford
Andrew S. Beard	Robert J. Heath	Liman Swan
William A. Becknell	Albert H. Latimore	William Walkup
George Birdwell	Robert W. Madden	William C. Ward
Thomas G. Birdwell	John Mankins	Josiah F. Wheat
Benjamin Blanton	M. W. Mathis	*Source:* Texas State Archives.

Linwood) was located on the San Antonio Road leading from Nacogdoches to Fort Lacy in present Cherokee County. A Kickapoo War veteran who had served in Captain Jacob Snively's ranger company, Durst pulled a quarter of his new men from companies returning to Nacogdoches County from the Cherokee campaign. First Lieutenant Hugh Kenner, another Kickapoo War veteran, had previously served with Captain James Durst's largely Indian ranger company. Joseph Durst's rangers served along the San Antonio Road through September 27, 1839.

In the more central settlements along the Colorado River, ranger companies had been in service during the first half of the year. The three-company battalion under captains George Erath, Nimrod Doyle, and James Mathews had served Robertson and Milam counties through early June. They had seen no action and were replaced by a single company to range both counties after they were disbanded.

Captain Nelson Merrill formed a new company of Bastrop County Rangers on June 10 from the remnants of Captain Micah Andrews' company which Merrill had previously served in. His first lieutenant was John J. Eakin, former orderly sergeant of Andrews' rangers. His

Captain Durst's Mounted Rangers: August 15–September 27, 1839

Captain:	Samuel M. Bean	Louis Rose
Joseph Durst	Isaac Durst	James Selmon
First Lieutenant:	Sylvester Gray [1]	Larry Simpson [2]
Hugh Kenner	John Howard [2]	Washington Sims
Second Lieutenant:	Pendleton Luckett	William Wooton
John Roark	Jose L. Mancha	
Privates:	Juan A. Padilla	
George A. Bass	F. D. Pickens	
Isaac T. Bean	Stephen Richards	

1 Joined Sept. 15, 1839.
2 Joined Sept. 21, 1839.

Source: Texas State Archives.

orderly sergeant was A. J. Adkisson, who was already a veteran of both the Córdova and Flores fights. Captain Merrill's company covered the capital area in its ranging circuit and his men were discharged at Austin on September 10, 1839.[31]

The vast frontier area of Red River County remained a key spot for monitoring Indian activity along the United States border following the Cherokee War. After Captain Joseph Sowell's Fannin County company was disbanded on August 31, only Captain John Emberson's rangers remained in service along the entire Fannin and Red River county areas..

On September 2, 1839, Emberson wrote a letter to Secretary of War Albert Sidney Johnston from Camp Bois d' Arc, which was located near Fort Inglish. He reported that his men had continued to find no enemy action since his last communication and also no signs of Indians crossing the Red River either to or from Texas. The only exception had been a small party of Shawnees during late August who were on their way from Texas to their village on the north side of the Red River. These Shawnees informed Emberson that a small party of Cherokees had settled on the east fork of the Trinity River, for whom Emberson informed Johnston he would keep an eye out.

Captain Emberson also warned of a new Indian invasion threat.

> I have just received a communication from Mr. Clark, sub agent for the Choctaw Indians of the United States, which informs me that a party of Cherokees are now embodying on the Arkansas River, for the purpose of invading Texas, and advising me to keep a close watch for them. I believe the United States Indian agents are doing all in their power to prevent the Indians from crossing Red River, to commit depre-

Capt. Merrill's Bastrop Co. Rangers: June 10–September 10, 1839

Captain:	Reuben L. Doan	Isaac Norris [1]
Nelson Merrill [1]	Francis Duncan [1]	Levi Paine
First Lieutenant:	Robert Finney	Isaac D. Parker
John J. Eakin [1]	L. B. Foster	C. S. Parrish [1]
Orderly Sergeant:	Samuel Fowler [1]	James Ogden Rice [1]
Allen J. Adkisson [1]	David Hudson [1]	Benjamin Roberts [2]
Privates:	John G. Jamison	R. T. Smith [1]
Henry Alderson [1]	William Johnson	S. J. Whatley
John Angel	Johnson Jones	Joseph G. Young
B. D. Bassford [1]	Augustine Kirkley	
John Blair	Winfield Lowe [1]	
John William Brown[1]	Elias Marshall	
R. S. Chandler [1]	Felix McCluskey	
Allen J. Davis [1]	William H. Moore	

[1] Previously served in Capt. Andrews' rangers through June 10, 1839.
[2] Enlisted June 11 per audited military claims.
Source: Texas State Archives.

dations upon our citizens. Yet it will be impossible to prevent it, so long as Red River remains the dividing line for two hundred miles between our settlements and the Indians, and no station or military post at any point upon said stream.[32]

Emberson's note to Johnston was forwarded on to the United States, whose own secretary of war promised that orders had been given to his commanders "stationed at and near the line of the two countries" to prevent any hostile invasion by these Indians.

During September, a detachment of Emberson's men under Lieutenant William M. "Buckskin" Williams was making camp at Camp Caldwell in present northeastern Grayson County. Williams' "West Detachment" had operated from this camp for a couple of months or more. Camp Caldwell was located on the farm of James A. Caldwell, who furnished supplies to these rangers during their service. Williams' detachment joined Emberson's main company by mid-September and all were mustered out at Camp Warren on September 16, 1839.[33]

By the end of September, only three companies of Texas Rangers remained in service east of the Trinity River. Captain James Box's men were still active in the Third Militia Brigade, while captains Mark Roberts and James Sims covered the Fourth Militia Brigade.

The mounted gunmen regiment authorized by President Lamar had also been mustered out of service. Led into battle during the

Cherokee War by Lieutenant Colonel Woodlief and Major Jones, these companies had operated with Colonel Burleson's army for much of their service period. Captains Mark Lewis and James Ownby disbanded their six-month companies on September 9.

The situation in central Texas would soon force Lamar to organize a new regiment. En route to Austin with Colonel Jacob Snively during the fall of 1839, Secretary of Treasury James H. Starr saw a band of fifteen "Texas cowboys" who were carrying on "predatory warfare" against the inhabitants of Chihuahua on the Rio Grande. The cowboys were murdering, burning houses, and driving off cattle, mules, and horses. Starr reported that these men were harboring hundreds of cattle and were boasting that no judge or jury could be found to punish them. They were even hopeful that the blame would be put on the Tonkawa Indians.[34]

The settlers at San Antonio were informed on September 2 that their government could not presently offer any force to stay at that place. They were offered Captain Reuben Ross, with a detachment of about seventy men, who were "well mounted and armed," and had been ordered to include that section of the country in their ranging circuit. Ross, who signed his military papers as "Capt. of Rangers," was to use his men to offer what protection they could. President Lamar also wrote to John Henry Moore on the Colorado to raise two hundred men to range "out your way."

Captain Ross' ranging company was raised in Houston and surrounding counties by August. From its camp opposite Richmond, the company moved west toward San Antonio. Ross received orders in early September to include San Antonio in his ranging circuit. Soon after arriving, however, he was visited by agents of Antonio Canales and other Mexican federalists. Captain Ross and his company were motivated to give up their ranging duties and march for San Patricio.[35]

During late 1839, Major Ross became a leader of a force of some 225 mercenary Texan soldiers known as the Texas Auxiliary Corps. These men allied with Canales and other Mexican revolutionaries who were attempting to liberate Mexico's northern provinces from Santa Anna's Centralist government.[36] Captain Richard Roman of Refugio County and Captain Samuel Jordan, who left the First Regiment of Infantry soon after the Cherokee War for this cause, commanded companies which participated in a November battle at Mier.

Canales' so-called Federalist War would continue along the Rio Grande through the summer of 1840 although President Lamar would never officially commit any troops to such a cause.

★ ★ ★ ★ ★

Removal of the Shawnees: October 1839

The treaty made with the Shawnees by Tom Rusk and company on August 2 after the Battle of the Neches was apparently carried out about two months after it had been signed. Rusk and James Mayfield sent a final report of their treaty to Secretary of War Johnston on October 2 from Nacogdoches.[37]

Two payments were made concerning the Shawnees' removal, the funds being drawn from Texas' secretary of treasury. Brigadier General Kelsey Douglass was to pay the Indian tribe $598 for improvements and T. Edwards & Co. was issued vouchers for

Capt. Emberson's Red River/Fannin Co. Rangers: March 16–Sept. 16, 1839		
Captain:	Mabel Gilbert [1]	A. Jackson Sage
John Emberson	Hardin Hart	Osa Santiago
First Lieutenant:	Meredith Hart	James Seymore
William M. Williams	Murden Hart	John Seymore
Second Lieutenant:	Isaac Houston [2]	Richard H. Sowell
Charles W. Sadler	Sam Johnson	Jesse Stiffle
First Sergeant:	Thomas Johnson [3]	J. P. Thornton
John C. Bates	George Kennedy	Thomas Tolbott
Second Sergeant:	Smith Largin	Francisco Travine
William S. Dillingham	Wiliam E. Leech	William C. Twitty
Third Sergeant:	Peter Maroney	William Tyler [5]
Sam Moss	William Martin	Elijah Underwood
Privates:	William Mason	Whitfield Viles [6]
William H. Anderson	Alexander McKinney	Henry F. Viser
Samuel Burk	Curtis Moore	William E. Wiley
Nice Canter	Jose Morea	Henry Williams
Gabriel Chinowith	James R. O'Neal	Samuel Wychard
William Cortely	Jason H. Petigrew	
Thomas Cousins	William M. Rice	
James Dalton	John Riley	
Benton B. Davis	Dr. E. L. Rogers [4]	
John Davis	Joseph Rogers	
William Davis	James Rutland	
Thomas Doudy	Thomas R. Sadler	
Jesse Francis	Gordon Sage	

[1] Sub for Thomas Lofton.
[2] Substitute for James S. Johnson.
[3] Sub for John Robbins.
[4] Replaced John Trimble and acted as physician.
[5] Sub for Franklin Powell.
[6] Sub for John Johnson.

$3,312.50. Rusk and Mayfield reported to Johnston that they were "anxious to have forwarded our account with the vouchers, but cannot procure all the items until the return of Mr. Patton, who is now absent with the Shawnees."

Captain Alexander Jordan and fellow Cherokee War veteran Moses L. Patton had been appointed as contractors to effect the removal of the Shawnees from Texas. Of the total payments to be paid by the Texas treasury, Rusk had already placed $3,850 in the hands of Patton. Mayfield and Rusk recommended:

> We agreed with Patton and Jordan at thirty five hundred dollars to furnish the transportation for the Indians. On starting with them, we found there were some other improvements, and some expenses amounting to a few hundred dollars more than the first valuation returned to us. Immediately upon Patton's return we will transmit to your department the original valuation.

The Texan commissioners formally thanked the local merchants for providing "their goods at good money prices, and but for their liberality, it would have been impossible for us to have removed the Indians with the means at our disposition."

★ ★ ★ ★ ★

Texas Military Status: September 30, 1839

Paymaster General Jacob Snively submitted an important report to Secretary of War Johnston on October 21, 1839. In it, he detailed all expenses incurred for Texas military units thus far for the present year.[38]

Snively presented summaries of funds paid out and funds yet to be paid. One of his estimates included a total cost of $33,049 still required to finish paying the militia companies under Major General Rusk which had served on campaigns in late 1838 and early 1839. Another showed Johnston that that it would take an estimated $21,000 to fully pay all the volunteer militia companies that had served under General Kelsey Douglass in the recent Cherokee War. This figure did not include expenses required to pay the First Regiment of Infantry troops which had participated.

Interestingly, Snively did not include the ranger companies of captains Henry Madison Smith, James Box, or Solomon Adams in his

Cherokee War cost estimate. These three companies instead show up on Snively's "Estimate of funds required for the payment of the Rangers for the present year, 1839."

The Texas military's chief paymaster officially recognized only eighteen companies of Texas Rangers to have operated at any time in the period of December 1, 1838–September 30, 1839. All other companies, by Snively's standards, officially operated in the form of Texas Militia or Texas Army.

Seven of these companies were listed in an estimate of funds required "for the payment of rangers, for services rendered on the Red River frontier, in 1838 and 1839":

Lieut. Col. Montague's Field and Staff	$3,100
Capt. Nathaniel T. Journey	6,900
Capt. Mark K. Robert's company	390
Capt. John Hart's company	1,300
Capt. Robert Sloan's	3,259
Capt. Jesse Stiff's	354
Lieut. John P. Simpson's	350
Total:	$15,643

The other dozen ranger companies were listed in the separate Snively report on funds required to pay "Rangers for the present year, 1839."

Commander/County:	*Estimated Funds:*
Field and Staff	$2,450
John Emberson, Red River	9,500
Henry Madison Smith, Nacogdoches and James Edward Box, Houston	7,000
George Bernard Erath, Milam	4,430
James D. Mathews, Robertson	4,500
Micah Andrews, La Grange	2,825
William Mosby Eastland, La Grange	2,400
Solomon Adams, Houston	7,820
Mathew Caldwell, Gonzales	4,572
Nimrod Doyle, Robertson	4,500
John Bird, Fort Bend	2,964
Noah Smithwick, Bastrop	2,225
Total:	$55,186

It should be noted that this is only one officer's perspective on which companies were paid as "rangers" and which ones were paid otherwise. Certainly other companies should be added to this list as having served as rangers, such as that of Captain Joseph Daniels' Milam Guards of the Second Militia Brigade.

Estimated funds required to pay the regular army for the year 1840 would be $306,649. This included $52,000 to maintain five companies of cavalry and $193,410 for fifteen companies of infantry. An additional $61,239 was estimated to cover the field and general staff.

These reports to the secretary of war are enlightening on the Texas military's status by the end of September 1839. Colonel Hugh McLeod also submitted a report showing the effectiveness of the Texas Militia to date. Each county had been ordered to be organized with mandatory militia enrollment for eligible males by a proclamation of President Lamar dated February 15, 1839. Each county was to organize regional companies whose men would elect their own officers.

Following such elections, a muster roll and return of officer elections was to be submitted for every company. Some counties failed to submit all their muster rolls in compliance with the president's orders. Others did, but these rolls have been lost or destroyed over time. McLeod's documentation gives the best record of the Texas Militia's enrollment between February 15 and September 30, 1839.

In McLeod's report, he found that of thirty-one Republic of Texas counties in 1839, sixteen had submitted complete muster rolls of their companies. Eight other counties had not submitted muster rolls but had submitted certificates of the formation of companies. Seven counties had submitted no information.

From the twenty-four counties submitting militia information, McLeod found that 111 total companies had been formed. From the sixteen counties submitting muster rolls, he found that 4,620 men had been received into service.

Nacogdoches County had been ordered to provide the largest number of companies (ten). Red River County had been ordered to produce the next greatest number (eight) followed by Béxar, Montgomery, and San Augustine counties (each with seven).

Strength of Texas Militia By County
February 15–September 30, 1839

Based on Documentation of Texas Secretary of War, published in *Journals of the Fourth Congress, Republic of Texas*, III: 85.

County:	Number of Companies:[1]	Number of Men In Each Company:[2]	Total No. of Men:[3]
Austin	5	55, 62, 73, 55, 57	302
Bastrop	5	*No muster rolls submitted*	-
Béxar	7	43, 54, 56, 24, 63, 59, 65	364
Brazoria	4	105 *(3 rolls not submitted)*	105
Colorado	3	39, 56, 37	132
Fannin	2	63, 48	111
Fayette	2	87, 48	135
Fort Bend	4	69, 60, 66, 56	251
Galveston	3	107 *(2 rolls not submitted)*	107
Goliad	-	*No companies organized*	-
Gonzales	2	33 *(1 roll not submitted)*	33
Harrison	-	*No companies organized*	-
Harris[burg]	-	*No companies organized*	-
Houston	4	44, 77, 66, 52	239
Jackson	2	47, 57	104
Jasper	6	*No muster rolls submitted*	-
Jefferson	3	57, 66, 68	191
Liberty	-	*No companies organized*	-
Matagorda	5	66, 60 (3 rolls not submitted)	125
Milam	1	60	60
Montgomery	7	84, 100, 125, 81, 103 *(2 rolls n.s.)*	493
Nacogdoches	10	42, 78, 39, 110, 42, 40, 80, 28, 35, 39	533
Red River	8	*No muster rolls submitted*	-
Refugio	1	71	71
Robertson	3	59, 65, 60	173
Sabine	6	69, 68, 64, 70, 81, 50	402
San Augustine	7	*No muster rolls submitted*	-
San Patricio	-	*No companies organized*	-
Shelby	2	46 *(1 roll not submitted)*	46
Victoria	9	64, 60, 84, 50, 110, 66, 59, 64, 76	642

[1] As ascertained by Secretary of War. [2] Per muster rolls submitted.

[3] Includes only numbers on muster rolls submitted.

Chapter 12

Colonel Neill's Gunmen On the Offensive

October 23–November 22, 1839

By the end of September, Colonel Edward Burleson's regular army was gearing up to move to the new capital city which was under construction. President Lamar and his cabinet would transfer the seat of Texas government to Austin by October 1. Colonel Pinckney Caldwell, quartermaster for the Frontier Regiment, was in Houston on September 27. In a letter written that date, Caldwell indicates that the bulk of the army was preparing to depart Fort Burleson.

> I returned to this place yesterday. I have been on a campaign against the Cherokees and other Indians for four months.
>
> They [the army] have been ordered to the city of Austin, our new site of government—I will return to the Falls of the Brazos tomorrow to join the Army again. From there I will go in a few days to the city of Austin where I will be stationed the balance of the winter.[1]

During early October, Burleson marched his troops toward Austin, leaving Company D behind to permanently man his namesake fort at the Falls of the Brazos River. The army marched from one old ranger post to another. Camp was next established near the site of Fort Colorado (once known as Fort Houston), the post built and manned by Colonel Coleman and Major William Smith's ranger battalions from late 1836 through early 1838.

Burleson and seventy of his men had reached the Austin area by October 12. The First Regiment settled on Walnut Creek near the road leading from the Colorado River settlements to the growing town of

Austin. Camp Walnut Creek was established and would remain in place for a little over a month as new recruits marched into the area. The site was located a little more than two miles northeast of the Montopolis bridge over the Colorado River in Austin.[2]

By late October, three companies of infantry were at Camp Walnut Creek. The October 31 muster roll of Company C shows that Captain John Kennymore had taken command on October 23 after Captain Samuel Jordan had resigned on September 2 to join Major Ross' Texan troops near the Mexican border. Captain Adam Clendenin remained in command of Company B at Walnut Creek.

Captain William Sadler and other officers of the Frontier Regiment had been ordered down to Galveston to work with the new recruits who were arriving from the United States. During the next two months, new companies were assembled, provisioned in Houston and marched toward Austin. The old Company A was completely rebuilt during this time and Sadler would take command of a new Company G by November 20.

The first new company to arrive was Captain John Holliday's Company E. Holliday had recruited soldiers for the Texas Army at Clarksville in Red River County prior to the Cherokee War. At Galveston following the campaign, he took command of Company E on September 17, 1839. His first lieutenant was William M. Dunnington, previously of the revamped Company C.[3]

Holliday sent the twenty-five man first detachment of his company to Houston on September 19 for provisions and the thirty-four man second detachment left Galveston on October 4. Company E was consolidated in Houston and departed for Austin on October 7, arriving at Camp Walnut Creek on October 27.

Soon after the army's main body established Camp Walnut Creek, Colonel Burleson ordered Captain Kennymore to take a nineteen-soldier detachment farther north to set up a second campground. In order to offer further protection to Austin-area settlers, Kennymore's men established Camp Caldwell on the south bank of Brushy Creek in present Williamson County, about 2.5 miles east of present Round Rock.[4]

The camp was named for Captain Mathew Caldwell, a former ranger captain who had recently joined the Frontier Regiment of Infantry. Camp Caldwell was adjacent to Kenney's Fort, a private fort built by Dr. Thomas Kenney and Joseph Barnhart in the spring of 1839 while construction continued on the capital of Austin twenty-five miles south. The fort was a single blockhouse with three or four log cabins enclosed by an eight-foot stockade.

The area around Kenney's Fort had previously been defended only by the local men of the small farming community. Starting with the arrival of Captain Kennymore's detachment, the community would enjoy the added protection of infantry troops during the next four months.

★ ★ ★ ★ ★

Captain Howard's Comanche Fight: October 24, 1839

Whether leading his company into a charge or taunting a superior force to charge him individually, George Howard was a model of early Texas Indian fighting. He was always ready for a fight and had recently proven his bravery on two separate Cherokee battlefields.

While the main army established camps closer to Austin, Captain Howard's Company D of the First Regiment of Infantry had been stationed at Fort Burleson at the Falls of the Brazos in September. Since the close of the Cherokee War, he struggled with keeping his soldiers in service. Between July 30 and October 15, Howard lost at least eight men to desertion.[5]

His company was down to thirty-four men as of October 24. On this date, Captain Howard and a group of his soldiers were accompanying an army wagon train of public stores commanded by Captain William H. Moore. A twenty-man detachment from Company C under Second Lieutenant Daniel Lewis had been sent from Camp Walnut Creek to escort the wagons on their journey to Fort Burleson.

Moore's wagons had crossed Brushy Creek on October 23 and were moving from the San Gabriel River in the direction of the old Little River Fort by morning on October 24. Captain Howard's men were riding in advance of the party when they encountered a large band of Comanche Indians.

> I discovered a number of Indians at a distance, and leaving the man to watch their movements and endeavor to ascertain their numbers, I joined my company to put them in a position for attack or defense, as circumstances might require.
>
> The scout came in and reported about one hundred and forty Indians. I then took a position in an island of timber, forming a breast-work with wagons, which I had barely completed when the enemy came upon us. There were from fifteen to twenty riding around, and, as I thought, endeavoring to draw me from my position. Finding that impossible, they drew

off to a point of timber, about two hundred and fifty yards distant.[6]

Captain Howard mounted his horse and rode in their direction to determine the number of Indians. Finding their number no more than twenty and that they appeared to be heading for reinforcements, Howard decided it prudent to start his men marching on for the Falls of the Brazos. He instructed Captain Moore and Lieutenant Lewis that he would try to provoke the enemy into making an attack, while his men were to hold themselves in readiness. Being in possession of the best horse, Captain Howard took up this duty alone.

Upon topping a summit of a hill on the prairie, the infantry captain found the Indians to be moving on. Spotting the lone Texan, the

Captain Howard's Comanche Skirmish: October 24, 1839

COMPANY D

Captain:
George Thomas Howard
First Lieutenant:
Samuel B. Carson
Second Lieutenant:
James M. Alexander [1]
First Sergeant:
William J. Johnson
Second Sergeant:
Eli Phillips
Third Sergeant:
Millard M. Parkerson
Fourth Sergeant:
Townsend Gardner
First Corporal:
Phillip Lyons
Second Corporal:
Ferdinand Booker
Privates:
James Burk
Daniel Burns
William Joseph Campbell
James Castillo
Stephen Cook
Horatio N. Eldridge
Nehemiah Hauckenbury
Joshua Hudson
George Jenkins
John R. Johnson [2]
Lewis Joseph
Robert P. Little
William McKain
Charles Mossenton
Richard D. Newman
John O'Neal
James Parker
John R. Richardson
Francis Riley
John Taite Smith
John Snider
William Stewart
William Wallace
James Warmsley
John A. Wimble

[1] Joined by transfer from Company B Oct. 12, 1839.
[2] Joined by transfer from Company C Oct. 12, 1839.

Source: Thompson, *Defenders of the Republic of Texas*, 126-30.

COMPANY C DETACHMENT

Captain:
William H. Moore *
Second Lieutenant:
Daniel Lewis
Second Sergeant:
William Appleton
First Corporal:
Robert R. Germany
Privates:
Charles S. Anderson
Alexander Bell
James Bird
Peter F. Craft
John Hare
John Harper
Jacob Hoodle
Augustus Kemper
James Kimberly
John Lewis
John Martin
John McDonald
George W. Miller
John Robinson
Adolphus Rousette
William Scott
Samuel Young

* Not regularly attached to Company C.

Source: Thompson, *Defenders of the Republic of Texas*, 95-98.

Captain George Thomas Howard (1814–1866) was a fierce Indian fighter. An army officer already a veteran of the Cherokee War, Howard valiantly led an ambush against hostile Comanches in October 1839.
Prints and Photographs Collection, Center for American History, University of Texas at Austin.

Indians quickly turned and gave chase, hoping to cut him down before he reached his own forces again. Howard cunningly led the warriors back toward his own wagon guard. When they arrived within two hundred yards, Lieutenant Lewis and twelve men met Howard. Captain Moore retained the balance of the men to guard the wagons while the others charged. Howard's report continues:

> A skirmish ensued, which lasted about fifteen minutes, when they retreated, leaving three men and three horses dead upon the field, besides several who rode off, evidently wounded. The state of our horses was such that I could not pursue them, as they were mostly mounted on fine American horses; and having seen a very large trail near Brushy the day before, I though it most prudent to proceed on my route.
>
> We sustained no injury, with the exception of one horse, which was wounded and left behind.

Captain Howard's Comanche fight occurred near Opossum Creek in present Williamson County north of the Austin area. Howard's command arrived at Fort Burleson on Monday, October 28, without further encounters. He wrote to Secretary of War Johnston that he was "convinced there is a large force hovering about the road from this place to Austin" based on the various trails and signs of Indians.

Howard also reported that Lieutenant James Alexander and several of his men had come down with fevers. Sick and wounded men at Fort Burleson were on their own, as no surgeon existed within seventy miles of their post. Deciding that the wagon guard was insufficient for its return to the Austin area, Captain Howard detailed First Lieutenant Samuel Carson with an additional thirteen soldiers to accompany Lieutenant Lewis' Company C detachment back.

Upon their return to the main army, Lewis' men found that there had been some excitement of another variety at Camp Walnut Creek. Company C's Captain John Kennymore had been attacked by a junior officer of another company. Third Corporal Robert Morris of Captain Clendenin's Company B was convicted by his peers of stabbing Kennymore.

Colonel Burleson would not tolerate such insubordination in his Frontier Regiment. Two soldiers found guilty of desertion two months earlier at Fort Houston were sentenced to death but their sentences had been commuted to less severe punishments by President Lamar. There was no mercy given Corporal Morris, who was executed in Austin on October 28, 1839. The Wednesday, December 11, issue of the *Telegraph and Texas Register* reveals that he was put to death

> in pursuance of the sentence of a court martial. His offense was the stabbing of Capt. Kennymore. An attempt to murder the officer of the day was clearly and conclusively proved against him, and he had met the punishment he deserved.

★ ★ ★ ★ ★

John Neill's First Regiment of Mounted Gunmen

On the day following Captain Howard's brazen battle with the Comanches, a Texan regiment of mounted gunmen attacked an Indian village on October 25, 1839.

The force making this attack had been organized two months prior. On August 24, 1839, President Mirabeau Lamar had issued a proclamation for a regiment of mounted gunmen to be raised for the purpose of conducting a campaign to the upper Brazos River area against the hostile Indians who had been plaguing the Austin area settlers.

The companies assembled during September represented a large number of southeastern Texas counties from the Neches River to the Brazos River. Captain Samuel Williams' Company A was largely from Jasper County, while Captain John P. Gill's Company B was formed in Brazoria County. In Liberty County, Captain Nathaniel H. Carroll organized

Company C. Captain Samuel Davis' Company D was largely from Harris County and Captain William F. Young recruited Company E from neighboring Montgomery County. Just southwest of Houston, Captain George W. Long formed Company F in Fort Bend County and Captain William F. Wilson's mounted gunmen were organized in Galveston County. Farther north of Houston than the other units, Company G was the final one organized on October 3 in Robertson County. It was commanded by Captain Henry Reed, a former officer of Captain Mathew's rangers through June.

An additional fifteen men were organized under Second Lieutenant Thomas H. Brennan to compose an artillery company. Brennan's men would man a light brass cannon that had been brought to Texas by General Thomas Jefferson Green following the Texas Revolution. Adjutant General McLeod wrote that "It was furnished with slugs of lead, and musket balls, which is such warfare will do great execution."

A twenty-nine-man mounted spy company was later formed on October 13 under veteran ranger Captain John Jackson Tumlinson Jr., his men largely pulled from the ranks of five of the existing mounted companies.

Since Henry Karnes had resigned his commission as colonel of the mounted gunman battalion of Texas a month prior, these troops elected their own senior officers. Colonel John C. Neill of Harrisburg County was chosen by the volunteers to lead the new battalion. Neill had recently commanded one of Karnes' mounted gunman companies on the frontiers during the summer's Cherokee War. His second-hand man was Lieutenant Colonel Alexander Somervell of Fort Bend County. William F. Young of Montgomery County was elected major and he turned command of his Company F to Captain William V. R. Hallum on September 14.

There is confusion among historians concerning the fact that Colonel John Neill led this campaign. In most official correspondence, his name is given simply as "J. C. Neill," which has almost always been incorrectly interpreted as James Clinton Neill, the San Jacinto artillery commander. James Neill was wounded at San Jacinto and was even provided a league of land for having suffered a severe loss during the revolution that cost a man either an eye, arm, or leg or other similar injury that "shows his incapacity for bodily labor."[7] Muster rolls of the companies participating in the fall 1839 Comanche campaign show the commanding officer of the First Regiment of Mounted Gunmen to be "John C. Neill."

The mounted companies ordered into the field by President Lamar all rendezvoused in Robertson County at Jeremiah Tinnon's crossing of the Old San Antonio Road over the Navasota River on October 9, 1839. From their home counties, each company covered a great distance to reach the rendezvous point. Captain Gill's Company B had to travel 180 miles, while Captain Williams' Company A covered two hundred miles in reaching the Navasota. The farthest distance of travel was for that of the Galveston Mounted Gunmen under Captain Wilson. His company did not join Colonel Neill's expedition but instead received new orders to join with Colonel Henry Karnes near San Antonio.

Shortly after the rendezvous of the regiment, Colonel Hugh McLeod, the adjutant general, provided information to the *Telegraph and Texas Register* on Colonel Neill's troops. This was published in the paper's October 16 issue in Houston.

> It is exceedingly gratifying to us to be able thus to testify to the readiness with which the citizens seem disposed to obey any call that is made upon them to assist in driving from our borders the only enemy whom we now have to dread. The troops were in fine spirits and determined to effect the objectives of the campaign.
>
> Colonel P. H. Bell, Inspector General, and Major H. Landers, Commissary, accompanied the troops.
>
> The route of march will be—unless diverted by the enemy —up the Brazos to the mouth of Noland's Fork; up Noland's Fork, and down the West Fork of the Trinity; and, if practicable, cross the Trinity, and attack and disperse the Indians, should it prove that the Cherokees or other hostile tribes are in that section of the country.
>
> The troops had forty days rations, and beeves enough with them for the whole campaign, and that the late rains having filled the streams, the supplies of water will be abundant.
>
> The troops from the different counties seemed to harmonize, and feel an honorable spirit of emulation to excel in the strife with the enemy.

Colonel Neill's gunmen proceeded up the Trinity River on horseback, with Lieutenant Brennan's artillery unit pulling their brass cannon with a team. Montgomery Bell Shackleford, who had served earlier in the year in Captain Erath's rangers, was employed on October 15, 1839, as a pilot to the troops on their expedition up the Brazos.

He performed his duties and was honorably discharged from the service. His papers were signed by Col. J. C. Neill at the Camp on Cedar Creek on November 22, 1839.

Among the private soldiers departing on this expedition was twenty-two-year-old William K. Hamblen, who had been born in Virginia and moved to Texas with his family in April 1834. He became a member of Company D and later wrote of his experiences on this campaign.

> In September 1839 [I] enlisted in a company for frontier service. We were enrolled by an officer of the regular Army of Texas. We elected our officers—Sam Davis Capt. Company D, [John] Phillips 1st Lt., [D. E.] Lawhorn 2nd, James Cooper orderly sergeant of same company. The above are the names of the officers of the company that I served in. The names of the officers of the other companies I have forgotten except Capt. Gill of Brazoria County.
>
> We crossed the Brazos River at old Nashville—thence to the Falls of the Brazos—thence to the old [Waco] Village on the Brazos River where the town of Waco now stands. We continued up the river and kept one Lord's day at the old Towash village. [We] had a sermon by [Nathan] Shook [of Company E], a Methodist minister.[8]

The following day, October 25, John Neill's regiment marched to an Indian village located where a United States military post named Fort Graham was later built on the east bank of the Brazos River in 1849 in present Hill County. The Texans attacked the Indian village but found their opponents unwilling to fight. "There were about 100 wigwams and said to be about 100 warriors," wrote Private Hamblen, "a part of two tribes, Ionis and Keechies." The Indians chose to flee instead of fight their foes and made their escape through thick brush except for "the Ioni chief, who was killed near the village. We captured all their camp equipage and about forty Indian ponies."

The Indian village located at the site of what later became Fort Graham was actually that of Anadarko Indian Chief José María, winner of the Bryant's Fight in January. In the days following this skirmish, Colonel Neill's gunmen continued their expedition up the Brazos. Several days later, Captain Tumlinson's spies captured an Indian woman and her two children. Shortly after their capture, Private Hamblen recalled that the Texan forces "routed another

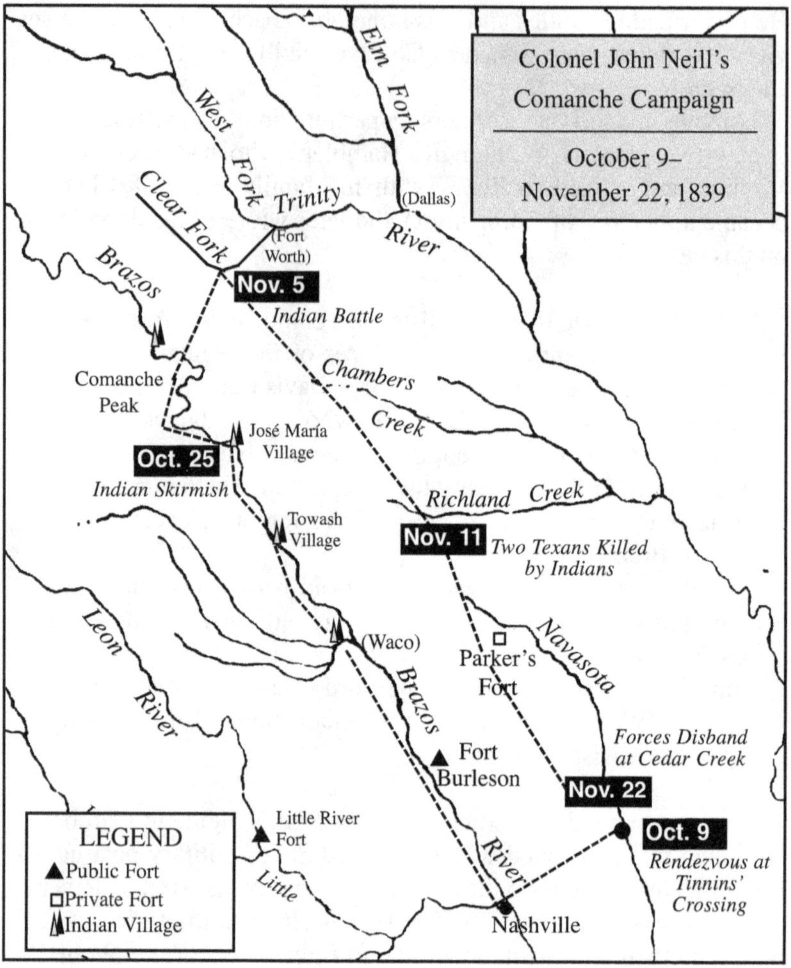

encampment of Indian hunters."

The Indian forces fled further on up the river and Neill's men continued to track them. The Indians were followed to a hill on the Brazos River known as Comanche Peak. It is located in Hood County west of the Brazos, between Brazos and Squaw creeks, just off present Highway 377 about four miles south of Granbury.

From Comanche Peak, the Texans moved to the Clear Fork of the Trinity River and there engaged the Indians again. From its point of origination in northwestern Parker County, the Clear Fork flows some forty-five miles before joining the West Fork of the Trinity River at the city of Fort Worth.

Comanche Peak, actually a mesa, was a prominent Indian and pioneer landmark. Rising 1,229 feet, Comanche Peak served as a lookout point and may have had ceremonial value for local tribes. This highway marker is located off State Highway 144 near Granbury in Hood County. In this area, Colonel Neill's gunmen fought two skirmishes with Indians in late 1839. *Author's photos.*

The engagement between Neill's troops and the Indians took place on November 5, 1839. Hamblen says that they fought "a small squad of Indians and killed two of them." The Indians likely fought with the advantage of good cover, for they killed as many as a dozen Texan horses. The muster roll of Company A shows that Inspector General Peter Bell allowed Captain Samuel Williams compensation for three horses valued at $90, $70, and $65, which were lost to "the Indians on the 5th Nov. 1839." Company C's muster roll shows that at least nine horses were lost, including those of Captain Nathaniel Carroll, First Lieutenant Jackson Griffin, and Second Lieutenant Thaxton Epperson.

No Texans were killed during the battle northeast of Comanche Peak, although Private Laban Menefee of Captain Henry Reed's Company G was wounded. He was hit by an arrow which passed through his thigh. The wound was not life threatening, but according to his family Menefee "was bothered with it the rest of his life."[9]

Unlike most Indian battles in Texas, Colonel Neill's entire campaign has received very little attention. Veteran ranger George Erath briefly noted several years later in a letter to Mirabeau Lamar that Neill's men had fought a battle near Comanche Peak in 1839.[10]

Henderson Yoakum's early history of Texas, published in 1855, mentions that near the José María Village a "bloody battle" was fought by Texans under Neill and "a portion of the Comanches located there." After a fierce conflict, "the Indians fled leaving a number of their warriors slain."[11]

Yoakum mistakenly gives the date of the battle as October 25, 1838. Other Texas historians have thus continued to use 1838 as the year of "James C." Neill's Comanche campaign instead of 1839. James T. DeShields in *Border Wars of Texas* does, however, correctly list the Texas leader as "Col. John C. Neill."[12]

Several days after John Neill's regiment had its second skirmish near Comanche Peak, Colonel Hugh McLeod wrote to Secretary of War Johnston on November 9 that "The regiment of drafted men is still in the field on the Brazos frontier, and have been thus far entirely successful."[13]

Colonel Neill's expedition did suffer two casualties, however, in the vicinity of Richland Creek. This creek rises in southeastern Hill County and crosses Navarro County before emptying into the Trinity in northern Freestone County. The muster roll of Captain Reed's Company G shows that privates John J. Earle and Phillip Whepler were killed by Indians on November 11. Another member of this company, William Hemblen, gives further information on their deaths.

> We continued our march between the Trinity and Brazos in the direction of home. On Richland Creek, we got two men killed by Indians. They left the command and were shot before they went two miles. Their names were Earle and Whepler and [were residents of] old Nashville on the Brazos.

First Regiment of Mounted Gunmen
Composition of Forces:
Field and Staff: October 5–November 22, 1839

John C. Neill	Colonel	Antonio Miller	Musician
Alexander Somervell	Lt. Colonel	G. D. Long	Asst. Surgeon
William Foster Young	Major	John C. Thomas	Sgt. Major
J. F. Garrett	Commissary		
Harley Price	Ast. Comm.	Army Officers on Expedition:	
Benjamin F. Smith	Adjutant	Peter H. Bell	Colonel
William H. McGee	Surgeon	Hillequist Landers	Major

Capt. Williams' Company A: September 11–December 2, 1839

Captain:
Samuel Williams
First Lieutenant:
Charles W. Blanchard
Second Lieutenant:
A. P. D. Sapp
First Sergeant:
John C. Thomas [1]
John Wilkinson [1]
Second Sergeant:
Stephen Williams
Third Sergeant:
John A. Smith
Fourth Sergeant:
Rufus Goodenow
First Corporal:
A. J. Youngblood
Privates:
T. K. Anderson
Drewery Anglin
Robert Bays [2]
William M. Beatty
John Bennett
Riley Bevil
John D. Brooks
William M. Brown
Ezekiel Champion
Andrew J. Chessher
George B. W. Cooke
Charles H. Delaney [3]
Wilson Dobbs [2]
Wilson Donoho
John Fishe
Pleasant Gathap [2]
John Hamilton
M. G. Hansby [3]
Ennis Hardin
John Harman
Berry Hawkins [4]
Henry H. Haygood
Stephen Heard
Wyatt Hickman
Charles Howard
Nathaniel Howard
John Ivy [5]
Levi Jewell
Frederick Jones [3]
James King
James Knight
Ashley Mahaffey
William Mansel
Jesse McGee
John McGee
Friend McMahon [6]
James McMahon [4]
Andrew Montgomery
George W. Nicks
Martin H. Prewitt
Robert Richardson
Owen Rosier
John R. Rostion
Nathaniel Ryons
John M. Sharp
Andrew F. Smyth
Adam L. Stewart
James Sturrick [3]
Pane Swift
George Thomason
Taylor Thomason
Jesse J. Webb
William Webb [3]
R. S. Welch
Elias Whitmore
Harrison Williams
John R. Williams
Thomas D. Williams
Washington Williams
William N. Williams
James Wilson
Monial Wilson
Richard Youngblood

1 Thomas promoted to sergeant major. Wilkinson promoted to 1st Sergeant.
2 Left the Republic.
3 Sick.
4 Left the county.
5 Transferred.
6 Unable to perform duty.

Source: All muster rolls for this regiment transcribed from copies from the Texas State Archives.

Capt. Gill's Company B: September 14–November 22, 1839

Captain:
John Porter Gill
First Lieutenant:
William H. McGee [1]
Second Lieutenant:
James Hays
First Sergeant:
Hardy Price
Second Sergeant:
George L. Bledsoe
Third Sergeant:
Samuel L. Wheeler
Fourth Sergeant:
Elijah Doyle
First Corporal:
George Rounds
Second Corporal:
Richard A. Abbott
Privates:
Samuel Allen
Powhattan Archer
P. H. Arklep
H. A. Bannister
L. M. Biddle
Charles Carman
James A. Dupong
Casper Escher
James J. George
Phillip Golden
William G. Goosley
Warren D. C. Hall
William M. Head
H. Holstein
John Houston
Samuel Huffer
Patrick Hufner
Thomas D. James
John Keiser
William A. Knox
Harvey W. Little
James Louis
John Loyd
James Lumbard
J. L. McMill
J. C. Moreland
Alec Mustard
John Prewitt
M. Robertson
Michael Roger
Nathaniel Rudder
John Ryon
Jordan Short
John Smelser
James E. Smith
Jordan Sweeney
Benjamin Talley
Theophilus Wells
H. A. Westall
Charles White
R. J. Whitehurst
Gilbert Winney
Henry Woodland
John Worrall

1 Appointed surgeon October 5.

Capt. Carroll's Company C: September 15–December 1, 1839

Captain:
Nathaniel H. Carroll
First Lieutenant:
Jackson H. Griffin
Second Lieutenant:
Thaxton Epperson
First Sergeant:
W. H. Knight
Second Sergeant:
John Ward [1]
Third Sergeant:
William Fitzgerald [2]
First Corporal:
Augustus B. Hardin
Second Corporal:
Thomas Johnson
Privates:
Aaron Armstrong
J. H. Avon
Reuben Barber
Preston J. Bland [5]
Francis Boshone [7]
William F. Brewer
W. Chevanno
J. F. Clark [1]
A. P. Davis
H. S. Davis
Charles E. Dugat
F. M. Fitzgerald
Robert Fletcher [1]
George Hodges
D. C. Hoover
John Jackson
Newton Jackson
B. F. Kerr
Reuben J. Lynch
S. W. Mathias [6]
Abram D. Mayes
Antonio Miller
Wiliam G. Newman [1]
William Norman
William H. Palmer [1]
James Polley
Newton Swinney
John W. White
Sidney B. White
Sebourne White
Harrison Williams [4]
John R. Williams [4]
James Williams
George C. Wiseman

1 Transfer to Tumlinson's spy company October 13/14.
2 Promoted to second sergeant on October 13.
3 Appointed chief musician on October 13, 1839.
4 Transfer to Company A October 7.
5 Transfer to Company D October 1.
6 Died Oct. 13 at Nashville.
7 Deserted October 12.

Capt. Davis' Company D: September 10–November 27, 1839

Captain:
Samuel Davis
First Lieutenant:
John Phillips
Second Lieutenant:
D. E. Lawhon
First Sergeant:
James Cooper
Privates:
Bartlett Anable
Andrew J. Beard
Robert S. Beard
William C. Beard
John Blackman
Payton Blank
James R. Brewster
Andrew Briscoe
M. H. Bush
John Clark
John D. Cottle
M. K. Dickerson
Meredith T. Duncan
Joseph Dunman
George Elliott
W. Fain
Richard Fork
W. R. Gilhene
James Gray
William R. Hamblen
Daniel Hanna
P. Heifner [1]
John House
Joseph House
Mumford House
Robert Howell
James Ingolls
John Ivy
Absolom Jett
John Jett
Joseph B. Jewell
Levi Jewell
N. Lado
James M. Land
P. B. McCurly
W. Mennett
W. E. Millen
William Mitchell
William N. Mock
John H. Moore
Benjamin F. Mott
George Mulin
Dempsey C. Pace
William C. Palmer
James Patillo
Eli Roberts
Archer Smith
John Smith
M. Smith
James H. Taylor
A. J. Tiviss
George White
Jesse White
John White
W. White
Peter Willer
Oliver H. Williams

[1] Joined on October 7.

Capt. Hallum's Company E: September 14–November 22, 1839

Captain:
William F. Young[1]
Wm V. R. Hallum[1]
First Lieutenant:
William H. Wood
Second Lieutenant:
James Wilson [2]
First Sergeant:
James W. Hacket
Privates:
Charles Armsdell
Wesley Berryman
William H. Bishop
Adam R. Bowen [4]
Samuel Brimberry [2]
George Brown
Franklin Bruger
John E. Buchannon
Warren Burgess[3]
John Carnes
Thomas Carson[9]
James M. Cartwright [2]
William Cartwright
Robert Childers [4]
George W. Clary
William Clure [4]
William R. Conner
W. Cooke
Thomas Crissup
S. L. Davis
William J. Duncan[5]
Joseph Durham
Nimrod Edwards
L. W. Estice [2]
Benjamin Franks
Smith Gammon
Daniel Garrant [7]
J. F. Garrett [6]
Jesse Gray
King S. Hadley [4]
Hugh Hampton
John Harper
J. J. Hunter [8]
Joseph B. Jewell [5]
W. Johnson
Lewis Jones
George M. Kirby[5]
Joseph Lang
S. Lauderdale
John D. Long
J. J. Mabury
W. R. Marsh
Anderson Martin
Charles McCoy
James McDonald
William McGee [7]
Mack McRoy [10]
W. Miller
Rudolph Mock
J. J. Music
William S. Norris
J. W. Overby
James H. Perry [5]
Isaac Prater
A. Pursivall
J. F. Ransdale
John S. Recter
Thomas Ringgold
Joseph Roark
Nathan Roarke
E. P. Robertson
Sidney Shepherd[4]
Nathan Shook
Henry Sikes
Benjamin F. Smith [6]
Leroy H. Smith
Patrick Smith
F. L. Smithey
B. B. Stancil
John J. Tumlinson [8]
Albert Vaughn [2]
William G. Walker
Benjamin Westers
Benjamin White
William Whitley
Wright Williams [8]
William C. Wines
Willis Winters

[1] Promoted Sept. 14.
[2] Transferred Oct. 28.
[3] Transferred Oct. 19.
[4] Transferred Oct. 12.
[5] Transferred Oct. 4.
[6] Transferred Oct. 5.
[7] Transferred Oct. 18.
[8] Transferred Oct. 12.
[9] Transferred Oct.27.
[10] Transferred Oct. 13.

Capt. Long's Company F: September 9–November 30, 1839

Captain:
George W. Long
First Lieutenant:
James Hughes
Second Lieutenant:
Solomon Squier
First Sergeant:
John C. Foster
Second Sergeant:
M. M. Ferguson
First Corporal:
G. W. Bruce
Second Corporal:
Samuel S. Smith
Privates:
John J. Bonds
William Bridge
T. R. Bryant
Samuel E. Bundick
Michael Doyle
Philip Fairchild
James P. Frances
Benjamin Gillick
Hiram Goodman
William B. Goodman
Austin Hagan
James Hodge
William Hodge
James F. Hunter
Robert H. Hunter
James F. Johnson
Robert H. Kuykendall
Alfred M. Liles
A. F. Mudd
George W. Pentacost
David Pierhouse
George W. Pleasant
William Randles
Amos J. Roark
James Sharp
Moses Shipman
Alexander Somervell [1]
Joseph Somervell
Jesse G. Thompson

[1]Elected Lieutenant Colonel.

Roster does not include eleven men who defaulted from company and were not paid.

Captain Reed's Company G: October 3–November 22, 1839

Captain:
Henry Reed
First Lieutenant:
John Marlin
Second Lieutenant:
James O. Butler
First Sergeant:
T. M. Springfield
Second Sergeant:
John R. Cummins [1]
Third Sergeant:
Eli Chandler
Fourth Sergeant:
Moses Griffin
First Corporal:
Harrison York
Second Corporal:
William B. Hill
Privates:
Montgomery Burch
David Cobbs
William Cox
Eli Davis
Thomas Drumgold
Charles Duncan
Thomas Duncan
John J. Earle [2]
John Fullerton
Alfred Hicks
Samuel W. Marlin
Bailey Martin
R. S. Mayfield [1]
T. P. Mayfield [1]
Andrew M. McMillan
Edward D. McMillan
James M. McMillan
Laban Menefee
Thomas S. Menefee
Buckner Milton [1]
Charles Nanny
John L. Robertson
Charles Smith [1]
Thomas Sykert [3]
John F. Underhill
James Walker
James B. Ware
Edmund Webb
Travis Webb
Phillip Whepler [2]

[1] Transfer to spy company on October 20, 1839.
[2] Killed November 11 by the Indians.
[3] Transfer to spy company on October 28, 1839.

Lt. Brennan's Artillery Company: Sept. 2–December 4, 1839

Second Lieutenant:
Thomas H. Brennan
First Sergeant:
G. W. Boswell
Privates:
Casper Escher [1]
Warren Goodman
Michael Green
Richard Hardy
Edward Jackson
Charles Johnson
John Loyd [1]
James Lumbard [1]
George McDougal
T. C. Moreland [1]
Robert St. Clair
William Smith
Charles White [1]

[1] Joined on October 7, 1839 from Company B.

Capt. Tumlinson's Spy Company: October 13–November 22, 1839

Captain:
John J. Tumlinson Jr. [1]
First Lieutenant:
Robert Childers [1]
First Sergeant:
John Ward [2]
Second Sergeant:
Wright Williams [1]
First Corporal:
Nathan Shook [1]
Second Corporal:
King S. Hadley [1]
Privates:
John S. Adams [3]
Adam R. Bowen [1]
J. F. Clark [2]
Albert Clois [4]
John Cottle [4]
John R. Cummins [5]
J. M. Eastern [7]
A. W. Elston [6]
Robert Fletcher [2]
Singleton House [4]
J. J. Hunter [1]
William Kennard [1]
George M. Kirby [4]
R. S. Mayfield [5]
T. P. Mayfield [5]
P. B. McCurly [4]
Mack McRoy [1]
Buckner Milton [5]
William G. Newman [2]
Sidney Shepherd [1]
Charles Smith [5]
Thomas Sykert [5]
Robert Withers [4]

[1] Transferred from Hallum's.
[2] Transferred from Carroll's.
[3] Volunteered on October 18.
[4] Transferred from Davis'.
[5] Transferred from Reed's.
[6] Transferred from Brennan's.
[7] Volunteered on October 28.

At the time that these men were killed, Colonel Neill's First Regiment of Mounted Gunmen was preparing to conclude its expedition. From "Camp above Parker's Fort," Neill gave written orders to Major Hillequist Landers to "proceed in advance of the army" to Cedar Creek. There he was to procure "a proficiency of corn for horses and beef and meal for subsistence for my command during our rendezvous at that point."[14]

Neill's men returned to Robertson County the following week and rendezvoused with Major Landers on November 22 at Cedar Creek. This tributary of the Navasota River rises just south of the town of Franklin and flows southeast for twenty miles. The mounted gunmen companies were discharged at Cedar Creek to return to their respective counties.

Muster rolls of the participating companies show that they were generally allowed an extra week of pay to cover the time spent returning home. Some had to travel as far as two hundred miles from Cedar Creek to reach their native counties. The men of Captain Carroll's Company C were entitled to pay through December 1 in order to cover their return. Lieutenant Thomas Brennan and his artillery company, forced to haul their cannon behind the others, did not disband until December 4.

Payroll records for Neill's troops were handled by Jacob Snively, paymaster of the Texas Army. The rate of pay for captains of this mounted gunman regiment was sixty dollars per month. First lieutenants were paid fifty dollars per month, first sergeants forty per month, and the privates each received twenty-five dollars per month.

Although these troops had not engaged a significant number of Indians, their campaign made yet another statement to the tribes along the Brazos River. Texas military forces were becoming more offensive by late 1839, carrying an organized fight well beyond the established settlements, right to the Indians' own villages.

Shortly after Colonel Neill's companies were discharged to return to their homes, the *Austin City Gazette* carried a brief mention of their campaign in its November 27, 1839, issue. The *Gazette* warned that the evidence of Indian settlements higher upriver predicated the need for continued ranger service.

> Col. Neill, who has command of the drafted forces ordered up the Brazos, has returned from the pursuit of the Indians. They are supposed to be embodied in considerable numbers, on that river, about 150 miles above the falls.
>
> The settlements on the Brazos are more exposed than any other portion of the frontier; and we hope the Government will place an adequate force on that river for their protection. They have suffered greatly, and some of our best citizens, with a large amount of property, may be sacrificed, unless timely protection be furnished.[15]

CHAPTER 13

Karnes' Hill Country Comanche Expedition

October 20–December 8, 1839

In Galveston County, the locals had wasted no time in organizing their sixty-man mounted gunmen company following President Lamar's August 24 requisition. Sheriff William F. Wilson volunteered his services and was quickly joined by the requisite number of young men from his county. The citizens preferred to raise their company voluntarily in order to avoid being drafted.

J. W. Benedict, a twenty-four-year-old New York native who had settled in Galveston with his family, joined this unit to help "quell the Indian disturbances upon our frontier." From the first organization of the Galveston Mounted Riflemen, Benedict kept a private journal of his experiences. He felt that many young Galveston businessmen saw this expedition as a chance

> to view the interior and thinking no better opportunity would offer itself of accomplishing their own desires and also of aiding their adopted country. On the 7th of September a list was circulated and on the 9th myself with the rest were on board the steamer *R. Putnam* on our way to the Capitol. As enlisted soldiers with light hearts intent on trusting to our fate in whatever may befall us in a savage wilderness. On arriving at Houston we were quartered in the Capitol (which was nearly empty as the Cabinet and archives were then in the act of removing to the new Seat of Government at Austin).
>
> The necessary requisites were made by the Government for our equipments by paying in advance for 3 months at 25% per Mo. This together with a considerable [sum] subscribed by the citizens of Galveston enabled us to equip our company.[1]

The Galveston company elected Sheriff William Wilson to be its captain. William Turner was elected his first lieutenant and James M. Branham became second lieutenant. Captain Wilson learned that his company would not be joining the other county gunmen companies under Colonel John Neill.

Private Benedict wrote,"We now learned with pleasure that we were destined to the Northwest Frontier under command of Colonel Karnes, Commandant at San Antonio." Wilson's men were to accompany Karnes north from San Antonio into the Comanche country.

Wilson's company was likely chosen for this task since it was the first of the new county gunmen companies to form. Henry Karnes was also suffering from a lack of cavalry and ranger-type units to man such an expedition. In addition to the regular army and the new mounted gunmen regiment, there were only two companies of mounted rangers in service during the time of Colonel Neill's expedition. In the Fourth Militia Brigade, Captain Mark Roberts' rangers covered the Red River area from September 16, 1839, through March 16, 1840. In the Third Brigade, Captain George K. Black's Nacogdoches County Rangers were in service from October 22, 1839, through January 29, 1840.

★ ★ ★ ★ ★

Galveston Mounted Gunmen Join Karnes

Henry Karnes had resigned his commission as colonel of the mounted gunmen battalion on July 29, but did not let that stop him from finding men to defend San Antonio from the Comanches. He returned to San Antonio in late August after a visit to the government in Houston. Intent upon making a new offensive against the Comanches, he spoke with some of the Mexican federalist officers who were idling about town. He found enough support to organize a forty-six-man company of Mexicans and Texans on September 8.[2]

Three former Mexican federalist officers would head up the mounted company. José María Gonzales, a former colonel in the army, was elected captain and selected Mauricio Carrasco and Agapito Galbán as his lieutenants. One of the Anglo-Texians attached to this San Antonio company was John James, who had also volunteered for Karnes' June expedition to Canyon de Uvalde. James' public debt claims state that Captain Gonzales' company formed and departed San Antonio on September 10, 1839.

José María Gonzales, by authority of the Sec. of War of the late Republic of Texas, organized a company in San Antonio, said county [Béxar], for the purpose of making an expedition against the hostile Indians then committing depredations on the frontier. That said company was composed of about 50 men. That they furnished themselves with horses, ammunition, arms, provisions, etc.[3]

The Galveston Mounted Gunmen departed Houston on Saturday evening, September 15, and made camp that night in an open prairie. There, they spent several days gearing up for their expedition to the northwestern frontier. From Private Benedict's personal diary, a rare and vivid portrait of 1830s ranger service is available.

Thursday Morning 19th. were ordered to get up our horses for marching. Then, such a bustling and fixing that none knew how to proceed. We were most of us provided with pistols, bowie knives, belt knives, etc.—which we could very easily manage to carry, but there was our cooking paraphernalia. No one seemed willing to take the responsibility of carrying [it]. They were therefore divided off into messes of 8 each—one taking his proportion of the cooking whereabouts . . .

The roll being called, we were ordered to mount and took up our line of march. Proceeded to Mr. Wheaton's. Slaughtered a beef. It may be well to describe the mode of keeping our horses together. Being about 60 in number, this required great care. Each horseman was required to have a cabrace or larietto by which means they were attached to a stake or tree so that a certain area of ground can be given to each horse without interrupting its neighbor.[4]

By September 20, Captain Wilson's company had moved far enough out beyond Houston as to be on the open prairies. Benedict noted that "vast herds of deer could be seen grazing in every direction, together with the vast variety of flowers." The company proceeded along in double file, making camp in the Brazos River bottoms on Friday, September 30, after an exhausting day of riding under the scorching Texas sun. Traveling up the river bottoms the next day, the company passed by the lonely town of San Felipe. Only a handful of new buildings had gone up since the town was burned during the Texas Revolution.

Henry Wax Karnes (1812–1840), was born in Tennessee and learned to be a woodsman growing up in Arkansas. Second in command of cavalry at San Jacinto in 1836, he served as colonel of Texas Cavalry from January 1837 through March 1838. Karnes commanded a mounted ranger battalion during 1839 and led at least three offensives against the Indians during 1838 and 1839. *Karnes sketch by early Texas painter Henry Arthur McArdle courtesy of Texas State Library and Archives Commission.*

By Sunday, September 22, Wilson's men had crossed the San Bernard and arrived at Columbus on the Brazos, having covered thirty-two miles from San Felipe. From Columbus, the rangers moved up country, passing occasional dwellings which had been deserted following Indian depredations. They camped on a small branch of the Navidad River, with lookouts posted that night to watch for Indians.

Colonel Henry Karnes joined Wilson's company on September 24. He was sick and ordered Wilson to take his men to a watering place a few miles away and camp until he was well enough to accompany them. For the next two days, Karnes lay sick with a fever while the horses fed and rested. Camp was made at the Stoney Fork of the Navidad River. The creek beds were dry due to the time of the year. This provided good hunting grounds for the men while they rested in camp, as Private Benedict recorded in his journal.

> During our stay here, I took a ramble up this fork one or two miles. I saw fresh tracks of several kinds of wild animals—deer, wolves, bear, wild hogs, etc.—which seemed to have but just departed. I returned, shouldering a noble fat

> turkey which was well received by us, for we were nearly destitute of any kind of food. We had been fasting already for nearly 24 hours. For some unaccounted for means, we had not been provided with bread since we left Houston. We subsisted entirely upon beef and were often days without that, trusting only to what game might be killed.

Colonel Karnes recovered from his fever and rejoined Captain Wilson's company. Together, they moved on and arrived at Gonzales on September 30. Here the citizens showed "great hospitality" towards them. Due to the great number of Indian attacks in the area, Gonzales residents were not opposed to putting up soldiers. The company departed Gonzales on October 1 and took up a course along the bank of the Guadalupe River. The following day, they crossed over the swift, clear waters of this river near a Mexican farm house located on the banks. After a long day's ride, Karnes had his men make camp on Cibolo Creek.

★ ★ ★ ★ ★

Hiatus in San Antonio

Karnes' men arrived in San Antonio on October 3 after riding a route of some 215 miles from Houston. Camp was made at San Antonio Springs, just north of present Brackenridge Park, on the west bank of the San Antonio River a mile north of town. Karnes soon moved his men into the buildings of Mission Concepción for a few days.[5]

Captain Wilson's Galveston Mounted Riflemen remained on station for two weeks while Karnes attended to business. The men had a chance to look about the town and take in the local festivities. Private Benedict took the opportunity to record his impressions of the Alamo City.

> San Antonio de Béxar is a somber looking town. The original town is built from hewn stone and from its antiquity presents a very Gothic appearance, being built about a century since. They were originally built connected from one street to the other and partitioned only for each inhabitant of only one story height and terrace-roofed so that those blocks in their present dilapidated state have only the appearance of a vast pile of rocks.

> The streets, which were once said to be distinguished for their cleanliness, is now irregular, filthy, and sooty. A water course has been dug around the town and is said to have once been running through each street. People nearly all of color except some few Americans. Many aged people. Children generally go naked, especially in wet weather . . .
>
> During our stay here, [we] had a good opportunity to observe the manners and customs of the inhabitants—which to say the most in their favor is but little superior [to] their neighbors and hostile enemies, the Comanches. Those Comanches keep them in such awe they dare not venture without the outskirts of the town without going armed and two or three in company, and very seldom lose sight of the spire and cross of their cathedral.
>
> The Alamo is situated on the opposite side of the river from the main town. It is the ruins of a very extensive building, built it is said about a century since. It was apparently built both for devotion and fortification. The main room (the Chapel) is very extensive, bearing on its walls several inscriptions to the Roman Catholic order, also vases and busts as large as life, beautifully carved from stone . . .
>
> The Alamo is distinguished as being the scene of cruel bloodshed, where Crockett and his brave comrades were slaughtered by the Mexicans. The place is still shown where he last placed himself against the wall and hewed down several. The marks of his cutlass are visible.

Benedict found that "extensive balls" were held in the evenings in small rooms with smooth earth floors. During the midday hours, the citizens scarcely stirred at all. At night, however, San Antonio came alive with the street being lighted and bowers being erected in the street for the fandango. Men and women alike gathered for dances, which included "the lascivious waltz and the Virginia Reel."

On October 15, Captain Wilson's company changed their place of encampment to within one mile of the San Antonio River. During their first night here, Indians managed to steal three of their horses. The horses had been tied or staked within the guards, but by sheer stealthiness the Indians managed to creep in on this particularly dark night and escape with the horses two hours before daybreak.

Several rangers immediately set out in pursuit of the thieves and shots were exchanged. One of the Indians was killed and one horse was recovered. The remaining Indians made off with the other two horses. Two of the fleeing Indians had bows and arrows and the third had used a musket with which he fired a shot that passed through the coat of a pursuing ranger without injuring him.

During the next three nights, the ranger camp was in a continual uproar due to alarms of Indians, who were apparently bent on vengeance for their dead comrade. On the night of October 19, one of the Texan guards thought he had spotted an Indian and opened fire. When others rushed to the scene, they found that this individual had mistakenly shot Second Corporal James C. Haskins. The rifle ball from his Yager struck Haskins in the groin, but fortunately created only a flesh wound, from which he recovered.

Following this mishap, Captain Wilson moved his camp to a more secure place that was free from nearby bushes and thickets which the Indians could use to their advantage.

★ ★ ★ ★ ★

Tracking the Comanche

On the morning of Sunday, October 20, Colonel Karnes finally headed up an expedition to go after the Comanches. He departed San Antonio for the San Saba mountain hill country. Karnes was accompanied by the volunteer company under Captain José María Gonzales that he had helped organize on September 8. This mixed unit was largely Tejanos, but included some white surveyors and former rangers, such as Jack Hays. There were also among this group some scientists who were interested in making discoveries and collecting samples of botany, geology, minerals, and the like.

Including the company of Captain Wilson, Karnes had a total of 105 men in his party. Private Benedict for one was impressed, as he noted, "Together with our pack mules, extra horses for the spies gave us quite a formidable appearance." The regiment was formally divided into two companies of cavalry. The first was commanded by Colonel Karnes himself and included Captain Gonzales' men. The second company was that under Wilson.

> We began now to have more strict order and discipline. At night a detachment was taken from each company for guard, under the direction of the officer of the day. Orders [were] strictly enforced to keep a strict watch. In the morning, we generally started early, always having an advance and rear

guard. Our marches were generally continued till about 2 o'clock p.m., when we would strike camp early in order to reconnoiter our position for the night.

On October 21, the Karnes expedition entered a valley about ten miles from San Antonio, where it encountered "picturesque scenery" with the hilltops in the distance. That night a bear was killed near the camp. The following day the men continued along through a valley filled with wild grass that grew as tall as four feet high in places.

Colonel Henry Karnes' Comanche Expedition
October 20–November 21, 1839

Capt. Wilson's Galveston Mounted Gunmen: Sept. 8–Dec. 8, 1839

Captain:
William F. Wilson [1]
First Lieutenant:
William Turner [2]
Second Lieutenant:
James M. Branham [3]
Surgeon:
Alfred S. Allen
Commissary:
G. Gould Dishon
Orderly Sergeant:
William Dunbar [4]
First Sergeant:
Elmanson Lewis
Second Sergeant:
Joseph P. Burger
Third Sergeant:
Jack R. Everitt [5]
First Corporal:
N. S. Hill
Second Corporal:
James C. Haskins
Third Corporal:
Thomas P. Mills
Fourth Corporal:
William R. Sisty [7]
Privates:
Lewis Beardsley
J. W. Benedict
J. H. F. Chapman
Thomas J. Church
Richard Clark
Robert Clark
Thomas Ryan Clark
William H. Emery
P. G. Evers
Samuel Fleury
Armaine Friedericks
Joseph S. Gamble
Macinio Garcia
James M. Harvey
James Henderson
John Hughes
John Johnson
James A. Jones
J. S. LeClere
Henry E. Looney
Robert Manning
John McDonald
John McIver
Joseph S. McKay
Ephraim McLane [6]
Jacob Myers
Robert Paris
John Parsons
James Peacock
H. W. Ridgway
William E. Roberts
Edward Ryan
John Sheal
William Stevens
Elias Stone
Alexander Thompson
George Toby
Henry Van Tassal
John J. Vaughan
H. Langdon Waldron
William Welch
Robert White
D. Williams
Francis F. Williams
William Y. Wood
A. B. Yard

[1] Resigned November 19.
[2] Resigned November 16.
[3] Elected First Lieutenant November 18.
[4] Elected 2nd Lt. Nov. 18.
[5] Elected Ord. Sgt. Nov. 18.
[6] Elected Captain Nov. 18.
[7] Accidentally killed on October 26, 1839.

Source: Muster rolls from Texas State Archives.

Captain Gonzales' Mounted Volunteers: Sept. 8–Nov. 21, 1839

Captain:
José María Gonzales
First Lieutenant:
Mauricio Carrasco
Second Lieutenant:
Agapito Galbán
First Sergeant:
James W. Lauderdale
Privates:
Juan Berban
Marino Bernan
José María Carn
Pike Cockrill
James Collingsworth
Simon Contieras
Fernando Curiel
Thomas Dennis
Isaac Donoho
José María Ebana
Cyrus Washburn Egery
Pedro Escamia
_______ Fuqua
Damacio Galbán
Jacinto de la Garza
Leandro Garza
Antonio Gonzales
C. K. Ham
John Coffee Hays
Ancelmo Hernandez
Antonio Hernandez
Juan Hernandez
Blays Herrera
Moses Heskew
John James
William Lindsay
Marino Mindiola *
Rodrigo Montalvo
Thomas Moody
Landers L. Nobles
Frank L. Paschal
Vitor Pedeasa
Antonio Pérez
Juan Ramos
Wilson J. Riddle
Gustarer Rubio
Rafael Sepeda
Joshua Threadgill
Roberto Tiferina
Eugenio Treviño
George Van Nepo

* Shot accidentally Oct. 22. Died on Oct. 28.

Coming to a steep ravine with huge rocks, the men were compelled to dismount their horses and make them slide down. The hillsides were covered with wild pine and junipers. Shortly after this descent, Private Benedict recorded a "shocking accident" which occurred when passing through this ravine. The lock of one man's gun caught on a limb and caused his gun to discharge, striking the chest of a nearby Tejano soldier, Private Marino Mindiola of Captain Gonzales' company.

The company made camp after passing the ravine. Karnes led his men three miles across another ravine and made camp again, this due to the fact that Mindiola was being carried on a litter. The following day, October 24, they managed to cover five miles in present Kendall County northwest of San Antonio. Camp was made on the Guadalupe River at a point about one hundred miles above where they had first crossed this river. Benedict recorded:

> We were now forbidden to fire a gun on any account whatsoever except in seeing Indians. Wild game passed almost within our reach. We had several beeves provided on starting, but by this time they were either killed and eaten or had escaped us. We had no breadstuffs provided. Within five days from starting from Béxar, our only stock of provisions consisted in coffee and salt. Five or six Mexicans were employed

as hunters, provided with spears, bows, and arrows and extra horses. On those we were to depend for sustenance.

On Friday, October 25, Henry Karnes led the Mexican hunters out with fresh horses. They returned to camp with three bears. The expedition was now generally believed to be in the area of the Tawakoni Indians, who were considered by some settlers to be more dangerous than the Comanches. "They are said to be very sly, cautious, more deadly, hostile and savage than the Comanches," wrote Benedict.

While the wounded Private Mindiola was suffering from his accidental wounding, another tragedy occurred on October 26. Corporal William R. Sisty of Captain Wilson's company was fatally wounded. Another member of the company had kept his rifle under a blanket at night to prevent dew from damaging it. Due to the threat of Indian attack at any time, this gun was kept loaded with the cap on the flintlock. As this man withdrew the rifle from under the blanket, it caught on the grass and discharged. The rifle ball first passed through Sisty's hand, then the knee of his pantaloons, and entered his left breast and finally lodged in his back. At about 2:00 p.m., one and a half hours after the accident, Sisty was pronounced dead.

On Sunday, October 27, Sisty was buried "with reversed arms with military honors about one-hundred yards from our encampment under a wild china tree, within the roar of the Guadalupe." The following day Private Mindiola passed away and was buried under the same tree. The week-old expedition had thus suffered two casualties to gunfire without the first sight of an enemy.

Following this burial, the Texans picked up camp and marched about six miles before making camp in a valley. On October 29, Karnes' forces marched another seventeen miles. They climbed a hill from whose summit they had a view of a great extent of the countryside. J.W. Benedict took note of the scenery before him.

> Never did I behold such a grand extension and sublime view. We had followed the course of a valley to attain the summit, which was with great difficulty. We were compelled to dismount in our progress. On attaining the eminence, we were at once on a rocky plateau from which we could view in every direction hilltops piercing one above another till they were closed from view behind the blue veil of distance. It looked like a vast ocean of which [we] were in the midst.
>
> This may be termed the dividing ridge between the

> Guadalupe and the San Saba or properly the San Saba Hills. We had a rocky descent into the valley through a broken surface covered with rocks and oak timber.
>
> Encamped on the River Pedernales. Found an Indian encampment deserted. Fresh signs of buffalo.

The following day, Colonel Karnes marched his men five miles. The men managed to kill a buffalo, which was a blessing for those who had been near starvation for days. Rainy weather set in on October 31, and forced the troops to maintain their encampment. A great number of pecan nuts were found to help feed the men.

Movement was resumed on November 1. Private Benedict found that the bad weather had made his horse ill to the point that he could move him along only "with great difficulty." The company travelled about sixteen miles before they were brought to a halt by the sight of one of the surveyors barreling down upon them. This man, acting as a spy, arrived "himself and horse nearly breathless. We could just hear ejaculated the word (Indians)."

The company was at this time in the area of present Fredericksburg. Karnes ordered his men to commence a "retrograde" for eight miles until he passed the order to halt. Camp was made at this point. Jack Hays, heading up a small party of spies from Captain Gonzales' company, wrote that the Tejano spies became alarmed at the sight of the Indians and refused to leave camp. Hays selected three others "as spies with orders not to return until the enemy should be ferreted out."[6]

The scouts under Hays located the Indian encampment after darkness fell. Under cover of night, they crawled slowly forward until they were close enough to discern the figures of sleeping Indians. With his companions covering him, Hays bravely crept toward the fire until he was within "80 yards" and able to count the slumbering forms. Hays counted thirty well-mounted Indians, whom he claimed to be led by one of the more prominent Comanche chiefs, Isomania.[7]

Hays' scouts fell back to the Texas camp and informed Colonel Karnes of their findings. About half of the company was left in camp under Lieutenant Branham to guard the horses, mules, and equipage. Karnes and the other half of Captain Wilson's company set out on the night of November 1 with Jack Hays and the spies to attack.

Hays and his men guided Karnes and Wilson's troops to the Comanche camp, "which they reached about an hour before day." Just as Karnes' rangers began closing in on these Indians, a horse belonging to one of the Comanches became frightened and alerted the sleeping Indians. The surprised Indians grabbed their weapons, and the shooting commenced. "The Indians were taken by surprise," wrote Hays, "and thought more of flight than fight."

By the time the fleeing Comanches had fired their way through their attackers, they had suffered heavy loss. At least ten Comanche bodies were found on the battlefield and one seriously wounded Indian was taken prisoner by Karnes' party. The Texans sustained no men killed or wounded. Private Benedict recorded that the Texan party "surprised about 25 Comanches just at daybreak and before the Indians could make their escape 10 or 12 were killed." Jack Hays took note of the Indian casualties.

> Twelve of them were found dead on the ground, among whom was Asa Minor, the leader—a chief of great note. He had been shot through by two balls, and lay as dead for three days—when he was found with life still in him. His countrymen recovered him and he was soon restored to health. He afterwards came to Béxar, and there related his fate, stating that he had lain dead three days, and then came to life.

Karnes, Wilson, and their men returned to camp around noon the following day. They had with them forty horses and mules, together with equipment, bridles, robes, and other loot.

The following day, November 3, the Texan party travelled ten miles and encamped on a small stream. Little food had been captured from the Comanches, so Colonel Karnes allowed the men to hunt for their food, as Benedict relates.

> Notwithstanding the prizes taken, we had had nothing to eat for 36 hours previous. The liberty was granted to every man to hunt with his gun. Not many hours elapsed before our camp could boast as many varieties of meats as any city—such as buffalo, bear, deer, turkeys, bullocks.[8]

On November 4, the Karnes expedition travelled eight miles and encamped near a ledge of rocks. Several of the riflemen went out hunting and killed several deer, plus a buffalo and a bear. Benedict noted that, "A Comanche Indian who had been taken prisoner wounded died and was thrown in the bushes by the Mexicans and left."

The Texan forces moved another four miles the following day and made camp on November 5 in the valley of the Llano River. Colonel

Karnes had fallen sick again, so the expedition remained in camp for several days while he recovered. Karnes had never fully recovered from the arrow wound he had sustained in his fight with Comanches on the Arroyo Seco fight nearly thirteen months prior.

The idle time on the cold Texas frontier did not bode well for the tired men. Jack Hays and other surveyors of Captain Gonzales' company were eager to return to Austin. Some considered leaving Karnes with Captain Wilson's riflemen and returning to their homes.

The passing days of inaction and cold weather did not improve spirits. Benedict noted that the men were eager to end the expedition.

> Much excitement and considerable speculation is manifested in camp concerning our future course, also considerable disaffection. At one time, Captain Wilson states that he shall leave with the surveyors and proceed home—numbers resolve to join him.
>
> [Nov.] 8—It being now two months since our enlistment, two thirds of our time had expired. Our provisions such as were laid in enumerated only under the head of salt and coffee being nearly exhausted, caused many a fond regret at not being in a civilized land.
>
> Every bosom now swells with fond recollections of home. Its cheerful fireside and withal its broiling steaks. Contrasting those with our situation exhibited an unhappy difference which will account for the dissatisfaction among many of us.
>
> The cold frosty nights in which we were compelled to stand sentinel without the necessary requisites for sustaining life made it extremely unpleasant and irksome to us all. And, too, [was] the idea [which was] being advanced that we were to take a westerly course through the mountains to the Rio Grande for a more successful accomplishment of our expedition, and also to escort Genl. Gonzales to his Ranchero de Laredo who had accompanied us thus far for this sole object.

Jack Hays' party of surveyors, attached to Captain Gonzales' mounted volunteers, decided to head for Austin on their own on November 10. Joining this group were Wilson J. Riddell, a doctor from New Orleans, and William E. Roberts from Captain Wilson's Galveston Riflemen.

Shortly after their departure, Private Benedict recalled that "one or two of the company returned, stating that they had discovered camp fires and dare[d] not proceed." Captain Wilson's company immediately went in pursuit of these campfires to check on Indians. They found only three or four deserted wigwams and no direct trail.

Wilson's men parted again with these surveyors and returned to camp. The ill health of Colonel Karnes, the cold weather, and inactivity took a toll on the Galveston riflemen during the next week. First Lieutenant William Turner resigned on November 16 to return home, followed by Captain Wilson on November 19. The remaining men elected as their new officers Captain Ephraim McLane, First Lieutenant James Branham, Second Lieutenant William Dunbar, and Orderly Sergeant Jack R. Everitt.

The expedition made its way back to San Antonio by November 21, on which date Captain Gonzales disbanded his volunteer company. Paymaster Jacob Snively paid the company $3,017.21 for two months and eleven days of service. Captain McLane's men saw no further action. His company, the last in service of Colonel John Neill's First Regiment of Mounted Gunmen, returned to Galveston County and was disbanded on December 8, 1839.

Henry Karnes' expedition received only a small writeup in the *Telegraph and Texas Register* on December 11. The paper noted that Captain Wilson's Galveston volunteers had recently had a skirmish with the Indians on the Pedernales River, killing eleven Indians and taking about forty horses. Some of the Comanches reportedly displayed garments believed to have been stolen from the John Webster party which had been slaughtered near the San Gabriel River.[9]

Chief Castro and some of his Lipan braves, bitter enemies of the Comanches, had brushed with these Indians shortly before Karnes. The *Telegraph* mentioned this skirmish in its January 8, 1840, issue.

> We have received a bundle of papers from Judge [James W.] Robinson, given to him by Castro, the Lipan chief, taken in Gonzales County about the 25th of October last, from the Comanches, in fight with them, in which none of the latter was killed, and one Mexican boy about 15 years old escaped, and came into Victoria.[10]

The papers captured after the battle were mainly "receipts for land taxes, a land certificate granted by the Board of Land Commissioners for Bastrop County, and other papers." From the names on the papers, the *Telegraph* editors deduced that these papers had also been taken from the bodies of the Webster Massacre victims.

CHAPTER 14

"Short But Decisive Affair"

December 1839

The summer's Cherokee War had scattered the people of Chief Bowles considerably. One small band of the Cherokees had a brush in late 1839 with Fort Houston settlers led by former General Nathaniel W. Smith, who had brought his family to Fort Houston from Athens, Tennessee, in late 1838. Smith's son-in-law, Dr. James Hunter wrote that, "All we have to fear is incursions from small bodies of Cherokee Indians, burning and pillaging the frontier settlements."[1]

Primarily along the Trinity River, General Smith had quickly purchased more than 50,000 acres of land in Houston County. He planned to locate some of his land in the former Cherokee Nation north of Fort Houston between the Neches and Angelina rivers. While out surveying, the party ran into a band of Cherokees, as Dr. Hunter wrote.

> Eighteen of us, General Smith among the number, went up to their country to look at lands. We were too careless, thinking they would not attack us. They fired on us about 8 o'clock at night before we had stationed our sentinel.
>
> We returned the fire as soon as we could gather our arms and establish some order, charging them in the dark and driving them off. There were seven lying in a tent and they fired at us about 30 feet distant right into the mouth of the tent. Eighteen balls were shot in a row directly above our heads, right through the tent. One man was wounded. General Smith had a ball to pass through his coat sleeve, another through his saddle which he was using as a pillow.

> Several had balls pass through their hats and clothes. I had one bullet through my overcoat and ten or twelve buckshot or slug holes through the same. I never knew of so many close licks given and so little damage done.
>
> We could not ascertain whether we killed any of them or not, as it was in a cane brake and they had opportunities of carrying off their dead and wounded. It was pretty scary times for a while but we come off safe but one man, a Mr. Dunniger from Kentucky, who received a rifle ball in his thigh.

The wounded man was helped back to Fort Houston, some forty miles south, where he was tended to by Dr. Hunter. General Smith's surveyors had been fortunate to escape the ambush with only one injury. This incident reminded the Fort Houston settlers that the relative peace they had enjoyed following the Cherokee War could not be taken for granted while out on the undeveloped frontier.

★ ★ ★ ★ ★

The Frontier Regiment's New Strength

While colonels Neill and Karnes were carrying out campaigns against Indians on the northern and western Texas frontiers, President Lamar's Frontier Regiment was busy rebuilding in preparation for making its own fall campaign.

Galveston Island was a hotbed of recruitment activity for these army companies during November 1839. The excitement generated by the summer's Cherokee War likely added to the increase in enlistments. Many of these men from the United States sailed from New Orleans to Galveston.

Captain Mark Skerrett, the chief recruiting officer stationed at Post Galveston, estimated to Secretary of War Sidney Johnston in early November that within weeks "there will be in service ten companies" of the Frontier Regiment.[2] Skerrett did manage to fill out five new companies by late December, the first being Captain John Holliday's new Company E. Holliday had long served in the Texas Army and was one of the few of James Fannin's men to escape the Goliad Massacre. Company E departed Houston on October 7 and arrived at Camp Walnut Creek on October 27.

The other new companies organized during late 1839 were Captain James January's Company F, Captain William Sadler's Company G, Captain George Laurence's Company H, and Captain Benjamin Gillen's Company I.

The original Company A was revamped by December 14 and was eventually placed under command of Captain William Redd. Due to the time required to provision these men and forward them on foot to the Austin area, only January and Holliday's companies would arrive in time to see action in 1839.

Further information on the status of the Texas Army is found in a War Department summary issued by Secretary of War Johnston in November 1839 to President Lamar. In it, he detailed all military expenditures, men enrolled, battles fought, and the casualties incurred over the past year by forces other than voluntary companies.[3]

Since the commencement of issuing bounties in 1837 through September 30, 1839, Johnston reported that 4,163,740 acres of Texas land had been issued in certificates of claim to donation and bounty lands. From January 1 through September 30, 1839, Texas issued bounty land grants, in varying quantities depending on length of service, for a total of 425,920 acres. During this same nine-month period, 135,680 acres of donation land in tracts of 640 acres each had been given away.

Johnston detailed the accomplishments of the Frontier Regiment from its creation in December 1838. He felt that this act had "been carried only partially into effect." Recruiting stations had been established throughout the republic, supervised by the field officers of the regiment. Recruiting had been poor until funds had been made available to help this process. Although many of the field officers had not been able to command his own company, Johnston noted that recruitment was picking up and that the officers might soon have their own commands.

> Many of them, after the suspension of the recruiting service, have been employed in various duties connected with the service of the regulars and volunteers, employed in the field . . .
>
> The recruiting has been commenced again, under very favorable auspices, and we have good grounds for the belief, that the ranks of the regiment will be filled at an early day.

Johnston attached a document that had been submitted to him on November 9 by Hugh McLeod, the military's adjutant general. McLeod's General Return of the Army of Texas showed the condition and number of men in service.

As for the officers and ranks of those currently "present for duty" there were three colonels: Edward Burleson over the First Regiment of Infantry; Lysander Wells over the Regiment of Dragoons (cavalry); and George Hockley over Ordnance. There was one lieutenant colonel of infantry, a lieutenant colonel for cavalry and various other staff officers. McLeod listed sixteen captains, two for cavalry and fourteen for the First Infantry. The fifteenth infantry captain as of this date was listed as "sick." In the First Infantry in November, there were ten first lieutenants, seven second lieutenants, fifteen sergeants, and thirteen corporals.

The army's ranks also included three musicians, three quartermaster sergeants, one sergeant major, and 158 privates assigned to companies in the First Regiment. Another eighty-three men were shown as "recruits and unattached soldiers" and three privates were listed as sick. McLeod's report also shows that there were an additional five captains of the First Regiment who were on detached services, apparently recruiting in the United States, and two other captains listed as with leave or on furlough. Per McLeod's count, this brought total strength of the Texas Army to 338 officers and men as of early November.

Armed with Captain Skerret's recruiting information, Johnston informed President Lamar that he was prepared to fill out ten companies of infantry and five of cavalry for the Frontier Regiment. Estimates for arms, cannon, and equipment had been forwarded to Colonel William Dangerfield in the United States. Colonel Hockley's ordnance department in Houston struggled to issue and repair hundreds of muskets and sabers to arm the new companies being organized in Galveston.[4]

In addition to the regular infantry and cavalry companies, Colonel Johnston reported on the act originally passed on December 29, 1838, for mounted volunteer companies. Colonel Henry Karnes had managed to raise only three companies since that time, those of captains Lewis, Ownby, and Garrett.

> Those best fitted for the service, by their experience, hardy habits, and physical qualifications, were generally unable to equip themselves. Three companies only were raised by this act, two of which were mounted and equipped at the public expense [those of captains Lewis and Ownby], and were attached to the regular force under Col. Burleson. The money advanced for this purpose has since been reimbursed to the Government, in the settlement of the accounts of these men, after the expiration of their term of service, by the Pay Department.[5]

In addition to the army and Karnes' companies, Johnston related that companies of citizens "were enrolled, for local defense in the most assailable districts, and received in the service as rangers." Many of these ranger companies, of course, had been government authorized units specific to various Texas counties.

★ ★ ★ ★ ★

Burleson's Northwestern Campaign

The recruiters in Galveston had added another one hundred soldiers to the Frontier Regiment's ranks by early December, bringing total army strength to about 440 men, including staff and field officers.[6] Secretary of War Johnston decided that the Texas Army was now strong enough to conduct its first major campaign since the Cherokee War.

Johnston sent orders to Colonel Burleson on December 11 to carry out a campaign against the Comanches and other hostile Indians. The army was operating from Camp Caldwell near Austin by this date and included four companies of infantry, Adam Clendenin's Company B, John Kennymore's Company C, John Holliday's Company E, and James January's Company F.

Captain January's company had only arrived at Camp Caldwell from Houston on December 5, 1839, one month after leaving their recruiting station. Captain Skerrett, commander of Post Galveston, had issued clothing to the men before sending them to Houston for additional jackets, pantaloons, and arms. Once properly equipped, January's men had marched from Houston for Camp Caldwell on November 12.[7]

Other companies were moving to join Burleson but would not arrive in time to make the new campaign. Secretary of War Johnston noted on December 12 that another company was en route from Houston and was "expected hourly" in Austin.[8]

This was Captain Sadler's Company G, which had been recruited between October 18 and November 11, 1839. He took acting command of this company on November 20. Army quartermaster records show that Company G departed Houston at the end of November and arrived in Austin by December 17. On this date, Sadler resigned from the Frontier Regiment after completing one year of service. A voucher from Adjutant General Hugh McLeod's office in Austin dated December 21, 1839, verified that Captain Sadler had been ordered from his Houston County residence "near the San Antonio crossing of the Neches" to Galveston to organize his company. Assistant quartermaster Robert Neighbors paid John Cheek for successfully furnishing

> one wagon and team for the transportation of the baggage and supplies of Capt. Sadler's company of the 1st Regt. of Infantry Texas Army from the city of Houston to the city of Austin by the best and most practicable route, subject to the order of the said Capt. Sadler.[9]

Johnston further noted that one and a half more companies were en route from Galveston by December 12. These were Company H and Company I, recruited through December 4. Both were under charge of Captain George Laurence, although Captain Benjamin Gillen would soon be given command of Company I. Private John W. Thompson had been appointed the acting sergeant major of the Company I Detachment until Gillen assumed command.[10]

The newly revamped Company A departed Galveston several days later and began its journey toward the Austin area. In addition to these eight companies, Captain George Howard and his Company D remained on station at Fort Burleson near the Falls of the Brazos during mid-December.

Sidney Johnston was encouraged by the army finally starting to show strength. In a letter to the Texas Senate on December 18, he laid out his plans to begin working on the string of blockhouses that had been originally planned when the Frontier Regiment was created a year prior. The posts would start near Coffee's trading house on the Red River. The next would be located in the Cross Timbers near the West Fork of the Trinity River. The final fort would be located at San Patricio near the mouth of the Nueces River. Johnston proposed that these posts be manned by two full regiments of infantry and one of cavalry. These troops would use the forts as bases to strike against any concentrations of hostile Indians worthy of attention.[11]

Construction on the new forts would remain on hold until Colonel Burleson could carry out the army's new campaign. The *Telegraph and Texas Register* reported that the combined tribes of Lipans, under Chief Castro, and Tonkawas, under Chief Placido, were in Austin on December 11 preparing to accompany Burleson on his expedition into Comanche country.

> About 300 troops under this officer and 200 of the Indians were to leave the encampment near Austin on or about the 13th inst. for this purpose.

The object of the expedition is to force the Comanches from the section of country near the San Saba and to establish a line of block houses from the Colorado to the Red River. These block houses, when erected and garrisoned, it is believed, will eventually shut out the prairie Indians from the country, and remove the frontier from 100 to 200 miles further northward. By this means an immense tract, the most fertile and healthy section of Texas, will be opened to the enterprising immigrants who are crowding into the country.[12]

Colonel Burleson's Northwestern Campaign
December 16, 1839–January 12, 1840

Field and Staff:		Wm. D. Houghton	Adjutant
Edward Burleson	Colonel	Shields Booker	Surgeon
William S. Fisher	Lt. Colonel	Richard Cochran	Ast. Surgeon
Peyton S. Wyatt	Major		

Captain Clendenin's Infantry Company B

Captain:	Andrew Benner	James Jack
Adam Clendenin	William Benson	John R. Johnson
Second Lieutenant:	William Berry	M. Henry Judd
Collier C. Hornsby	John L. Bray	William Kelly
Matthew McGovern[1]	Thomas Casey	John M. Krauss
First Sergeant:	John Cassidy	Tiba Lesley [2]
Sylvanus Dunham	John Cavitt	Andrew Moore
Second Sergeant:	John Chappel	Abner Pitcher
James Alston	Michael Daily	William Redfield
Third Sergeant:	David Davis	Louis Reuter
Richard Nixon	Henry S. Day	John Riley
Fourth Sergeant:	Thomas Denning	John Shaw
James H. Pollard	John Dennison	Thomas Simpson
First Corporal:	William Dial	Ephraim Stansberry
John J. Johnson	Cornelius Diggons	Charles Stroud
Second Corporal:	Joseph Dubignon	William Walker
Hiram Bell	Oliver Farnsworth	Daniel S. Ward
Third Corporal:	James Farrell	James Wyatt
Samuel Woods	William Gray	
Musician:	Thomas Harrison	
Daniel Smith	Andrew Hay	
Privates:	Henry Hays	
David Anderson [2]	John Horan	
Matthew Anderson	Horrace H. Houghton	
William Barton	John Humrich	

[1] Acting Assistant Commissary.
[2] Deserted company while marching on January 2, 1840. Bodies were found January 4, apparently killed by Comanches.

Captain Kennymore's Infantry Company C

Captain:
John C. P. Kennymore
Second Lieutenant:
Daniel Lewis
First Sergeant:
Washington Stephens
Second Sergeant:
George W. Miller
Third Sergeant:
Robert R. Germany
Privates:
Charles L. Anderson
William Appleton [1]
Alexander Bell
James Bird
Abraham Bradley
Abel A. Chapman
Peter F. Craft
Michael Dunn
Michael Fanning [1]
John Hare
John Harper
Jacob Hoodle
Zephelin Islin
Augustus Kemper
James Kimberly
Justinien Laroque
Adolphus Lefebore
John Lewis
John Martin
John McCoon
John McDonald
John Robinson
William Scott
Christoper Trouts
James Tweed
Joseph B. Young
Samuel Young

[1] Discharged Jan. 10, 1840 by surgeon's certificate of disability.

Source: Thompson, *Defenders of the Republic of Texas*, 95–103.

Captain Holliday's Infantry Company E

Captain:
John Holliday
First Lieutenant:
William M. Dunnington
Second Lieutenant:
Abram Scott
First Sergeant:
Edward Fitzgerald
Second Sergeant:
Pasqual Leo Buquor
Third Sergeant:
John R. Welch
Fourth Sergeant:
Patrick Doherty
First Corporal:
Thomas W. Murray
Second Corporal:
Edward Dunn [1]
Third Corporal:
John Florey
Fourth Corporal:
Arthur Edwards
Privates:
William Aberly
William Allison
John Anderson
Samuel Arnold
William Barry
David Beattie
Joseph Bergen
William Bloom
C. G. Burckle
Jasper Bursh
John Connolly
Augustus Davis
Isaac Delamere
Thomas Donagan [1]
Amos Donaldson
Daniel Donovan
Josiah R. Edgar
Henry Fowle
Ferdinand Ham [2]
Phillip Haslocher
Charles Landover
Thomas Maguire
James McClaskey
John McCreney
Archibald McMillan
Jacob McMindus
Jacob Mushback
Bernard Norton
Walter Palmer
John Quimby
Lorenzo Rice
John Rogers
Lawrence Rourke [3]
Frederick Rudge
Robert Russell
Frederick Sackman
John Stein
Wiley P. Stewart
George Taylor
George Thomas
Nicholas Tumeltey [4]
Henry Webber
Robert G. Whitney
William Kerr York

[1] Discharged for disability by surgeon's certificate January 8, 1840.
[2] Discharged for disability by surgeon's certificate January 10, 1840.
[3] Discharged for disability by surgeon's certificate January 3, 1840.
[4] Discharged for disability by surgeon's certificate February 15, 1840.

Source: Thompson, *Defenders of the Republic of Texas*, 158–69.

Captain January's Infantry Company F

Captain:	John R. Connor	John J. Mitchell
James B. P. January	John A. Crawford	W. W. Morgan
First Lieutenant:	James Cullennin	Martin Northorn
Martin Moran	James Drugan	S. Renner
Second Lieutenant:	George Fehl	Thomas Riley
John S. Sutton	James Franklin [1]	Richard M. Ross
First Sergeant:	James Hall	John Shay
Andrew Manttee	Peter Hazel	James Smith
Second Sergeant:	Solomon Jones	Isaac Stewart
Edward Kirkland	Bernard Kaump	Jacob Tator
First Corporal:	Peter Keizer	David M. Taylor
Charles Stroube	William Kelly	Smith B. Thomas
Second Corporal:	Edward LeGrand	John Vervats
Levi Sellick	Charles Maher	Gaetano Volta
Privates:	John Manning	John Webster
Joseph Adams	John Martin	Robert West
Charles Banks	Mack Mason	Charles White
Frederick Brands	J. B. McClyman	John Wilson
James Brannon	Robert McCormick	
John F. Butler	Niel McNeal	
Lewis Calhoun	William Mead	
Alexander Campbell	Thomas Menzies	
John Connolly	John Miller	

[1] Deserted December 21.

Source: Thompson, *Defenders of the Republic of Texas*, 181–93.

Other Units on Northwestern Campaign:

Mounted Volunteer Scouts	Captain Mathew Caldwell
Mounted Lipan Scouts	Chief Castro
Mounted Tonkawa Scouts	Chief Placido

Muster rolls unavailable for these units.

In addition to Tonkawa and Lipan Indian scouts, Burleson had four infantry companies, plus "a few mounted volunteers under the charge of Capt. Caldwell."[13] Elected captain of the volunteers, Mathew Caldwell had most recently commanded a three-month company of rangers in spring 1839 which had been involved in the tracking of Flores. Among Caldwell's volunteers was former ranger captain John L. Lynch, who had also commanded a spy detachment during the Cherokee War which was employed by the First Regiment through August 25, 1839.

Burleson's forces departed the Austin area on December 16, hoping to follow up on the recent successful expeditions by colonels Karnes and Neill. Perhaps only about fifty of Burleson's men were mounted. All others were foot soldiers.[14]

The troops were originally under command of Lieutenant Colonel William Fisher and Major Peyton Wyatt. The official report written by Burleson, "Winter Campaign against the Comanches," shows that the army proceeded north toward the San Gabriel River, which was six miles distance from Camp Caldwell on Brushy Creek. Fisher had his men make camp for the night on the San Gabriel.

The troops marched throughout December 17, covering about twelve miles in a northwesterly direction. The Frontier Regiment maintained a steady pace up the San Gabriel, covering fifteen miles on December 18 before making camp "on the sources of the same stream." An additional eight miles in a northwesterly direction were covered the following day.

After making camp on the evening of December 19, the troops were joined by Colonel Burleson. He took command and on the following day marched his troops eighteen miles to the Lampasas River before making camp. The troops had marched through present Williamson and Burnet counties into present Lampasas County. Burleson moved his men another eighteen miles on December 21 before making camp on a branch of the Lampasas River.

On December 22, the expedition continued on its course "about eight miles and encamped for the purpose of affording our spies an opportunity of reporting." The spies, mostly the Lipans and Captain Caldwell's small mounted group, went out on December 23 while the infantry companies moved slowly forward in the same general direction as the previous day.

The spies returned with the report that they had found fresh signs a short distance ahead. Burleson's men marched about eight miles this day, moving from the Lampasas River more westerly toward the Colorado River. By the time camp was established that evening, his men had traveled about one hundred miles northwest of Austin and were in present Mills County.

After daybreak on Christmas Eve, Burleson moved his troops about two miles "to avoid discovery." The ground soldiers were then rested while he waited for his spies to "make a thorough examination" of the countryside during the morning hours.

> The spies came in and reported, having found an Indian camp on the Colorado, about nine miles distant. Upon this

information I made a movement, about three o'clock, P.M., in the direction of the camp, so as to enable me to reach and surprise it during the night. Having marched some six miles, and arrived, as I was led to believe, within a few miles of the enemy, I halted the troops, and sent the spies on, in advance, for the purpose of discovering the position of their camp. I remained, resting on our arms, until one o'clock at night, when the spies coming in, reported they were unable to find the enemy.

I immediately, however, dispatched other spies, with orders to search out their camp and report as early as possible.

★ ★ ★ ★ ★

Christmas Cherokee Battle: December 25, 1839

This spy group returned to camp around 8:00 a.m. on December 25. They had found the Indian camp about six miles distant on the west side of the Colorado. In his report, Burleson noted, "Upon marching the distance, we found it to be about twelve." Camp was quickly broken down and the troops were ordered "to prepare immediately for action." The line of march was taken up about 9:00 a.m. Colonel Burleson feared that if he wanted to surprise the enemy after dark, there was a good chance the Indians' hunters or spies might find them first during the daylight.

The Indian camp discovered by scouts proved to be Cherokees under chiefs Egg and John Bowles, who was son of the old war chief who had been slain in East Texas. Chief Bowles was attempting to reach Mexico with his people by passing beyond the outermost white settlements.[15]

Approaching the Cherokee camp unseen during the daylight was not an easy chore. Burleson took his men a short distance upriver from the camp and there crossed over to the other side. "Considerable precaution and circumspection was necessary" to maintain the surprise element.

Burleson's men arrived within a few hundred yards of the Cherokee camp and were met by one Indian who had been sent out to parley with them. Burleson felt that this brave was basically detaining them until the others could either flee or prepare for battle.

It was not my intention to fire upon them, could they have been induced to surrender; but perceiving their messenger taken into custody, they commenced a brisk fire from a creek

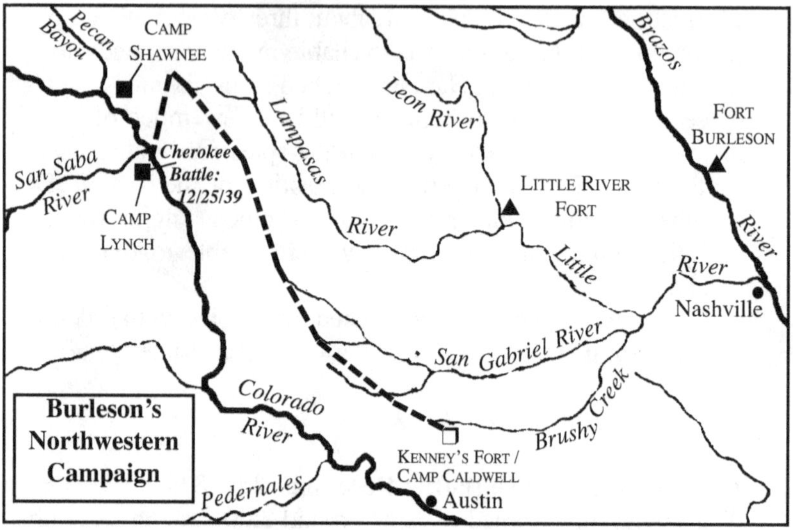

> or ravine, in the rear of their encampment, which was immediately returned by (B) company, under Capt. Clendenin, which was formed under cover of some trees and fallen timber, while the rest of the command filed to the right, in order to flank their left, or surround them.

While the other companies moved around to surround the Cherokees, the Indians took panic and fled the battlefield. The Texan forces in the advance charged the Indians and started them to flight. The Indians were hotly pursued for two miles by the entire Texas force. The surrounding terrain favored the Indians and most of their warriors succeeded in escaping.

In the running fight, at least six Indians were killed and left dead on the battlefield. Conspicuous among the bodies were Chief Egg and Chief John Bowles. Both were fatally wounded and found dead on the battlegrounds. The remaining Cherokees made the best of the prevailing dense cedar brakes, the rocky terrain, and a precipitous ravine to escape the battlefield.

In overrunning the Indian camp, Colonel Burleson's men managed to capture one elderly Indian, five women, and nineteen children. Among the prisoners were the widow of Chief John Bowles (Duwali), three children, and two of Bowles' sisters. The Texans also captured the entire campground equipage, including horses and cattle. Among the written documents found was an account book belonging to the

Killough family of East Texas, which belied Sam Houston's claim that Cherokees had never killed white men in Texas.[16]

The Texans' after-action report states that they had suffered one man killed and one Tonkawa wounded. Burleson regretted the loss of his "gallant comrade, Captain Lynch, of the volunteers." Lynch was killed while charging among the foremost in the advance. He was shot through the chest and died almost instantly. Burleson was equally pleased with the battlefield conduct of his other troops, as he wrote on December 26 to Sidney Johnston in his action report from Camp Lynch, named for the fallen John Lynch.

> In praise of the officers and men, who were engaged in this short but decisive affair, I cannot say too much. Each appeared anxious and determined to do his duty, and I feel gratified in being thus enabled to bear testimony to their gallant conduct.
>
> The Lipan and Tonkawa Indians have also performed their duty with fidelity as scouts, and with bravery in the field.
>
> The number of Cherokees engaged in this affair I have not been able to ascertain with any degree of correctness.[17]

Burleson's men did their best to interrogate the elderly Cherokee Indian they had captured. "From his own assertions, and the great anxiety manifested by the squaws, the old Cherokee, whom we had taken prisoner on the previous day, could probably induce the remaining portion of this party to come in and surrender themselves up as prisoners of war." Colonel Burleson then liberated this old Cherokee and furnished him with a horse, ordering him to leave and spread the truce offering to the remaining Indians of his party.

Also on December 26, the Texans paid their last respects to their slain comrade John Lynch. "He was interred with the honors of war, and received the attention due to a gallant soldier," wrote Burleson.

The army camped overnight again at Camp Lynch, but by December 27 the old Cherokee had not returned as promised. Burleson then decided to pursue the Indians. He sent the other Indian women and children prisoners to Austin under an armed guard patrol led by Lieutenant Martin Morran of Company F. Burleson sent his first battle report and all captured papers with Morran's men. Before concluding this report on the evening of December 26, Burleson noted that he would take up the line of march on the following day for Pecan Bayou, twelve to fifteen miles distant. He planned to "scour the country, on both sides of that stream, to the forks; from thence I shall proceed to the Brazos."

Camp Lynch was broken at 3:00 p.m. on December 27 and the men marched four miles. On December 28, the expedition marched to Pecan Bayou. Upon arrival at that river, the advance spies spotted two Indians running away. The Tonkawa scouts immediately sent up a cry of "Comanches" and commenced the chase.

"I happened to be near [this spot] myself, at the time," Burleson recorded, "and ordered them pursued, which was done immediately by Capt. Caldwell and those mounted on the best horses, for about two miles."[18] They followed these Indians back to their camp, which had been hastily abandoned. The Indians had "left everything they had, together with three horses." They were judged to be Shawnees from the appearances of their equipage, skins, and valuable furs they left behind. They were not seen again on the campaign, however.

Burleson's troops camped near the junction of Pecan Bayou and the Colorado River, calling their site Camp Shawnee. They remained here until January 1, 1840, and conducted searches for the Indians. Burleson sent out spies who spent two days scouring the area. They traveled across the San Saba about twenty-five miles while others traveled about the same distance up the Colorado River and Pecan Bayou.

These scouts returned to Camp Shawnee on the night of December 31. Burleson wrote Secretary of War Johnston that his men had made

> no discovery that will authorize proceeding further. I shall therefore take up the line of march tomorrow morning in the direction of the Brazos, and shall lose no time in accomplishing my expedition, contemplated by your order.

★ ★ ★ ★ ★

Thus the Texas Army closed out the final day of 1839 chasing and chastising Indians in central Texas. Things had changed considerably in five years of Indian wars on the Texas frontier. Expeditions had once been carried out by volunteer posses on missions of vengeance against Indians who had attacked fellow settlers. By 1839, with President Lamar's ethnic cleansing policy, offensive sweeps were being carried out by infantry companies, ranger units and even a mounted gunmen battalion.

These offensives were often accompanied by volunteer scouts, including small units of Indian scouts cooperating with Texan forces to drive away their own enemies.

The wheels of change were undeniably in motion on the Texas prairies. The once vulnerable settlers had become the hunters. The Shawnees and Cherokees had been largely driven from Texas. The rangers and frontiersmen would develop new weapons and new tactics in the coming years which would enable them to fight more effectively against the aggressive Comanches.

Texas Rangers, used since Stephen F. Austin's early days, were formally organized and revamped during the late 1830s. The legendary men of law and order were born of the necessity to defend the early settlements from Indian forces. In these early years, this task had been accomplished by operating in small numbers with little support on the frontier. Entering the 1840s, depredations in eastern Texas were becoming less frequent. The new offensive sweeps by Anglo-Texian forces were making the frontier a less inhabitable place for Native Americans.

Afterword

Colonel Edward Burleson's Frontier Regiment was two weeks into 1840 before returning from its final Indian campaign of 1839. His troops marched out of Camp Shawnee on January 1, 1840, and headed east toward the Brazos River. They crossed a chain of small mountains dividing the Colorado and Brazos rivers, making camp on the night of January 3 on the Leon River, one of the forks of the Little River.

On January 3, Doctor Shields Booker and Captain James January of Company F were scouting out ahead of the main party. They returned to camp that night and reported to Burleson "the discovery of twenty-five or thirty Indians a few miles from camp."

During the early hours of January 4, Burleson detached Lieutenant Colonel Fisher, Major Wyatt, and all the mounted men at his discretion to pursue these Indians. He took the balance of the foot soldiers about six miles on down the stream and made camp, awaiting their report. The Tonkawa scouts soon joined Burleson at this camp and reported having seen a large force of some ninety or one hundred Indians near the party under Fisher. The Tonkawas also reported having found the bodies of two infantrymen on the Leon River who had deserted the army two days previous.

The two soldiers were privates David Anderson and Tiba Lesley of Captain Clendenin's Company B. According to the muster roll, these men had "absented themselves from the company while on the march without leave on the 2nd of January." The Texans believed that these men "were murdered by the Comanches."[1]

Burleson immediately marched out with his troops to assist. They proceeded to the area on the Leon indicated, but found no signs of Indians.

Fisher and Wyatt's mounted party had turned and made its way back toward camp by that time, also. On their return, Fisher's men did encounter a large group of Comanches, whom they instantly charged upon. The enemy fled and were chased for three miles "as rapidly as the weak condition of our horses would permit." The Indians managed to escape into the mountains and further pursuit was not attempted.

The Texans had fortified their newest camp. Burleson left Second Lieutenant Daniel Lewis in command of a small guard detail, and took the balance of the men in pursuit of the Indians on the morning of January 6. They found a large trail about ten miles from camp which led south. It appeared to have been made by four or five hundred mules. At the same time, they discovered "extensive fires in the direction of the Upper Brazos. We followed the trail, however, to their camp, which they had abandoned in the greatest confusion and haste."

It was obvious that Burleson's men were pushing the Indians farther and farther along, following just slightly behind them. The Lipan and Tonkawa scouts reported to him that the enemy Indians had fled to the Upper Brazos area, which Burleson firmly believed.

At this point, he determined that further pursuit would be fruitless. "Our provisions were growing somewhat short, our men fatigued and our mules and horses much jaded," wrote Burleson. He therefore decided to close out his Northwestern Campaign for the winter.

The army moved back toward Austin and reached Camp Caldwell on January 12, 1840. Other new companies had arrived in the Austin area during Burleson's absence. With nine infantry companies at their disposal, Burleson and Lieutenant Colonel Fisher began assigning various companies to improve upon the chain of frontier forts that the Frontier Regiment was designed to maintain. Frontier posts were manned and/or established during 1840 at Fort Burleson, Mission San Jose, Mission Concepción, the Alamo, San Gabriel, Little River Fort, Fort Johnston, and Fort Skerrett (in Cherokee Nation). Troops were also stationed during the year at Houston, Post Galveston, and a new arsenal established in Austin under command of Captain James P. Goodall.

The Frontier Regiment's most serious encounter of 1840 was the famed Council House Fight in San Antonio. The army attempted to hold some of the Comanche tribal leaders for failing to bring all of their white captives into San Antonio, but the meeting turned to violence. Most of the Comanche leaders were slain in the fight. All told, thirty-five Indians were killed, including three women and two children, and twenty-seven were captured. The Texans suffered seven killed and eight wounded.[2]

The result of the Council House Fight was that the Comanches would observe no peace with Texans for nearly four years. Six months after their terrible losses at San Antonio's council house, the Comanches exacted revenge by raiding coastal towns in August. After nightfall on August 8, the Indians turned back for the west with two to three thousand horses and mules, many loaded with the clothing and goods they had plundered from Linnville. Texas frontier leaders gathered volunteers and moved to meet the Comanches as they moved back from the coast. Major General Felix Huston, now commanding the Texas Militia, took the command of some two hundred total Texian volunteers. In the ensuing battle of Plum Creek on August 12, an estimated sixty to eighty Comanches were killed and several captives were recovered. Many a veteran Texas Ranger captain of past and future fame participated in the Plum Creek battle, including Jesse Billingsley, Mathew Caldwell, Daniel Friar, Jack Hays, Ben McCulloch, Henry McCulloch, Rufus Perry, and William "Bigfoot" Wallace.

Other expeditions were made during 1840 into Indian territories of Texas, the most notable of which was made by Colonel John Henry Moore with ninety-odd volunteers. On the Red Fork of the Colorado River, his forces attacked a Comanche village at dawn on October 24. The Texans charged the unsuspecting village from all sides and opened fire. Some of the Comanches managed to cross the river and flee for cover. Men, women, and children were slaughtered and pursuit was carried out by mounted volunteers for four miles.

Command of the army's First Regiment passed from Edward Burleson to Colonel William G. Cooke. During late 1840 into the early months of 1841, he worked diligently on building the military road from Red River down to Austin. This was the greatest accomplishment of Lamar's Frontier Regiment by the time he was forced to disband his army in the spring of 1841.

In the absence of an army, the Texas government once again relied upon regional ranging units to protect the settlements. Specific counties were allowed to call up company of "minutemen" to range out during perceived emergencies.

The frontier clashes during 1840 and 1841 would mark the beginning of a new era in Texas frontier warfare with the Indians. The Texans began to use mounted men firing from horseback and learned that determined charges into their enemy had a noticeable effect on their opponent. The first repeating firearms would make their way into ranger hands during the 1840s and would significantly change the way battles were fought. Micah Andrews, a former ranger captain, had used a new Colt repeating rifle in Moore's Comanche fight. He reported that he was able to fire the Colt ten times while his companions were able to fire their rifles only twice.[3]

The frontier weapons would continue to improve in the 1840s. Samuel Colt's new pistol could fire off five rounds as quickly as a man could get off one round from any other pistol of the day. Some of these new pistols found their way to Texas, including at least two orders placed by the Frontier Regiment.

During the early 1840s, Texas Ranger companies generally became smaller units which often struggled to provision themselves properly. They were more mobile than volunteer militia units, however, and served as the true scouts for any impending danger. South Texas along the so-called Nueces Strip, a disputed area between the Nueces and Rio Grande rivers, became a hotbed for bandits and adventurers who robbed and killed Mexicans, Texans, and Indians.

The exploits of Jack Hays' rangers are legendary in Texas. They took the fight to the Comanche offensively and adapted their fighting techniques much like some of the Indians' own methods. The advancement of firearm technology helped the rangers to rule the frontiers. Sam Colt's .36 caliber "Paterson five-shooter" pistol with its revolving cylinder was reportedly first used by Hays in the early 1840s.[4]

The Colt revolver and the subsequent Walker Colt, a .44 caliber six-shot revolver Samuel H. Walker helped Colt to design, allowed the Texas Rangers new freedom in fighting. With this new weapon, the Texans could continue to fire and charge on horseback. The Comanches were shocked to find that their foes were no longer the riflemen who had been forced to dismount to fight.

The rangers became adept at fighting and would help hold the line against all enemies during the final years of the Republic of Texas. The rangers patrolled and fought raiders along the Nueces Strip, helped thwart attempts by Mexican soldiers to seize San Antonio in 1842, and continued to engage Comanches with their new six-shooters.

The Congress of the United States of America accepted the new Constitution of the State of Texas on December 29, 1845. Although officially annexed this date, the state government of Texas was not formally organized until February 19, 1846.

Armed with their Colts, the rangers became a formidable fighting machine in their frontier conflicts during the next decade. Jack Hays' rangers served ably with U.S. forces during the Mexican War of 1846–1848. Following this war, John "Rip" Ford took command of the Texas Rangers, dubbing his men the Cavalry of the West. His men would fight in the Cortina War of 1859–1860, incited by the siege of Brownsville by Mexican forces, and throughout the Civil War.

During the next century, the Texas Rangers survived as the law and order keepers of their new state. They gained fame in tracking some of the more famous outlaws, such as John Wesley Hardin in 1877, Sam Bass in 1878, and Bonnie Parker and Clyde Barrow in 1934. The Texas Rangers have received international recognition as recently as July 1999, when Sergeant Drew Carter negotiated the peaceful surrender of one of the FBI's most wanted murderers. Today, they operate with just over one hundred rangers as an elite investigative unit of the Department of Public Safety. These men and women do not wear uniforms, but operate from a handful of field offices while covering all 254 Texas counties.

These fabled lawmen have been forced to evolve with their changing state and its rapidly changing technologies. Once scouting from a fast horse on the isolated frontiers, the ranger of modern day is just as likely to track a foe via laptop computer, cell phone, or the Internet.

Stephen F. Austin's vision in 1823 of employing a small, very mobile group of frontiersmen to protect the remote settlements was prolific. The ranging service was legally adopted in 1835 during the Texas Revolution. It was refined and thoroughly tested during the ensuing five years.

The frontier leaders during the late 1830s had immigrated to Texas from many different states. Some were well-educated and were involved in the republic's political process, while others gained command from their reputations as able spies, good horsemen, and fearless fighters. Only a select few of these early freedom fighters are household names of Texas history.

Many Texas frontier leaders of the late 1830s continued to serve their republic and future state for decades in military or legislative roles. Others took their talents on to other prospective new lands. After much recognition in Texas, Jack Hays and Noah Smithwick, for example, both later moved to California.

The famed Henry Karnes died of yellow fever on August 16, 1840. Other 1830s era frontier leaders would meet their maker in Indian skirmishes. Jacob Snively was killed by Apaches in 1871 while working as a surveyor and prospector in the Arizona Territory. Captain John Denton, a company leader during the Cherokee War, was killed in 1841 during the battle of Village Creek about six miles east of present Fort Worth. Captain John York was killed on Escondida Creek in 1848 while leading volunteers in a battle against marauding Indians. George Barnett, an 1835 ranger captain, was killed by Lipan Apaches in 1848 while deer hunting fifteen miles west of Gonzales.

Some of the brighter stars of the Lone Star State's early history ended their lives early. First Regiment Captain Samuel Jordan committed suicide in 1841. Tom Rusk, former major general of the Texas Militia and United States Senator for Texas, also took his own life in Nacogdoches in 1857.

Ranger Captain Michael Costley had been fatally shot in a dispute in Nacogdoches in 1837. Ranger and infantry company commander Mark Lewis was killed in an Austin shooting quarrel in 1843. Veteran ranger and Indian fighter Albert Gholson died in 1860 as a result of a fight with his neighbor.

Others gave their lives in service against foes other than Indian. Many early rangers participated in the ill-fated Mier Expedition of 1842 and were captured and held as prisoners. Joe Berry, one of Captain Tumlinson's 1836 rangers, was murdered by Mexican soldiers while lying helpless in bed with a broken leg during the Mier imprisonment. Captain William Eastland, a ranger commander from late 1836 through early 1838, was one of the seventeen Mier prisoners who drew a black bean from a jar and was put to death before a firing squad. During the Civil War, Ben McCulloch and Albert Sidney Johnston were each shot down and killed while leading forces in combat in 1862.

Many Texas counties were named in honor of the early 1830s frontiersmen. Among those honored with a county name are Peter Hansborough Bell, Edward Burleson, Mathew Caldwell, Robert Morris Coleman, James Coryell, Nicholas Mosby Dawson, John Bunyan Denton, William Mosby Eastland, George Bernard Erath, William S. Fisher, John Coffee Hays, Henry Wax Karnes, George C. Kimbell (Kimble County), Benjamin McCulloch, Daniel Montague, José Antonio Navarro, John Henninger Reagan, Sterling Clack Robertson, Thomas Jefferson Rusk, Erastus Smith (Deaf Smith County), James Smith (Smith County), Edward H. Tarrant, and Robert McAlpin Williamson.

Although these men and a few others have been well recognized for their service, scores others have been all but forgotten. They fought with what little they had for everything they did not have: independence, freedom from Indian depredations, and security for their families. An enemy was anyone who endangered the settlers' land, families, or sense of security. Little regard was given to what rights the Native Americans claimed to have who had lived on the same lands years before the Anglo settlers arrived.

Those who served as Texas Rangers and frontiersmen in the later 1830s had been born in numerous countries. Many other rangers were Tejanos and Indians who shared a common goal of quelling any frontier menance. Some men volunteered and fought without ever signing their names to a muster roll. Many of those who were dutifully inscribed have been forgotten by muster rolls long since lost or destroyed. Not lost, however, are the courage and sense of duty carried by each who volunteered for frontier service in the late 1830s. The spirit and determination of the Texas Rangers was legendary in these early years and is a daily prerequisite for the rangers that wear the badge today.

Appendix

Texan Casualties of the Frontier Indian Wars

1835–1839

This compilation includes Texas Rangers and militiamen killed *in the line of duty* during hostile encounters with Indian forces. Ranger losses to Mexican forces during the Texas Revolution, such as Lieutenant George Kimble's Gonzales rangers killed at the Alamo, are not included. Likewise, the two men wounded in Captain Deaf Smith's 1837 Laredo fight with Mexican cavalrymen are not listed.

Other casualties not listed are: men accidentally wounded and who subsequently died from these wounds during the course of a campaign; individuals killed during Indian depredations; and deserters who were killed by Indians after they left their companies on campaign.

1835

Killed In Action

Name:	Date Killed:	Action:
John Williams	July 11, 1835	Coleman's Tawakoni Village Attack
Moses Smith Hornsby	Sept. 1, 1835	Colonel Moore's Ranger Campaign (killed by friendly fire)

Wounded In Action

Name:	Date Wounded:	Action:
___ Bliss	July 11, 1835	Coleman's Tawakoni Village Attack
Jesse Halderman	July 11, 1835	Coleman's Tawakoni Village Attack
___ Wallace	July 11, 1835	Coleman's Tawakoni Village Attack

1836

Killed In Action

Name:	Date Killed:	Action:
Robert B. Frost	May 19, 1836	Parker's Fort Massacre
Benjamin Parker	May 19, 1836	Parker's Fort Massacre

Silas Mercer Parker Sr.	May 19, 1836	Parker's Fort Massacre
____ Robinett	August 22, 1836	Coleto Creek Indian Fight
Thomas J. Robinson	August 22, 1836	Coleto Creek Indian Fight

Author's Note: Information on the above August 22, 1836, Indian fight was made available to me after Volume 1 of *Savage Frontier* was published. Edwin G. Pierson Jr. provided information on his ancestors including biographies of John Goodloe Warren Pierson and John Hogue Pierson, as well as a muster roll of Captain Pierson's 1836 cavalry company. A detachment of John G. W. Pierson's company fought a battle with Comanche Indians on Coleto Creek near Victoria and suffered two men killed and two wounded. A fifth man, named only as "De Orman" escaped.

Wounded In Action

Name:	Date Wounded:	Action:
Hugh M. Childress	Jan. 20, 1836	Tumlinson's Walnut Creek Fight
Elijah Ingram	Jan. 20, 1836	Tumlinson's Walnut Creek Fight
Andrew Houston	August 1836	Capt. Hill's Yegua River Battle
John H. Pierson, Sgt.	August 22, 1836	Coleto Creek Indian Fight
Alexander Whitaker	August 22, 1836	Coleto Creek Indian Fight

1837

Killed In Action

Name:	Date Killed:	Action:
Francis Childers	Jan. 7, 1837	Sgt. Erath's Elm Creek Fight
David Clark	Jan. 7, 1837	Sgt. Erath's Elm Creek Fight
Columbus Anderson	Jan. 28, 1837	Trinity River Indian Attack
David Faulkenberry	Jan. 28, 1837	Trinity River Indian Attack
Evan Faulkenberry	Jan. 28, 1837	Trinity River Indian Attack
Philip Martin	March 1837	Lieut. Wren's Comanche Fight
Jesse Bailey	May 6, 1837	Post Oak Springs Massacre
Aaron Cullins	May 6, 1837	Post Oak Springs Massacre
David M. Farmer	May 6, 1837	Post Oak Springs Massacre
John Hughes	May 6, 1837	Post Oak Springs Massacre
Claiborne Neal	May 6, 1837	Post Oak Springs Massacre
James Barnes	May 10, 1837	Mustang Prairie Indian Fight
Daniel McLean	May 10, 1837	Mustang Prairie Indian Fight
John Sheridan	May 10, 1837	Mustang Prairie Indian Fight
James Coryell	May 27, 1837	Perry Springs Indian Attack
Jesse Blair	Nov. 10, 1837	Stone Houses Fight
Alexander Bostwick	Nov. 10, 1837	Stone Houses Fight
James Christian	Nov. 10, 1837	Stone Houses Fight
Joseph Cooper	Nov. 10, 1837	Stone Houses Fight
James Joslen	Nov. 10, 1837	Stone Houses Fight

Alfred H. Miles	Nov. 10, 1837	Stone Houses Fight
Westley Nicholson	Nov. 10, 1837	Stone Houses Fight
William Nicholson	Nov. 10, 1837	Stone Houses Fight
Dr. William Sanders	Nov. 10, 1837	Stone Houses Fight
Lewis P. Scheuster	Nov. 10, 1837	Stone Houses Fight

WOUNDED IN ACTION

Name:	Date Wounded:	Action:
Abram Anglin	Jan. 28, 1837	Trinity River Indian Attack
Samuel K. Blisk	Nov. 10, 1837	Stone Houses Fight
Robert Fletcher	Nov. 10, 1837	Stone Houses Fight
John Zekel	Nov. 10, 1837	Stone Houses Fight

1838

KILLED IN ACTION

Name:	Date Killed:	Action:
Dr. Bigham	Late May 1838	Settlers' Fight near Fort Oldham
Joseph Reed	Late May 1838	Settlers' Fight near Fort Oldham
James Neil	Oct. 9, 1838	Surveyors' Fight on Battle Creek
Euclid M. Cox	Oct. 9, 1838	Surveyors' Fight on Battle Creek
Samuel T. Allen	Oct. 9, 1838	Surveyors' Fight on Battle Creek
Thomas Barton	Oct. 9, 1838	Surveyors' Fight on Battle Creek
J. Bullock	Oct. 9, 1838	Surveyors' Fight on Battle Creek
David Clark	Oct. 9, 1838	Surveyors' Fight on Battle Creek
Richard Davis	Oct. 9, 1838	Surveyors' Fight on Battle Creek
J. Hard	Oct. 9, 1838	Surveyors' Fight on Battle Creek
Alexander Houston	Oct. 9, 1838	Surveyors' Fight on Battle Creek
Elijah Ingram	Oct. 9, 1838	Surveyors' Fight on Battle Creek
Joseph P. Jones	Oct. 9, 1838	Surveyors' Fight on Battle Creek
P. M. Jones	Oct. 9, 1838	Surveyors' Fight on Battle Creek
Asa T. Mitchell	Oct. 9, 1838	Surveyors' Fight on Battle Creek
____ Spikes	Oct. 9, 1838	Surveyors' Fight on Battle Creek
William Tremier	Oct. 9, 1838	Surveyors' Fight on Battle Creek
Rodney Wheeler	Oct. 9, 1838	Possible Surveyor's Fight victim
J. W. Williams	Oct. 9, 1838	Surveyors' Fight on Battle Creek
Julius Bullock	Oct. 12, 1838	Maj. Mabbitt's Cordova Skirmish
John W. Carpenter	Oct. 12, 1838	Maj. Mabbitt's Cordova Skirmish
Thomas M. Scott	Oct. 12, 1838	Maj. Mabbitt's Cordova Skirmish
John Wilson	Oct. 12, 1838	Maj. Mabbitt's Cordova Skirmish
James Hall	Oct. 16, 1838	Mortally wounded during battle of Kickapoo. Died December 17, 1838.
Benjamin F. Cage	Oct. 20, 1838	Captain Cage's Comanche Fight
Robert M. Lee	Oct. 20, 1838	Captain Cage's Comanche Fight
Dr. Henry G. McClung	Oct. 20, 1838	Captain Cage's Comanche Fight

Peter Conrad	Oct. 20, 1838	Captain Cage's Comanche Fight
____ Green	Oct. 20, 1838	Captain Cage's Comanche Fight
____ King	Oct. 20, 1838	Captain Cage's Comanche Fight
Daniel O'Boyle	Oct. 20, 1838	Captain Cage's Comanche Fight
John Pickering	Oct. 20, 1838	Captain Cage's Comanche Fight

WOUNDED IN ACTION

Name:	Date Wounded:	Action:
____ Lawson	Late May 1838	Settlers' Fight near Fort Oldham
Henry Wax Karnes	August 10, 1838	Arroyo Seco Comanche Fight
One unnamed ranger	Sept. 18, 1838	Montague's Caddo Village Raid
Nathan W. Baker	Oct. 9, 1838	Surveyors' Fight on Battle Creek
Walter Paye Lane	Oct. 9, 1838	Surveyors' Fight on Battle Creek
William Smith	Oct. 9, 1838	Surveyors' Fight on Battle Creek
John T. Violet	Oct. 9, 1838	Surveyors' Fight on Battle Creek
Richard G. Dunlap	Oct. 20, 1838	Captain Cage's Comanche Fight
Joseph L. Hood	Oct. 20, 1838	Captain Cage's Comanche Fight
Robert Patton	Oct. 20, 1838	Captain Cage's Comanche Fight

1839

KILLED IN ACTION

Name:	Date Killed:	Action:
Hale Barton	Jan. 16, 1839	Captain Bryant's Fight
L. Dorsey	Jan. 16, 1839	Captain Bryant's Fight
Alfred P. Eaton	Jan. 16, 1839	Captain Bryant's Fight
William Fullerton	Jan. 16, 1839	Captain Bryant's Fight
Henry Haigwood	Jan. 16, 1839	Captain Bryant's Fight
Hugh A. Henry	Jan. 16, 1839	Captain Bryant's Fight
William N. P. Marlin *	Jan. 16, 1839	Captain Bryant's Fight
G. Washington McGrew	Jan. 16, 1839	Captain Bryant's Fight
Jacob Plummer	Jan. 16, 1839	Captain Bryant's Fight
Andrew Jackson Powers	Jan. 16, 1839	Captain Bryant's Fight
Charles Sauls *	Jan. 16, 1839	Captain Bryant's Fight
Cyrus L. Ward	Jan. 16, 1839	Captain Bryant's Fight
Andrew Jackson Webb	Jan. 16, 1839	Captain Bryant's Fight
Joseph S. Martin	Feb. 14, 1839	Col. Moore's Comanche Raid
Edward Blakey	Feb. 25, 1839	Battle of Brushy Creek
Jacob Burleson	Feb. 25, 1839	Battle of Brushy Creek
James Gilliland	Feb. 25, 1839	Battle of Brushy Creek
John B. Walters	Feb. 25, 1839	Battle of Brushy Creek
John Bird	June 26, 1839	Capt. Bird's Comanche Battle
Thomas Gay	June 26, 1839	Capt. Bird's Comanche Battle
H. M. C. Hall	June 26, 1839	Capt. Bird's Comanche Battle
Jesse E. Nash	June 26, 1839	Capt. Bird's Comanche Battle

William H. Weaver	June 26, 1839	Capt. Bird's Comanche Battle
John Crane	July 15, 1839	Battle Creek Cherokee Engagement
Henry P. Crowson *	July 15, 1839	Battle Creek Cherokee Engagement
Henry M. Rogers	July 15, 1839	Battle Creek Cherokee Engagement
John Ewing *	July 16, 1839	Battle of the Neches
George F. Martin *	July 16, 1839	Battle of the Neches
John S. Thompson *	July 16, 1839	Battle of the Neches
John L. Lynch	Dec. 25, 1839	Burleson's Cherokee Engagement

* Mortally wounded.

WOUNDED IN ACTION

Name:	Date Wounded:	Action:
Benjamin F. Bryant	Jan. 16, 1839	Captain Bryant's Fight
Chadison Jones	Jan. 16, 1839	Captain Bryant's Fight
Enoch M. Jones	Jan. 16, 1839	Captain Bryant's Fight
George W. Morgan	Jan. 16, 1839	Captain Bryant's Fight
Lewis B. Powers	Jan. 16, 1839	Captain Bryant's Fight
William M. Eastland	Feb. 14, 1839	Col. Moore's Comanche Raid
Smallwood S. B. Fields	Feb. 14, 1839	Col. Moore's Comanche Raid
Ira Leffingwell	Feb. 14, 1839	Col. Moore's Comanche Raid
James Martin	Feb. 14, 1839	Col. Moore's Comanche Raid
Martin Felix Taylor	Feb. 14, 1839	Col. Moore's Comanche Raid
One unnamed Lipan	Feb. 14, 1839	Col. Moore's Comanche Raid
3 unnamed men	Feb. 25, 1839	Battle of Brushy Creek
3 unnamed rangers	Mar. 29, 1839	Burleson's Mill Creek Battle
James Milford Day	Mar. 30, 1839	Scouts' Skirmish Near Seguin
David Reynolds	Mar. 30, 1839	Scouts' Skirmish Near Seguin
Solomon Allbright	July 15, 1839	Battle Creek Cherokee Engagement
John S. Anderson	July 15, 1839	Battle Creek Cherokee Engagement
John A. Harper	July 15, 1839	Battle Creek Cherokee Engagement
John McAnulty	July 15, 1839	Battle Creek Cherokee Engagement
George T. Slaughter	July 15, 1839	Battle Creek Cherokee Engagement
John B. Thacker	July 15, 1839	Battle Creek Cherokee Engagement
James R. Wilehart	July 15, 1839	Battle Creek Cherokee Engagement
Henry W. Augustine	July 16, 1839	Battle of the Neches
William Bell	July 16, 1839	Battle of the Neches
John N. Brimberry	July 16, 1839	Battle of the Neches
J. J. Caskey	July 16, 1839	Battle of the Neches
James Elijah Gilliland	July 16, 1839	Battle of the Neches
David S. Kaufman	July 16, 1839	Battle of the Neches
Felix Grundy Lemmon	July 16, 1839	Battle of the Neches
Thomas McLaughlin	July 16, 1839	Battle of the Neches
Hugh McLeod	July 16, 1839	Battle of the Neches
Edward Ratcliffe	July 16, 1839	Battle of the Neches
David Rusk	July 16, 1839	Battle of the Neches
Henry Madison Smith	July 16, 1839	Battle of the Neches
J. M. Smith	July 16, 1839	Battle of the Neches
M. Tansell	July 16, 1839	Battle of the Neches

George Willman	July 16, 1839	Battle of the Neches
Laban Menefee	Nov. 5, 1839	Neill's Fight on the Clear Fork
Unnamed Tonkawa	Dec. 25, 1839	Burleson's Cherokee Engagement

TEXAS ARMY CASUALTIES OF THE CHEROKEE WAR:

Killed In Action

John Day	July 15, 1839	Battle Creek Cherokee Engagement
Martin Tutts	July 16, 1839	Battle of the Neches
Timothy O'Neill	July 26, 1839	Indian Ambush near Fort Lamar

Wounded In Action

James Ball	July 15, 1839	Battle Creek Cherokee Engagement
Ferdinand Booker	July 16, 1839	Battle of the Neches
Wm. Joseph Campbell	July 16, 1839	Battle of the Neches
William Clements	July 16, 1839	Battle of the Neches
Samuel W. Jordan	July 16, 1839	Battle of the Neches
Millard M. Parkerson	July 16, 1839	Battle of the Neches
Joseph B. Young	July 16, 1839	Battle of the Neches

Chapter Notes
Volume II

Abbreviations to the Republic Claims Papers, 1835–1846.
Texas State Library and Archives Commission, Austin.

AC Audited Claims are those military-related claims submitted to the Comptroller or Treasurer of the Republic of Texas that were audited, approved and paid by the republic government.

PD Public Debt Claims are claims for services provided between 1835 and 1846 that could not be paid until after Texas' annexation in 1846. These were largely paid between 1848 and the early 1860s, mainly from the 1850 Boundary Compromise money Texas was paid for its lost territory.

PP Republic Pension Papers were generally filed from the 1870s to the early 1900s by veterans who served in the Texas Revolution and other republic-era military units.

UC Unpaid Claims are those documents which do not fit in one of the above categories or those whose final payment disposition is unknown.

Chapter 1
The Texas Militia Takes The Field

1. Gerald Swetnam Pierce, *Texas Under Arms: The Camps, Posts, Forts, and Military Towns of the Republic of Texas* (Austin, Tex: Encino Press, 1969), 131.

2. Noah Smithwick, *The Evolution of a State/Recollections of Old Texas Days* (Austin: University of Texas Press, 1983), 144.

3. Noah Smithwick AC, R 98, F 482.

4. Smithwick, *The Evolution of a State*, 145–147.

5. Worth S. Ray, *Austin Colony Pioneers: Including History of Bastrop, Fayette, Austin, Grimes, Montgomery and Washington Counties, Texas* (Austin, Tex: Jenkins Publishing Company, 1970), 306.

6. P. B. Norton AC, R 78, F 367.

7. William H. Smith AC, R 98, F 370, 387.

8. Micah Andrews AC, R 3, F 68.

9. Malcolm D. McLean, *Papers Concerning Robertson's Colony in Texas*, 19

vols. (Fort Worth, Tex. and Arlington, Tex.: Texas Christian University Press and The University of Texas at Arlington Press), 16: 375.

10. Joseph Hornsby AC, R 47, F 30–31; Malcolm M. Hornsby AC, R 47, F 47; Reuben Hornsby AC, R 47, F 79.

11. Joseph M. Nance, *After San Jacinto: The Texas-Mexican Frontier, 1836–1841* (Austin: University of Texas Press, 1963), 38–40.

12. (Karl) Hans Peter Marius Nielsen Gammell, *The Laws of Texas, 1822–1897*, 10 vols. (Austin, Tex: The Gammel Book Company, 1898), 1:1427–28.

13. Nance, *After San Jacinto*, 39.

14. James T. DeShields, *Border Wars of Texas* (1912; repr., Austin, Tex: State House Press, 1993), 221.

15. William M. Eastland AC, R 28, F 255–259.

16. Henry Wilson AC, R 116, F 556; Richard J. Lloyd AC, R 61, F 523.

17. Noah Smithwick AC, R 98, F 482.

18. Smithwick, *The Evolution of a State*, 151.

19. DeShields, *Border Wars*, 223.

20. McLean, *Papers*, 16: 419–20.

21. These facts reported in *Telegraph and Texas Register* on May 2, 1838, also in McLean, *Papers*, 16: 458–59.

22. McLean, *Papers*, 16: 420, 425–26, 435–36, 438–43.

23. John Wesley Wilbarger, *Indian Depredations in Texas* (1889; repr., Austin, Tex: State House Press, 1985), 609–10.

24. DeShields, *Border Wars*, 221–23.

25. McLean, *Papers*, 16: 451–53 and 50.

26. Nance, *After San Jacinto*, 42.

27. McLean, *Papers*, 16: 509.

28. Nance, *After San Jacinto*, 42–43.

29. McLean, *Papers*, 16: 538–540.

30. Ibid, 16: 559; see also *Telegraph and Texas Register* of May 29, 1838.

31. DeShields, *Border Wars*, 224; McLean, *Papers*, 16: 541–43; *Texas Indian Papers*, I: 50-52.

32. McLean, *Papers*, 16: 447–49.

33. Pierce, *Texas Under Arms*, 116.

34. McLean, *Papers*, 15: 488–89.

35. Charles A. Gulick Jr., Winnie Allen, Katherine Elliott, and Harriet Smither, *The Papers of Mirabeau Buonaparte Lamar* 6 vols. (1922; repr., Austin, Tex: Pemberton Press, 1968), 3: # 1648, T. Ragsdale, "Early Settlements and Indian Fights in Red River County," 276–77.

36. Nance, *After San Jacinto*, 117–119. Gary Clayton Anderson, *The Conquest of Texas: Ethnic Cleansing in the Promised Land, 1820–1875* (Norman: University of Oklahoma Press, 2005), 158–64.

37. Article reprinted in *Telegraph and Texas Register* on Saturday, August 25, 1838. See *Gone to Texas*, 83.

38. "Recollections of S. F. Sparks." *Quarterly of the Texas State Historical Association*. 12: No. 1 (July 1908), 75–76.

39. Nance, *After San Jacinto*, 120; Anderson, *The Conquest of Texas*, 164.

40. John Henry Brown, *Indian Wars and Pioneers of Texas* (1880; repr., Austin, Tex: State House Press, 1988), 50–51.

41. James Kimmins Greer, *Texas Ranger: Jack Hays in the Frontier Southwest* (College Station, Tex: Texas A&M University Press, 1993), 28. This book was originally published by E.P. Dutton and Company, Inc. as *Colonel Jack Hays: Texas Frontier Leader and California Builder* in 1952. Gulick, *Lamar Papers*, 4: # 2432, George T. Howard to Lamar, 230.

42. Brown, *Indian Wars*, 51.

43. Nance, *After San Jacinto*, 120. Thanks to Professor James E. Crisp for his letter of May 18, 2005, which clarifies the Spanish translation of Córdova's letter.

44. Kevin Ladd, *Gone to Texas: Genealogical Abstracts from The Telegraph and Texas Register 1835-1841* (Bowie, Md.: Heritage Books, 1994), 83.

45. McLean, *Papers*, 16: 583–84.

46. John Salmon Ford, edited by Stephen B. Oates, *Rip Ford's Texas* (Austin: University of Texas Press, 1994), 35.

47. Ibid.

48. Mary Whatley Clarke, *Thomas J. Rusk: Soldier, Statesman, Jurist* (Austin, Tex: Jenkins Publishing Company, 1971), 110–11.

49. Ford, *Rip Ford's Texas*, 36.

50. Hulen M. Greenwood, *Garrison Greenwood: Ancestors and Descendants* (Privately published by author in Houston, Tex: 1986), 65.

51. Leonard H. Mabbitt AC, R 63, F 446.

52. Clark, *Rusk*, 111.

53. Ford, *Rip Ford's Texas*, 36.

54. Clarke, *Rusk*, 111–12.

55. W. Y. Lacy narrative from *Lone Star State*, 238–239; contained in Mary Kate Hunter Notebooks in Palestine Library.

56. "A Brief Study of Thomas J. Rusk Based on His Letters to His Brother, David, 1835–1856," *Southwestern Historical Quarterly* 34 (April, 1931): 279–80.

Chapter 2

"Shoulder Your Arms And Chastize The Enemy"

1. McLean, *Papers*, 16: 587-92.

2. Gerald Swetnam Pierce, *The Army of the Republic of Texas, 1836–1845* (Dissertation from the University of Mississippi, copyright 1964, on file in the Texas Room of the Houston Public Library), 137–38.

3. W. Y. Lacy account from *Lone Star State*, 238–39, in Mary Kate Hunter Notebooks.

4. Nance, *After San Jacinto*, 54–55.

5. August 25, 1838 Letter from Citizens of Fort Houston to President Sam Houston, from Original Rusk Papers, Stephen F. Austin State University Library in Nacogdoches, Texas. See also Edna McDonald Wylie, "Fort Houston Settlement" (August 1958 thesis in the collections of the Houston Public Library's Clayton Genealogy Branch), 126–27.

6. DeShields, *Border Wars*, 224.

7. McLean, *Papers*, 16: 596–97.

8. Army Correspondence, Box 1214–23, Texas State Archives.

9. Gulick, *Lamar Papers*, 4: William B. Stout to Lamar, # 2465, 273.

10. Pierce, *Texas Under Arms*, 176–77.

11. Ibid, 78–79.

12. The key source for the account on Montague's campaign is Judge John P. Simpson from W. A. Carter, *History of Fannin County, Texas (*1885; repr., Honey Grove, Tex: Fannin County Historical Society, 1975). He participated in the expedition, although his name does not appear on either Journey or Sloan's muster rolls, perhaps because he soon joined Captain Jesse Stiff's mounted gunmen on December 1. Simpson's account is also contained in Wilbarger, *Indian Depredations*, 426–28.

13. Gulick, *Lamar Papers*, IV: William B. Stout to Lamar, # 2465, 273.

14. Simpson as quoted in Wilbarger, *Indian Depredations*, 427–28.

15. McLean, *Papers*, 16: 624.

16. Ibid, 16: 260–61.

17. Wylie, "Fort Houston Settlement," 128, 41.

18. Ibid, 129. From the Original Rusk Papers in Stephen F. Austin State University Library in Nacogdoches.

19. *Cherokee County History.* First Edition, 1986. Crockett, Tex: Published by the Cherokee County Historical Commission and the Publications Development Co. of Texas.

20. Albert Woldert, "The Last of the Cherokees in Texas, and the Life and Death of Chief Bowles," *Chronicles of Oklahoma*, Issued by The Oklahoma Historical Society in Oklahoma City, Okla., vol. I, no. 3, (June 1923): 179–226. W. B. Killough account on pages 202–6.

21. McLean, *Papers*, 16: 260–62.

22. Ladd, *Gone to Texas*, 89.

23. Harry McCorry Henderson, "The Surveyors Fight," *Southwestern Historical Quarterly* 56 (July 1952): 25. Henderson's article shows a total of twenty-seven surveyors present for the fight. Henderson's grandfather was William F. Henderson, who gave his account to historian John Henry Brown (as did survivor William Smith) in the 1850s. Walter Lane wrote in 1885 that there were twenty-two surveyors "and a boy," as printed in DeShields, *Border Wars*, 225. John Henry Brown agrees that twenty-five surveyors set out from Franklin and that twenty-three were in the battle. See Brown, *Indian Wars*, 47–50. The most modern account of the battle also agrees on twenty-three in the fight. For this detailed coverage see Jimmy L. Bryan Jr., "More Disastrous Than All: The Surveyors' Fight, 1838," *The East Texas Historical Journal* 38, no. 1 (2000): 3–14. John Ingram biographical sketch of the Louis Wiltz Kemp Papers from the San Jacinto Museum of History confirms Elijah Ingram as one of the victims.

24. Carolyn Reeves Ericson, *Nacogdoches: Gateway to Texas. Volume I. A Biographical Directory, 1773–1849* (Nacogdoches: Ericson Books, 1991), 168.

25. Henderson, "The Surveyors' Fight," 26–27.

26. Walter P. Lane to DeShields in DeShields, *Border Wars*, 226.

27. Henderson, "The Surveyors' Fight," 28.

28. DeShields, *Border Wars*, 226 and Henderson, "The Surveyors' Fight," 29. The pistol later made its way into the possession of the San Jacinto Museum of History.

29. Henderson, "The Surveyors' Fight," 30. Bryan, "More Disastrous Than All: The Surveyors' Fight, 1838."

30. DeShields, *Border Wars*, 227.

31. Henderson, "The Surveyors' Fight," 31–33.

32. DeShields, *Border Wars*, 231–32; Groneman, *Battlefields of Texas*, 82; Henderson, "The Surveyors' Fight," 34–35.

CHAPTER 3
THE KICKAPOO WAR

1. *Telegraph and Texas Register*, November 3, 1838. This entire article is reprinted in McLean, *Papers*, 16: 628–30.

2. Pierce, *Texas Under Arms*, 45.

3. Brown, *Indian Wars*, 56.

4. David F. Webb PD, R 195, F 83.

5. Lacy account from *Memorial and Biographical History of Navarro, Henderson, Anderson, Limestone, Freestone and Leon Counties, Texas*, 240. Lacy's account is also contained in the Mary Kate Hunter Notebooks in the Palestine Library.

6. Wylie, "The Fort Houston Settlement," 103.

7. Louis Blount, "A Brief Study of Thomas J. Rusk," *Southwestern Historical Quarterly* 34 (April 1931): 279–80.

8. Gulick, *Lamar Papers*, II: 263–67.

9. Brown, *Indian Wars*, 56.

10. Rusk letter from *Telegraph and Texas Register*, November 3, 1838.

11. Gulick, *Lamar Papers*, 2: # 846, McLeod to Lamar, 263–67.

12. Brown, *Indian Wars*, 56.

13. Gulick, *Lamar Papers*, II: # 846, McLeod to Lamar, 266.

14. Judge Andrew J. Fowler article on "The Edens Massacre" from *Historical Sketch of Anderson County* notebook in Palestine Library.

15. McLean, *Papers*, 16: 260–61.

16. Gulick, *Lamar Papers*, 2: # 846, McLeod to Lamar, 266.

17. Rusk letter from *Telegraph and Texas Register*, November 3, 1838.

18. Gulick, *Lamar Papers*, 2: # 846, McLeod to Lamar, 266.

19. McLean, *Papers*, 16: 625.

20. Daniel L. Crist PP, R 211, F 9-16.

21. Woldert, "The Last of the Cherokees in Texas," 205.

22. George W. Wilson AC, R 116, F 545.

23. Wylie, "The Fort Houston Settlement," 84.

24. George H. Duncan AC, R 124, F 208–10. James Cook AC, R 123, F 539.

25. John Walker AC, R 108, F 499–500. Robert Madden AC, R 63, F 652. John Murchison AC, R 126, F 304–6. Joseph Walker PD, R 193, F 352. William Charles Brookfield PD, R 159, F 10. Captain Robert W. Smith AC, R 26, F 534. D. H. Edens AC, R 28, F 389.

26. Dianna Everett, *The Texas Cherokees: A People Between Two Fires, 1819–1840* (Norman: University of Oklahoma Press, 1990), 96.

CHAPTER 4
TO THE BORDER AND BEYOND

1. For a detailed account of the Edens-Madden Massacre, see Stephen L. Moore, *Taming Texas: Captain William T. Sadler's Lone Star Service* (Austin, Tex: State House Press, 2000), 131–40. Other informative accounts include: Judge Andrew J.

Fowler's "The Edens' Massacre" account, from the Mary Kate Hunter Notebooks in Palestine, Texas; *History of Houston County*, 12–13; *The Edens Adventure: A Brief History of the Edens Family in America (*Published by the Edens Family Association, 1992), 32–41; and David H. Campbell letter to President-Elect Mirabeau B. Lamar in Gulick, *Lamar Papers*, 2: 263–65.

2. McLean, *Papers*, 16: 260–61.

3. DeShields, *Border Wars*, 243–44. See also Moses Lapham and John Pickering biographical sketchs in L. W. Kemp papers, San Jacinto Museum of History, Houston, Texas.

4. Ladd, *Gone to Texas*, 98.

5. *Biographical Directory of the Texan Conventions and Congresses, 1832–1845* (Austin, Tex: Book Exchange, 1941), 106.

6. DeShields, *Border Wars*, 244; Benjamin Franklin Cage biographical sketch in L. W. Kemp papers, San Jacinto Museum of History, Houston, Texas.

7. Ibid, 245 and Ladd, *Gone to Texas*, 95. See also Miles Squier Bennett diary; Center for American History, University of Texas at Austin.

8. Pierce, *Army*, 142.

9. Gulick, *Lamar Papers*, 2: #849, Duffield to J. S. Mayfield, 268.

10. William Smith AC, R 98, F 304. Stephen Crist AC, R 21, F 587–90. Roland W. Box AC, R 10, F 213-14. Joseph Jordan AC, R 55, F 317. Reason Crist AC, R 21, F 569. Samuel G. Wells AC, R 112, F 136.

11. Oliver Lund PD, R 63, F 141.

12. William T. Sadler Pension Papers, courtesy of Howard C. Sadler.

13. *The Edens Adventure*, 41–44. Captain Jacob Snively received 38 bushels of corn on October 30, 1838, from Armstead Bennett and 3 bushels of corn from Daniel Parker. This is evidenced by Audited Claims of the Republic of Texas on microfilm reel 7. Joel Daniel Leathers of the Mustang Prairie community in Houston County also furnished 700 bushels of corn to the Texas Army, as evidenced by a receipt from December 29, 1838, which was endorsed by Quartermaster Martin Lacy. See *History of Houston County*, 445. Martin Murchison submitted a claim for furnishing fodder, hay, and five cattle to the army on October 22, 1838. Murchison had previously supplied Captain Jewell's Fort Houston rangers in 1836. See Murchison's audited claims, R 126, F 307–314.

14. Gulick, *Lamar Papers*, 2: # 875, McLeod to Lamar, 293; Pierce, *Army*, 142–43.

15. Pierce, *Army*, 143.

16. Gammell, *The Laws of Texas*, II: 3–5.

17. *Journals of the Fourth Congress of the Republic of Texas* (Austin, Tex: Von Boeckmann-Jones Co. Printers, 1930), 3: Reports and Relief Laws, 90–91.

18. Colonel James Chessher to Brig. Genl. K. H. Douglass. K. H. Douglass Papers from James Harper Starr Papers. Courtesy of The Center for American History, The University of Texas at Austin.

19. Adele B. Looscan, "Captain Joseph Daniels," *Texas Historical Association Quarterly* 5, no. 1 (1901–1902): 19–21.

20. Fourth Sergeant James G. Claud AC, R18, F195 and Private Samuel W. Lincoln AC, R 61, F 74.

21. William F. Allison AC, R 2, F 320.

22. Looscan, "Captain Joseph Daniels," 22.

23. Captain John Wortham to General Rusk, December 2, 1838. K. H. Douglass Papers from James Harper Starr Papers. Courtesy of The Center for American History, The University of Texas at Austin.

24. Gulick, *Lamar Papers*, 4: # 2162, Daniels to Lamar, Gulick, 29–30.

25. Wilbarger, *Indian Depredations*, 1–4.

26. Gulick, *Lamar Papers*, V. R. Palmer to Lamar, 2: # 893, 303–4.

27. Ibid, Palmer to Lamar, 2: # 896, 306–7.

28. Gulick, *Lamar Papers*, 2: # 875, McLeod to Lamar, 293.

29. Ibid, 2: # 876, Rusk to Lamar, 294; 2: # 878, Rusk to Lamar, 295; 2: # 877, Rusk to Lamar, 295; 2: # 884, McLeod to Lamar, 298–99.

30. Major General Thomas J. Rusk to General Douglass from Shawnee Town, November 21, 1838. K. H. Douglass Papers from James Harper Starr Papers. Courtesy of The Center for American History, The University of Texas at Austin.

31. Ibid, 4: # 2465, William B. Stout to Lamar, 274; 2: # 890, McLeod to Lamar, 302; 2: # 901, McLeod to Lamar, 308–9; 2: # 943, McLeod to Lamar, 341; Anderson, *The Conquest of Texas*, 169–70.

32. McLean, *Papers*, 16: 187–88.

Chapter 5
Campaigns of the Red River Riflemen

1. B. C. Walters to Gen. K. H. Douglass from Camp Shawnee Town, December 14, 1838. K. H. Douglass Papers, James Harper Starr Collection, The Center for American History, The University of Texas at Austin.

2. B. C. Walters to Gen. K. H. Douglass from Camp Shawnee Town, December 20, 1838. Douglass Papers, Starr Collection.

3. Capt. J. E. Box to Gen. K. H. Douglass, December 24, 1838, from Fort Houston. Douglass Papers, Starr Collection.

4. DeShields, *Border Wars*, 251.

5. Jacob Snively to Gen. K. H. Douglass, January 13, 1839, from Camp Williams. Douglass Papers, Starr Collection.

6. Jacob Snively to Gen. K. H. Douglass, January 14, 1839, from Camp at Killough's. Douglass Papers, Starr Collection.

7. Gulick, *Lamar Papers*, 4: William B. Stout to Lamar, # 2465, 274.

8. Pierce, *Texas Under Arms*, 30.

9. McLean, *Papers*, 15: 489.

10. Gulick, *Lamar Papers*, 4: William B. Stout to Lamar, # 2465, 274.

11. Isaac Lyday PD, R 169, F 560–62; Pierce, *Texas Under Arms*, 98.

12. Isaac Lyday AC, R 33, F 563; Cornelius B. Tollett PD, R 191, F 335; Curtis Jernigan PD, R 164, F 514–24.

13. Pierce, *Texas Under Arms*, 98-99.

14. Gulick, *Lamar Papers*, 4: William B. Stout to Lamar, # 2465, 274.

15. Pierce, *Texas Under Arms*, 156–57.

16. Gulick, *Lamar Papers*, 4: William B. Stout to Lamar, # 2465, 275.

17. Carter, *History of Fannin County*, 28–29.

18. Pierce, *Texas Under Arms*, 81.

19. *Journals of the Fourth Congress, Republic of Texas. Vol. 3: Reports and Relief Laws*, 89.

20. Gulick, *Lamar Papers*, 2: 352; Anderson, *The Conquest of Texas*, 174.

21. Ibid, 2: Shaw and Hill to Lamar, # 942, 340–41.

22. Gammell, *The Laws of Texas*, II: 15–20.

23. Gulick, *Lamar Papers*, 2: Johnston to Lamar, # 953, 371.

24. Pierce, *Texas Under Arms*, 61.

25. Gammel, *The Laws of Texas*, 2: 29-30.

26. DeShields, *Border Wars*, 251.

27. General E. Morehouse to Major William Jefferson Jones, January 21, 1839. Adjutant General's Papers, Texas State Archives.

28. Betty Dooley Awbrey and Claude Dooley. *Why Stop? A Guide to Texas Historical Roadside Markers* (4th ed. Houston, Tex: Lone Star Books, 1999), 182.

29. Gulick, *Lamar Papers*, 2: McLeod to Lamar, # 997, 406.

30. Ibid, 4: William B. Stout to Lamar, # 2465, 273.

31. Ibid, 2: Rusk to Lamar, # 996, 405.

32. *Journals of the Fourth Congress, Republic of Texas. Vol. 3: Reports and Relief Laws*, 89.

33. Gulick, *Lamar Papers*, 2: McLeod to Lamar, # 1024, 423–24.

Chapter 6

Morgan Massacre And Bryant's Defeat

1. Gulick, *Lamar Papers*, 2: Johnston to Lamar, # 995, 404–5.

2. Gammell, *Laws of Texas*, 2: 31.

3. Ibid, 2: 44.

4. Gulick, *Lamar Papers*, 2: Lamar to Congress, # 988, 402–3.

5. Gammell, *Laws of Texas*, 2: 78.

6. Ibid, 2: 93.

7. Greer, *Texas Ranger*, 33.

8. DeShields, *Border Wars*, 254; Wilbarger, *Indian Depredations*, 362; Dudley G. Wooten, *A Comprehensive History of Texas, 1685 to 1897* (Dallas: William G. Scharff, 1898), 1: 750–51. It should be noted that early historian John Henry Brown wrote the original account of the Morgan Massacre and Bryant's Defeat, upon which most all other accounts are based. Brown originally published his account in an early issue of the *Farmer's Almanac*.

9. Account of Isaac Marlin as related to Reverend A. B. Lawrence in 1840. Excerpts of this text are found in McLean, *Papers*, 16: 68–70. See also DeShields, *Border Wars*, 254.

10. Wilbarger, *Indian Depredations*, 362–63.

11. DeShields, *Border Wars*, 255.

12. Looscan, "Captain Joseph Daniels," 22.

13. Gulick, *Lamar Papers*, 4: Daniels to Lamar, # 2162, 30.

14. Looscan, "Captain Joseph Daniels," 23-24.

15. Gulick, *Lamar Papers*, 4: Daniels to Lamar, # 2162, 30.

16. DeShields, *Border Wars*, 255–56 is the principal source of this account unless otherwise noted.

17. DeShields, 256; Gulick, *Lamar Papers*, 4: Daniels to Lamar, # 2162, 30.

18. DeShields, *Border Wars*, 256–57.

19. Gulick, *Lamar Papers*, 4: Daniels to Lamar, # 2162, 30.

20. DeShields, *Border Wars*, 257–58. Mary Foster Hutchinson, *Texian Odyssey. The Life and Times of a Forgotten Patriot of the Republic of Texas: Colonel Eleazar Louis Ripley Wheelock, 1793-1847* (Austin, Tex.: Sunbelt Eakin, 2003).

21. Bill Groneman, *Battlefields of Texas* (Plano: Republic of Texas Press, 1998), 83. "José María." The New Handbook of Texas Online, accessed 6/5/05 (http://www.tsha.utexas.edu/handbook/online/articles/JJ/fjo74.html).

22. Gulick, *Lamar Papers*, 2: Ethan Melton Circular Letter, # 1016, 420.

23. Ibid, 4: Daniels to Lamar, # 2162, 30.

24. Albert G. Gholson AC, R 33, F 295; Looscan, "Captain Joseph Daniels," 25.

25. Looscan, "Captain Joseph Daniels," 25.

Chapter 7
Moore's Comanche Raid and the Battle of Brushy Creek

1. Wylie, "The Fort Houston Settlement," 133–34.

2. Ibid, 49.

3. Brown, *Indian Wars*, 57–58.

4. McDonald letter previously cited.

5. Brown, *Indian Wars*, 58.

6. Nance, *After San Jacinto*, 41.

7. George W. Wilson AC, R 116, F 545.

8. Capt. J. E. Box letter of January 29, 1839. Army Papers, Quartermaster Correspondence, Box 1217-4, Texas State Library and Archives Commission.

9. *Journals of the Fourth Congress*, 3: 102–3. Also reproduced in Winfrey, *Texas Indian Papers*, 1: 55–56.

10. Nance, *After San Jacinto*, 89.

11. Pierce, *Army*, 154–57.

12. Karen R. Thompson, ed., *Defenders of the Republic of Texas* (Austin, Tex.: Laurel House Press by the Daughters of the Republic of Texas, 1989), 15–16.

13. Gulick, *Lamar Papers*, 4: Stout to Lamar, # 2465, 274–75; Pierce, *Texas Under Arms*, 158.

14. Mark R. Roberts to A. S. Johnston on May 28, 1839. *Texas Indian Papers*, 59-61.

15. Gulick, *Lamar Papers*, 4: Stout to Lamar, # 2465, 275–76.

16. Sowell, *Rangers*, 53.

17. William M.Eastland AC, R 28, F251.

18. Brown, *Indian Wars*, 74–75. Brown's research consistently proves itself to be accurate and is considered to be the most reliable for the figure of Moore's troops. Chief Castro's muster roll, for example, shows that Brown is exactly right in stating that forty-two Lipans accompanied the expedition. Brown states that fifty-five Anglos comprised the companies of captains Smithwick and Eastland. A. J. Sowell, on the other hand, says that sixty-five Anglos were on this expedition in *Rangers and Pioneers of Texas*, 54.

19. Smithwick, *The Evolution of a State*, 154–55.

20. John Holland Jenkins, *Recollections of Early Texas. The Memoirs of John Holland Jenkins.* Edited by John Holmes Jenkins III. (1958; repr., Austin: University of Texas Press, 1995), 183–84. Hereafter cited as Jenkins, *Recollections*.

21. Smithwick, *The Evolution of a State*, 155; Jenkins, *Recollections*, 184.

22. “Biography of Cicero Rufus Perry, 1822–1898. Captain, Texas Rangers.” Special collections of Daughters of the Republic of Texas Library, San Antonio, Tex. See page 6.

23. Smithwick, *The Evolution of a State*, 155.

24. Ibid; Jenkins, *Recollections*, 184.

25. “Capt. J. H. Moore’s report of a battle with the Comanches, on the 15th of February, 1839. La Grange, March 10th, 1839.” *Journals of the Fourth Congress*, 3: 108–109. Hereafter cited as Moore Report.

26. Smithwick, *The Evolution of a State*, 156.

27. Brown, *Indian Wars*, 75.

28. Moore Report, 109.

29. Jenkins, *Recollections*, 186.

30. Brown, *Indian Wars*, 75; Smithwick, *The Evolution of a State*, 157.

31. Wilbarger, *Indian Depredations*, 145.

32. Smithwick, *Evolution of a State*, 156.

33. Jenkins, *Recollections*, 186.

34. Moore Report, 109.

35. Smithwick, *Evolution of a State*, 157; and Brown, *Indian Wars*, 75.

36. Noah Smithwick AC, R 98, F 467–69.

37. Moore Report, 110.

38. “Biography of Cicero Rufus Perry, 1822–1898,” 5–6.

39. Smithwick, *Evolution of a State*, 157.

40. William M. Eastland AC, R 28, F 251.

41. Moore, *Taming Texas*, 165–66; Gulick, *Papers*, 2: 464–65. Original letter is housed in the Texas State Archives.

42. John H. Jenkins and Kenneth Kesselus, *Edward Burleson: Texas Frontier Leader* (Austin, Tex: Jenkins Publishing Co., 1990), 181. See also Colonel Burleson’s report of an “engagement with a party of Northern Indians, near Bastrop.” This report, dated March 2, 1839, from Bastrop County, is contained in *Journals of the Fourth Congress*, 3:112–13. Hereafter cited as Burleson’s “Engagement” Report. David F. Crosby, “Texas Rangers in the Battle of Brushy Creek,” *Wild West* 10, no. 2 (August 1997): 63.

43. Brown, *Indian Wars*, 61.

44. Burleson’s “Engagement” Report and Brown, 61, are the key sources for the Coleman depredation.

45. Jenkins, *Recollections*, 56–57. See also Sowell, *Rangers*, 55–56, who states that this volunteer force included sixteen men.

46. Brown, *Indian Wars*, 61.

47. Jenkins, *Recollections*, 71.

48. Brown, *Indian Wars*, 61; Wilbarger, *Indian Depredations*, 148.

49. Wilbarger, *Indian Depredations*, 148.

50. Jenkins, *Recollections*, 58. The main account of Burleson trying to save Winslow Turner is from editor John Holmes Jenkins III’s notes to his great-great grandfather John Holland Jenkins’ original recollections. Jenkins in his editorial names “Samuel Highsmith” as the participant who narrowly avoided being killed when Captain Burleson was shot in the head. A. J. Sowell, however, in his *Early Settlers and Indian Fighters of Southwest Texas* (aka *Texas Indian Fighters*, State

House Press, 1986 reprint, 1–17) names Benjamin Franklin Highsmith as the man actually present. The other key chroniclers of this period, J. W. Wilbarger, John Henry Brown, and James DeShields, do not mention either Highsmith by name. For his account of Brushy Creek, Sowell interviewed Ben Highsmith in 1897 at the latter's home in Bandera County, Texas.

51. Sowell, *Rangers*, 56–57.

52. Wilbarger, *Indian Depredations*, 149.

53. Burleson's "Engagement" Report, 112.

54. Wilbarger, *Indian Depredations*, 149–50.

55. Account of Ben Highsmith as related to A. J. Sowell in *Texas Indian Fighters*, 17.

56. Jenkins, *Recollections*, 248, 268–69.

57. Wilbarger, *Indian Depredations*, 150.

58. Groneman, *Battlefields of Texas*, 86.

59. Jenkins, *Recollections*, 59–60, xvii–xviii.

60. Ibid, 60 and 246.

61. Burleson's "Engagement" Report, 113.

62. Sowell, *Rangers*, 57.

CHAPTER 8
THE CÓRDOVA AND FLORES FIGHTS

1. Brown, *Indian Wars*, 73–74; DeShields, *Border Wars*, 264; *Handbook of Texas*, 2: 106–107. John Henry Brown heard his account of the Indian battle firsthand from Henry McCullough on August 19, 1887, in Dallas.

2. Jenkins, *Burleson*, 186.

3. Nance, *After San Jacinto*, 90–91.

4. William H. Weaver PD, R 195, F71.

5. *Handbook of Texas*, Vol. 1: 163.

6. Gammell, *Laws of Texas*, 2: 78.

7. Gulick, *Lamar Papers*, 4: Erath to Lamar, "Sketches on Milam and Robertson County," # 2164, 32–33.

8. Pierce, *Texas Under Arms*, 62.

9. Nance, *After San Jacinto*, 123.

10. McLean, *Papers*, 16: 209–11.

11. Nance, *After San Jacinto*, 123–26.

12. Jenkins, *Recollections*, 84–85.

13. Nance, *After San Jacinto*, 126–27.

14. Catherine W. McDowell, ed., *Now You Hear My Horn. The Journal of James Wilson Nichols, 1820–1887* (Austin: University of Texas Press, 1961), 35.

15. Groneman, *Battlefields of Texas*, 88.

16. The two principal accounts of this episode are Jim Nichols' in McDowell, *Now You Hear My Horn*, 32–34, and Sowell, *Rangers and Pioneers of Texas*, 185–89. A. J. Sowell occasionally confused dates in his early writings. He believed his uncle was serving under Captain James H. Callahan at the time of the Mill Creek battle and that he later served under Captain Caldwell. Sowell actually served as a private in Caldwell's rangers from March 16–June 16, 1839, and served under Captain Callahan in 1840.

In *Early Settlers and Indian Fighters of Southwest Texas* (417–18), published in 1900, sixteen years after his *Rangers and Pioneers of Texas*, Sowell correctly wrote that Captain Caldwell commanded Seguin's rangers in March 1839.

Interestingly, Jim Nichols also wrote that he was a member of Captain Callahan's minutemen at the time of the Mill Creek battle. He is also shown on Captain Caldwell's muster roll for this period. The versions of Nichols and Sowell differ slightly. It should be noted, however, that Sowell wrote from what he heard from uncles John and Andrew Sowell. Nichols wrote from his personal experiences.

18. Brown, *Indian Wars*, 64; see also Nance, *After San Jacinto*, 128–29.

19. McDowell, *Now You Hear My Horn*, 34–35. Jim Nichols only mentions four rangers present for this attack, but Sowell wrote that D. M. Poor was also present in *Rangers*, 189.

20. D. N. Poore PD, R 176, 604.

21. McDowell, *Now You Hear My Horn*, 35; Sowell, *Texas Indian Fighters*, 417–25.

22. Nance, *After San Jacinto,* 127–29; Brown, *Indian Wars*, 64; Sowell, *Rangers*, 189-90.

23. McDowell, *Now You Hear My Horn*, 35–36.

24. Ibid, 36–37.

25. Sowell, *Rangers*, 188.

26. Ibid, 190.

27. Brown, *Indian Wars*, 64–66.

28. Nance, *After San Jacinto,* 129.

29. Army Correspondence, Quartermaster's File, Texas State Archives. See also Pierce, *Texas Under Arms*, 167.

30. Captain Samuel Jordan letter of April 22, 1839. Army Correspondence, Quartermaster's File, Texas State Archives.

31. Pierce, *Texas Under Arms*, 4.

32. Gulick, *Lamar Papers*, 2: Jones to Lamar, # 1198, 529-31.

33. Pierce, *Texas Under Arms*, 5.

34. Brown, *Indian Wars*, 65; Nance, *After San Jacinto,* 131-32.

35. Miles Squier Bennett diary entries and "Experiences on the Western Frontier, Republic of Texas, 1838–1842" sketch from Valentine Bennett Scrapbook, The Center for American History, University of Texas at Austin.

36. Burleson Report "of a fight with the Mexicans and Indians, in May, 1839, on the St. Gabriel." Written to Secretary of War Johnston on May 22, 1839, from Austin. Contained in *Journals of the Fourth Congress*, III: 113–14.

37. Wilbarger, *Indian Depredations*, 158–63. Nance in *After San Jacinto,* 132–34, agrees with Wilbarger's version of the Córdova and Flores fights. For additional detail, Burleson's May 22 report was used in recounting these battles.

38. Special thanks to historian Jack Jackson for sending me this point, which he has done considerable research on.

39. Groneman, *Battlefields of Texas*, 90.

40. Nance, *After San Jacinto,* 137–39; Wilbarger, *Indian Depredations*, 165.

41. Richardson, T. C. *East Texas*, 1: 116.

Chapter 9
Bird's Creek Fight

1. Everett, *The Texas Cherokees*, 51.

2. *Journals of the Fourth Congress of the Republic of Texas*, 3: 77.

3. Pierce, *Texas Under Arms*, 125; Journals, 77–78.

4. Franklin Madis, *The Taking of Texas. A Documentary History* (Austin, Tex: Eakin Press, 2002), 97–99.

5. Aldrich, *The History of Houston County, Texas*, 201. Quartermaster's orders of May 21 and May 22, 1839. Letters courtesy of the Archives Division of the General Land Office of Texas.

6. Everett, *The Texas Cherokees*, 102–103; Clark, *Thomas J. Rusk*, 124.

7. Woldert, "The Last of the Cherokees," 197-98.

8. McLean, *Papers*, 16: 248–52; Gulick, *Lamar Papers*, 2: 590–94. See also Dorman Winfrey and James M. Day, *The Texas Indian Papers, 1825-1843* (Austin, Tex: Austin Printing Co., 1911), 2: 61-66.

9. John H. Reagan, "Expulsion of the Cherokees from East Texas," *Quarterly of the Texas State Historical Association* 1 (1897): 40. Hereafter cited as Reagan, "Expulsion."

10. John H. Reagan, *The Memoirs of John H. Reagan*. Edited by John F. Jenkins (Austin, Tex: The Pemberton Press, 1968), 30. Hereafter cited as Reagan, *Memoirs*.

11. Brown, *Indian Wars*, 70.

12. McLean, *Papers*, 16: 225–27.

13. Jenkins, *Recollections*, 179.

14. Brown, *Indian Wars*, 70.

15. Report of Nathan Brookshire from Camp Nashville, May 31, 1839. The latter is contained in *Journals of the Fourth Congress of the Republic of Texas*, 3: 110–11. Hereafter cited as Brookshire report. Brookshire's report, John Henry Brown, *Indian Wars*, 70–72, and DeShields, *Border Wars*, 260, serve as the principal sources for the Bird's Creek Battle unless otherwise noted.

16. Quartermaster's records, May 20, 1839. Courtesy of the Archives Division of the General Land Office of Texas.

17. Brown, *Indian Wars*, 71.

18. William H. Weaver PD, R 195, F 70.

19. *Handbook of Texas*, 1: 222; Brown, *Indian Wars*, 71–72.

20. DeShields, *Border Wars*, 262; Brown, *Indian Wars*, 72.

21. Brookshire report, *Journals*, 111.

22. George W. Tyler, *The History of Bell County* (San Antonio, Tex: The Naylor Company, 1936), 62–64.

23. Wilbarger, *Indian Depredations,* 370.

24. DeShields, *Border Wars*, 262–263.

25. Army Papers, Quartermaster Correspondence 1835–1841, Box 1217-8, Texas State Archives.

26. Quartermaster's records, May 29, 1839. Courtesy of the Archives Division of the General Land Office of Texas.

27. Brown, *Indian Wars*, 72.

28. McLean, *Papers*, 16: 85.

29. C. W. Webber, *Tales of the Southern Border* (Philadelphia: J. B. Lippincott

& Co., 1856), 54–55. See also Greer, *Texas Ranger: Jack Hays in the Frontier Southwest*, 34–35.

30. Miles Squier Bennett diary entry from Valentine Bennett Scrapbook, The Center for American History, University of Texas at Austin. See also Bennett's "Reminiscences of Western Texas."

31. John James PD, R 164, F 349–62.

32. Ibid, F 354–60. See also Jesus F. de la Teja, ed., *A Revolution Remembered: The Memoirs and Selected Correspondence of Juan N. Seguin* (Austin, Tex: State House Press, 1991), 184–86.

33. Miles Squier Bennett is the key source for the June 1839 Henry Karnes campaign, unless otherwise noted. His recollections are contained in the Valentine Bennett Scrapbook, The Center for American History, University of Texas at Austin. This scrapbook includes several compilations or articles that were later published in the *Cuero Star* and *Houston Post*. Among them are "Reminiscences of Western Texas" and "Experiences on the Western Frontier, Republic of Texas, 1838–1842."

34. Greer, *Texas Ranger*, 35. Rena Maverick Green, (ed.), *Memoirs of Mary A. Maverick* (1921; repr., Lincoln: University of Nebraska Press, 1989), 23–24.

35. Miles Squier Bennett diary and compilations cited above.

36. Jenkins, *Recollections*, 90–92, 241, 268.

37. John Harvey Biography from Louis Wiltz Kemp Papers, San Jacinto Museum of History, Houston, Texas.

Chapter 10

The Cherokee War

1. Reagan, *Memoirs*, 31-32.

2. Woldert, "The Last of the Cherokees in Texas," 209–12.

3. Peterson Lloyd AC, R 61, F 515.

4. Jenkins, *Burleson*, 198–99.

5. Pierce, *Texas Under Arms*, 23.

6. Clarke, *Thomas J. Rusk*, 127.

7. Ben H. Procter, *The Life of John H. Reagan* (Austin, Tex: The University of Texas Press, 1962), 22–23.

8. William Hart to J. H. Starr, July 11, 1839. James Harper Starr Papers. Courtesy of The Center for American History, The University of Texas at Austin.

9. Everett, *The Texas Cherokees*, 104–5.

10. Johnston to Lamar, *Journals of the Fourth Congress*, 3: 78.

11. Everett, *The Texas Cherokees*, 105.

12. G. G. Alford to J. H. Starr, July 10, 1839. Starr Papers. Courtesy of The Center for American History, The University of Texas at Austin.

13. William Hart to J. H. Starr, July 11, 1839. Starr Papers. Courtesy of The Center for American History, The University of Texas at Austin.

14. Charles S. Taylor to J. H. Starr, July 11, 1839. Starr Papers. Courtesy of The Center for American History, The University of Texas at Austin.

15. Everett, *The Texas Cherokees*, 105.

16. Clarke, *Thomas J. Rusk*, 129–30; Everett, *The Texas Cherokees*, 105.

17. Hart to Starr, July 24, 1839. Starr Papers. Courtesy of The Center for American History, The University of Texas at Austin.

18. Clarke, *Thomas J. Rusk*, 129–30; Everett, *The Texas Cherokees*, 105–6.

19. Jenkins, *Burleson*, 200.

20. K. H. Douglass, July 15, 1839. K. H. Douglass Papers in Starr Papers. Courtesy of The Center for American History, The University of Texas at Austin.

21. *History of Houston County*, 618; Clarke, *Thomas J. Rusk*, 131.

22. Hart to Starr, July 24, 1839. Starr Papers. Courtesy of The Center for American History, The University of Texas at Austin.

23. DeShields, *Border Wars*, 300; Ford, *Rip Ford's Texas*, 29.

24. Reagan, "Expulsion," 43.

25. Reagan, *Memoirs*, 33.

26. "Report of K. H. Douglass of the Campaign Against the Cherokees," August 1839. Provided by Donaly E. Brice, Supervisor of Reference Services with the Texas State Library and Archives Commission. Hereafter referred to as Douglass Cherokee Campaign Report. See also Winfrey, *The Texas Indian Papers, 1825–1843,* 1: 76–77.

27. Hart to Starr, July 11, 1839. Starr Papers. Courtesy of The Center for American History, The University of Texas at Austin.

28. Woldert, "The Last of the Cherokees in Texas." Article and supplement notes of Woldert courtesy of Texas State Archives.

29. K. H. Douglass to A. S. Johnston, 16 July 1839. This rough draft of the July 15 action was written by James S. Mayfield from Camp Carter. See Gulick, *Lamar Papers*, 3:45–46.

30. Procter, *The Life of John H. Reagan*, 24–25.

31. Hart to Starr, July 24, 1839. Starr Papers. Courtesy of The Center for American History, The University of Texas at Austin.

32. Procter, *The Life of John H. Reagan*, 24–25.

33. The companies which were truly "Texas Rangers" during the Cherokee War have been and will likely continue to be debated. The companies of captains Mark Lewis and James Ownby were raised by Karnes, Woodlief, and Major William Jones. The Third Congress referred to this battalion as "Companies of Mounted Volunteers" on December 29, 1838. They were to be paid according to "Mounted Riflemen in the Ranging Service." General Edwin Morehouse to Major Jones on January 21, 1839, "for the Corps of Rangers in which you have the honor of holding a command." See Adjutant General's Papers, Texas State Archives.

Colonel Karnes raised a third "mounted gunman" company which saw service during the Cherokee War fights, that of Captain Greenberry Harrison. From the Third Militia Brigade's Nacogdoches Regiment, Captain Alexander Jordan names his company "Mounted Rangers" on his muster roll. Similarly, Captain Lewis Sanchez commanded "Mounted Gunmen" per his muster roll. These companies were organized prior to the volunteer companies that moved out from Nacogdoches.

Captains James Box, Henry Madison Smith, and Solomon Adams also commanded rangers during the Cherokee War. Their companies had all been in service for months prior to the July battles. Each of these three can be clearly tracked in republic-era documents as being classified rangers. There will be arguments that other companies participating in the Cherokee War should be dubbed "Texas Rangers." All others, however, were attached to the Frontier Regiment or were volunteer militia units called up specifically to serve during the immediate crisis.

Of the companies participating in the Cherokee War, there is mention of one other unit which I have been unable to determine. Samuel M. Dalton of the Red

River area noted that he and other men under a "Captain Ward" joined forces with an existing company. "I found a little squad or part of a company under Capt. Ward of Clarksville, Red River Co., and arrived in the Cherokee country, and attached ourselves to a company just in time to see the fight." See McLean, *Papers*, 15: 489.

P. F. Rodden to David Rodden, October 26, 1839. See Madis, *The Taking of Texas*, 98.

34. Reagan, *Memoirs*, 34.

35. Sowell, *Texas Indian Fighters*, 292; Woldert, "The Last of the Cherokees in Texas," 217–18.

36. Hart to Starr, July 24, 1839. Starr Papers. Courtesy of The Center for American History, The University of Texas at Austin. See also Spellman, *Forgotten Texas Leader*, 39, 153.

37. Jenkins, *Burleson*, 202.

38. Hart to Starr, July 24, 1839. Starr Papers. Courtesy of The Center for American History, The University of Texas at Austin.

39. Pierce, *Texas Under Arms*, 89–90 and 205–206.

40. Douglass Cherokee Campaign Report.

41. Brown, *Indian Wars*, 67–68.

42. Hart to Starr, July 24, 1839. Starr Papers. Courtesy of The Center for American History, The University of Texas at Austin.

43. Reagan, *Memoirs*, 33.

44. Procter, *The Life of John H. Reagan*, 26.

45. Douglass Cherokee Campaign Report.

46. Hart to Starr, July 24, 1839. Starr Papers. Courtesy of The Center for American History, The University of Texas at Austin. Also referenced was "July 26, 2005," a Battle of the Neches ceremony and historical facts paper supplied by Eagle Douglas to author on June 11, 2005. Eagle also lists several Caddo of the Neches, Tahocullake, and Mataquo Indians to have been present.

47. Burleson letter published in *Telegraph and Texas Register*, October 23, 1839.

48. McLean, *Papers*, 16: 334–35.

49. Jenkins, *Burleson*, 203–204.

50. Hart to Starr, July 24, 1839. Starr Papers. Courtesy of The Center for American History, The University of Texas at Austin.

51. Willis Bruce biography in McLean, *Papers*, 12: 432.

52. Procter, *The Life of John H. Reagan*, 26.

53. Reagan, *Memoirs*, 33–34. P. F. Rodden to David Rodden, October 26, 1839. See Madis, *The Taking of Texas*, 98.

54. Hart to Starr, July 24, 1839. Starr Papers. Courtesy of The Center for American History, The University of Texas at Austin.

55. Burleson letter published in *Telegraph and Texas Register*, October 23, 1839.

56. Douglass Cherokee Campaign Report.

57. Hart to Starr, July 24, 1839. Starr Papers. Courtesy of The Center for American History, The University of Texas at Austin.

58. Brown, *Indian Wars*, 68.

59. Reagan, *Memoirs*, 34.

60. Clarke, *Rusk*, 133; Brown, *Indian Wars*, 68; Reagan, "Expulsion," 45.

61. Ernest Jones, "Captain W. T. Sadler Helped Create County," *Palestine Herald-Press*, February 5, 1969, 10. See also Moore, *Taming Texas*, 191–92.

62. Winfrey, "Chief Bowles and the Texas Cherokee," 32n.; Mary Whatley Clarke, *Chief Bowles and the Texas Cherokees* (Civilization of the American Indian Series, No. 113; Norman: University of Oklahoma Press, 1971), 109; Brown, *Indian Wars*, 68.

63. Reagan, *Memoirs*, 46.

64. Hart to Starr, July 24, 1839. Starr Papers. Courtesy of The Center for American History, The University of Texas at Austin.

65. Burleson letter published in *Telegraph and Texas Register*, October 23, 1839.

66. Everett, *The Texas Cherokees*, 108.

67. Hart to Starr, July 24, 1839. Starr Papers. Courtesy of The Center for American History, The University of Texas at Austin.

68. Burleson letter published in *Telegraph and Texas Register*, October 23, 1839.

69. Carolyn Reeves Ericson, *Nacogdoches—Gateway to Texas. A Biographical Directory, Vol. I* (Nacogdoches, Tex: Ericson Books, 1977), 45–46.

70. Spellman, *Forgotten Texas Leader*, 39–42.

71. Clarke, *Thomas J. Rusk*, 134.

72. Hart to Starr, July 24, 1839. Starr Papers. Courtesy of The Center for American History, The University of Texas at Austin.

73. Clarke, *Chief Bowles and the Texas Cherokees*, 111.

74. Woldert, "The Last of the Cherokees in Texas," 223–24.

Chapter 11
Pursuit And Removal

1. Clarke, *Chief Bowles and the Texas Cherokees*, 110.

2. *Republic of Texas Pension Application Abstracts*. Published by the Austin Genealogical Society (Austin, Tex: Morgan Printing and Publishing, 1987), 49.

3. Ford, *Rip Ford's Texas*, 30.

4. Hart to Starr, July 24, 1839. Starr Papers. Courtesy of The Center for American History, The University of Texas at Austin. Upon returning to Nacogdoches, Hart found that several of the sick and wounded men had already arrived there. David Rusk was "home and doing well" from his leg wound. David Kaufman, wounded in the cheek, was also at home. Judge Charles Taylor had returned sick with "a return of fever." Major James Reily had also returned home and was guarding "twenty-five thousand dollars in silver" which was apparently to be used to pay the troops in the field for the Cherokee War.

5. Douglass Cherokee Campaign Report.

6. Clarke, *Thomas J. Rusk*, 135–36.

7. Douglass Cherokee Campaign Report.

8. Gulick, *Lamar Papers*, 4: William B. Stout to Lamar, 275.

9. Walter Paye Lane, *The Adventures and Recollections of General Walter P. Lane* (Austin, Tex: Pemberton Press, 1970), 41.

10. Army Correspondence, Quartermaster Papers, Box 1217-8. Texas State Library and Archives Commission.

11. Douglass Cherokee Campaign Report.

12. Ladd, *Gone to Texas*, 145.

13. Everett, 108–9.

14. Johnston to Lamar, *Journals of the Fourth Congress*, 3: 79; also 108–9.

15. Peterson Lloyd AC, R 61, F 515.
16. Pierce, *Texas Under Arms*, 136.
17. *Journals of the Fourth Congress*, 3: 88–89.
18. Ladd, *Gone to Texas*, 146–47.
19. Roland, *Albert Sidney Johnston*, 96.
20. Army Correspondence, Box 1214-35. Texas State Library and Archives Commission.
21. Pierce, *Texas Under Arms*, 102–105.
22. Spellman, *Forgotten Texas Leader*, 42.
23. Gulick, *Lamar Papers*, 3: # 1425, 84–86.
24. Jenkins, *Recollections*, 80–82.
25. McLean, *Papers*, 16: 356–61. Reprinted from *Frontier Times*, Bandera, Tex., June 1937, 373–76.
26. Jenkins, *Recollections*, 81.
27. Ladd, *Gone to Texas*, 153; Jenkins, *Recollections*, 82; Washington Perry Reese biographical sketch, Kemp Papers, San Jacinto Museum of History, Houston, Texas.
28. McLean, *Papers*, 16: 346–68.
29. Jenkins, *Recollections*, 81–82.
30. Pierce, *Texas Under Arms*, 76.
31. Benjamin Roberts AC, R 88, F 375.
32. *Journals of the Fourth Congress*, 3: 18.
33. Pierce, *Texas Under Arms*, 25.
34. Nance, *After San Jacinto*, 140–41.
35. Pierce, *Texas Under Arms*, 137.
36. Spellman, *Forgotten Texas Leader*, 43–45.
37. "Report of the Commissioners appointed to make a treaty with the Shawnee Indians." Nacogdoches, October 2, 1839. Contained in *Journals of the Fourth Congress, Republic of Texas*, 3: 114–15.
38. *Journals of the Fourth Congress*, 3: 88–91.

Chapter 12
Colonel Neill's Gunmen on the Offensive

1. McLean, *Papers*, 16: 334–35.
2. Pierce, *Texas Under Arms*, 175.
3. Thompson, *Defenders of the Republic of Texas*, 71–75, 95–98, 158–62.
4. Pierce, *Texas Under Arms*, 25–26, 81–83.
5. Thompson, *Defenders of the Republic of Texas*, 129–30.
6. Captain Howard's report of "Engagement with Indians on the 24th. Oct., 1839" from *Appendix to the Journals of the House of Representatives: Fifth Congress* (Printed at the Gazette Office, Austin: 1841) 125–26.
7. McLean, *Papers*, 16: 300.
8. Ibid, VIII: 347-49.
9. Doris Daniel Powell, *The Genealogy of Hugh Alva Menefee Jr.* (Cleburne, Tex: Privately published, 1972), 49. "According to tradition in the family," Laban Menefee was wounded during the Battle of Bird's Creek in 1839. He *was* in service in this area as a ranger, but was actually among the men who remained at Fort Milam

during the fight. Laban's nephew Thomas S. Menefee *did* participate in Bird's fight. Due to the fact that there are very few records of Colonel Neill's campaign, the family is understandably unaware of which 1839 Indian engagement Laban was wounded in.

10. Erath to Lamar, "Sketches on Milam and Robertson County," Gulick, *Lamar Papers*, 4: # 2164, 32–33.

11. Yoakum, *History of Texas*, 2: 247.

12. DeShields, *Border Wars*, 248. See also Wilbarger, *Indian Depredations*, 81.

13. *Journals of the Fourth Congress, Republic of Texas*, 3: 82.

14. Col. J. C. Neill to Major H. Landers, Texas State Library and Archive Commission, Army Correspondence, Box 1214-38.

15. McLean, *Papers*, 16: 412.

Chapter 13
Karnes' Hill Country Comanche Expedition

1. J. W. Benedict, "Diary of a Campaign Against the Comanches," *Southwestern Historical Quarterly* 32 (April 1929): 300–10. Hereafter cited as Benedict, "Diary."

2. Pierce, *Texas Under Arms*, 137–38.

3. John James PD, R 164, F 355–57.

4. Benedict, "Diary," 301–309.

5. Pierce, *Texas Under Arms*, 138.

6. Hays to Lamar, Gulick, *Lamar Papers*, 4: 231.

7. Greer, *Texas Ranger*, 36; see also Hays to Lamar, Gulick, *Lamar Papers*, 4: 231–32.

8. Benedict, "Diary," 309.

9. Ladd, *Gone to Texas*, 160.

10. McLean, *Papers*, 16: 348.

Chapter 14
"Short But Decisive Affair"

1. Dr. James Hunter letter of January 12, 1840, presented to the University of Texas by Mary Kate Hunter. See Wylie, "The Fort Houston Settlement," 77–78, 119–22.

2. Secretary of War Albert Sidney Johnston to President Lamar, from the War Department, City of Austin, December 12, 1839. From the Army Papers (Correspondence, 1837–1839), Texas State Archives, Texas State Library, Austin.

3. Johnston to Lamar, *Journals of the Fourth Congress*, 3: 75–84.

4. Hockley to Johnston, Gulick, *Lamar Papers*, III: 136–38.

5. Johnston to Lamar, *Journals of the Fourth Congress*, 3: 76.

6. Pierce, *The Army of the Republic of Texas*, 179.

7. Thompson, *Defenders of the Republic of Texas*, 181–187.

8. Johnston to Lamar, December 12, 1839, from Army Papers (Correspondence), Texas State Archives. Johnston's letter does not mention any company commanders by name. He lists four companies under Burleson stationed on the Colorado River above Austin, one company marching toward Austin that was expected hourly, one company stationed at the Falls of the Brazos, and one and a half more companies en

route from Galveston.

9. Army Papers (Quartermaster Records), Texas State Library and Archives Commission. Captain William T. Sadler 1839 payment vouchers, Army Papers.

10. Thompson (ed), *Defenders of the Republic of Texas*, 223–27, 243–47.

11. Roland, *Albert Sidney Johnston*, 96–98.

12. December 18, 1839, *Telegraph and Texas Register;* DeShields, *Border Wars*, 284–285.

13. Details of this campaign are taken primarily from Edward Burleson's "Winter Campaign against the Comanches" report, written on December 26, 1839, from Camp Lynch. See *Appendix to the Journals of the House of Representatives: Fifth Congress*, 126–31.

14. Gerald S. Pierce, "Burleson's Northwestern Campaign," *Texas Military Monthly* 6, no. 3 (Fall 1967): 195.

15. Jenkins, *Burleson*, 216, and Pierce, *Army*, 179.

16. Jenkins, *Burleson*, 218.

17. Burleson's Report from Camp Lynch on December 26, 1839, of "Engagement with the Cherokees," reprinted as Document B in *Appendix to the Journals of the House of Representatives: Fifth Congress*, 126–28.

18. Burleson's "Report of the Destruction of a Shawnee Village, on Pecan Bayou, Dec. 31st, 1839," from *Journals of the Fourth Congress*, Document C, 132.

AFTERWORD

1. Thompson, *Defenders of the Republic of Texas*, 79.

2. For accounts of the Council House Fight, see Spellman, *Forgotten Texas Leader*, 46–50; Webb, *The Texas Rangers*, 55–57; Brice, *The Great Comanche Raid*, 21–26; DeShields, *Border Wars*, 288–93.

3. Brice, *The Great Comanche Raid*, 62–63.

4. Knowles, *They Rode For the Lone Star*, 96–98.

BIBLIOGRAPHY

DOCUMENTS, MANUSCRIPTS AND COLLECTIONS

Aldrich, Armistead Albert. Papers. Center for American History, University of Texas, Austin.

Appendix to the Journals of the House of Representatives: Fifth Congress. Printed at the Gazette Office for the Republic of Texas, Austin, 1841.

Army Papers, Republic of Texas. Archives and Library Division, Texas State Library in Austin, Texas.

Bennett, Miles Squier diary from Valentine Bennett Scrapbook, The Center for American History, University of Texas at Austin. Also includes "Experiences on the Western Frontier, Republic of Texas, 1838–1842," sketch by Miles S. Bennett.

"Biography of Cicero Rufus Perry, 1822–1898. Captain, Texas Rangers." Special collections of Daughters of the Republic of Texas Library, San Antonio, Tex.

Bishop, Eliza H. John Wortham Biographical Sketch.

Edens, Frank N. Unpublished research on Daniel Parker family.

General Land Office of Texas: records and papers collection.

Hunter, Mary Kate. Unpublished Papers of, located in Carnegie Library in Palestine, Texas. Miss Hunter was a school teacher who collected statements in the early 1900s from many of the county's earliest citizens. Some of her collected works are referenced, including, "Statement of Mr. R. R. Sadler - Taken Down by Kate Hunter, June 20, 1923"; "Some Early History of Palestine" by Bonner Frizzell; and Judge A. J. Fowler's "The Edens' Massacre" and "Historic Sketches of Anderson County."

Journals of the Fourth Congress of the Republic of Texas. Austin, Tex: Von Boeckmann-Jones Co. Printers, 1930.

Muster Rolls of the Texas Army and the Texas Militia, courtesy of the Texas State Archives. See individual chapter footnotes and appendices for those referenced.

Nicholson, James. Papers. Center for American History, University of Texas, Austin.

Pierce, Gerald Swetnam. "The Army of the Republic of Texas, 1836–1845." Dissertation from the University of Mississippi, copyright 1964, on file in the Texas Room of the Houston Public Library.

Pierson, Edwin G. Jr. Collection. Mr. Pierson, after reading Volume 1 of *Savage Frontier*, was kind enough to send me a biography of his great-great grandfather, Captain John Goodloe Warren Pierson, and another on the captain's son, John Hogue Pierson. Among other muster rolls provided by Mr. Pierson was that of Captain Pierson's 1836 cavalry company.

"Report of K. H. Douglass of the Campaign Against the Cherokees," August 1839. Courtesy of Donaly E. Brice, Texas State Library and Archives Commission.

Republic Claims Papers, 1835–1846 (microfilmed). Texas State Library and Archives Commission, Austin.

Rusk, Thomas Jefferson. Original Papers of. East Texas Research Center in Stephen F. Austin State University Library, Nacogdoches.

Sadler, Robert H. "Notes Relative to the Edens Massacre." Written on January 1, 1971. "Facts related to Robert H. Sadler by Lula Sadler Davis of Grapeland, Texas, widow of John A. Davis." Courtesy of Howard C. Sadler collection.

Sadler, William Turner. Texas Pension Papers and Audited Military Claims. Provided courtesy of Howard C. Sadler. Also referenced: William Turner Sadler land documents provided by the General Land Office of Texas.

Starr, James Harper. Papers. Center for American History, University of Texas, Austin. Includes papers of Brigadier General Kelsey H. Douglass.

Uniform of the Army of the Republic of Texas. Prescribed and published by order of the President.

Wimberly, Dan B. "Daniel Parker: Pioneer Preacher and Political Leader." History dissertation submitted to the Graduate Faculty of Texas Tech University in May 1995. Courtesy of Dr. Frank N. Edens.

Wylie, Edna McDonald. "The Fort Houston Settlement." A Thesis from August 1958 in the collections of the Houston Public Library's Clayton Genealogy Branch.

BOOKS

Aldrich, Armistead Albert. *History of Houston County, Together with Biograhical Sketches of Many Pioneers*. San Antonio, Tex: The Naylor Co., 1943.

Anderson, Gary Clayton. *The Conquest of Texas. Ethnic Cleansing in the Promised Land, 1820–1875*. Norman: University of Oklahoma Press, 2005.

Avera, Carl. *Centennial Notebook: A Collage of Reminenece of Palestine's First Century*. Palestine: Royall National Bank, 1976.

———. *From Steamboats to Spacecraft: Between the Neches and the Trinity. A History of Anderson County's First 125 Years*. Palestine, Tex: Express Books, an Imprint of the Word Factory, ca. 1970s.

Awbrey, Betty Dooley and Claude Dooley. *Why Stop? A Guide to Texas Historical Roadside Markers*. 4th ed. Houston, Tex: Lone Star Books, 1999.

Barker, Eugene C. *The Life of Stephen F. Austin: Founder of Texas, 1793–1836*. Austin: University of Texas Press, 1985.

Bate, W. N. *General Sidney Sherman: Texas Soldier, Statesman and Builder.* Waco, Tex: Texian Press, 1974.

Battles of Texas. Waco, Tex: Texian Press, 1987.

Binkley, William C. *Official Correspondence of the Texas Revolution*. New York: Appleton-Century, 1936.

Biographical Directory of the Texan Conventions and Congresses, 1832–1845. Austin, Tex: Book Exchange, 1941.

Biographical Gazetteer of Texas. Austin, Tex: W. M. Morrison Books, 1987.

Brice, Donaly E. *The Great Comanche Raid: Boldest Indian Attack of the Texas Republic.* Austin, Tex: Eakin Press, 1987.

Brown, Gary. *The New Orleans Greys: Volunteers in the Texas Revolution.* Plano, Tex: Republic of Texas Press, 1999.

Brown, John Henry. *Indian Wars and Pioneers of Texas.* 1880. Reprint, Austin, Tex: State House Press, 1988.

Carter, W. A. *History of Fannin County, Texas.* Originally published in Bonham, Texas, by the *Bonham News*, 1885. Reprint, Honey Grove, Tex: Fannin County Historical Society, 1975.

Chariton, Wallace O. *Exploring the Alamo Legends.* Plano, Tex: Republic of Texas Press, 1992.

Cherokee County History. Crockett, Tex: Published by the Cherokee County Historical Commission and the Publications Development Co. of Texas, 1986.

Clark, Sara. *The Capitols of Texas: A Visual History.* Austin, Tex: Encino Press, 1975.

Clarke, Mary Whatley. *Chief Bowles and the Texas Cherokees.* Civilization of the American Indian Series, No. 113. Norman, Okla.: University of Oklahoma Press, 1971.

———.*Thomas J. Rusk: Soldier, Statesman, Jurist.* Austin, Tex: Jenkins Publishing Company, 1971.

Connor, Seymour V., et al. *Capitols of Texas.* Waco, Tex: Texian Press, 1970.

Cox, Mike. *Texas Ranger Tales II.* Plano, Tex: Republic of Texas Press, 1999.

Day, James M. *Post Office Papers of the Republic of Texas, 1836–1839.* Austin, Tex: Texas State Library, 1966.

———compiler. *The Texas Alamanac 1857–1873. A Compendium of Texas History.* Waco, Tex: Texian Press, 1967.

De Bruhl, Marshall. *Sword of San Jacinto: A Life of Sam Houston.* New York: Random House, 1993.

DeShields, James T. *Border Wars of Texas.* 1912. Reprint, Austin, Tex: State House Press, 1993.

———. *Tall Men with Long Rifles.* San Antonio, Tex: Naylor Company, 1935.

Dixon, Sam Houston and Louis Wiltz Kemp. *The Heroes of San Jacinto.* Houston, Tex: The Anson Jones Press, 1932.

The Edens Adventure: A Brief History of the Edens Family in America. Published by the Edens Family Association, 1992.

Erath, George Bernard as dictated to Lucy A. Erath. *The Memoirs of Major George B. Erath, 1813–1891.* Austin, Tex: Texas State Historical Society, 1923. Reprinted by The Heritage Society of Waco in 1956.

Ericson, Carolyn Reeves. *Nacogdoches—Gateway to Texas. A Biographical Directory, Vol. I.* Nacogdoches, Tex: Ericson Books, 1977.

Everett, Dianna. *The Texas Cherokees: A People Between Two Fires, 1819–1840.* Norman: University of Oklahoma Press, 1990.

Fehrenbach, T. R. *Lone Star: A History of Texas and the Texans.* Reprint, New York: American Legacy Press, 1983.

Ford, John Salmon, edited by Stephen B. Oates. *Rip Ford's Texas*. Austin: University of Texas Press, 1994.

Gambrell, Herbert. *Anson Jones: The Last President of Texas*. 1947. Reprint, Austin: University of Texas Press, 1988.

Gammell, (Karl) Hans Peter Marius Nielsen. *The Laws of Texas, 1822 - 1897*. 10 vols. Austin, Tex: The Gammel Book Company, 1898.

Gonzales County History. Published by Gonzales County Historical Commission and Curtis Media Corp., 1986.

Green, Rena Maverick, editor. *Memoirs of Mary A. Maverick*. 1921. Reprint, Lincoln: University of Nebraska Press, 1989.

Greenwood, Hulen M. *Garrison Greenwood: Ancestors and Descendants*. Privately published by author in Houston, Tex: 1986.

Greer, James Kimmins. *Texas Ranger: Jack Hays in the Frontier Southwest*. College Station: Texas A&M University Press, 1993. This book was originally published by E.P. Dutton and Company, Inc. as *Colonel Jack Hays: Texas Frontier Leader and California Builder* in 1952.

Groneman, Bill. *Alamo Defenders. A Genealogy: The People and Their Words*. Austin, Tex.: Eakin Press, 1990.

———. *Battlefields of Texas*. Plano: Republic of Texas Press, 1998.

Gulick, Charles A. Jr., Winnie Allen, Katherine Elliott, and Harriet Smither. *The Papers of Mirabeau Buonaparte Lamar*. 6 vols. 1922. Reprint, Austin, Tex: Pemberton Press, 1968.

History of Houston County: 1687–1979. Compiled and edited by the History Book Committee of Houston County Historical Commission of Crockett, Texas. Tulsa, Okla.: Heritage Publishing Company, 1979.

Hohes, Pauline Buck. *A Centennial History of Anderson County, Texas*. San Antonio, Tex: Naylor, 1936.

Huston, Cleburne. *Deaf Smith: Incredible Texas Spy*. Waco, Tex: Texian Press, 1973.

———. *Towering Texan: A Biography of Thomas J. Rusk*. Waco, Tex: Texian Press, 1971.

Hutchinson, Mary Foster. *Texian Odyssey. The Life and Times of a Forgotten Patriot of the Republic of Texas: Colonel Eleazar Louis Ripley Wheelock (1793–1847)*. Austin, Tex.: Sunbelt Eakin, 2003.

Jenkins, John H. and Kenneth Kesselus. *Edward Burleson: Texas Frontier Leader*. Austin, Tex: Jenkins Publishing Co., 1990.

Jenkins, John Holland. *Papers of the Texas Revolution 1835-1836*. 10 vols. Austin, Tex: Presidial Press, 1973.

———. *Recollections of Early Texas. The Memoirs of John Holland Jenkins*. Edited by John Holmes Jenkins III. 1958. Reprint, Austin: University of Texas Press, 1995.

Knowles, Thomas W. *They Rode for the Lone Star. The Saga of the Texas Rangers. The Birth of Texas—The Civil War*. Dallas, Tex: Taylor Publishing Company, 1999.

Koury, Michael J. *Arms For Texas: A Study of the Weapons of the Republic of Texas*. Fort Collins, Colo.: The Old Army Press, 1973.

Ladd, Kevin. *Gone to Texas: Genealogical Abstracts from The Telegraph and Texas Register 1835–1841*. Bowie, MD: Heritage Books, 1994.

Lane, Walter Paye. *The Adventures and Recollections of General Walter P. Lane*.

Austin, Tex: Pemberton Press, 1970.

Lord, Walter. *A Time To Stand: The Epic of the Alamo as a Great National Experience*. New York: Harper & Row Publishers, 1961.

Madis, Franklin. *The Taking of Texas. A Documentary History.* Austin: Eakin Press, 2002.

McDowell, Catherine W., ed.. *Now You Hear My Horn. The Journal of James Wilson Nichols, 1820–1887.* Austin: University of Texas Press, 1961.

McLean, Malcolm D. *Papers Concerning Robertson's Colony in Texas*. 19 vols. Fort Worth, Tex. and Arlington, Tex.: Texas Christian University Press and The University of Texas at Arlington Press, 1974-93.

Memorial and Biographical History of Navarro, Henderson, Anderson, Limestone, Freestone and Leon Counties, Texas. Chicago: Lewis, 1893.

Miller, Thomas Lloyd. *Bounty and Donation Land Grants of Texas: 1835–1888*. Austin: University of Texas Press, 1967.

Moore, Stephen L. *Taming Texas. Captain William T. Sadler's Lone Star Service*. Austin, Tex: State House Press, 2000.

Muster Rolls of the Texas Revolution. Austin: Daughters of the Republic of Texas, 1986.

Nacogdoches County Families: Texas Sesquisentinneal, Vol. I. Published by The Nacogdoches County Genealogical Society. Dallas, Tex: Curtis Media Corporation, 1985.

Nance, Joseph M. *After San Jacinto: The Texas-Mexican Frontier, 1836–1841*. Austin: University of Texas Press, 1963.

Nevin, David. *The Texans (The Old West Series)*. 1975. Reprint, Alexandria, Va: Editors of Time-Life Books, 1980.

The New Handbook of Texas. 6 vols. Austin: The Texas State Historical Association, 1996.

Newcomb, W. W. Jr. *The Indians of Texas: From Prehistoric to Modern Times*. Austin: University of Texas Press, 1961.

Neyland, James. *Palestine (Texas): A History.* Palestine, Tex: Empress Books, 1993.

Pierce, Gerald Swetnam. *Texas Under Arms. The Camps, Posts, Forts, and Military Towns of the Republic of Texas*. Austin, Tex: Encino Press, 1969.

Pioneer Families of Anderson County Prior to 1900. Palestine, Tex: Anderson County Genealogical Society, 1984.

Plummer, Rachel (Parker). *Narrative of the Capture and Subsequent Sufferings of Mrs. Rachel Plummer.* Houston, Tex: Privately published, 1839.

Pohl, James W. *The Battle of San Jacinto*. Austin: Texas State Historical Association, 1989.

Powell, Doris Daniel. *The Genealogy of Hugh Alva Menefee Jr.* Cleburne, Tex: Privately published, 1972.

Procter, Ben H. *The Life of John H. Reagan*. Austin: The University of Texas Press, 1962.

Purcell, Robert Allen. *The History of the Texas Militia*. Austin: University of Texas Press, 1981.

Ramsay, Jack C. Jr. *Thunder Beyond the Brazos: Mirabeau B. Lamar.* Austin, Tex: Eakin Press, 1985.

Ray, Worth S. *Austin Colony Pioneers: Including History of Bastrop, Fayette, Austin,*

Grimes, Montgomery and Washington Counties, Texas. Austin, Tex: Jenkins Publishing Company, 1970.

Reagan, John H. *The Memoirs of John H. Reagan*. Edited by John F. Jenkins. Austin, Tex: The Pemberton Press, 1968.

Republic of Texas Pension Application Abstracts. Published by the Austin Genealogical Society. Austin, Tex: Morgan Printing and Publishing, 1987.

Richardson, Rupert N. *Texas, The Lone Star State*. New York: Prentice-Hall, 1943.

Roberts, Madge Thornall, editor. *The Personal Correspondence of Sam Houston. Volume I: 1839–1845*. Denton: University of North Texas Press, 1996.

Robinson, Duncan W. *Judge Robert McAlpin Williamson. Texas' Three-Legged Willie*. Austin: Texas State Historical Society, 1948.

Robinson, Charles M. III. *The Men Who Wear the Star: The Story of the Texas Rangers*. New York: Random House, 2000.

Roland, Charles P. *Albert Sidney Johnston: Soldier of Three Republics*. Austin: University of Texas Press, 1964.

Scott, Zelma. *History of Coryell County*. Austin: Texas State Historical Society, 1965.

Smithwick, Noah. *The Evolution of a State/Recollections of Old Texas Days*. Austin: University of Texas Press, 1983.

Sowell, A. J. *Texas Indian Fighters. Early Settlers and Indian Fighters of Southwest Texas*. 1900. Reprint, Austin, Tex: State House Press, 1986.

———. *Rangers and Pioneers of Texas*. 1884. Reprint, Austin, Tex: State House Press, 1991.

Spellman, Charles E. *The Texas House of Representatives: A Pictorial Roster, 1846–1992*.

Spellman, Paul N. *Forgotten Texas Leader: Hugh McLeod and the Texan Santa Fe Expedition*. College Station: Texas A&M University Press, 1999.

Stroud, Harry A. *Conquest of the Prairies*. Waco: Texian Press, 1968.

Supplement to Pioneer Families of Anderson County Prior to 1900. Palestine, Tex: Anderson County Genealogical Society, January, 1991.

Teja, Jesus F. de la, editor. *A Revolution Remembered. The Memoirs and Selected Correspondence of Juan N. Seguin*. Austin, Tex: State House Press, 1991.

Thompson, Karen R., editor. *Defenders of the Republic of Texas*. Austin, Tex: Daughters of the Republic of Texas via Laurel House Press, 1989.

Tolbert, Frank X. *The Day of San Jacinto*. New York: McGraw-Hill Book Co., 1959.

Tyler, George W. *The History of Bell County*. San Antonio, Tex: The Naylor Company, 1936.

Utley, Robert M. *Lone Star Justice. The First Century of The Texas Rangers*. New York: Oxford University Press, 2002.

Wallace, Ernest, David M. Vigness and George B. Ward. *Documents of Texas History*. Austin, Tex: State House Press, 1994.

Webb, Walter Prescott, editor. *The Handbook of Texas: A Dictionary of Essential Information*. 3 vols. Austin: The Texas State Historical Association, 1952.

———. *The Texas Rangers: A Century of Frontier Defense*. Austin: University of Texas Press, 1991.

Webber, C. W. *Tales of the Southern Border*. Philadelphia: J. B. Lippincott & Co., 1856.

White, Gifford. *1830 Citizens of Texas: A Census of 6,500 Pre-Revolutionary Texians*. Austin, Tex: Eakin Press, 1983.

———. *1840 Census of Texas*. Austin, Tex: The Pemberton Press, 1966.

———. *1840 Citizens of Texas Land Grants*. Austin, Tex: 1988.

Wilbarger, John Wesley. *Indian Depredations in Texas*. 1889. Reprint, Austin, Tex: State House Press, 1985.

Wilkins, Frederick. *The Legend Begins: The Texas Rangers, 1823–1845*. Austin, Tex: State House Press, 1996.

Williams, Amelia W. and Eugene C. Barker. *Writings of Sam Houston*. Austin: The University of Texas Press, 1938–43.

Winchester, Robert Glenn. *James Pickney Henderson: Texas' First Governor.* San Antonio, Tex: The Naylor Company, 1971.

Winfrey, Dorman, and James M. Day. *The Texas Indian Papers, 1825–1843*. Four volumes. Austin, Tex: Austin Printing Co., 1911.

Wooten, Dudley G., ed. *A Comprehensive History of Texas, 1685 to 1897*. 2 vols. Dallas: William G. Scharff, 1898.

Yoakum, Henderson. *History of Texas From its First Settlement in 1685 to its Annexation to the United States in 1846*. 2 vols. 1855. Reprint, Austin, Tex: Steck Company, 1935.

ARTICLES

Barker, Eugene C., ed. "Journal of the Permanent Council." *The Quarterly of the Texas State Historical Association* 7 (1904).

Benedict, J. W. "Diary of a Campaign against the Comanches." *Southwestern Historical Quarterly* 32 (April 1929): 300-10.

Blount, Lois. "A Brief Study of Thomas J. Rusk Based on His Letters to His Brother, David, 1835–1856." *Southwestern Historical Quarterly* 34 (April 1931).

Brown, Jennifer. "Their Spirits Still Live On Battleground: Indian Group Buys East Texas Site of Famed Battle of Neches." *Tyler Morning Telegraph*, December 14, 1997.

Bryan, Jimmy L. Jr. "More Disastrous Than All: The Surveyors' Fight, 1838." *The East Texas Historical Journal* 38, no. 1 (2000): 3-14.

Chriesman, Horatio. "Reminiscences of Horatio Chriesman." *The Quarterly of the Texas State Historical Association* 6 (1903).

Crosby, David F. "Texas Rangers in The Battle of Brushy Creek." *Wild West* 10, no. 2 (August 1997): 60–64, 89–90.

Fuquay, John W. "The Smith Family." *Tyler Today* (Summer 1996): 24–26. Courtesy of the Smith County Historical Society.

Henderson, Harry McCorry. "The Surveyors' Fight." *Southwestern Historical Quarterly* 56 (July 1952): 25–35.

Hiatt, James. "James Parker's Quest." *Wild West* 3, no. 3 (October 1990): 10, 16, 62–63.

Johnson, Norman K. "Chief Bowl's Last Charge." *Wild West* 2, no. 2 (August 1989): 12–16, 62–66.

Jones, Ernest. "Captain W. T. Sadler Helped Create County." *Palestine Herald-Press*, February 5, 1969, 10.

Looscan, Adele B. "Capt. Joseph Daniels." *Texas Historical Association Quarterly*, 5, no. 1 (1901-1902): 19–21.

Mann, William L. "James O. Rice, Hero of the Battle on the San Gabriels." *Southwestern Historical Quarterly* 55 (July 1951): 30–42.

Pierce, Gerald S. "Burleson's Northwestern Campaign." *Texas Military Monthly* 6, no. 3 (Fall 1967): 191–201.

Reagan, John Henninger. "Expulsion of the Cherokees from East Texas." *Quarterly of the Texas State Historical Association*, 1 (1897): 38–46.

"The Records of an Early Texas Baptist Church." *The Quarterly of the Texas State Historical Association.* Volume I (1833–1847) of the church's history is published in 11, no. 2 (October 1907) and Volume II (1847-1869) is published in 12, no. 1 (July 1908).

"Recollections of S. F. Sparks." *Quarterly of the Texas State Historical Association* 12, no. 1 (July 1908).

"Sadler Descendant of County Pioneer." *Palestine Herald-Press*, January 10, 1975.

Telegraph and Texas Register. See source notes from individual chapters for dates between 1836 and 1839 copied from microfilm in the Texas Room of the Houston Public Library.

Wilcox, S. S. "Laredo During the Texas Republic." *Southwestern Historical Quarterly* 42, no. 2 (1939): 83–107.

Williams, Amelia. "A Critical Study of the Siege of the Alamo," *Southwestern Historical Quarterly* 36, no. 4, through 37, no. 4 (July 1933–April 1934).

Winfrey, Dorman. "Chief Bowles of the Texas Cherokee." *Chronicles of Oklahoma* 32 (Spring 1954): 29–41.

Woldert, Albert "The Last of the Cherokees in Texas, and the Life and Death of Chief Bowles." *Chronicles of Oklahoma*, Issued by The Oklahoma Historical Society in Oklahoma City, Okla., 1, no. 3 (June 1923): 179–226. Copy provided by the Texas State Archives, which included supplemental notes made by Woldert after the original publication of this article.

Yates, Becky. "Historical Date Line: Edens-Madden Massacre." *The East Texas Roundup*, Crockett, Texas, December 17, 1970, 6. Courtesy of Howard C. Sadler.

Index

Note: Military ranks shown, captain and above, indicate the highest rank held by an individual during the 1830s.

CPSIA information can be obtained
at www.ICGtesting.com
Printed in the USA
JSHW042058260421
14006JS00002B/2